Starting an e-Bay® Business

FOR

DUMMIES®

2ND EDITION

Starting an e-Bay® Business FOR DUMMIES® 2ND EDITION

by Marsha Collier

WILEY

Wiley Publishing, Inc.

Starting an eBay® Business For Dummies; 2nd Edition
Published by
Wiley Publishing, Inc.
111 River Street
Hoboken, NJ 07030-5774
www.wiley.com

WILEY

About the Author

Marsha Collier spends most of her time on eBay. She loves buying and selling — she's a PowerSeller — as well as meeting eBay users from around the world. As a columnist, an author of four best-selling books on eBay, a television and radio expert, and a lecturer, she shares her knowledge of eBay with millions of online shoppers. Thousands of eBay fans also read her monthly newsletter, *Cool eBay Tools*, to keep up with the changes on the site.

Out of college, Marsha worked in fashion advertising for the *Miami Herald* and then as special projects manager for the *Los Angeles Daily News*. She also founded a home-based advertising and marketing business. Her successful business, the Collier Company, Inc., was featured in *Entrepreneur* magazine in 1985, and in 1990, Marsha's company received the Small Business of the Year award from her California State Assemblyman and the Northridge Chamber of Commerce.

More than anything, Marsha loves a great deal. That's what drew her to eBay in 1996, and that's what keeps her busy on the site now. She buys everything from light bulbs to parts for her vintage Corvette to designer dresses. Marsha knows how to apply her business acumen to eBay, and in this book, she shares that knowledge with you. In *Starting an eBay Business For Dummies*, Marsha combines her knowledge of business, marketing, and eBay savvy to help you make a smooth and quick transition from part-time seller to full-time moneymaker.

Dedication

I dedicate this book to the eBay entrepreneurs who have a zest for knowledge and the "stick-to-it-iveness" to follow through on their projects and stare success straight in the eye. I dedicate this book also to those who are convinced that get-rich-quick schemes don't work and that, in the long run, hard work and loving what you do get the job done and lead to financial achievement and contentment.

Good luck in your endeavors. I hope this book will help you along the way.

Author's Acknowledgments

Updating a book like this is a challenge. Lots of people have helped, but the lion's share of assistance comes from the encouragement that I receive from the eBay community and those I've met when "doing it eBay."

Ron Johnson, thank you for managing to squeeze time into your hectic schedule to take my calls. Thank you also to the eBay sellers referred to in this book for helping me show the best of eBay to the world: Jillian Cline (PreservationPublishing), Joe Cortese (Noblespirit); Robin Le Vine (Bubblefast), Steve Lindhorst (ListingRover), Bob Miller (BobMill), SallyJo Severance (SallyJo), Marjie Smith (Abovethemall), Jeff Stannard (Melrose_Stamp) Ken Tate (Cardking4), and Jonathan and Ellen White (Magic-By-Mail).

Then, of course, I thank the upper crust at Wiley. My publisher, Andy Cummings, always has a new idea, and Steven Hayes, my acquisitions editor, tries hard to help me in my endeavors (although sometimes I make him crazy).

In this book, I had an amazing editor (who I think is now hooked on eBay): Susan Pink. Thank you for allowing me the leverage to make this book different from the others and putting in your quality input to help me make it even better. Once again, thanks to Patti "Louise" Ruby, my technical editor. This is the fourth book of mine that she's worked on as tech editor; I just can't think of a smarter person to go to for bouncing off ideas.

Publisher's Acknowledgments

We're proud of this book; please send us your comments through our online registration form located at www.dummies.com/register/.

Some of the people who helped bring this book to market include the following:

Acquisitions, Editorial, and Media Development

Project Editor: Susan Pink

Acquisitions Editor: Steve Hayes

Technical Editor: Patti Louise Ruby

Editorial Manager: Carol Sheehan

Media Development Supervisor: Richard Graves

Editorial Assistant: Amanda Foxworth

Cartoons: Rich Tennant, www.the5thwave.com

Composition

Project Coordinator: Adrienne Martinez

Layout and Graphics: Amanda Carter, Andrea Dahl, Lauren Goddard, Joyce Haughey, Stephanie D. Jumper, Michael Kruzil, Barry Offringa, Lynsey Osborn

Proofreaders: Brian H. Walls, TECHBOOKS Production Services

Indexer: TECHBOOKS Production Services

Publishing and Editorial for Technology Dummies

Richard Swadley, Vice President and Executive Group Publisher

Andy Cummings, Vice President and Publisher

Mary Bednarek, Executive Acquisitions Director

Mary C. Corder, Editorial Director

Publishing for Consumer Dummies

Diane Graves Steele, Vice President and Publisher

Joyce Pepple, Acquisitions Director

Composition Services

Gerry Fahey, Vice President of Production Services

Debbie Stailey, Director of Composition Services

Contents at a Glance

Introduction 1

Part 1: Getting Serious about eBay 7

Chapter 1: Using eBay to Launch Your Business 9
Chapter 2: The Finer Points of eBay Selling 29
Chapter 3: Cool eBay Tools 57
Chapter 4: Practicing Safe Selling 83
Chapter 5: Your Very Own eBay Store 107

Part 11: Setting Up Shop 123

Chapter 6: Stocking the Store 125
Chapter 7: Knowing the Value of What You're Selling 145
Chapter 8: Establishing a Base of Operations: Your Web Site 157

Part 111: Business Is Business — No Foolin' Around! 175

Chapter 9: Software Built for Online Auctions 177
Chapter 10: Dollars and Sense: Budgeting and Marketing Your Auctions 199
Chapter 11: Jazzing Up Your Auctions 213
Chapter 12: Providing Excellent Customer Service 231
Chapter 13: When the Money Comes Rolling In 239
Chapter 14: Getting It from Your Place to Theirs 263

Part 1V: Your eBay Back Office 277

Chapter 15: Going Legit 279
Chapter 16: Practicing Safe and Smart Record-Keeping 289
Chapter 17: Building an eBay Back Office 309

Part V: The Part of Tens 325

Chapter 18: Ten Successful eBay Sellers and Their Stories 327
Chapter 19: Ten Other Places to Move Merchandise 341

Part V1: Appendixes 349

Appendix A: Glossary 351
Appendix B: The Hows and Whys of a Home Network 357

Index 367

Table of Contents

Introduction 1

  About This Book 1
  What You're Not to Read 2
  Foolish Assumptions 3
  How This Book Is Organized 3
    Part I: Getting Serious about eBay 3
    Part II: Setting Up Shop 4
    Part III: Business Is Business — No Foolin' Around! 4
    Part IV: Your eBay Back Office 4
    Part V: The Part of Tens 4
    Part VI: Appendixes 5
  Icons Used in This Book 5
  Where to Go from Here 5

Part 1: Getting Serious about eBay 7

  Chapter 1: Using eBay to Launch Your Business 9

    Getting Down to Bidness (er, Business) 10
      Budgeting your time: eBay as a part-time money maker 10
      Jumping in with both feet: Making eBay a full-time job 12
    Deciding What to Sell 13
      Turning your hobby into a business 14
      Including the whole family in the business 17
      Bringing your existing business to eBay 18
    Getting What It Takes to Sell 19
      Computer hardware 20
      Connecting to the Internet 20
      Choosing your eBay user ID 22
      Finding your eBay feedback 24
    Making Your Auctions Run More Smoothly 24
      Software you can use 25
      Collecting the cash 26
      Home base: your Web site 27
      Setting up your shop 27

  Chapter 2: The Finer Points of eBay Selling 29

    Finding Where to Sell Your Stuff 29
      Automotive? Go eBay Motors 31
      Live auctions 34
      Real estate: Not quite an auction 35

Fixed-Price Sales on eBay 37
Types of eBay Auctions 38
        Traditional auctions 38
        Dutch auctions 39
        Reserve price auctions 40
        Restricted access auctions 42
        Private auctions 43
Running Your Auction 43
        Starting the bidding 44
        Auction timing 45
        Marketing your auctions 47
        A second chance 50
Listing Violations 50
        Listing policies 51
        Linking from your auctions 53
        Linking from your About Me page 55

Chapter 3: Cool eBay Tools **57**

My eBay 58
        All Buying 60
        Selling 64
        All Favorites 67
        My Account 69
The About Me Page 71
eBay Seller Services 73
        Bidder-management tools 73
        ID Verify 76
        Feedback: Your permanent record 76
        The eBay PowerSeller program 79
        eBay auction software 80
        eBay Fraud Protection 80
        eBay education 81

Chapter 4: Practicing Safe Selling **83**

Is What You Want to Sell Legal? 84
        Prohibited items 86
        Questionable items 87
        Potentially infringing items 89
Trading Violations 91
        When the competition doesn't play fair 91
        Baaad bidders 94
        Not knowing who's who 98
Taking Action: What to Do When Someone Breaks the Rules 99
        SquareTrade to the rescue 100
        eBay's Security Center 104

Chapter 5: Your Very Own eBay Store 107

Online Stores Galore 108
Your eBay Store Name 109
Setting up Shop 110
Running Your Store 115
    Store design and marketing 115
    Manage your items 118
    Promotions 120
Marketing Your Wares 121
Making a Sale 121

Part II: Setting Up Shop *123*

Chapter 6: Stocking the Store 125

Dollar Stores 126
    99¢ Only Stores 126
    Big Lots 126
    Tuesday Morning 127
Discount Club Stores 127
    Sam's Club 127
    Costco 128
Garage Sales 128
Going-Out-of-Business Sales 129
Auctions 129
    Liquidation auctions 130
    Estate auctions 130
    Charity silent auctions 130
Goodwill, Salvation Army, and Resale Shops 132
Freebies 133
Salvage: Liquidation Items, Unclaimed Freight, and Returns 134
    Items by the pallet 136
    Job lots 138
Wholesale Merchandise by the Case 138
Resale Items on eBay 139
Consignment Selling 141

Chapter 7: Knowing the Value of What You're Selling 145

The Easy Way: eBay Search 146
    Advanced searching methods 148
    Using eBay Advanced Search 148
Useful Publications 152

Online Sources of Information 153
        Web sites 153
        Online appraisals 154
    Authentication Services 154

Chapter 8: Establishing a Base of Operations: Your Web Site 157
    Free Web Space — a Good Place to Start 158
    Paying for Your Web Space 161
        ReadyHosting.com 163
        Interland.com 164
        Microsoft Small Business Center 165
        Yahoo! Web site services 166
    What's in a Web Site Name: Naming Your Baby 167
    Registering Your Domain Name (Before Someone Else Takes It) 168
    Marketing Your Web Site (More Visitors = More Business) 170
        Banner ad exchanges 171
        Getting your URL into a search engine 172

Part III: Business Is Business — No Foolin' Around! 175

Chapter 9: Software Built for Online Auctions 177
    Considering Tasks for Automation 177
        Setting up images for automatic FTP upload 178
        Setting up an auction photo gallery 179
        Sorting auction e-mail 181
        Automating end-of-auction e-mail 181
        Keeping inventory 182
        Generating HTML 182
        One-click relisting and selling similar items 183
        Scheduling your listings for bulk upload 184
        Researching your statistics 184
        Photo hosting 186
        Automating other tasks 186
    Managing Your Business with Online Resources and Software 188
        Online auction management sites 189
        Auction management software 193

**Chapter 10: Dollars and Sense: Budgeting and Marketing
Your Auctions 199**
    Listing Your Items 200
    eBay's Optional Listing Features 201
        Home-page featured auctions 202
        Featured Plus 203
        Subtitle 204

Highlight option 205
Listing Designer 205
Boldface option 206
View counter 206
The gallery 207
Buy It Now 208
eBay's Cut of the Action 210
Insertion (listing) fees 210
eBay Final Value Fees 212

Chapter 11: Jazzing Up Your Auctions **213**
Writing Winning Text 213
Your eBay Photo Studio 214
Digital camera 215
Other studio equipment 217
Props 219
Taking Good Pictures 223
Using a Scanner 224
Image-Editing Software 224
A Home for Your Images 225
Free ISP space 226
Auction management sites 226
eBay Picture Services 226
HTML and You 229

Chapter 12: Providing Excellent Customer Service **231**
Meeting Your Customers 231
Communicating with Your Customers 233
The initial inquiry 234
The winner's notification letter 235
The payment reminder 236
The payment received and shipping notice 237
The "Your item is on the way" e-mail 238

Chapter 13: When the Money Comes Rolling In **239**
It Doesn't Get Any Simpler: Money Orders 239
7-Eleven (and other convenience stores) 240
United States Postal Service 240
Western Union 241
Pay Me When You Get This: Cash On Delivery 242
The Check's in the Mail: Personal Checks 243
Paper checks 243
Bank debits (e-checks and instant transfers) 244
Hold This for Me: Escrow Service 245
I Take Plastic: Credit Cards 247

Credit card payment services 248
Your very own merchant account 256
Costco member's credit card processing 258
The VeriSign Payflow link service 260

Chapter 14: Getting It from Your Place to Theirs 263

Finding the Perfect Shipping Carrier: The Big Three 263
Federal Express 265
United Parcel Service 268
United States Postal Service 270
Protecting Packages with Universal Parcel Insurance Coverage 274
Occasional shipper program 276
Offline standard program 276

Part IV: Your eBay Back Office 277

Chapter 15: Going Legit 279

Types of Businesses 280
Sole proprietorship 280
Partnership 281
LLC (Limited Liability Company) 282
Corporation 282
Taking Care of Regulatory Details 284
Fictitious business name statement 284
Business license or city tax certificate 284
Sales tax number 287
Don't withhold the withholding forms 288

Chapter 16: Practicing Safe and Smart Record-Keeping 289

Keeping the Books: Basics That Get You Started 290
Records Uncle Sam May Want to See 292
Supporting information 293
How long should you keep your records? 294
Bookkeeping Software 295
QuickBooks: Making Bookkeeping Uncomplicated 296
QuickBooks Pro 297
QuickBooks EasyStep Interview 298
QuickBooks chart of accounts 301
QuickBooks on the Web 307

Chapter 17: Building an eBay Back Office 309

The Warehouse: Organizing Your Space 309
Shelving your profits 310
Box 'em or bag 'em? 310

Inventory: Keeping Track of What You Have and Where You Keep It 311
The Shipping Department: Packin' It Up 312
    Packaging clean up 312
    Packing materials 313
    Packaging — the heart of the matter 316
The Mail Room: Sendin' It Out 317
    ClickStamp Internet Postage from Pitney Bowes 318
    Endicia.com 319
    PayPal Shipping Services 321
    Stamps.com 323

Part V: The Part of Tens **325**

Chapter 18: Ten Successful eBay Sellers
and Their Stories **327**
    Abovethemall 327
    BobMill 329
    Bubblefast 330
    Cardking4 332
    ListingRover 333
    Magic-By-Mail 334
    Melrose_Stamp 336
    Noblespirit 337
    PreservationPublishing 338
    SallyJo 339

Chapter 19: Ten Other Places to Move Merchandise **341**
    Donate to Charitable Organizations 341
        Classy gifting 342
        Online charities 342
    Have a Garage Sale 343
    Rent a Table at the Local Swap Meet 344
    Consign Merchandise to the Local Antique Mall 345
    Take a Booth at a Community Event 345
    Resell to Sellers on eBay 345
    Visit a Local Auctioneer 346
    Find Specialty Auction Sites 347
    Run a Classified Liquidation Ad 348
    Sell Everything on eBay for a $.99 Opening Bid 348

Part VI: Appendixes 349

Appendix A: Glossary 351

Appendix B: The Hows and Whys of a Home Network 357

Variations of a Home Network 358
Powerline network 359
Home phoneline 360
Hooking up with wireless 363
Internet Security and Your Home Network 365
Firewall software 365
Antivirus software 366

Index..367

Introduction

. . . .

*T*hank you for taking a look at the second edition of *Starting an eBay Business For Dummies.* I've written this book to serve as a manual to get you organized and get your eBay business off the ground. From handling your selling time on eBay more efficiently to stocking your store to the *real* way to set up your books and daily operations, I give you all the details about running a successful eBay business. From my own years of experience and numerous interactions with hundreds of eBay sellers, I offer countless time-saving and money-saving tips — and secret eBay hints — along the way.

I've made a successful living while working out of my home for the past 20 years, and I share my personal experiences to show you that you, too, can run a successful home business. I started my own marketing and advertising business so that I could be at home and near my preschool daughter. She's graduated college now (don't start counting the years — it's not polite), and I devote my time to selling on eBay (I'm a PowerSeller) and writing and teaching for eBay University. Through perseverance and dedication, my small homegrown business financed my home and my daughter's upbringing, twelve years of private school, and college education. I know that the only limits to my eBay business are time. With the information in this book, and some hard work, you too can expand your eBay business.

One thing that I can't guarantee is how much money you can earn selling on eBay. I've discovered — perhaps the hard way — that it takes a good deal of discipline to run a home business. The time you spend and the amount of devotion you give your business will help you boost your success.

About This Book

Success awaits you! If you've read *eBay For Dummies,* you know just how fun and profitable eBay can be. You've probably picked up this book because you've heard lots of stories about people making big money online, and you're interested in getting your piece of the pie. If you have a retail business, establishing an eBay Store can be a profitable extension of it.

Is selling on eBay something that you'd like to do more of? Do you have a full-time job, but you'd like to sell on eBay part-time? eBay can easily supplement your income for the better things in life — such as vacations or even private school for the kids. Perhaps you're looking to make a career change, and jumping into an eBay business with both feet is just what you have in mind. If so, this is the book for you.

I've watched eBay change from a homey community of friendly collectors to a behemoth Web site with tens of thousands of categories of items and more than 100 million registered users. I'll bet you've been buying and selling with positive results, and you can see the benefits of taking this a bit more seriously. What are you waiting for? There's no time like the present to get started on your new career. Thousands of people across the world are setting up businesses online, and now is your time to take the leap of faith to begin a profitable enterprise. eBay gives you the tools, the customers, and the venue to market your wares. All you need is a bit of direction.

Starting an eBay Business For Dummies picks up where my *eBay For Dummies* leaves off. The tips I include give you the opportunity to improve your eBay money-making ability and just might turn an eBay novice into a professional running a booming eBay business. I also show the experienced user the prudent way to turn haphazard sales into an organized business. This book has it all! I've combined the fine points of eBay with real business and marketing tools to help you complete the journey from part-time seller to online entrepreneur.

In this book, you can find the answers to some important questions as I take you through the following tracks:

- ✔ Reviewing what you know and introducing some of the finer points of eBay auctions
- ✔ Sprucing up your auctions to attract more bidders
- ✔ Dealing with customers
- ✔ Setting up your business in a professional manner
- ✔ Deciding how to handle inventory (and where to find it)
- ✔ What you need to be in an eBay business . . . for *real*

What You're Not to Read

If you use this book the way you'd use a cookbook, jumping around from recipe to recipe (or chapter to chapter), you'll be able to find the answers to your particular questions all at once. Read the book from beginning to end if you'd like, and keep it handy to look up future questions as they come to you. You don't have to memorize a thing; the information you need is at arm's length.

Foolish Assumptions

Because you're reading this, I assume you're serious about selling on eBay and want to find out the fine points of just how to do that. Or perhaps you want to know how much is involved in an eBay business so that you can make the decision whether to give it a go.

If I have you figured out and you've decided that it's time to get serious, here are some other foolish assumptions I've made about you:

- ✔ You have a computer and an Internet connection.
- ✔ You've bought and sold on eBay and are fairly familiar with how it works.
- ✔ You have an existing small business or you'd like to start one.
- ✔ You like the idea of not having to work set hours.
- ✔ You feel that working from home in jeans and a t-shirt is a great idea.

If you can say yes to my foolish assumptions, you're off and running! Take a few moments to read the following section to get a feel for how I've put together this book.

How This Book Is Organized

This book has five parts. The parts stand on their own, which means that you can read Chapter 12 after reading Chapter 8 and maybe skip Chapter 13 altogether (but I know you won't because that's where I discuss the money!).

Part 1: Getting Serious about eBay

Reviewing what you know is always a great place to start. Considering the way eBay constantly changes, you'll probably find a little review worthwhile. So in this part, I delve into the finer points of eBay. Perhaps you'll discover a thing or two you didn't know — or had forgotten.

Setting up your eBay store is important, and in this part I show you step by step the best way to do it — and give you tips to figure out when the timing is right for you to open your store.

Part II: Setting Up Shop

You need to decide what type of business you plan to run and what type of inventory you'll sell. Here's where I discuss how to find merchandise and the best way to sell it. I also give you the lowdown on eBay Motors, real estate, and some of the other unusual areas where you can sell.

You'll also find out how to research items — before you buy them to sell — so you'll know for how much (or whether) they'll sell on eBay.

I also discuss the importance of your own Web site for online shopping and how to set one up quickly and economically.

Part III: Business Is Business — No Foolin' Around!

In Part III, I discuss exactly how to use available online and offline tools, implement auction management software, jazz up your auctions, and handle shipping efficiently and effectively. Because working with customers and collecting payments is important, too, you'll find that information here as well.

Most importantly, you also find out how to obtain free shipping material for your business delivered to your door, get your postal carrier to pick up your boxes at no charge, and insure your packages without standing in line at the post office.

Part IV: Your eBay Back Office

Setting up your business as a real business entity involves some nasty paper-work and red tape. I try to fill in the blanks here, as well as show you how to set up your bookkeeping. This is the place where you'll find a checklist of the items you'll need to run your online business.

You also need to know how to set up your home business space and how to store your stuff. I cover that here plus bunches more!

Part V: The Part of Tens

You can't write a For Dummies book without including the traditional Part of Tens. So in an untraditional manner, here are ten real-life stories of successful (and happy) people selling at eBay. You also find out about ten places to move your merchandise (if you want to sell elsewhere than eBay).

Part VI: Appendixes

I include a random collection of terms in Appendix A. You're probably already familiar with many of these words, but others will be new to you. Refer to this appendix often as you peruse other parts of the book. In Appendix B, I briefly discuss home networking, a perk you'll want to have when your eBay business grows.

Icons Used in This Book

If there's something I need to interject — okay, something I'm jumping up and down to tell you but it won't fit directly into the text — I indicate it by placing this tip icon in front of the paragraph. You'll know the tip to follow will be right on target!

Do you really know people who tie string around their fingers to remember something? Me neither; but this icon gives me the opportunity to give you a brief reminder to note. Kinda like a sticky note.

I like this picture of a petard. Yep, that's what it's called; the round bomb device that Wile E. Coyote slam-dunks in the cartoons is called a petard. In that vein, if you don't heed the warning indicated by the small petard, you may be "hoisted by your own petard," or made a victim of your own foolishness.

Here I share some of the interesting thoughts I've picked up from eBay sellers over the years. Because I believe that knowledge is enhanced through learning from the successes and mistakes of others, I include these little auction factoids so that you might gain some insight from them. After all, if someone else has learned from a unique trick, you can benefit by taking heed.

Where to Go from Here

Time to hunker down and delve into the book. If you have time, just turn the page and start from the beginning. If you're anxious and already have some questions you want answered, check out the handy index at the end of the book and research your query.

Take this information and study it. Being a success on eBay awaits you. I can't wait to hear your success stories if I meet you at eBay Live or a book signing in your town.

My goal is to help you reach your goals. Feel free to contact me through my Web site and sign up for my free newsletter. That way you can stay up to date:

```
www.coolebaytools.com
```

Please e-mail me with any suggestions, additions, and comments. I want to hear from you and hope to update this book with your words of wisdom. (Humorous stories are also gratefully accepted!)

Part I
Getting Serious about eBay

The 5th Wave   By Rich Tennant

"I don't understand why no one at eBay is bidding on Junior's old baby clothes."

In this part . . .

Because eBay continually makes improvements, some of its features are like hidden golden nuggets. In this first part, I delve into the finer points of eBay with you. Perhaps you'll discover a thing or two you didn't know or had forgotten.

Chapter 1

Using eBay to Launch Your Business

. . . .

In This Chapter

▶ Getting serious about your business

▶ Making decisions about what to sell

▶ Having what it takes to make a living online

▶ Running an efficient auction

. . . .

*Y*ou've decided to get serious about your sales on eBay, so now you have to step up to the plate and decide how much time you have to devote to your eBay business. I talk about all kinds of eBay businesses in this book. Even though you're not quitting your day job and selling on eBay full time (yet!), I still think you're serious. A large portion of sellers, even eBay PowerSellers (those who gross more than $1,000 a month in sales), work on eBay only part time.

eBay sellers come from all walks of life. A good number of stay-at-home moms are out there selling on eBay. And so many retirees are finding eBay a great place to supplement their income that I wouldn't be surprised if the AARP creates a special eBay arm. If you're pulled out of your normal work routine and faced with a new lifestyle, you can easily make the transition to selling on eBay.

In this chapter, I talk about planning just how much time you'll be able to devote to your eBay business — and how to budget that time. I also talk about figuring out what to sell. Your eBay business won't grow overnight, but with dedication and persistence, you may just form your own online empire.

Getting Down to Bidness (er, Business)

Before launching any business, including an eBay business, you need to set your priorities. And to be successful at that business, you must apply some clear level of discipline.

I won't bore you with the now-legendary story of how Pierre Omidyar started eBay to help fulfill his girlfriend's Pez dispenser habit, blah, blah, blah. I *will* tell you that he started AuctionWeb with a laptop, a regular Internet Service Provider (ISP), and an old school desk. He and his buddy Jeff Skoll (a Stanford MBA) ran the twenty-four-hours-a-day, seven-days-a-week AuctionWeb all by themselves. When I began using the service, I had a lot of questions — and I always got prompt, friendly answers to my e-mails. When the site started attracting more traffic, Pierre's ISP began to complain about all the traffic and raised his monthly fees. To cover the higher costs, Pierre and Jeff began charging 25 cents to list an auction. Pierre was so busy running the site that the envelopes full of checks began to pile up — he didn't even have time to open the mail.

When Pierre incorporated eBay AuctionWeb in 1996 with his partner Jeff, they were each drawing a salary of $25,000. Their first office consisted of one room, and they had one part-time employee to handle the payments. They started small and grew.

Budgeting your time: eBay as a part-time money maker

A part-time eBay business can be very profitable. One thing that I stress in this book is that the more time and energy you spend on your eBay business, the more money you can make. That said, I now move on to the lowest possible level of time that you should devote to your business.

Maybe you enjoy finding miscellaneous items to sell on eBay. You can find these items somehow in your day-to-day life. So let's suppose that you could spend at least a few hours (maybe three) a day on eBay. Now you must include the time it takes to write up your auctions. If you're not selling only one type of item, allow about fifteen minutes to write your auction, take your picture or scan your image, and of course, upload it to eBay or a photo-hosting site.

How much time it takes to perform these tasks varies from person to person and will improve according to your level of expertise. Regardless, every task in your eBay auction business takes time, and you must budget for that time. See the sidebar "Some handy eBay timesaving tips" for pointers.

Some handy eBay timesaving tips

Crunched for time? The following are some features that you're sure to find useful — and handy:

✔ **HTML templates:** In Chapter 11, I give you some tips on finding basic HTML format templates for attractive auctions. These HTML templates cut your auction design time to a few minutes. Most experienced eBay sellers use preset templates to speed up the task of listing auctions, and this should be your goal.

✔ **TurboLister program:** When you want to list a bunch of auctions at once, I recommend using the eBay TurboLister program. I estimate that TurboLister enables you to put together and upload ten auctions in just fifteen minutes. In Chapter 9, I run down the details on how to use this very cool tool.

✔ **Relisting (or Sell Similar) feature:** When you sell the same item time after time, you can use TurboLister (it archives your old listings so you can repeat them) or the handy eBay relisting or Sell Similar features. When your auction ends on eBay, links pop up offering to relist your listing or to Sell Similiar. If you want to run a different auction with a similar HTML format to the one that just ended, simply select the Sell Similar option and cut and paste the new title and description into the Sell Your Item page of your new listing.

✔ **Auction management software:** See the "Software you can use" section in this chapter and see also Chapter 9, in which I detail various programs to integrate into your eBay business.

Only you can decide how much time you want to spend researching going rates for items on eBay and deciding which day or time your item will sell for the highest price. You can take great photos and write brilliant descriptions, but cashmere sweaters won't sell for as much in the heat of summer as they do in winter. Doing your research can take up a good deal of time when you're selling a varied group of items.

You also have to consider how much time it takes to shop for your merchandise. You may have to travel to dealers, go to auctions, or spend time online discovering new ways to find your auction merchandise. Many sellers set aside a full day each week for this undertaking. Your merchandise is what makes you money, so don't skimp on the time you spend identifying products. The time you spend on this comes back to you in higher profits.

Here's a list of various activities that you must perform when doing business on eBay:

✔ Photograph the item

✔ Clean up and resize the images in a photo editor (if necessary)

✔ Upload the images to eBay Picture Services when you list or before listing to your ISP or third-party hosting service

- ✔ Weigh the item and determine the shipping cost
- ✔ Choose an auction title with keywords
- ✔ Write a concise and creative description
- ✔ List the auction on eBay
- ✔ Answer bidder questions
- ✔ Send end-of-auction e-mails
- ✔ Carry out banking
- ✔ Perform bookkeeping
- ✔ Pack the item safely and securely
- ✔ Address the label and affix postage
- ✔ Go to the post office

Time yourself to see how long it takes to accomplish each of these tasks. The time varies when you list multiple items, so think of the figures that you come up with as your *baseline,* a minimum amount of time that you must set aside for these tasks. This information can help you decide how many hours per month you need to devote to running your part-time eBay business.

Jumping in with both feet: Making eBay a full-time job

As you can see in the list in the preceding section, the tasks required for your eBay business can be time consuming. But careful planning and scheduling can turn your business into an online empire.

The best way to go full time on eBay is to first run your business part time for a while to iron out the wrinkles. After you become comfortable with eBay as a business, you're ready to make the transition to full-time seller. The minimum gross monthly sales for a Bronze-level PowerSeller is $1,000. If you plan your time efficiently, you can easily attain this goal. Head to Chapter 3 for more information on the PowerSeller program.

Running a full-time business on eBay is the perfect option for the working parents who prefer staying at home with their children, retirees looking for something to do, or those who'd just rather do something else than work for their boss. Read some real-life profiles of happy full-time sellers in Chapter 18.

See Figure 1-1 for an example of the eBay home page, the first stop for most buyers on eBay. Note how eBay makes an effort to reflect some sort of promotion to better market the items you put up for sale.

Deciding What to Sell

What should I sell? That is *the* million dollar question! In your quest for merchandise, you're bound to hear about soft goods and hard goods. *Soft,* or nondurable, goods are generally textile products, such as clothing, fabrics, and bedding. *Hard* goods are computer equipment, housewares, and anything else that's basically nondisposable.

Following are just a few points to consider when you're deciding what to sell:

- ✔ **Shipping costs:** Some differences exist between shipping hard and soft goods. Soft goods can fold up and be packed in standard box sizes, available from the USPS, or (better yet) in bubble or Tyvek envelopes for much lower shipping costs. Most hard goods come in their own boxes, which may or may not be individually shippable. You'll also need to use Styrofoam peanuts or bubble cushioning or double package the item in an oddly sized box. See Chapter 17 for the lowdown on shipping and packing.

- ✔ **Other shipping considerations:** Do you want to handle large boxes and deal with the hassles of shipping them?

- ✔ **Possible storage problems:** Do you have the room to store enough merchandise to keep you going? Soft goods can take up considerably less space than hard goods.

You don't always have to buy your items in bulk to make money on eBay. The first things you sell might be items you find in your garage or attic. To find out about some other fun ways to acquire goods to sell, check out the next section.

Turning your hobby into a business

C'mon, you've got a hobby; everyone does! Did you collect stamps or coins as a kid? Play with Barbie dolls? Maybe your hobby is cars? Did you inherit a bunch of antiques? Been collecting Hummel figurines for a few years? eBay has a market for almost anything.

You can't possibly be an expert on everything. You need to keep up-to-date on the market for your items, and following more than four or five basic item groups may divert your attention from selling.

Selling within a particular category or two can be a good idea for repeat business. Should you decide to major in miscellany and sell anything and everything, you may not realize the highest possible prices for your items. This can be okay if you have a source that permits you to buy items at dirt-cheap pricing.

Collectibles: Big business on eBay

Pierre Omidyar started eBay with the idea to trade collectible Pez dispensers. eBay now lists fifty main categories of collectibles (see Figure 1-2), and those categories are divided into thousands of categories, subcategories, and sub-subcategories. Almost anything that you'd want to collect is here, from advertising memorabilia to Girl Scout pins to Zippo lighters!

If you have a collection of your own, eBay is a great way to find rare items. Because your collection is something dear to your heart and you've studied it on and off for years, you could probably call yourself an expert. Bingo — you're an expert at something! I recommend that you hone your skills to find things in your area of expertise at discount prices (you're liking this more and more, aren't you?) and then sell them on eBay for a profit. Start small and start with something you know.

If there's one thing you know, it's fashion!

Are you one of those people who just knows how to put together a great outfit? Do you find bargains at Goodwill but people think you've spent hundreds on your garb? Do you know where to get in-season closeouts before anyone else does? Looks like you've found your market (see Figure 1-3).

Figure 1-2:
The eBay
Collectibles
hub with
links to
categories.

Figure 1-3:
eBay area
for clothing,
shoes, and
accessories.

Buy as many of those stylish designer wrap dresses (you-know-whose at you-know-where) as you can, and set them up on the mannequin you've bought to model your fashions for eBay photos. (For more on setting up fashion photos on eBay, check out Chapter 11.) Within a week, you just may be doubling your money — 'cause sweetie-darling, who knows fashion better than you?

If a ball, a wheel, or competition is involved — it's for you

I don't want to preach in generalities, but I think I'm pretty safe in saying that most guys like sports. Guys like to watch sports, play sports, and look good while they're doing it. I see that as opening up venues for a profitable empire on eBay. I don't want to leave out all the women out there who excel and participate in many sports. Women may have even more discriminating needs for their sporting endeavors! I know I do. My golf game stinks — but I do make a point to at least look good when I go out there, with respectable equipment and a fabulous outfit.

eBay has an amazing market going on right now for soccer equipment, and I don't even want to go into how much football and golf stuff is selling on eBay. And the last time I looked, golf items totaled more than 57,000 listings! What a bonanza! New stuff, used stuff — it's all selling on eBay (see Figure 1-4). It's enough to put your local pro shop out of business — or perhaps put *you* in business.

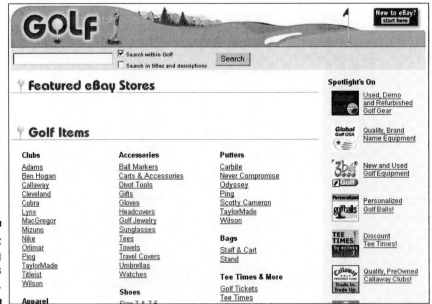

Figure 1-4:
Sporting
goods
on eBay.

Including the whole family in the business

Sometimes just the idea of a part-time business can throw you into a tizzy. After all, don't you have enough to do? School, work, soccer, kids glued to the TV — you might sometimes feel as if you've no time for family time. However, the importance of family time is what brought me to eBay in the first place. I was working long hours in my own business, and at the end of the day, when my daughter Susan wanted to go shopping, perhaps for some Hello Kitty toys or a Barbie doll, I was just too tired. (Can you relate?)

I'd heard about AuctionWeb from a friend and had bought some things online for my own collections. (Okay, you got me; I collected Star Trek stuff — call me geek with a capital *G*.) I'd also browsed around the site and found some popular toys selling for reasonable prices. So one evening I introduced Susan to eBay, and life has never been the same. We'd go to toy stores together right when they opened on Saturday morning, so we'd get first dibs on shipments of the hottest, newest toys. She'd go to the dolls and I'd go to the action figures. We'd buy several, go home, and post them for sale on eBay. We made money, yes, but the best part was our toy runs. They will always remain a special memory.

Susan has since graduated from college (she majored in business and marketing — must have been inspired by our eBay enterprise) but she still calls home when she finds a hot CD or closeouts of a top-selling item. We still purchase and list items together. The family that eBays together . . . always does.

My short trip down memory lane has a point: A family business can succeed and everyone can enjoy it. I was in charge of the financing and the packing while Susan looked up ZIP codes on the Internet and put pins in a 4' x 5' map showing every city that we bought or sold from. She learned some excellent lessons in marketing, advertising, and geography, all in one swoop.

Toys, books, and music — oh MY!

Having children in your home brings you closer to the latest trends than you could ever imagine. I remember sitting at a Starbucks a couple of years ago watching some dads and their sons pouring over notebooks full of Pokémon cards. (Actually, the kids were off playing somewhere and the dads were coveting the cards.)

And what about Star Wars? Star Trek? G.I. Joe? Can you say action figures? (If guys have them, they're not dolls — they're action figures.) If you have access to the latest and greatest toys, buy them up and sell them to those who can't find them in their neck of the woods.

If your home is like mine, books pile up by the tens! Old educational books that your children have outgrown (even college textbooks) can be turned into a profit. Remember that not every book is a classic that needs to be part of your library forever. Let another family get the pleasure of sharing children's tales!

If anything piles up faster than books, it's CDs and videos. Somehow the old lambada or macarena music doesn't hold the magic it once did. Or maybe, those zany kid comedies don't mesmerize you the way they used to. You can get rid of your own items and find plenty of stock at garage sales. Buy them cheap and make a couple of dollars.

Selling children's clothes

When I recently checked eBay for the number of infant and toddler clothes auctions in progress, I found more than 130,000 — and the bidding was hot and heavy. For stay-at-home parents, selling infant and children's clothing is a super way to pick up extra income.

If you've had a baby, you know all too well that friends and relatives shower new moms with lots of cute outfits. If you're lucky, your baby gets to wear one or two of these (maybe only for a special picture) before outgrowing them. These adorable portrait outfits can earn you a profit on eBay. Many parents, with children a few steps behind yours, are looking for bargain clothing on eBay — a profitable hand-me-down community. As your children grow up (and out of their old clothes), earn some money while helping out another parent.

Bringing your existing business to eBay

Do you already have an existing business? eBay isn't only a marketplace where you're able to unload slow or out-of-season merchandise. You can also set up your store right on eBay (see Figure 1-5). An eBay store allows you to list a fixed-price item at a reduced fee and keep the item online until it's sold. When you run your regular auctions for special items, they will have a link to your store, thereby drawing in new shoppers to see your store merchandise.

Here are a few ways you can expand your current business with eBay:

✔ **Opening a second store on eBay:** How many people run stores that sell every item, every time? If you're a retailer, you've probably made a buying mistake. Many times the item that *isn't* selling in your store *is* selling like hotcakes in similar stores elsewhere in the country. eBay gives you the tools to sell those extra items to make room for more of what sells at your home base.

Perhaps you just need to raise some cash quickly. eBay has tens of thousands of categories in which you can sell regular stock or specialty items. For a caveat on what's verboten, check out Chapter 4.

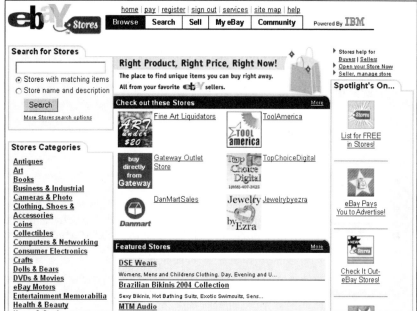

Figure 1-5:
eBay Stores
central.

✔ **Selling by mail order:** If you've been selling by mail order, what's been holding you back from selling on eBay? It costs you far less to list your item on eBay than to run an ad in any publication. Plus, on eBay, you get built-in buyers from every walk of life. If your item sells through the mail, it will sell through eBay.

✔ **Licensed real estate agents:** Plenty of land, homes, and condos are selling on eBay right now. List your properties online so that you can draw from a nationwide audience. When you offer listings on the Web, you're bound to get more action. Give it a whirl and read more about selling real estate on eBay in Chapter 2.

You won't find a cheaper landlord than eBay. Jump over to Chapter 5 if you really can't wait for more information about how to set up your eBay store.

Getting What It Takes to Sell

I've heard many sellers-to-be say they want to start a business on eBay so that they can relax. Since when is running any business a way to relax? Granted, you don't need a whole lot of money to get started on eBay and you won't have a boss breathing down your neck. But to run a successful eBay business, you need drive, determination, and your conscience to guide you, as well as a few solid tools, such as a computer, and an Internet connection. In this section, I give you the lowdown on these things and more.

Computer hardware

First, you're gonna need a computer. In my basic assumptions about you (see the book's introduction), I figure that you have one and know how to use it. Your computer doesn't have to be the latest, fastest, and best available. It does help if your computer has a good deal of memory to process your Web browsing and image touchups. One of my eBay selling computers is an antique Pentium 3, an absolute turtle next to my new 4.3GHz model. But combined with a speedy Internet connection, my little machine enables me to run many eBay auctions easily.

One thing to keep in mind is that hard drives are getting cheaper by the minute. The bigger your hard drive, the more space you'll have to store images for your auctions. (Individual pictures shouldn't take up much space because each should max at 50K.) A caveat: The bigger the hard drive, the more chance for making a mess of it by losing files. When you get started, be sure that you set up a sensible filing system by using folders and subdirectories.

Check out Chapter 11, in which I talk more about the other stuff you might need, such as a scanner and a digital camera.

Connecting to the Internet

If you've been on eBay for any length of time, you know that your Internet connection turns into an appendage of your body. If your connection is down or you can't log on due to a power outage, you can't function and instead flounder around, babbling to yourself. I understand because I've been there. If you're selling in earnest, I recommend pulling the plug on your dial-up connection unless you have no choice.

Before investing in any broadband connection, visit www.broadbandreports.com (see Figure 1-6) and read the reviews of ISPs in your area. Users from around the country post their experiences with the many providers across the country, so you can get a good idea of what's in store in your neighborhood in the connection arena. The site also has more testing tools than you can imagine and will test the speed of your (or your friend's) Internet connection at no charge.

Dial-up connections

If you must use a dial-up connection, avail yourself of the many free trials that different Internet Service Providers (ISPs) offer to see which one gives your computer the fastest connection. After you find the fastest, be sure that it's reliable and has at least a 99 percent uptime rate.

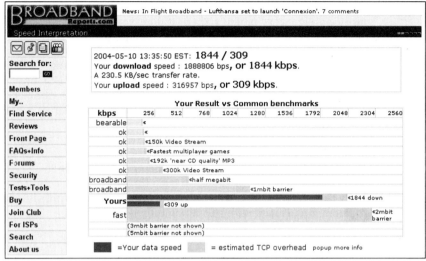

Figure 1-6:
The results
of the free
speed test
of my cable
connection.

Most of the United States still logs on to the Internet with a dial-up connection, so what can be so wrong? This type of connection is painfully slow. An auction with lots of images can take minutes to load. The average eBay users want to browse many auctions and won't wait while your images load; they'll just go to the next auction.

To make the best use of your time when running your auctions and conducting research, you need to blast through the Internet. You need to answer e-mail, load images, and conduct your business without waiting around for snail's-pace connections. Although a modem is supposed to link up at 56K, FCC regulations state that it can't connect any faster than 53K. In practice, the highest connection I've ever experienced on a dial-up was 44K.

DSL

A confusing bunch of Digital Subscriber Line (DSL) flavors (ASDL, IDSL, SDSL, and more) are available these days, ranging from reasonably priced to out of sight. DSL, when it works as advertised, is fast and reliable. A DSL line depends on the reliability of your telephone service: Crackling or unreliable phone lines can be a barrier to using DSL.

The main problem with a DSL connection is that your home or office needs to be no farther than 18,000 feet from your local telephone office. The service runs from $25 to $100 a month, and it might cost even more if you get DSL through a *booster* that boosts the signal to a location farther away than the minimum 18,000-foot border.

Many homes and offices in this country fall out of range for DSL. If you can get it, true DSL service can give you a connection as fast as 1.5MB per second download. (IDSL is only 144K.)

I had DSL for about a year and was initially blown away by the speed. Unfortunately, every time it rained (it does rain occasionally in Southern California), my service went out. I had to call time after time to get a service call. Sadly, this is a well-known drawback of DSL. Your local telephone company (Telco in DSL-speak) owns your home or office phone lines. Because DSL goes over POTS (plain old telephone service), your DSL provider has to negotiate connection problems with the folks at your telephone company. As you might guess, one company often blames the other for your problems.

A friend of mine tried to get around this issue by getting DSL from the local phone company, which sounded great to me. It turned out to be not so great because it seems that the local phone companies tend to form companies to handle high-speed connections. So even though the two companies are technically the same, the two will still argue about who's responsible for your problems. Broadband with this much difficulty can be too much trouble.

Digital cable

Eureka, I think I've found the motherlode of connections: cable. If you can get cable television, you can probably get a blazingly fast cable Internet connection. Your cable company is probably replacing old cable lines with newfangled digital fiber-optic lines. These new lines carry a crisp digital TV signal and an Internet connection as well. (These fancy new lines have plenty of room to carry even more stuff, and I'm sure it won't be long before cable companies have some hot new services to sell us.)

My digital cable Internet connection is generally fast and reliable. I just did a speed test on my line, and I'm downloading data at 1844 kilobauds per second. Compare that to the old-fashioned baud rate of dial-up (remember the old 300 baud modems?). So far, the service has been very reliable, and I've experienced little downtime. For $40 a month, I consider my cable connection well worth the investment.

As far as the myth about more users on the line degrading the speed, a cable connection is more than capable of a 10Mbps transfer. That's already about 10 times faster than DSL. It would take a whole lot of degrading to noticeably slow down your connection. (Your computer still has to load the browser.)

Choosing your eBay user ID

"What's in a name?" I believe that's how the old quote goes. On eBay, there's a whole lot in your name! When you choose your eBay user ID, it becomes your name — your identity — to all those who transact with you online. They don't know who you are; they know you only by the name they read in the seller's or bidder's spot.

The lowdown on user IDs

When choosing your user ID, keep the following points in mind:

✔ Your ID must contain at least two characters.

✔ It doesn't matter if you use uppercase or not; eBay displays your ID in all lowercase letters.

✔ You may use letters, numbers, and any symbol except @ and &.

✔ You can't use URLs as your ID.

✔ You can't use the word *eBay* in your user ID; that privilege is reserved for eBay employees.

✔ You can change your ID every 30 days if you want to. When you do, you get a special icon next to your name, signifying that you've changed to a new ID. Your feedback profile (permanent record) follows you to your new ID.

✔ Spaces aren't allowed; if you want to use two words, you can separate them by using the underscore key (press Shift+hyphen to type the underscore key). You may not use consecutive underscores.

✔ Do I have to tell you this? Don't use a name that's hateful or obscene; eBay (and the community) just won't permit it.

Ever wonder why you don't see many banks named Joe and Fred's Savings and Loan? Even if Joe is the President and Fred is the Chairman of the Board, the casual attitude portrayed by their given names doesn't instill much confidence in the stability of the bank. Joe and Fred might be a better name for a plumbing supply company — or a great name for guys who sell plumbing tools on eBay! Joe and Fred strike me as the kind of friendly, trustworthy guys who might know something about plumbing.

Does your retail business have a name? If you don't have your own business (yet), have you always known what you'd call it if you did? Your opportunity to set up your business can start with a good, solid respectable sounding business name. If you don't like respectable (it's too staid for you), go for trendy. Who knew what a Verizon was? Or a Cingular? Or a Bubblefast, which is one of my favorite eBay shipping suppliers.

Are you selling flamingo-themed items? How about pink_flamingos for your selling identity? Be creative; *you* know what best describes your product.

Stay away from negative sounding names. If you really can't think up a good user ID, using your own name is fine.

You've no doubt seen a bunch of lousy user IDs out there. Here are a few examples of what not to use: ISellJunk, trashforsale, mystuffisgarbage.

eBay protects and does not reveal your e-mail address. If another user wants to contact you, he or she can do so by clicking your user ID. The e-mail will be sent to you through eBay's e-mail system.

If you decide to change your user ID, don't do it too often. Customers recognize you by name, and you may miss some repeat sales by changing it. Besides, eBay places a special icon next to your user ID on the site to show others that you've changed your ID. This icon will stick with you for 30 days.

Finding your eBay feedback

The number that eBay lists next to your name is your feedback rating; see Figure 1-7 for my rating. Anyone on the Internet has only to click this number to know how you do business on eBay — and what other eBay users think of you. At the top of every user's feedback page is an excellent snapshot of all your eBay transactions of the past six months. For the lowdown on feedback, go to Chapter 3.

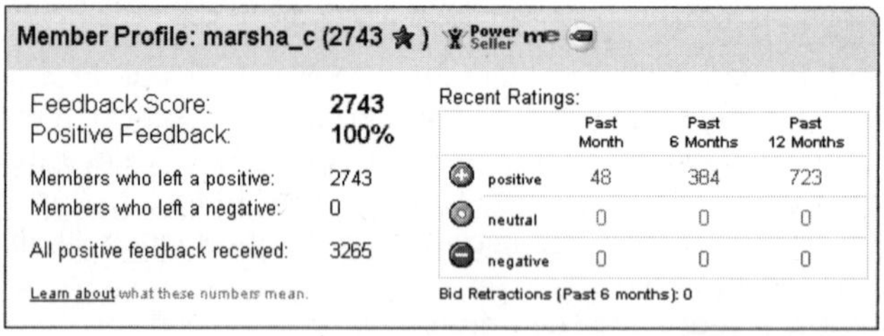

Member Profile: marsha_c (2743 ⭐)   🏆 Power Seller   me

		Recent Ratings:		
			Past Month	Past 6 Months	Past 12 Months
Feedback Score:	2743				
Positive Feedback:	100%				
Members who left a positive:	2743	😊 positive	48	384	723
Members who left a negative:	0	😐 neutral	0	0	0
All positive feedback received:	3265	☹ negative	0	0	0
Learn about what these numbers mean.		Bid Retractions (Past 6 months): 0			

Figure 1-7:
My eBay
feedback.

If you're really serious about this business thing, and your feedback rating isn't as high as you'd like it to be, go online and buy some stuff. Even though eBay now distinguishes between Buyer and Seller feedback, the numbers will still grow. Feedback should always be posted for both buyers and sellers. Every positive feedback increases your rating by +1; a negative decreases it by –1. To get a high rating, you'd better be racking up those positives.

Making Your Auctions Run More Smoothly

In this section, I discuss a few more niceties that you'll need to round out your eBay home base. The following tools are important, but you must decide which ones you'll use. Some people prefer a totally automated office while others prefer to do things the old-fashioned way. One of my favorite eBay PowerSellers works with file folders, a hand-written ledger book, and hand-written labels. If it makes you happy, do it your way. I'm going to suggest a few options that will ease the pain of paperwork.

Software you can use

These days, software is available to accomplish just about anything. It would seem fitting that an all-encompassing software package exists that can help you with your auction, right? Well, maybe. It depends on how much you want your software to do and how much of your business you want to fully control. In this section, I describe some software examples that you might find useful.

Auction management

Auction management software can be a very good thing. It can automate tasks and make your record keeping easy. You can keep track of inventory, launch auctions, and print labels using one program. Unfortunately, most of these programs can be daunting when you first look at them (and even when you take a second look).

You have choices to make regarding the software: How much are you willing to spend for the software, and do you want to keep your inventory and information online? Maintaining your listing information online enables you to run your business from anywhere; you just log on and see your inventory. Online management software is tempting and professional, and may be worth your time and money.

A good many sellers prefer to keep their auction information on their own computers. This method is convenient and allows sellers to add a closer, more personal touch to their auctions and correspondence. Some folks say that keeping information local, on their own computer, is more suited to the small-time seller. I think it's a matter of preference.

In Chapter 9, I discuss the wide selection of management software available, including AuctionWorks.com, Auction Wizard 2000, and the eBay-owned Selling Manager.

HTML software

You may want to try some basic HTML software to practice your ad layouts. I tell you where to find some templates in Chapter 11, but you'll want to preview your auctions before you launch them.

You can use a full-blown Web page software package, such as FrontPage, to check out how your auction will look, or you may want to keep it simple. I use software called CuteHTML all the time because it's about as simple as it can get. Go to the following to download a 30-day free trial:

```
www.globalscape.com/cutehtml
```

If you like it, you can buy it for only $19.99.

Spreadsheets and bookkeeping

Many sellers keep their information in a simple spreadsheet program such as Excel. The program has all the functionality you need to handle inventory management and sales info.

For bookkeeping, I like QuickBooks, which is as complete as it gets. It's straightforward, but only if you have a basic knowledge of accounting. It also integrates with spreadsheets. In Chapter 16, I discuss QuickBooks in some detail.

Collecting the cash

Credit cards are the way to go for the bulk of your auctions. Often, credit cards make the difference between a sale and no sale. People are getting savvy (and more comfortable) about using their credit cards online because they're becoming better informed about the security of online transactions and certain guarantees against fraud. So although you might truly love money orders, you need to take credit cards as well. In this section, I discuss another decision you need to make: Do you want your own private merchant account or would you rather run your credit card sales through an online payment service? For more about these options, read on.

Online payment services

Until you hit the big time, you may want to go with the services of an online payment service such as the eBay-owned PayPal. PayPal offers excellent services and their rates are on a sliding scale, according to your monthly dollar volume. Online payment services accept credit cards for you. They charge you a small fee and process the transaction with the credit card company. The auction payment will be deposited in an account for you. Unless your sales go into tens of thousands of dollars a month, an online payment service can be more economical than your own merchant account. For more about these services and accounts, see Chapter 13.

Your own merchant account

As you may or may not know (depending on the amount of spam in your e-mail), thousands of merchant credit card brokers guarantee that they can set you up so that you can take credit cards yourself. These people are merely middlemen. You have to pay for their services, either in an application fee or as part of a hefty percentage as a processing software. Some of these brokers are dependable businesses and others are nothing more than hustlers. If you have decent credit, you don't need these guys: Go straight to your bank!

Your bank knows your financial standing and credit worthiness better than anybody. It's the best place to start to get your own *merchant account,* an account in which your business accepts credit cards directly from your buyers. You pay a small percentage to the bank, but it's considerably less than you pay to an online payment service. Some banks don't offer merchant accounts for Internet transactions because ultimately the bank is responsible for the merchandise related to the account if you fail to deliver the goods. Remember that your credit history and time with the bank play a part in whether or not you can get a merchant account.

The costs involved in opening a merchant account can vary, but you'll need between $300 and $2,000 to get started. Here are some of the possible costs you may face:

✔ A monthly processing fee if you don't reach the monthly minimum set by your bank

✔ The discount rate (your bank's cut) of 15–45 cents per transaction

✔ About $700 for software that processes your transaction costs

✔ A monthly gateway fee of as much as $40

This is quite an investment in time and effort. In Chapter 13, I get into the details of a merchant account and explain exactly where all these costs go.

Home base: your Web site

eBay offers you a free page — the About Me page — that's the most important link to your business on eBay; see Chapter 3 for more information. The About Me page is part of your eBay store if you have one. You can insert a link on your About Me page that takes bidders to your auctions. You can link also to your own Web site from the About Me page!

If you don't have your own Web site, I recommend that you get one, especially if you're serious about running an eBay business. Check out Chapter 8, where I provide some tips on finding a Web host and a simple way to put up your own Web site.

You can keep your complete inventory of items on your Web site and list them as auctions or in your eBay store as their selling season comes around. Remember that there's no listing or final value fee when you have repeat customers on your Web site.

Setting up your shop

Office and storage space are a must if you plan to get big. Many a business was started at the kitchen table (that's how Pierre started eBay), but to be serious with a business, you must draw definite lines between your home life and your online ventures. Concentrating when you have a lot of noise in the background is difficult, so when I say draw a line, I mean a physical line as well as an environmental one.

Your dedicated office

You must first separate the family from the hub of your business. Many eBay sellers use a spare bedroom. (I started my home business in a 10-by-12-foot room.) As time progresses and your business grows, you might have to move. I chose to sacrifice my detached two-car garage. I guess I could have made it into a one-car garage, but I decided to take over the whole thing instead.

Here's what I did: Zoning laws in Southern California require me to have a garage, so I put a false office wall in the back so that the garage door could open normally. I used that area for extra storage. My garage had been wired (for some guy who was going to use big-time power tools, I suppose) and had its own breaker box. I hired an electrician to come in and place outlets around my office and had a large window cut into the wall overlooking my backyard (to remove the claustrophobic feeling and for ventilation). I now had a window and electricity.

The phone man came by and brought a line into the garage; a friend installed double jacks all around to accommodate the two phone lines. I picked out some reasonably priced paneling and hired workmen to install it and to drop a paneled ceiling with florescent lights. Finally, I bought furniture from my local Goodwill store. Presto-chango — I had successfully transformed what was once a dark garage into a bright, gleaming 18-by-20-foot *private* office. And here I successfully ran my advertising and marketing business for more than ten years.

You, too, have adjustments and decisions to make, just as I did, because you're going to need office space and storage space too.

One PowerSeller that I know moved all the junk out of his basement and set up shop there. He now has three computers and employs his wife and a part-time *lister* (who put his auctions up on eBay) to run the show. His basement office is networked and is as professional as any office.

Your eBay room

If you're able to set up an office similar to mine, your storage space should be covered for a while. For a real business, a closet just won't do, even though most sellers begin their eBay careers with an eBay closet. Seclude your stuff from your pets and family by moving it into another room. You'll also have to get shelving and more supplies to organize things. I talk more about this in Chapter 17.

Chapter 2

The Finer Points of eBay Selling

In This Chapter

▶ Finding the right category on eBay

▶ Figuring out fixed-price sales

▶ Selecting the auction type that works for you

▶ Pondering auction philosophies

▶ Breaking the rules: What you can't do on eBay

*A*t first glance, eBay is this behemoth Web site that seems way too large for any novice to possibly master. In a superficial way, that's right. eBay is always growing and undergoing facelifts. Under all the cosmetic changes, however, you find the basics. eBay is still the same old trading site: a community of buyers and sellers who follow the same rules and policies, making eBay a safe place to trade.

As anything gets larger, it must become compartmentalized to be manageable. The folks at eBay have done this most handily. The original basic eight categories now number in the thousands. The category breakdown is clearer and more concise. When a trend begins, the eBay tech gurus evaluate the sales and, when necessary, add new categories.

All this growth has forced eBay to expand. Aside from the traditional eBay auctions, you'll now find Dutch, private, restricted, and more. It can get confusing! In this chapter, I explain the new eBay features by reviewing how the site does business. Armed with this knowledge, you can effectively do your business.

Finding Where to Sell Your Stuff

The Internet is crowded with auctions, with many major portals including auctions as part of their site. But most bidders and sellers go to eBay. Why? More computers and electronics are sold on eBay than at Buy.com; more used cars are sold on eBay than at Autotrader; and more toys are probably sold on eBay than at KBKids. Even the United States Post Office found a niche on eBay, selling the contents of undeliverable packages in odd lots and excess equipment.

Whether you're selling auto parts, toys, fine art, or land, you must find your niche on eBay. Sounds easy enough. After all, deciding where to put your stuff for sale is pretty straightforward, right? Not necessarily. The task is complicated by the inclusion of thousands of categories on the eBay Category Overview page, shown in Figure 2-1.

Consider the example of a Harry Potter toy. Harry Potter toys are becoming increasingly popular with the continuing saga in both the books and the movies. The easy choice is to list the item under Toys & Hobbies: TV, Movie Character Toys: Harry Potter. But what about the category Collectibles: Fantasy, Mythical & Magic: Harry Potter? This is the point where you must decide whether you want to list in two categories and pay more (see the review of extra charges in Chapter 10) or count on the fact that your beautifully written Auction Title will drive those using the search engine directly to your item.

eBay supplies you with a great tool: *Find a Main Category* in the Sell your item pages. Type a few keywords for your item, and you're presented with a list of categories where items similar to yours are listed, as in Figure 2-2.

Figure 2-1:
The eBay Category Overview page; numbers next to categories reflect active auctions.

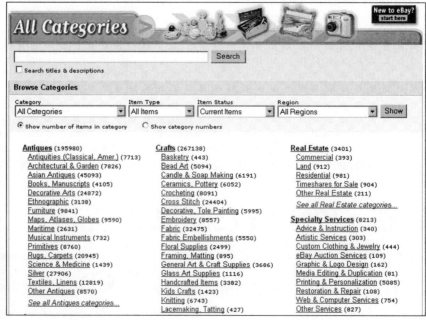

Find a Main Category

8 categories found for **baccarat vase**

You can select a suggested main category below and click **Sell In This Category**, or use different keywords to refine your search.

Enter item keywords to find a category

baccarat vase   Find | Tips

For example, "gold bracelet" not "jewelry"

Category

⊙ Pottery & Glass : Glass : Art Glass : French : Baccarat	(81%)
○ Home & Garden : Home Decor : Other	(3%)
○ Home & Garden : Home Decor : Vases : Other	(3%)
○ Pottery & Glass : Glass : Art Glass : North American : Other Makers	(3%)
○ Pottery & Glass : Glass : Art Glass : Other Countries	(3%)
○ Pottery & Glass : Glass : Glassware : Contemporary Glass : Crystal	(3%)
○ Pottery & Glass : Glass : Glassware : Elegant : Other Makers	(3%)
○ Pottery & Glass : Glass : Glassware : Waterford	(3%)

Figure 2-2:
eBay's category finder feature.

So you aren't selling Harry Potter toys? Suppose you're selling a DVD of the movie *The Red Violin*. Would listing it in DVD & Movies: DVD be the right choice? Or would you reach the proper audience of category browsers in Music: Musical Instruments: String: Violin?

Should a book on 1960s fashion be placed in Books: Antiquarian and Collectible? I had good luck going directly to the fans of 60s fashion in the category Clothing Shoes & Accessories: Vintage: Women's Clothing: 1965-76 (Mod, Hippie, Disco): Dresses.

The popularity of categories varies from time to time. News stories, the time of year, hot trends, or whether Katie Couric makes a comment about something all can change a particular category's popularity. How can you possibly know the best category for your item? Research your items regularly using my favorite tool: the awesome eBay search engine. (Visit Chapter 7 for more about using the search engine.) After you've found the right category for the item you're listing, give it a try. However, be sure to occasionally try alternatives as well.

Even when you've been selling a particular item for a while — and doing well with it — selling your item in a different but related category can boost your sales. A little research now and then into where people are buying can go a long way to increasing your eBay sales.

Automotive? Go eBay Motors

Anything and everything automotive can go in the eBay Motors category (see Figure 2-3), and it will sell like giant tires at a monster truck rally. Following are just a few of the car-related items that fit in this category.

Figure 2-3:
The eBay
Motors
home page.

Car parts

Got used car parts? eBay has an enormous market in used car parts. One seller I know goes to police impound sales and buys wrecks — just to save some valuable parts that he can resell on eBay.

New car parts are in demand, too. If you catch a sale at your local auto parts store when it's blasting out door handles for a 1967 Corvette (a vehicle for which it's hard to find parts), it wouldn't hurt to pick up a few. Sooner or later, someone's bound to search eBay looking for them. If you're lucky enough to catch the trend, you'll make a healthy profit.

Cars

Yes, you can sell cars on eBay. In fact, used car sales have skyrocketed online thanks to all the people who find eBay to be a trusted place to buy and sell used vehicles. Check out Figure 2-4 for an example of a used car auction. Selling vehicles on eBay is a natural business for you if you have access to good used cars, work as a mechanic, or have a contact at a dealership that lets you sell cars on eBay for a commission or on a consignment basis. (For the ins and outs of consignment selling, check out Chapter 6.

eBay Motors and its partners offer useful tools to complete your sale. eBay Motors features a free passenger Vehicle Purchase Protection up to $20,000 (with a $100 buyer co-pay should you have a claim), one-click access to Carfax

Figure 2-4:
An eBay
Motors
auction for a
previously
owned van
from seller
e.vehicles.

reports, vehicle inspection and escrow services, and vehicle shipping quotes from Dependable Auto Shippers. Access eBay Motors and its services from the eBay home page or go directly to www.ebaymotors.com.

Here are just a few things to keep in mind if you plan to sell cars on eBay:

✔ Selling a car on eBay Motors is a bit different from selling on regular eBay, mainly in the fees area. Take a look at Table 2-1 for significant differences. In Chapter 10, I include a table of all basic eBay fees for listings, options, and final values.

✔ To sell a vehicle on eBay Motors, you must enter the Vehicle Identification Number (VIN) on the Sell Your Item page. This way, prospective buyers can always access a Carfax report to get an idea of the history of the car.

✔ Although many people who have found the vehicle of their dreams on eBay are more than happy to take a one-way flight to the vehicle location and drive it home, shipping a vehicle is a reasonably priced alternative. You can make arrangements to ship a car quickly and simply. In Table 2-2, I list some sample costs for shipping cars around the country from various sites.

✔ If your reserve isn't met in an eBay Motors auction, you may still offer the vehicle to the high bidder through the Second Chance option. More information on that later in this chapter. You may also reduce your reserve during the auction if you feel you've set your target price too high.

Table 2-1	eBay Motors Vehicle-Specific Fees
Type of Fee	*Fee Amount*
Vehicle insertion (listing) fee	$40
Vehicle transaction service fee	$40*
Motorcycle insertion (listing) fee	$30
Motorcycle transaction service fee	$30*
Reserve price in listing (refundable if the vehicle sells)	$5
10-day listing (except pocket bikes)	$8

* There is no final value fee for selling on eBay Motors. The transaction service fee is what you pay when your item gets a bid (or if you've used a reserve, when bidding meets your reserve price)

Table 2-2	Estimated Costs for Shipping a Car	
From Here to There	*Terminal-to-Terminal Cost*	*Door-to-Door Cost*
Manhattan to Los Angeles	$899	$1102
Los Angeles to Chicago	$600	$770
Newark to Dallas	$860	$1030
Boston to Orlando	$650	$750
Phoenix to Houston	$690	$890

An item that you've listed on eBay Motors will appear in any search, whether a potential buyer conducts a regular eBay search or executes a search in eBay Motors.

Live auctions

eBay also holds live auctions, where you'll find rare and unusual items for sale. You can access the live auction area from a link on the home page or by going directly to

```
www.ebayliveauctions.com
```

To sell on eBay Live Auctions (shown in Figure 2-5), you must be a registered, licensed auction house. eBay Live Auctions supply non-stop, live auction action right on your desktop. Joining a live auction is a great deal of fun. These auctions happen in real-time; you can see (and participate in) the bidding action on your screen as it's happening.

Figure 2-5:
Non-stop
bidding
action on
eBay Live
Auctions!

Licensed auction houses run the live auctions from their locations, which are broadcast worldwide through eBay. You have to register individually for each auction in which you want to participate, and a buyer's premium is involved. More and more auctioneers are using this format to expand their customer bases.

As an eBay community member, you're able to bid on items featured in live auctions. As a matter of fact, I got waylaid for a few hours while writing this chapter, getting involved in bidding (and buying) in a coin auction! It's a good way to increase your own stock of merchandise to sell.

Real estate: Not quite an auction

eBay Real Estate isn't quite an auction. Because of the wide variety of laws governing the sale of real estate, eBay auctions of real property aren't legally binding offers to buy and sell. Putting your real estate up on eBay is an excellent way to advertise and attract potential buyers. When the auction ends, however, neither party is obligated (as they are in other eBay auctions) to complete the real estate transaction. The buyer and seller must get together to consummate the deal.

Nonetheless, eBay real estate sales are popular and the gross sales are growing by leaps and bounds. You don't have to be a professional real estate agent to use this category, although it may help when it comes to closing the deal. If you know land and your local real estate laws, eBay gives you the perfect venue to subdivide those 160 acres in Wyoming that Uncle Regis left you in his will.

For less than the cost of a newspaper ad, you can sell your home, condo, land, or even timeshare on eBay Real Estate (see Figure 2-6) in the auction format. You can also choose to list your property in an ad format, accepting not bids but inquiries from prospective buyers from around the world. On the Sell Your Item form, shown in Figure 2-7, you must specify special information about your piece of real estate.

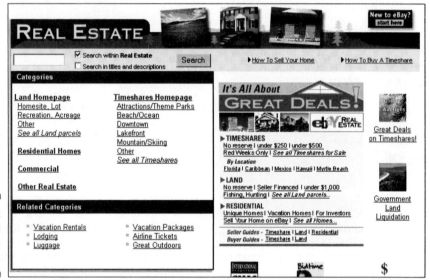

Figure 2-6: eBay Real Estate home page.

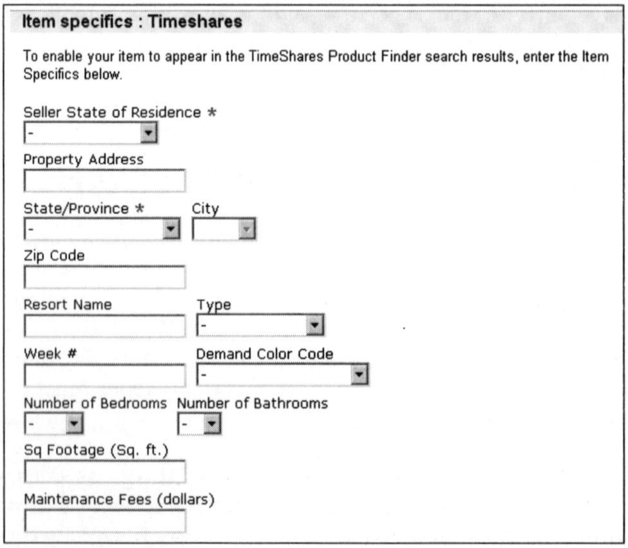

Figure 2-7: Item specifics for selling a Timeshare.

In Tables 2-3 and 2-4, I provide a listing of fees that you can expect to encounter on eBay Real Estate.

Table 2-3	eBay Real Estate Timeshare and Land Fees
Type of Fee	*Fee Amount*
Insertion (listing) for 1-, 3-, 5-, 7-, or 10-day auction	$35
30-day auction	$50
Ad format 30 days	$150
Ad format 90 days	$300
Reserve less than $200 (refundable if reserve is met)	$2
Reserve $200 or more	1% of reserve (maximum $100)
Final value fee	None

Table 2-4	eBay Real Estate Residential & Commercial
Type of Fee	*Fee Amount*
Insertion (listing) for 1-, 3-, 5-, 7-, or 10-day auction	$100
30-day auction	$150
Ad format 30 days	$150
Ad format 90 days	$300
Reserve $200 or more (refundable if reserve is met)	$2
Final value fee	None

Fixed-Price Sales on eBay

eBay is branching out (as if you weren't expecting it) into new arenas. To compete with Amazon.com and Yahoo!, eBay now includes *fixed-price sales* on its site. Fixed-price sales are an extension of the eBay Buy It Now feature. You put an item up for sale at a fixed price, and buyers pay the price that you're asking. Simple as that. Sellers are doing a great job at it too.

You can also find fixed-price sales at the new eBay Stores. Each eBay store is run by an eBay auction seller. eBay Stores has its own space on eBay — accessible in the following ways:

- ✓ Through the navigation bar by clicking Browse and then Stores
- ✓ By clicking the <u>eBay Stores</u> link on the eBay home page
- ✓ By going straight to `www.ebaystores.com` from the Web

Potential buyers will be able to access your items from anywhere on the eBay site. The cost of eBay Stores (see Table 2-5) compares favorably to any of the Web's megasite stores and are part of the eBay Stores Hub.

Table 2-5	eBay Store Fees
Type of Fee	*Fee Amount*
Monthly subscription fee	$15.95
Listing fee	$0.02
Gallery picture	$0.01
Final value fee	1.25%–5%

To get a complete overview on how to set up your own eBay Store, check out Chapter 5.

Types of eBay Auctions

An auction is an auction is an auction, right? Wrong! eBay has five types of auctions for your selling pleasure. Most of the time you'll run traditional auctions, but other auctions have their place, too. After you've been selling on eBay for a while, you may find that one of the other types of auctions better suits your needs. In this section, I review these auctions so that you fully understand what they are and when to use them.

Traditional auctions

Traditional auctions are the bread and butter of eBay. You can run a traditional auction for 1, 3, 5, 7, or 10 days, and when the auction closes, the highest bidder wins. I'm sure you've bid on several and at least won a few. I bet you've also made money running some of your own.

Not quite adult enough. . . .

I was surprised to see a private auction listed on one of my favorite eBay seller's list. She usually doesn't sell items like "Fringe Black BRA 36B SEXY SEXY SEXY," so I looked through this seller's past auctions. I saw that she didn't get any bids when she listed the bra in the restricted (Adult Only) area of eBay in the category Everything Else: Mature Audiences: Clothing, Accessory. When she put the bra up for private auction in the category Clothing & Accessories: Women's Clothing: Lingerie: Bras: General, she got five bidders and sold the item. I guess it wasn't sexy enough for the "adult" crowd!

You begin the auction with an opening bid, and bidders (I hope) will bid up your opening price into a healthy profit for you.

Dutch auctions

When you've purchased an odd lot of 500 kitchen knife sets or managed (legally, of course) to get your hands on a truckload of televisions that you want to sell as expeditiously as possible, the Dutch (multiple item) auction is what you'll want to use. In the *Dutch auction* (see Figure 2-8 for an example), which can run for 1, 3, 5, 7, or 10 days, you list as many items as you'd like, and bidders can bid on as many items as they'd like. The final item price is set by the lowest successful bid at the time the auction closes.

Figure 2-8:
A Dutch auction for United States proof sets in the U.S. Coins category.

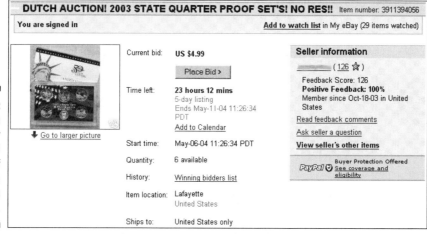

For example, suppose you want to sell five dolls on eBay in a Dutch auction. Your starting bid is $5 each. If five bidders each bid $5 for one doll, they each get a doll for $5. But, if the final bidding reveals that two people bid $5, one person bid $7.50, and another bid $8, all five bidders win the doll for the lowest final bid of $5.

In the following list, I highlight the details of the Dutch auction:

- ✔ The listing fee is based on your opening bid price (just like in a traditional auction), but it's multiplied by the number of items in your auction to a maximum listing fee of $4.80.

- ✔ The final auction value fees are on the same scale as in a traditional auction, but they're based on the total dollar amount of your completed auctions.

- ✔ When bidders bid on your Dutch auction, they can bid on one or more items at one bid price. (The bid is multiplied by the number of items.)

- ✔ If the bidding gets hot and heavy, rebids must be in a higher total dollar amount than the total of that bidder's past bids.

- ✔ Bidders may reduce the quantity of the items for which they're bidding in your auction, but the dollar amount of the total bid price must be higher.

- ✔ All winning bidders pay the same price for their items, no matter how much they bid.

- ✔ The lowest successful bid when the auction closes is the price for which your items in that auction will be sold.

- ✔ If your item gets more bids than you have items, the lowest bidders are knocked out one by one, with the earliest bidders remaining on board the longest in the case of tie bids.

- ✔ The earliest (by date and time) successful high bidders when the auction closes win their items.

- ✔ Higher bidders get the quantities they've asked for, and bidders can refuse partial quantities of the number of items in their bids.

For a large quantity of a particular item, your Dutch auction may benefit from some of the eBay featured auction options, which I detail in Chapter 10.

Reserve price auctions

In a *reserve price auction,* you're able to set an undisclosed minimum price for which your item will sell, thereby giving yourself a safety net. Figure 2-9 shows an auction in which the reserve has not yet been met. Using a reserve price auction protects the investment you have in an item. If, at the end of the auction, no bidder has met your undisclosed reserve price, you aren't obligated to sell the item and the high bidder isn't required to purchase the item.

This seller has set a reserve price
that hasn't been met by a bidder yet

Figure 2-9:
Note that a
reserve has
been set for
this auction.

For example, if you have a rare coin to auction, you can start the bidding at a low price to attract bidders to click your auction and read your infomercial-like description. If you start your bidding at too high a price, you might dissuade prospective bidders from even looking at your auction, and you won't tempt them to even bid. They may feel that the final selling price will be too high for their budgets.

Everyone on eBay is looking for a bargain or a truly rare item. If you can combine the mystical force of both of these needs in one auction, you have something special. The reserve price auction enables you to attempt — and perhaps achieve — this feat.

The fees for a reserve price auction are the same as those for a traditional auction with one exception. eBay charges between $2.00 and $100.00 for the privilege of running a reserve price auction. If the reserve price is $200.00 or more, the reserve price fee is 1% of the reserve price (with a maximum of $100.00). When your item sells, you get that money back.

The reserve price auction is a safety net for the seller but often an uncomfortable guessing game for the prospective bidder. To alleviate buyer anxiety, many sellers put reserve prices in the item description, allowing bidders to decide whether the item will fit into their bidding budgets.

You can't use the reserve price option in a Dutch auction.

Restricted access auctions

eBay won't allow certain items to be sold in nonrestricted categories, so you must list them in the Adult Only area of eBay. eBay makes it easy for the user to find or avoid these types of auctions by making this area accessible only after the user enters a password and agrees to the terms and conditions of the area (see Figure 2-10).

Items in the Adult Only area are not accessible through the regular eBay title search, nor are they listed in Newly Listed Items.

Anyone who participates in Adult Only auctions on eBay, whether as a bidder or a seller, must have a credit card on file on eBay for verification.

Do not attempt to slip an adult only auction into a nonrestricted category. eBay doesn't have a sense of humor when it comes to this violation of policy and may relocate or end your auction. eBay might even suspend you from its site.

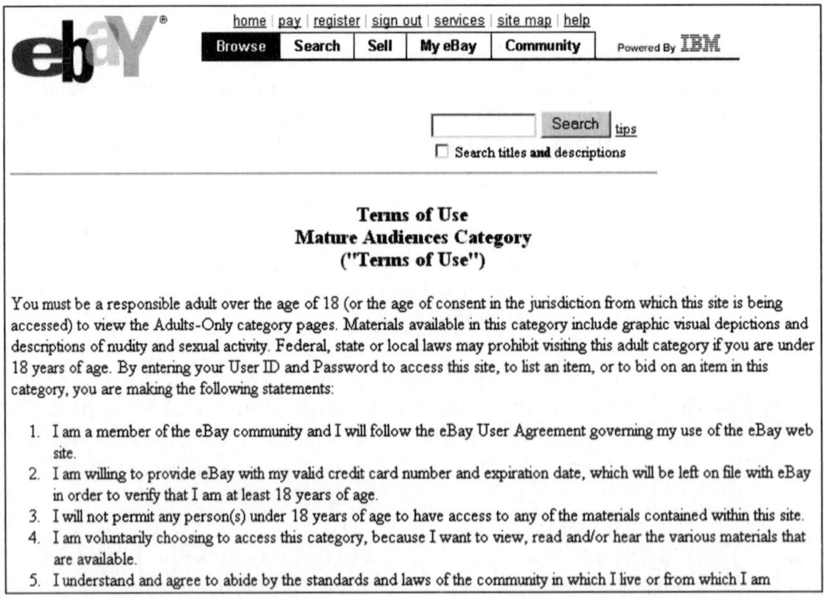

Figure 2-10: You must agree to the legalities to enter the Mature Audiences category.

home | pay | register | sign out | services | site map | help

Browse | Search | Sell | My eBay | Community | Powered By IBM

Search | tips
☐ Search titles **and** descriptions

Terms of Use
Mature Audiences Category
("Terms of Use")

You must be a responsible adult over the age of 18 (or the age of consent in the jurisdiction from which this site is being accessed) to view the Adults-Only category pages. Materials available in this category include graphic visual depictions and descriptions of nudity and sexual activity. Federal, state or local laws may prohibit visiting this adult category if you are under 18 years of age. By entering your User ID and Password to access this site, to list an item, or to bid on an item in this category, you are making the following statements:

1. I am a member of the eBay community and I will follow the eBay User Agreement governing my use of the eBay web site.
2. I am willing to provide eBay with my valid credit card number and expiration date, which will be left on file with eBay in order to verify that I am at least 18 years of age.
3. I will not permit any person(s) under 18 years of age to have access to any of the materials contained within this site.
4. I am voluntarily choosing to access this category, because I want to view, read and/or hear the various materials that are available.
5. I understand and agree to abide by the standards and laws of the community in which I live or from which I am

Private auctions

Bidders' names are often kept private when dealing in the expensive fine art world. Likewise, to protect the innocent, eBay *private auctions* don't place bidders' names on the auction listing. No one needs to know just how much you choose to pay for something, especially if the item is rare and you really want it.

As a seller, you have the option (at no extra charge) of listing your auction as a private auction.

The eBay search page features an area where you can conduct a bidder search. You — and everyone else including your family — can find the items that you've bid on. One December my daughter told me that she didn't want a particular item — something that I had just bid on — for Christmas. My creative daughter had been regularly perusing my bidding action on eBay to see what I was buying for the holidays! A private auction would have kept my shopping secret.

The private auction is a useful tool for sellers who are selling bulk lots to other sellers. It maintains the privacy of the bidders, and customers can't do a bidder search to find out what sellers are paying for the loot they then plan to re-sell on eBay.

A great option for sales of items that are a bit racy or perhaps for purchases of items that may reveal something about the bidder, the private auction can save you the potential embarrassment associated with buying a girdle or buying the tie that flips over to reveal a racy half-nude female on the back.

Although the private auction is a useful tool, it may intimidate the novice user. If your customer base comes from experienced eBay users and you're selling an item that may benefit by being auctioned in secret, you might want to try this option.

Running Your Auction

The basic plan for running an auction is the same for everyone, except for decisions regarding the timing of the auction and the starting price. If you speak to 20 different eBay sellers, you'll probably get 20 different answers about effective starting bids and when to end your auction. Until you develop your own philosophy, I'd like to give you the tools to make a sound decision.

You can also successfully promote your auctions online and offline, and now you can legally offer your item to the next highest bidder if the auction winner doesn't come through with payment. I discuss a few of these ideas in this section.

Starting the bidding

The most generally accepted theory about starting bids is that setting the bidding too high scares away new bids. Also, as in the case of the reserve price auction, if the bidding begins too high, novices might be afraid that the bidding will go too high and they'll never win the auction.

Some sellers begin the bidding at the price they paid for the item, thereby protecting their investment. This is a good tactic, especially if you bought the item at a price far below the current going rate on eBay.

To determine the current going value for your item, I recommend using the completed auctions search, which I explain in Chapter 7. If you know that the item is selling on eBay for a certain price and that there is a demand for it, starting the bidding at a reasonably low level can be a great way to increase bidding and attract prospective bidders to read your auction.

Years of advertising experience can't be wrong. If your item is in demand and people are actively buying, start the bidding low. Retail stores have done this for years with ads that feature prices starting at $9.99 or $14.98. Even television commercials advertising automobiles quote a low starting price. To get the car as shown in the ad, you may end up paying twice the quoted price.

When sellers know that they have an item that will sell, they begin their bidding as low as a dollar or even a penny. Because of the eBay *proxy bidding system* (which maintains your highest bid as secret, increasing it incrementally when you're bid against), it takes more bids (due to the smaller bidding increments) to bring the item up to the final selling price.

The downside is that new bidders who aren't familiar with the system may bid only the minimum required increment each time they bid. This can be frustrating, and they may quit bidding because it might take them several bids to top the current bid placed by someone who's familiar with the proxy bid system.

Very few of us know the proxy increments by heart, so as a refresher, I give you the goods in Table 2-6.

Table 2-6	Proxy Bidding Increments
Current High Bid	*Bid Increment*
$.01–$.99	$0.05
$1.00–$4.99	$0.25
$5.00–$24.99	$0.50
$25.00–$99.99	$1.00
$100.00–$249.99	$2.50
$250.00–$499.99	$5.00

Auction timing

Another debatable philosophy is auction timing. People are always asking me how long to run auctions and what's the best day to end an auction. You have to evaluate your item and decide the best plan:

- ✔ **One-day auction:** This format can be very successful if you have an item that's the hot ticket for the moment on eBay. I used this format when I sold some *Friends* TV show memorabilia. The 24-hour auction opened mid-day before the final show and ended the next day — at a very healthy profit!

  One-day auctions also give you the benefit of pushing your auction to the top of the heap in the listings. Because eBay defaults to show the items ending first at the top of the page (just below featured auctions) a one-day listing posts right up there!

- ✔ **Three-day auction:** If, as in the heyday of Beanie Babies, the item's price will shoot up right after you post it, a three-day auction works just fine. And it's great for those last-minute holiday shoppers looking for hard-to-find items.

  With the eBay Buy It Now feature, you can pretty much accomplish the same thing. When you list your item for sale, set a price at which you will sell the item; this is your target price. This price can be any amount, and if someone is willing to pay, it sells.

- ✔ **Five-day auction:** Five days will give you two days more than three and two days less than seven. That's about the size of it. If you just want an extended weekend auction, or if your item is a hot one, use it. Five-day auctions are useful during holiday rushes, when gift buying is the main reason for bidding.

✔ **Seven-day auction:** Tried-and-true advertising theory says that the longer you advertise your item, the more people will see it. On eBay, this means that you have more opportunity for people to bid on it. The seven-day auction is a staple for the bulk of eBay vendors. Seven days is long enough to cover weekend browsers and short enough to keep the auction interesting.

✔ **Ten-day auction:** Many veteran eBay sellers swear by the ten-day auction. Sure, eBay charges you an extra forty cents for the privilege, but the extra three days of exposure (it can encompass two weekends) can easily net you more than a dime in profits.

If you're selling an esoteric collectible that doesn't appear on eBay often, run a ten-day auction to give it maximum exposure. Start it on a Friday, so it will cover the aforementioned two weekends worth of browsers. In my book, *eBay Timesaving Techniques For Dummies*, I examine in depth the opinions on how long to run an auction and what day or time to begin it.

Your auction closes exactly one, three, five, seven, or ten days — *to the minute* — after you start the auction. Be careful not to begin your auctions when you're up late at night and can't sleep: You don't want your auction to end at two in the morning when no one else is awake to bid on it. If you can't sleep, make your time productive and prepare listings ahead of time with the TurboLister program to prepare your auctions and upload them for future launching when the world is ready to shop.

The specific day you close your auction can also be important. eBay is full of weekend browsers, so including a weekend of browsing in your auction time is a definite plus. Often, auctions that end late Sunday afternoon through Monday close with high bids.

Pirates of the Caribbean, er, Carribean?

Just before the *Pirates of the Caribbean* movie premiered; Disneyland gave out exclusive movie posters to their visitors. My daughter, savvy eBayer that she is, snagged several copies to sell on the site. She listed them (one at a time) when the movie opened and couldn't get more than the starting bid, $9.99, for each of them.

When we searched eBay for *pirates poster*, we found that the very same posters with a misspelled title, Pirates of the Carribean, were selling for as high as $30 each. We immediately changed her auctions to have the more popular (misspelling) *Carribean* in the title and quickly saw those dollar signs! After selling out her initial stock, she found another seller who had 10 for sale — in one auction — with the proper spelling in the title. She bought those as well (for $5 each) and sold them with misspelled titles on the site for between $15 and $27!

You'll need to do some research to determine the best times to run your auctions and for how long. In Chapter 10, I show you how to combine your search engine research with a special kind of statistical counter to help you identify the best closing time for your items. (See Chapter 7 for the details about using the search engine as a valuable research tool.) The best person to figure out the closing information for your auctions is you. Use the tools and over time you'll work out a pattern that works best for you.

A definite time *not* to close your auctions? Experience has taught many sellers never to close an auction on a national holiday. Memorial Day, the Fourth of July, and Veteran's Day may be bonanza sales days for retail shops, but eBay auction items closing on these days go at bargain prices. I guess everyone is out shopping the brick and mortars.

Marketing your auctions

How do you let people know about your auctions? What do you do if all 100 million users on eBay happen to not be on the site the week that your items are up for sale? You advertise.

Many mailing lists and newsgroups permit self-promotion. Find a group that features your type of items and post a bit of promotion. This works best if you have your own e-commerce Web site. Your site, which should be the hub for your sales, can give you an identity and level of professionalism that makes your business more official in the eyes of buyers. In Chapter 8, I detail the ins and outs of business sites on the Web.

eBay Merchant Kit

If you have your own family (non-commercial) Web site, it might just behoove you to spruce it up, pointing to your eBay listings. (You never know, Aunt Patti may just be in the market for your goods!) eBay has a fantastic Merchant Kit that turns your web page into a mini-eBay featuring your listings. In Figure 2-11, you can see the Merchant Kit in action on my family Web site, with active links to my eBay sales.

This page is run by eBay's magic API (application program interface) which is far too technical for the likes of me — I'm an expert at buying and selling — not techie coding! Luckily, we don't need to be techies to use this tool. It's automatically put on your site after you insert a bit of eBay-supplied HTML code into your Web page. The eBay API updates your listings every 10 minutes.

Picture	All Items	Price		Ends PDT
	TRUE COLOR Task Lamp LIGHT 13w 5000K Cloud Dome w Bulb	$33.95	*Buy It Now*	May-11 13:56
	New/Box CLOUD DOME Digital Lighting Kit 7" Ext Collar	$168.99	*Buy It Now*	May-11 13:59
	Deluxe CLOUD DOME Digital Complete Lighting Kit w Case	$231.99	*Buy It Now*	May-12 17:43
	NEW 2 Photography Photo Flood Lights Lighting Kit w Box	$119.99	*Buy It Now*	May-12 17:44
	CLOUD DOME Lighting Kit w Angled & Straight TWO COLLARS	$188.99	*Buy It Now*	May-12 17:49

Figure 2-11: The eBay Merchant Kit on my personal Web site.

To get your code, go to www.eBay.com/api/merchantkit.html and follow these steps:

1. **On the Marketplace page, click the Get Merchant Kit Now button.**

   You'll be taken to a place where you can select a few options to create an HTML sniplet to insert on your page. As with most eBay tasks, you are required to sign in again and agree to the official license agreement before you can get down to business.

2. **Choose the items that you want to appear.**

   Your choices are All Categories, a selected eBay category number, and (if you have an eBay store) one of your eBay Store categories. If your Web site is devoted to classic VHS tapes, for example, you might want to point your selection to eBay category 309 (DVDs & Movies:VHS).

3. **Choose the number of items you want to show: 25 or 50.**

4. **Choose the way in which you'd like to display your items.**

   You can display your items in order by items ending first, items ending last, highest prices first, or highest prices last.

5. **Indicate whether you'd rather have a different font face than the default, Verdana, or vary the type size.**

   I think Verdana is a perfect face to use. It was developed for clarity on the Internet. The default for the size is 2, which fits perfectly on the page — why monkey with it?

6. **Decide whether you want the PayPal icon (if you offer PayPal for your listings) and the highlight feature option (if you use it) to appear on the Marketplace page.**

7. **Click the Preview Sniplet button.**

   You see a representation of how your Marketplace will look and are presented with the proper HTML code to insert on your page.

8. **Copy the HTML code and paste it into your Web page where you want the Marketplace to appear.**

   Voila! a marketplace.

TipLink Buttons

eBay supplies some nice link buttons (see Figure 2-12) that you can use on your Web site. Visit the following address to add these links to your site's home page:

```
http://pages.ebay.com/services/buyandsell/link-buttons.html
```

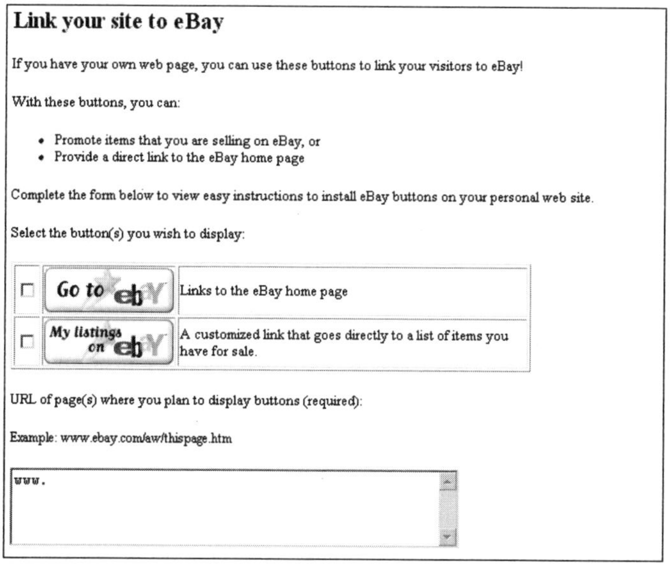

Link your site to eBay

If you have your own web page, you can use these buttons to link your visitors to eBay!

With these buttons, you can:

- Promote items that you are selling on eBay, or
- Provide a direct link to the eBay home page

Complete the form below to view easy instructions to install eBay buttons on your personal web site.

Select the button(s) you wish to display:

| ☐ | Go to eBaY | Links to the eBay home page |
| ☐ | My listings on eBaY | A customized link that goes directly to a list of items you have for sale |

URL of page(s) where you plan to display buttons (required):

Example: www.ebay.com/aw/thispage.htm

```
www.
```

Figure 2-12: The Shop eBay with Me link buttons.

I'm guessing that you already know all about your About Me page, a handy tool when it comes to marketing your auctions. In Chapter 3, I discuss the values of the About Me page. You should link to your Web site from your little home page on eBay.

Here's a great way to market future auctions: When you're sending items after making a sale on eBay, include a list of items that you'll be selling soon (along with your thank-you note, of course) — especially ones that may appeal to that customer. When you schedule your auctions, you're given the auction number before the item is listed.

Do not link your auction to your Web site. It's against eBay policy to possibly divert sales away from the auction site. *Do* link from your About Me page. See the "Linking from your auctions" section, later in this chapter, to find out just what you can and cannot link to and from.

A second chance

The new Second Chance feature on eBay helps sellers legitimize something that previously went on behind closed doors and in violation of eBay policy. When a winner doesn't complete a sale, the Second Chance feature allows sellers to offer the item to the next highest bidder.

You must still go through the proper channels and file your non-paying bidder notice with eBay. After doing that, you can then send a Second Chance offer to any under bidder no more than 60 days after the end of the auction. Your final value fee is based on the price you receive when the offer is accepted.

In the Second Chance Offer scenario, the seller can leave two feedbacks: one for the winner (non-paying bidder) and one for the person who bought the item through the Second Chance Offer transaction. The bidder to whom you proffer your Second Chance offer is covered by the eBay fraud protection program.

The Second Chance feature does not apply to Dutch auctions.

Listing Violations

eBay does not sell merchandise. eBay is merely a venue that provides the location where others can put on a giant, e-commerce party (in other words, sell stuff). To provide a safe and profitable venue for its sellers, eBay must govern auctions that take place on its site. eBay makes the rules; you and I follow the rules. I like to think of eBay as the place that lets you hold your senior prom in its gym. When I was in school, my classmates and I had to follow the rules or see our prom cancelled. If we don't agree to follow eBay's rules, a safe and trusted eBay community can't exist.

Listing policies

eBay has some hard-and-fast rules about listing your items. You must list your item in the appropriate category (that only makes sense), and I highlight here a few other rules that you should keep in mind when listing. What I discuss in this section isn't a definitive list of eBay listing policies and rules. Take time to familiarize yourself with the User Agreement (which details all eBay policies and rules) at the following:

```
pages.ebay.com/help/policies/user-agreement.html
```

I recommend regularly checking the eBay User Agreement for any policy changes.

Choice auctions

Your auction must be for one item only: The item that you specifically list in your auction. It's against the rules to give the bidder a choice of items, sizes, or colors. eBay protects you with its Purchase Protection program, which covers all online eBay transactions. When you give your bidders a choice, it's an illegal sale on eBay and isn't covered. Anything that's negotiated outside the eBay system can lead to either misrepresentation or fraud. You don't want to be caught up in that sort of grief and misery.

If eBay catches you offering a choice, they will end the auction and credit the insertion fee to your account.

Duplicate auctions

Remember the old supply and demand theory from your economics class? When people list the same items repeatedly, they drive down the item's going price while ruining all the other sellers' opportunities to sell the item during that time frame.

eBay allows you ten identical listings at any time. If you're going to list an item that many times, be sure to list it in different categories. That's a rule, but it also makes sense. Nothing drives down the price of an item faster than closing identical auctions, one after another, in the same category. eBay also requires that you list your auction in a category that's relevant to your item.

If you have multiple copies of something, a better solution is to run a Dutch auction for the total number of items you have for sale. Or perhaps run two Dutch auctions in different (but appropriate) categories.

If you're caught with more than ten identical auctions, eBay may end the additional auctions (any over ten). eBay will credit the insertion fees.

Pre-sale listings

eBay doesn't like it when you try to sell something that's not in your hands (known as a *pre-sale listing*). Doing so is a dangerous game to play anyway. In many situations, being the first seller to put a very popular item up for sale can get you some pretty high bids. And if you can guarantee in your auction description that the item will be available to ship within 30 days of the purchase or the auction closing, you can run a pre-sale. However, I don't recommend even attempting a pre-sale listing if you're not completely sure that you'll have the item in time.

If you know that you'll have the item to ship — and it won't be lost on its way to you — you may list the item with the following requirement: You must state in your auction description that the item is a pre-sale and will be shipped by the 30th day from the end of the listing or purchase. You'll also have to use a little HTML here because the text must be coded with an HTML font no smaller than font size 3.

Before you set up such an auction, check out the Federal Trade Commission 30-day rule covering these matters, which you can find at the following address:

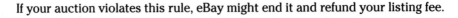

```
www.ftc.gov/bcp/conline/pubs/buspubs/mailorder.htm
```

Bonuses, giveaways, raffles, or prizes

Because eBay sells to every state in the United States, it must follow explicit laws governing giveaways and prizes. Each state has its own set of rules and regulations, so eBay doesn't allow individual sellers to come up with their own promotions.

If your auction violates this rule, eBay might end it and refund your listing fee.

Pre-selling: Not worth the hassle

A seller I once knew pre-sold Beanie Babies on eBay. She had a regular source that supplied her when the new toys came out, so she fell into a complacent attitude about listing pre-sales. Then her supplier didn't get the shipment. Motivated by the need to protect her feedback rating (and by the fear that she'd be accused of fraud), she ran all over town desperately trying to get the beanies she needed to fill her orders. The Beanies were so rare that she ended up spending several hundred dollars more than what she had originally sold the toys for, just to keep her customers happy.

Keyword spamming

Keyword spamming is when you add words, usually brand names, to your auction description that don't describe what you're selling (for example, describing that little black dress as Givenchy-style when Givenchy has nothing to do with it). Sellers use keyword spamming to pull viewers to their auctions after viewers have searched for the brand name. To attract attention to their listings, some sellers use "not" or "like" along with the brand name, such as "like Givenchy".

Keyword spamming actually causes your auction to fall under "potentially infringing" items for sale on eBay. Keyword spamming is a listing violation, and I mention it here because it affects all listings. The wording you choose when you run this kind of auction manipulates the eBay search engine and prospective bidders. For a complete discussion of keyword spamming and its complexities as an item that is an infringement of eBay's policies, see Chapter 4.

Linking from your auctions

Few issues set sellers to arguing more than the rules on linking. eBay has some rules that govern linking, which I describe in this section.

In your auction item description, you *can* use the following links:

- ✔ One link to an additional page that gives further information about the item you're selling.

- ✔ A link that opens an e-mail window on the prospective buyer's browser so that the buyer can send you an e-mail.

- ✔ Links to more photo images of the item you're selling.

- ✔ Links to your other auctions on eBay and your eBay Store listings.

- ✔ One link to your About Me page, besides the link next to your user ID that eBay provides.

- ✔ Links to vendors' sites that help you with your auctions. eBay considers listing services, software, and payment services to be third-party vendors. You can legally link to them as long as the HTML font is no larger than size 3; if you're using a logo, it must be no larger than 88 x 33 pixels.

   Most third-party vendors are well aware of these restrictions. They don't want their credits pulled from eBay, so the information they supply as a link generally falls within eBay's parameters.

eBay Giving Works (charity) auctions

Tens of millions of dollars has been raised on eBay for charitable organizations (see the figure). If you represent a legitimate charity, you may run auctions on eBay to raise funds. Just follow these simple steps:

1. **Register your charity as an eBay member.**

2. **Prepare an About Me page describing your charity.**

   Explain what it is, what it does, where the money goes, and so on. Set up the page to "Show no feedback" and indicate for the page to "Show all items." eBay will link this page to the Giving Works area.

3. **E-mail all the following information to eBay at** `charity@eBay.com`:

   ✔ User ID and e-mail address you registered with on eBay

   ✔ The completed About Me page

   ✔ Your 501c3/EIN number for your non-profit organization

✔ The time frame in which you expect to run your auction

✔ A brief description of your organization

✔ Examples of the items you'd like to list

✔ Name, e-mail address, and telephone number of the organization's main contact person

✔ The Web site address for your organization (if it has one)

You'll hear back from eBay when your charity has been approved. Your charity will then appear on Giving Works, and you can start planning your charity auctions. The eBay Giving Works page is accessible from a link on the home page or directly through the following:

`http://pages.ebay.com/givingworks`

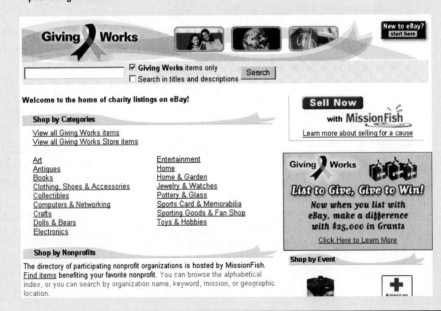

In your auction description, you _cannot_ link to the following:

- ✔ A page that offers to sell, trade, or purchase merchandise outside the eBay site.
- ✔ Any area on the Internet that offers merchandise considered illegal on eBay. See Chapter 4 for information on illegal items.
- ✔ Any site that encourages eBay bidders to place their bids outside eBay.
- ✔ Sites that solicit eBay user IDs and passwords.

Linking from your About Me page

eBay rules are pretty much the same as the rest of the site when it comes to your About Me page. Because eBay gives you this page for self-promotion, _you_ may link to your own business Web site from it (e-commerce or personal). Be sure not to link to other trading sites or to sites that offer the same merchandise for the same or lower price. Read more about the About Me page do's and don'ts in Chapter 3.

Chapter 3

Cool eBay Tools

In This Chapter

▶ Making My eBay your home page

▶ Taking advantage of your About Me page

▶ Managing the business of your auction: eBay seller services

*e*Bay offers you an amazing variety of tools. Because the site is constantly changing, very few of us know where these tools are, how to find them, or how to use them. I must admit that I have fallen victim to the "Oh, I didn't know I could do that" syndrome. When I poke around eBay and find a new cool tool or neat shortcut, it's always an eye-opener!

Aside from the tools I tell you about in this chapter, the most important shortcut I can give you is to remind you to sign in and click the box that says "Keep me signed in on this computer unless I sign out" before you attempt to do anything at eBay. This will permit you to do all your business at eBay without being bugged for your password at every turn.

If you have more than one user ID, or share a computer with other people, be sure to sign out when you're finished. The cookie system has been changed on eBay. Now, as on other Web sites, your computer will hold your sign-in information until you sign out. For your protection, you still have to type your password for actions involving financial information. To specify the tasks for which you want eBay to remember your sign-in information, go to the Preferences area of the My eBay page.

Many eBay users frequently share with me some nugget of information that has helped them along the way. And now I share these nuggets with you.

In addition, eBay has developed some incredibly useful features, such as My eBay, which allows you to customize eBay for your home page. Another feature, the About Me page, lets you tell the story of your business to the world as well as find out (with a click of the mouse) about the people you plan on buying from. To get the lowdown on my favorite cool eBay tools, read on.

My eBay

My own home at eBay pops up on my screen every morning with a cheery, "My eBay — Hello, marsha_c," followed by my current feedback rating. My eBay is no longer a step-by-step list of what you're bidding on and selling, but a veritable Swiss Army knife of eBay tools.

Access the My eBay page by clicking the My eBay button above the eBay navigation bar. The navigation bar, which is shown in Figure 3-1, appears at the top of every eBay page. You can also click the My eBay link at the bottom of the eBay home or Search page. Why? I don't really know why anyone would take two steps instead of one, but it's there and you can.

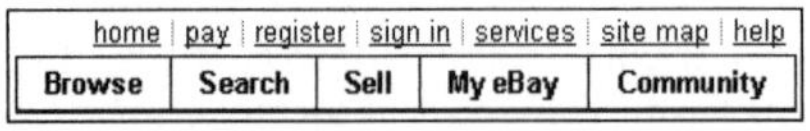

Figure 3-1:
The eBay navigation bar appears at the top of every eBay page.

| home | pay | register | sign in | services | site map | help |
| Browse | Search | Sell | My eBay | Community |

When you arrive at your My eBay page, you'll see a summary of the business that you have in progress on the site (see Figure 3-2). Each comment has a link, so you can investigate the progress of the transactions.

My eBay is divided into five areas (My Summary, All Bidding, All Selling, All Favorites, and My Account), which you can visit by clicking links in the My eBay Views box on the left side of the page. The top link of each My eBay area presents you with a summary of the activity in that area. The links below the top link take you to specific data, without having to scroll through a long page.

Setting a desktop shortcut to your My eBay page

People often tell me that they'd like a direct link from their computer desktop to their My eBay page. If you use Internet Explorer as your browser, just follow these steps:

1. **Sign in and go to your My eBay page.**

2. **In your browser's toolbar, choose File⇨ Send⇨Shortcut to Desktop.**

That's it. A clickable shortcut to your My eBay area is placed on your computer's desktop.

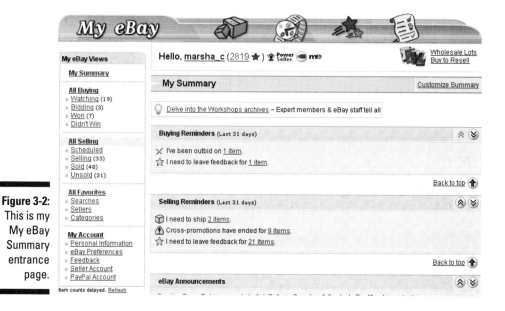

Figure 3-2:
This is my
My eBay
Summary
entrance
page.

At the bottom of My eBay Views is another box with convenient links to services and to answers you may need while doing business at eBay (see Figure 3-3). The task-specific pages of my eBay may show a <u>more</u> link in this additional links box. Click the <u>more</u> link and you're presented with a page of links related to the page you're on.

Selling Links

View Selling Manager
PayPal
Seller's Guide
Seller Central
Seller Tools
Manage My Store
Non-Paying Buyer Policy
more...

Figure 3-3:
The Related
Links box on
the My eBay
Selling page.

The links in the Related Links box are different depending on the page, with buying-related links on the All Buying page, selling-related links on the All Selling page (as in Figure 3-4), account-related links on the My Account page, and favorites-related links on the All Favorites page. When you have a question regarding some eBay procedure, you'll find these links very handy.

Selling-Related Links

Managing Your Items:	Billing/Payment:	Help Boards:
Sell Your Item	Billing Frequently Asked	Auction Listings board
Revise Your Item	Questions (FAQ)	Feedback board
Add to Item Description	PayPal	Packaging & Shipping board
Cancel Bids on My Item	Apply for an eBay Platinum Visa	PayPal Board
End My Listing Early		Photos/HTML board
	Trust and Safety:	Tools - Turbo Lister
Send A Second Chance Offer	Listing policies	Tools - Selling Manager
Promote Your Item	Items Not Allowed	Tools - Selling Manager Pro
	Non-Paying Bidder Program	Tools - Seller's Assistant Basic
Manage/Edit Andale counters	Trading Violations	Tools - Seller's Assistant Pro
Block or Pre-Approve Bidders	Dispute Resolution	
eBay Picture Services		Escrow/Insurance Board
	Services:	International Trading Board
eBay Seller Tools	Item Authentication	
	All about Escrow	**Shipping:**
Selling information:	SquareTrade Seal	eBay Shipping Calculator
Seller's Guide	Graphic & Web Design - eBay	eBay Shipping Center
Selling Frequently Asked	Professional Services	Shipping with US Postal Service
Questions (FAQ)		Order US Postal Service Shipping
After the Auction		Supplies
Seller Services		Shipping with UPS
		Find a UPS Store near you

Figure 3-4:
Selling-related links on the All Selling page.

At the top of each of the Views is a mini tote board, giving you a snapshot of your financial business dealings. In the Bidding area, it displays the number of items you're bidding on and the dollar amount of all your winning bids. In the Selling area, you see the number of items and the dollar amounts bid. The other views have a similar summary tote at the top of the page.

All Buying

Here it is: the hub for keeping track of your bids, your wins, items you're watching, and any items you didn't win. Although you plan to sell more than buy at eBay, I'm sure you'll occasionally find something to buy if only to turn around and resell it. I've found many a bargain item at eBay that I've re-sold immediately at a profit. Plus, I purchase most of my shipping supplies at eBay. (In Chapter 17, I reference a few eBay sources with great prices and fast shipping.)

Items I'm Bidding On

When you place a bid, eBay automatically registers it in the Items I'm Bidding On area, like the one shown in Figure 3-5.

Make the bidding page a daily stop at eBay so you can see the status of your bids:

✔ Bid amounts in green indicate that you're the high bidder in the auction.

✔ Bid amounts in red indicate that your bid is losing. If you decide to increase your bid, simply click the auction title to go to the auction.

✔ Dutch auctions appear in black. To determine whether you retain high bidder status in a Dutch auction, you have to go to the actual auction.

✔ The My Max Bid column reminds you of the amount of your highest bid; if you see a bid that surpasses your own, you'll know it's time to throw in another bid.

✔ The Bidding Totals box, at the top of the Bidding page, lists the current dollar amount you're spending and the number of items you're currently winning in pending auctions. You'll see the total amount you've bid and a separate total representing auctions you're winning.

✔ As auctions on which you've bid end, they automatically transfer to the Won and Didn't Win pages, based on your success or failure in the bidding process.

Figure 3-5:
Keeping track of your bidding at My eBay.

TIP

You can make notations on your bidding or item-watching, for example, to help you organize your gift giving. (See the note I added in Figure 3-6.) Click to place a check mark next to the item you want to annotate, click the Add Note button, and then add the information.

Items I'm Bidding On (5 items)				🖨 Print Customize ⌃ ⌄	
Show: **All** | Winning (3) | Not Winning (2)					
☐ Picture	Current Price	My Max Bid	Shipping Cost	Time Left △	Action
☐ **NEW Wireworks Designer Kitchen Spoon Rest NR**					
	$1.25	$3.01	--	44m	--
☐ **NobleSpirit~LIMITED EDITION Autographed BUCK KNIFE**					
	$18.01	$17.51	--	23h 20m	Bid Now!
My Note: For Dad on Father's day?				Edit	
☐ **-LIMITED-*TIME* Barbera pods QTY. (70) *Wholesale***					
	$20.00	$20.00	--	3d 21h 40m	--
eBay Note: Dutch Auction - You bid on 1 item. You are currently winning 1 item.					

Figure 3-6:
My Father's
Day notation
on my bid.

Items I've Won

Clicking the Won link in the bidding area displays all the items you've won as far back as the last 60 days. The default is 31 days, which should suffice for most transactions. The Items I've Won page is a great place to keep track of items that you're waiting to receive from the seller. It's also a convenient way to keep track of your expenditures, should you be buying for resale. Helpful features on this page include the following:

- ✔ **Check box:** Click the box to add a check mark, and you can indicate that you'd like to add a note to your record or remove it from the list.

- ✔ **Seller's user ID:** It always helps to remember the seller's name, and this link sends you to the seller's Member Profile (feedback page) where you can send an e-mail to the seller.

- ✔ **Auction title:** A link to the auction. I always use this when an item arrives so that I can be sure that the item I received is exactly as advertised.

- ✔ **Item number:** The auction number for your records.

- ✔ **Auction sale date:** Convenient way to see whether your item is slow in shipping. After a week, it doesn't hurt to drop the seller an e-mail to check on the shipping status.

- ✔ **Sale price** and **quantity:** Helps you keep track of the money you've spent. Works with the totals in the tote board.

✔ **Action:** Displays different commands based on the status of your transaction. You can click a link to pay for the item through PayPal, view the payment status on paid items, mark the item paid if you paid through other payment methods, or leave feedback once you've received the item and are satisfied that it's what you ordered.

✔ **Icons:** At the end of each item's listing are three icons that appear dimmed until the selected action is taken. A dollar sign indicates whether you've paid for the item, a star indicates that you've left feedback, and a quote bubble indicates whether feedback has been left for you.

When you receive an item and leave feedback, click the box and then click the box next to it and press the Delete Selected Items button to remove the completed transactions from view.

Items I'm Watching

Have you ever seen an auction that made you think, "I don't want to bid on this just now, but I'd like to buy it if it's a bargain"? Clicking the Watching link from the My eBay Views box will bring you to the Items I'm Watching page (see Figure 3-7), one of the most powerful features of the My eBay area, is just the tool to help you. This page lists each auction with a countdown (time left) timer, so you know exactly when the auction will close. When an auction on your watch list gets close to ending, you can swoop down and make the kill — if the price is right.

Figure 3-7:
Sit back and
observe at
My eBay.

Also a handy marketing tool, the Watching page allows you to store auctions from competitive sellers. That way, you can monitor the status of items similar to ones you plan to sell later and see whether the items are selling high or low, helping you to decide whether it's a good time to sell.

You've probably seen the <u>Add to watch list</u> link at the top of each auction page. If you're watching items (eBay allows you to monitor 100 auctions at a time), you'll see a notation on the page, indicating how many auctions you're currently watching.

My number-one reason for using the watch list function is that it allows me to keep my bargain hunting quiet. Everybody — including the competition — knows when you're bidding on an item; nobody knows when you're watching the deals like a hawk. When you're looking for bargains to buy and resell, you may not want to tip off the competition by letting them know you're bidding.

Selling

eBay provides some smooth management tools on your Selling page. You can track items you currently have up for auction and items you've sold. It's a quick way to get a snapshot of the dollar value of your auctions, as they proceed. Although this page isn't as good for marketing information (detailed counters are best — see Chapter 9), it's a pretty good way to tell at a glance how your items are faring.

Items I'm Selling

With the Items I'm Selling page, shown in Figure 3-8, you can keep an eye on your store items, your fixed-price sales, and the progress of your auctions. You can see how many bids your auctions have, whether your reserves have been met, and how long before the auction will close. By clicking an auction title, you can visit the auction to make sure your pictures are appearing or to check your counter.

Many people watch auctions and don't bid until the last minute, so you may not see a lot of bidding activity on your page. The # of Watchers feature can give you important information on the progress of your auctions.

The auctions that appear in green have received one or more bids (and met any reserves you've set). Auctions in red haven't received any bids or the set reserve price hasn't been met. Dutch auctions aren't color-coded and appear in black.

Figure 3-8:
Items I'm
Selling at
My eBay.

At the top of the Items I'm Selling area, eBay lists the current price of all items, including bidding on items that haven't met your reserve. The total dollar amount of the items that will sell when the auction is over appears beneath these totals. On the right side of your listings, eBay has a column for icons.

Items I've Sold

As you scroll down the All Selling page, you'll come to the Items I've Sold area. To avoid a lot of scrolling, you can reach an abbreviated version of this area (missing the detailed Selling Totals box) by clicking the Sold link in the Views box, under All Selling.

The Items I've Sold area keeps your sales in a concise place, as shown in Figure 3-9. I use it in lieu of fancy auction management software. If you're selling hundreds of items, your list will probably be too long to monitor individual auctions — but you can view the total current price of the items that will sell.

If you're selling more than 20 items a week, you might consider using eBay's Selling Manager to give you an even more complete auction management solution. See Chapter 9 for the lowdown on how to make this tool work for you.

The Items I've Sold page has the following features, which I'm sure you'll find helpful in completing your transactions:

- ✔ **Check box:** Click here to add a personal note to your record or to remove an item from your list.

- ✔ **Buyer's user ID** and **feedback rating:** The eBay ID of the winner of the sale. Click it to go to the User's Member Profile, where you can use eBay's e-mail sever to contact the buyer.

- ✔ **Quantity:** If the sale was for multiple items, the number of items is displayed here.

- ✔ **Item title:** A direct link to the auction. You can click this link to check on your auction and see the other bidders, should you want to make a Second Chance offer.

- ✔ **Item number:** The auction number for your records.

- ✔ **Sale price:** The final selling price for your item.

- ✔ **Total price:** The final selling price plus the shipping amount.

- ✔ **Sale date:** Keep an eye on the end date so that you can be sure you get your payment as agreed.

✔ **Action:** Here's where you find a hidden, drop-down menu that works with the icons to the left and offers links to various actions that you can take:

- **Mark paid:** If the customer hasn't paid using PayPal, you can indicate their method of payment (after you receive it).

- **View payment status:** See a copy of the payment receipt if the buyer paid using PayPal or a notation you inserted regarding other payment methods.

- **Print shipping label:** You can print a shipping label from here. See Chapter 14 for more professional options.

- **Leave feedback:** Leave feedback with a single click once you've heard that the item arrived safely and your customer is happy. For more information on leaving feedback, check out the section "Feedback: Your permanent record," later in this chapter.

- **Mark shipped**. After you've shipped the item, click here to indicate that it's on the way.

- **Second chance offer:** Click here to make a second chance offer to one of your underbidders if you have multiple items for sale.

- **Relist:** Here you can relist your item on the site.

✔ **Icons:** My eBay has several icons that appear dimmed until you perform an action with the Action command. You may also click the icons at the top of the list to sort your listings by actions completed, although most sellers prefer to keep the listings in the default chronological order.

- **Shopping cart:** The buyer has completed checkout (supplying a shipping address and planned payment method).

- **Dollar sign:** The buyer has paid using PayPal, or you've used the drop-down menu to indicate that the buyer has paid with a different form of payment (such as a money order or a personal check).

- **Shipping box:** The item has shipped.

- **Star:** You've left feedback.

- **Comment bubble:** The buyer has left feedback. A plus sign (+) indicates a positive comment, and a minus sign (-) indicates a negative comment.

All Favorites

If you sell and have an interest in a few categories, look no further than the My eBay All Favorites page, which gives you some links for checking out what's hot and what's not. The All Favorites page helps you track trends and find some bargains to resell at eBay.

Favorite Categories

eBay allows you to store hot links for four categories. These links give you the chance to quickly check out the competition.

Before you list some auctions on a popular item, estimate the date and hour that other auctions selling that item will close. Then go into the category and check to be sure that your auction won't be closing during a flood of auctions for the same item. Nothing kills profits more than closing an auction in the middle of a series of auctions selling the same thing. You can watch the final values drop one at a time.

Favorite Searches

Another tool that comes in handy for sellers as well as buyers is My Favorite Searches (see Figure 3-10). You can list as many as 100 favorite searches; when you want to check one out, simply click the <u>Search Now</u> link next to the item.

You can view saved searches, change them, delete them, or indicate that you'd like to receive e-mail notification when a new item is listed. To add an item to the list, run a search from any search bar on any eBay page and click the <u>Add to Favorites</u> link that appears at the top of the search results. The next time you reload your My eBay All Favorites page, your new favorite will be listed.

	My Favorite Searches (19 searches; 6 emails)			Add new Search
Delete				
☐ Name of Search △		Search Criteria	Email Settings	Action
☐ Search Now	"case of" Sort: Ending Soonest			Edit Preferences ▾
☐ Search Now	rodrique Sort: Ending Soonest			Edit Preferences ▾
☐ Search Now	"fred stone" partners			Edit Preferences ▾
☐ Search Now	"star trek" figure (autographed, signed) -photo			Edit Preferences ▾
☐ Search Now	(debox, deboxed, deboxer) Sort: Ending Soonest			Edit Preferences ▾
☐ Search Now	Broguiere's Sort: Ending Soonest			Edit Preferences ▾
☐ Search Now	"ex wife" -vhs -cd -dvd -videos -book Sort: Ending Soonest			Edit Preferences ▾
☐ Search Now	(macys, macy's) parade Sort: Ending Soonest			Edit Preferences ▾
☐ Search Now	(cemetery, cemetary) (plot, plots) Sort: Ending Soonest			Edit Preferences ▾

Figure 3-10: Some of my favorite searches (this month).

Keeping track of favorite searches is a valuable tool when you're looking for particular items to resell and want to find them at bargain-basement prices. Be sure to take advantage of asterisks (wildcard characters) and alternate spellings so you can catch items with misspellings in the title. These are your best bets for low prices. (See Chapter 7 for the lowdown on the search engine and how it can help your sales.)

If you choose to receive e-mail when your search locates a new listing, you can request that you receive notification from 7 days to a year. You're allowed to receive new listing e-mails on 30 of your 100 searches. Just click the Edit Preferences link in the far-right column (refer to Figure 3-10). eBay sends its robot to check listings each night, so you'll get notification of a new listing the next morning.

Favorite Sellers

Favorite Sellers is where I keep a list of people who sell items similar to what I sell. I can check up on them and see what they're selling, when they're selling it, and for how much. It's a helpful tool that has prevented me from listing an item right next to one of their auctions.

Favorite Sellers is handy also when your competition is selling an item that you plan to sell, but at a deeply discounted price. When that happens, don't offer yours until they sell out of the item, at which time the price will most likely go back up — supply and demand, remember? I have a few quality wholesalers and liquidators under my favorite sellers, too, and search for lots that I can resell at a profit.

To add a seller to your Favorite Sellers list, click the Add New Seller link in the upper-left corner of the page. On the page that appears, type the seller's user ID. You may add a maximum of 30 sellers to your list.

My Account

Your eBay account summary page (see mine in Figure 3-11) lets you know how much you owe eBay and how much they will charge your credit card that month. This is a quick and easy way to check your last invoice, payments and credits, and your account; all the links are located in one area.

You can also access your PayPal account to see, for example, when deposits were credited to your checking account. (For a complete picture of how to sign up and use PayPal, visit Chapter 13.)

Figure 3-11:
The My
Account
summary
page.

Personal Information

The Personal Information page holds all the links to your personal information at eBay. This is where you can change your e-mail address, user ID, password, and credit card information, and edit or create your About Me page. You can also change or access any registration or credit card information that you have on file at eBay.

The Personal Information page has a link for adding a wireless e-mail address for your cell phone or Palm. What a great idea: eBay can send End of Auction notices right to your WAP-enabled cell phone. The trouble is, sometimes these messages are sent out hours (days?) after the listing ends. So don't count on always getting immediate updates.

eBay Preferences

A nifty feature of the eBay Preferences page is the opportunity to customize how you see your My eBay pages (see Figure 3-12). If you run many auctions, you can show as many as 200 items on these pages.

You can also customize your eBay Sign In activities by clicking the <u>Change</u> link in the eBay Sign In Preferences section of the screen. You may as well select everything, so that you won't be constantly hammered for your password while conducting business at eBay.

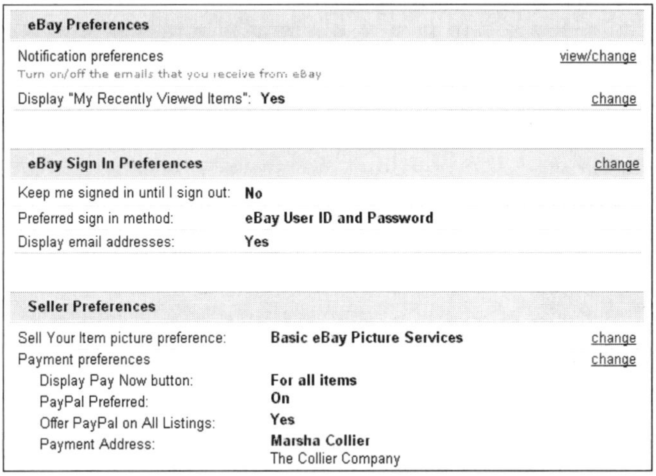

eBay Preferences	
Notification preferences	view/change
Turn on/off the emails that you receive from eBay	
Display "My Recently Viewed Items": **Yes**	change

eBay Sign In Preferences	change
Keep me signed in until I sign out: **No**	
Preferred sign in method: **eBay User ID and Password**	
Display email addresses: **Yes**	

Seller Preferences	
Sell Your Item picture preference: **Basic eBay Picture Services**	change
Payment preferences	change
Display Pay Now button: **For all items**	
PayPal Preferred: **On**	
Offer PayPal on All Listings: **Yes**	
Payment Address: **Marsha Collier**	
The Collier Company	

Figure 3-12:
Your eBay
Preferences
page.

The Microsoft Passport sign-in service may be available for signing in at eBay when you read this. eBay users with Microsoft Passport can sign in to eBay with either their Passport or their regular user ID and password. You can request to use the Passport single sign-in service on the eBay Preferences page. You can change your sign-in preference at any time.

The About Me Page

If you're on eBay, you *need* an About Me page. I hate to harp on this, but eBay is a community and all eBay members are members of that community. Checking out the About Me page of people you conduct business with gives you an opportunity to get to know them. Because eBay is a cyberspace market, you have no other way to let prospective bidders know that you're a real person. Don't you shop at some stores because you like the owners or people who work there? The About Me page takes a first step toward establishing a professional and trusted identity at eBay.

The About Me page enables you to personalize your business to prospective bidders. (See Figure 3-13 for an example.) Your About Me page also becomes your About the Seller page if you have an eBay store.

An About Me page benefits you also when you buy. Sellers usually like to know about their bidders to build confidence in their trading partners. If you've put up an About Me page, you're halfway there.

Figure 3-13:
An excellent example of an About Me page from member NobleSpirit!

If you don't have an About Me page, put this book down and set one up immediately. It doesn't have to be a work of art; just get something up there to tell the rest of the community who you are. You can always go back later and add to or redesign it.

When you plan your About Me page, consider adding the following:

✔ Who you are and where you live.

✔ Your hobbies. If you collect things, here's where to let the world know.

✔ Whether you run your eBay business full time or part time and whether you have another career. This is more integral information about you; let the world know.

✔ The type of merchandise that your business revolves around. Promote it here; tell the reader why your merchandise and service are the best!

✔ Your most recent feedback and a list of your current auctions.

To create your page, click the Me icon next to any user's name, scroll to the bottom of the About Me page that appears, find the line that reads "To create your own About Me page, click here," and click. You can also click the About Me link on the Personal Information page at My eBay. Or go to the following:

```
http://members.ebay.com/aw-cgi/eBayISAPI.dll?AboutMeLogin
```

Then follow the simple preformatted template for your first page and work from there.

eBay Seller Services

Most eBay users don't know the extent of eBay's seller-specific services. And sometimes sellers are so involved with their auctions that they don't take the time to find out about new helper tools. So I've gone deep into the eBay pond to dig up a few excellent tools to help you with your online business. Even if you've used some of these before, it might be time to revisit them because eBay has implemented quite a few changes during the past year.

Bidder-management tools

Did you know that you don't have to accept bids from just anyone? Although many people include notices in their auction descriptions attempting to qualify bidders ahead of time, this doesn't always prevent them from bidding on your auction. Alas, part of the business is watching your bidders. With bidder management tools, you can save yourself a good deal of grief.

Canceling bids

You could have any number of reasons for wanting to cancel someone's bid. Perhaps an international bidder has bid on an auction in which you clearly state you don't ship overseas. Here are a few more legitimate reasons for canceling a bid:

- ✔ The bidder contacts you to back out of the bid; choosing to be a nice guy, you let him or her out of the deal.
- ✔ Your bidder has several negative feedbacks and hasn't gone through with other transactions that he or she has won.
- ✔ You're unable to verify the bidder's identity through e-mail or the phone.
- ✔ You need to cancel the auction (see following tip).

I don't recommend canceling an auction unless you absolutely have to because it's just bad business. People rely on your auctions being up for the stated amount of time. They may be planning to bid at the last minute, or may just want to watch the action for a while. You may lose potential buyers by ending your listing early.

For whatever reason you're canceling someone's bid, you should first e-mail that person and clearly explain why you're doing so. Your bid cancellation appears in the auction's bidding history and becomes part of the auction's official record. For that reason, I recommend that you leave a concise, unemotional, one-line explanation on the cancellation form as to why you've cancelled the bid.

To get to the bid cancellation form, start on your My eBay All Selling page and scroll to Selling Links. You can also get to the cancellation form directly by typing the following in your browser:

```
http://pages.ebay.com/services/buyandsell/seller-cancel-
        bid.html
```

End your listing early

You may decide to end a listing early for any number of reasons. If any bids are on your auction before you end it, you'd be duty-bound to sell to the highest bidder. So before ending an auction early, it's polite to e-mail everyone in your bidder list, explaining why you're canceling bids and closing the auction. If an egregious error in the item's description is forcing you to take this action, let your bidders know whether you're planning to relist the item with the correct information.

After you've e-mailed all the bidders, you must then cancel their bids by using the bid cancellation form; for the link to this form, see the preceding section, "Canceling bids."

Only after canceling all bids should you go ahead and close your auction. To close your auction, use the <u>more</u> link at the bottom of your Selling Links box to get to the Managing Your Items box. Click the link there that says <u>End My Listing Early</u>. You can also go directly to

```
http://cgi3.ebay.com/aw-cgi/eBayISAPI.dll?EndingMyAuction
```

Following are some legitimate reasons for closing your auction:

✔ **You no longer want to sell the item.** Your account may be subject to a "Non-Selling Seller" warning unless you really have a good reason. (See Chapter 4 for more details.)

✔ **An error occurred in the minimum bid or reserve amount.** Perhaps your wife said that she really loves that lamp and you'd better get some good money for it, but you started the auction at $1.00 with no reserve.

✔ **The listing has a major error in it.** Maybe you misspelled a critical keyword in the title.

✔ **The item was somehow lost or broken.** Your dog ate it?

Blocking buyers

If you don't want certain buyers bidding on your auctions, you can remove their capability to do so. Setting up a list of bidders that you don't want to do business with is legal at eBay. If someone that you've blocked tries to bid on your auction, the bid won't go through. A message will be displayed notifying the person that he or she is not able to bid on the listing and to contact the seller for more information.

You can block as many as 1000 users from bidding on your auctions. However, I recommend that you use this option only when absolutely necessary. Situations — and people — change, and it's best to try to clear up problems with particular bidders.

You can reinstate a bidder at any time by going to the Buyer Blocking box at

```
http://pages.ebay.com/services/buyandsell/biddermanagement.
            html
```

and deleting the bidder's user ID.

Preapproving bidders

Suppose that you're selling a big-ticket item and want to prequalify your bidders. If the bidder has taken advantage of the ID Verify feature, which I explain in the next section, you can be sure that your bidders are who they say they are. You can scroll through a bidder's bidding history to see the amounts they've successfully bid in previous auctions and whether the feedback on those transactions is okay. Although eBay gives you the tools, you still have to do the research to determine whether you deem particular bidders trustworthy enough to bid on your special auction.

In your auction, state that bidders must prequalify by sending you an e-mail claiming their intent to bid. As you receive e-mails and approve bidders' intentions, you can build your preapproved bidder list.

Your preapproved bidder list is applicable only on an auction-by-auction basis. Using preapproved bidders means that only bidders in the listings you indicate must be preapproved. To use this feature, you must supply eBay with the auction number. You can add approved bidders right up to the close of the auction. Access the form and type in the preapproved bidders at

```
http://cgi3.ebay.com/aw-cgi/eBayISAPI.dll?PreApproveBidders
```

If someone who isn't preapproved tries to bid on your auction, eBay asks that bidder to contact you by e-mail before placing a bid. After you've investigated the bidder to your satisfaction and are comfortable with that person bidding on your auction, you can add the bidder's name to your preapproved bidder list for that auction.

ID Verify

ID Verify establishes proof that you are who you say you are. It also enables you to perform specialized eBay functions if you choose not to supply eBay with a credit card when you register. ID Verify has a one-time charge of $5, and VeriSign (one of the nation's largest credit security companies) conducts the verification. It is not a credit check. Your personal information is checked alongside consumer and business databases for consistency so that VeriSign can verify that you are who you say you are.

If you aren't quite ready to get the SquareTrade seal (see Chapter 4) for your auctions or you find the monthly fees involved in the seal currently prohibitive, ID Verify is the next best thing. Following are the extra functions you can perform without supplying your credit card:

- Buy an item through the eBay Buy It Now feature
- Place a bid above $15,000
- Bid on eBay Premier auctions
- Sell items in the eBay Mature Audiences category

Feedback: Your permanent record

Just like your high school permanent record, your eBay feedback follows you forever at eBay. If you change your user ID, it's there. If you change your e-mail address, it's there.

When you click the feedback number next to a user's ID, the user's eBay ID card (see Figure 3-14) is displayed. The information shown will tell you a lot about your bidder.

The most obvious tip-off to someone's feedback is the star you see next to the user ID. Different colored stars are awarded as folks reach milestones in their feedback ratings. To decipher the star colors and see what they mean, click the help link, and type the word *star*.

Your feedback means a great deal to people who visit your auctions. By glancing at your feedback page, they can see

- Whether you're an experienced eBay user
- Your eBay history
- When you started at eBay
- How many bid retractions you've had in the past six months

Figure 3-14:
The eBay
Feedback
page with
an overall
profile and
an ID card,
summarizing
recent
comments.

This is valuable information for both the buyer and the seller because it helps to evaluate whether you're the type of person who would make a responsible trading partner.

Worried about negative feedback? One possible way exists for getting negative feedback expunged from your record. You can file for mediation with SquareTrade (see Chapter 4 on how to do this), or if you're both in agreement, you can file for Mutual Feedback Withdrawal by going to

```
http://feedback.ebay.com/ws1/eBayISAPI.dll?MFWrequest
```

Enter the item number and continue filing the form. If the person who posted the feedback agrees to remove the negative feedback, eBay will oblige.

Leaving feedback

Everyone in the eBay community is honor-bound to leave feedback. Sometimes when you've had a truly dreadful experience, you hate to leave negative or neutral feedback, but if you don't, you're not helping anyone. The point of feedback is not to show what a great person you are, but to show future sellers or bidders where the rotten apples lie. So, when leaving feedback, be truthful and unemotional, and state just the facts.

Feedback is important, so you should be sure to leave some for every transaction you take part in. If a week has passed since you've shipped an item, and you haven't heard from the bidder or seen any new feedback, drop that bidder an e-mail. Write "Thanks for your purchase. Are you happy with the item?" Also emphasize that you'll be glad to leave positive feedback after you've heard a reply, and ask for the same in return.

Never leave feedback on a sale until you're absolutely, positively sure that the buyer has received the product and is happy with the deal. Many inexperienced sellers leave feedback the minute they get their money, but experience can teach them that it ain't over till it's over. A package can get lost or damaged, or the bidder may be unhappy for some reason. A buyer may also want to return an item for no good reason, turning a seemingly smooth transaction into a nightmare. You get only one feedback per transaction, so use it wisely. You can't go back and say that the buyer damaged the product and then tried to return it.

eBay provides so many different links to leave feedback that I could probably write an entire chapter on it. But I don't want you to fall asleep while reading, so I go through only the most convenient methods:

- ✔ Go to your auction page and click the <u>Leave Feedback</u> link, which appears on the left

- ✔ Click the number (in parentheses) next to the other user's name. When you're on that user's feedback page, click the <u>Leave Feedback</u> link

- ✔ Click the <u>Leave Feedback</u> link next to the completed sale on your My eBay page

- ✔ Visit the feedback forum (this link shows up on the bottom of every page) and click the link that shows you all pending feedback for the past 90 days. When you've fallen behind in leaving feedback, this is a super-fast way to catch up.

Responding to feedback

You may occasionally get feedback that you feel compelled to respond to. Did you know that you could? If the feedback is neutral or negative, I recommend that you cover yourself by explaining the situation for future bidders to see.

If you receive a negative feedback rating, a well-meaning admission of guilt would work. You could say something like, "Unfortunately, shipping was delayed and I regret the situation." Prospective bidders will see that you've addressed the problem instead of just letting it go.

To respond to feedback, follow these steps:

1. **In the My eBay Views box on your My eBay page, click the <u>Feedback</u> link under My Account.**

2. **On the feedback page, find Go to Feedback Forum at the top of the page, and click the <u>Reply to feedback received</u> link.**

    The Review and Respond to Feedback Comments Left for You page appears, as shown in Figure 3-15.

3. **Scroll to find the feedback comment that you want to respond to and click the <u>Respond</u> link.**

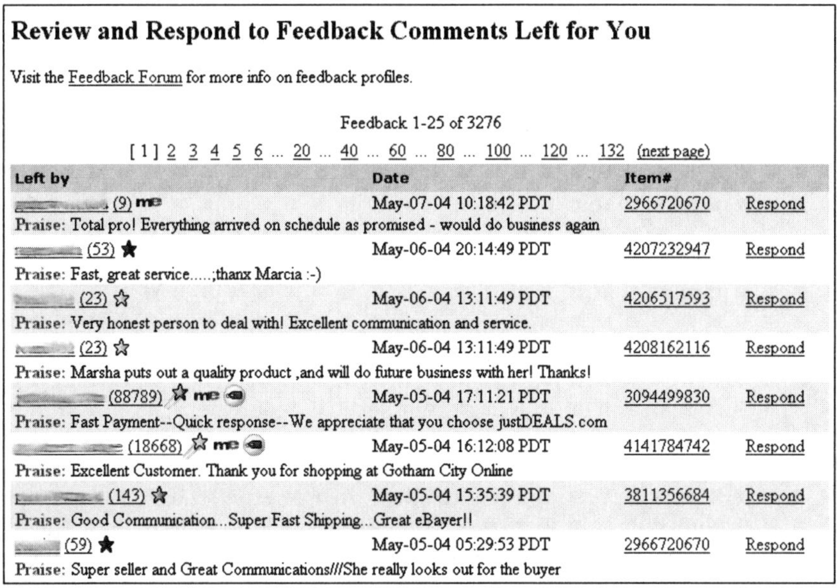

Review and Respond to Feedback Comments Left for You

Visit the Feedback Forum for more info on feedback profiles.

Feedback 1-25 of 3276

[1] 2 3 4 5 6 ... 20 ... 40 ... 60 ... 80 ... 100 ... 120 ... 132 (next page)

Left by	Date	Item#	
▬▬▬ (9) me	May-07-04 10:18:42 PDT	2966720670	Respond
Praise: Total pro! Everything arrived on schedule as promised - would do business again			
▬▬▬ (53) ★	May-06-04 20:14:49 PDT	4207232947	Respond
Praise: Fast, great service.....;thanx Marcia :-)			
▬▬▬ (23) ☆	May-06-04 13:11:49 PDT	4206517593	Respond
Praise: Very honest person to deal with! Excellent communication and service.			
▬▬▬ (23) ☆	May-06-04 13:11:49 PDT	4208162116	Respond
Praise: Marsha puts out a quality product ,and will do future business with her! Thanks!			
▬▬▬ (88789) ☆ me ⬤	May-05-04 17:11:21 PDT	3094499830	Respond
Praise: Fast Payment--Quick response--We appreciate that you choose justDEALS.com			
▬▬▬ (18668) ☆ me ⬤	May-05-04 16:12:08 PDT	4141784742	Respond
Praise: Excellent Customer. Thank you for shopping at Gotham City Online			
▬▬▬ (143) ☆	May-05-04 15:35:39 PDT	3811356684	Respond
Praise: Good Communication...Super Fast Shipping...Great eBayer!!			
▬▬▬ (59) ★	May-05-04 05:29:53 PDT	2966720670	Respond
Praise: Super seller and Great Communications///She really looks out for the buyer			

Figure 3-15:
Review and
respond
to your
feedbacks.

4. Type your response, and then click the Leave Response button.

The eBay PowerSeller program

I'm sure you've seen that big, giant PowerSeller logo on auctions that you browse. eBay PowerSellers represent the largest gross sales users at eBay. The requirements for becoming a PowerSeller follow:

✔ You must have a gross monthly dollar volume of $1000 (Bronze level); $3000 (Silver level); $10,000 (Gold level), $25,000 (Platinum level) or $50,000 (Titanium level). To remain a PowerSeller, you must maintain your level's minimum gross sales for the past three months and keep current with all the other requirements. To advance up the PowerSeller chain, you must reach and maintain the next level of gross sales for an average of three months.

If you miss your minimum gross sales for three months, eBay gives you a grace period. After that time, if you don't meet the minimum gross figures for your level, you may be moved down to the prior level or be removed from the PowerSeller program.

✔ You must have at least 100 feedback comments, with 98 percent positive. To calculate your feedback percentage, divide your number of positive feedbacks by your number of total feedbacks (negatives plus positives).

✔ You must average a minimum monthly total of 4 listings in the past three months.

PowerSellers enjoy many benefits:

Level	Priority eSupport	Toll-free phone	Account Manager
Bronze	Yes	No	No
Silver	Yes	Yes	No
Gold	Yes	Yes	Yes
Platinum	Yes	Yes	Yes
Titanium	Yes	Yes	Yes

The best thing about being a PowerSeller is the awesome level of customer service you receive, called Priority eSupport. When a PowerSeller dashes off an e-mail to a special customer service department, a reply comes back at the speed of light.

eBay doesn't require you to show the PowerSeller logo in your descriptions when you attain that level. Some PowerSellers don't include the logo in their auctions because they'd rather be perceived as regular folks at eBay.

eBay auction software

eBay has developed a fantastic software program called Turbo Lister, which is free and downloadable from the site. They also have an online Selling Manager to manage your auctions. For a breakdown of these software products and others to ease the seller's burden, skip to Chapter 9.

eBay Fraud Protection

The minute an auction payment hits the mailbox, or the moment that a winner pays with an online payment service, eBay covers the buyer with its fraud protection program. The program covers the bidder for $200 of the final auction price, with a $25 deductible.

The plan covers only fraud, not lost or damaged packages. The United States Postal Service offers insurance as an option, so I guess this means if your package arrives damaged and isn't insured, the bidder is out of luck. The eBay fraud protection program covers eBay buyers only when they're defrauded, the item is never shipped, or the item is significantly different from the auction description. The policy does *not* cover sellers for anything — so don't ship that item until you're darn sure the check has cleared!

When you get down to the nuts and bolts of the program, it has a lot of ifs. Buyers can apply only if they did not pay with cash. Bidders, if they paid by credit card, need to first apply to their credit card companies to see whether they're covered through them. The insurance will not cover the bidder if the seller has a negative feedback rating. The bidder also can't file any more than three claims within a six-month period.

eBay education

eBay offers many forms of training and education. No matter how advanced you are, its fun to go to eBay University and take a refresher course on the basics. You can also find some cool online interactive tutorials as you make your way through eBay. Take a moment when you can and watch them — you might just see one or two new features that you didn't know about. More information about eBay education is available at the following address:

```
www.eBay.com/education
```

eBay University

The eBay traveling tent show goes across the country, hosting thousands of eBay members, spreading the eBay word to the masses. You get a chance to meet some wonderful people who work for eBay and enjoy answering questions. eBay University follows two tracks:

- **Basic Selling:** A beginning class for new sellers that lays out the basics so they can progress from there.
- **Beyond the Basics:** A tutorial on eBay tools for advanced sellers.

Live, in-person seminars

Auction Advisor, an officially eBay licensed seminar series, visits cities around the county with an advanced, personalized form of eBay University. They specialize in small classes so that you can get answers to your questions. Their instructors are experts and can help you with getting your business up to speed. I teach at many of their seminars, so I look forward to seeing you. You can visit their Web site for a schedule at the following:

```
www.auctionadvisor.com
```

Online workshops

eBay has ongoing online workshops that allow you to participate through a chat screen. eBay experts give the one-hour workshops. eBay records and archives many interesting classes in the eBay education area, so you can see the classes after they premiere as well.

Chapter 4

Practicing Safe Selling

In This Chapter

▶ Understanding the rules

▶ Watching out for violations

▶ Protecting yourself — and helping make eBay a safe place to trade

There are a lot of *shoulds* in this world. You *should* do this and you *should* do that. I don't know who's in charge of the *shoulds,* but certain things just make life work better. You may or may not take any of the advice on these pages, but they'll make your eBay business thrive with a minimum of anguish. If you've ever had an auction pulled by eBay, you know what anguish truly feels like.

In the real world, we have to take responsibility for our own actions. If we buy a television set for $25 from some guy selling them out of the back of a truck, who do we have to blame when we take it home and it doesn't work? You get what you pay for, and you have no consumer protection from the seller of the possibly "hot" TVs. Responsible consumerism is every buyer's job. Lawsuit upon lawsuit gets filed — and some are won — when someone feels they've been ripped off, but my best advice is that if you stay clean in your online business, you'll keep clean.

eBay is a community, and the community thrives on the following five basic values:

✔ We believe people are basically good.

✔ We believe everyone has something to contribute.

✔ We believe that an honest, open environment can bring out the best in people.

✔ We recognize and respect everyone as a unique individual.

✔ We encourage you to treat others the way that you want to be treated.

eBay is committed to these values, and it says so right on its Web site. eBay believes that community members should "honor these values — whether buying, selling, or chatting." So *should* we all.

Is What You Want to Sell Legal?

Although eBay is based in California and therefore must abide by California law, sellers do business all over the United States. Therefore, items sold at eBay must be governed by the laws of every other state as well. As a seller, you're ultimately responsible for the legality of the items you sell and the way that you transact business on eBay. Yes, you're able to sell thousands of different items on eBay. But do you know what you aren't allowed to sell on eBay?

When alcohol becomes collectible

Many people collect rare and antique bottles of liquor or wine. I even sold a bottle of Korbel champagne designed by Frank Sinatra on eBay in 1998. Korbel bottles have featured artwork by designer Nicole Miller and comedienne Whoopi Goldberg as well as designs by Tony Bennett, Frank Sinatra, and Jane Seymour.

People also collect Jim Beam bottles, Dug decanters, and miniatures that are even more valuable when they're full. You *can* sell these on eBay as long as you fulfill the following requirements:

✔ The value of the item is in the collectible container, not its contents.

✔ The auction description should state that the container has not been opened but any incidental contents are not intended for consumption.

✔ The item must not be available at any retail outlet, and the container must have a value that substantially exceeds the current retail price of the alcohol in the container.

✔ Sellers should take steps to ensure that the buyer of these collectibles is of lawful age in the buyer's and seller's jurisdiction (generally 21 years old).

The eBay User Agreement outlines all eBay rules and regulations regarding what you can and can't sell as well as all aspects of doing business at eBay. If you haven't read it in a while, do so. You can find it at the following address:

```
http://pages.ebay.com/help/policies/user-agreement.html
```

These policies can change from time to time. As an active seller, you should make sure that you're notified of any changes. To request that you be notified when eBay makes changes to the User Agreement, as well as to control any correspondence you receive from eBay, follow these steps:

1. **In the My eBay Views section of the My eBay page, click the eBay Preferences link under My Account. Click the View/Change link, next to Notification Preferences.**

    Alternatively you can go to the following address:

    ```
    http://pages.ebay.com/services/myebay/optin-login.html
    ```

2. **Sign in with your user ID and password.**

    The Change Your Preferences page appears.

3. **Scroll down to the Legal and Other Emails area (see Figure 4-1), and check or uncheck any option you want to invoke.**

    To receive important information that may affect how you run your auctions, be sure that you click the User Agreement Changes option and Privacy Policy Changes option.

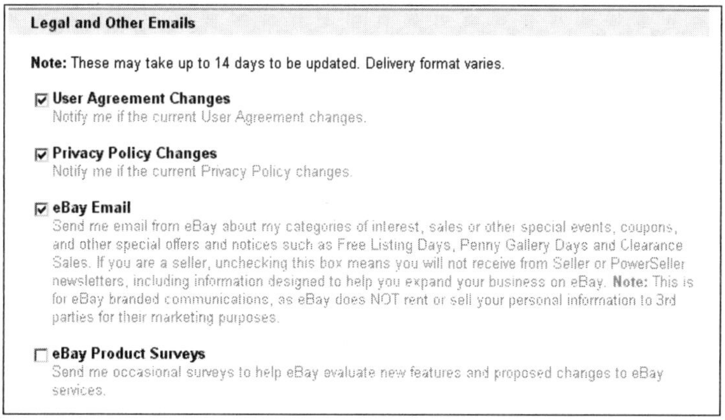

Legal and Other Emails

Note: These may take up to 14 days to be updated. Delivery format varies.

☑ **User Agreement Changes**
Notify me if the current User Agreement changes.

☑ **Privacy Policy Changes**
Notify me if the current Privacy Policy changes.

☑ **eBay Email**
Send me email from eBay about my categories of interest, sales or other special events, coupons, and other special offers and notices such as Free Listing Days, Penny Gallery Days and Clearance Sales. If you are a seller, unchecking this box means you will not receive from Seller or PowerSeller newsletters, including information designed to help you expand your business on eBay. **Note:** This is for eBay branded communications, as eBay does NOT rent or sell your personal information to 3rd parties for their marketing purposes.

☐ **eBay Product Surveys**
Send me occasional surveys to help eBay evaluate new features and proposed changes to eBay services.

Figure 4-1:
The Legal
e-mails
area of the
Change Your
Preferences
form.

By now, you should have a firm grasp of the rules and regulations for listing auctions (if not, check out Chapter 2). But in addition to knowing the rules for listing items, you must consider the items themselves. In this section, I detail the three categories of items to be wary of: prohibited, questionable, and infringing. Some are banned, period. Others fall in a gray area. You're responsible for what you sell, so you'd better know what's legal and what's not.

You may think it's okay to give away a regulated or banned item as a bonus item with your auction. Think again. Even giving away such items for free doesn't save you from potential legal responsibility.

Prohibited items

A *prohibited item* is banned from sale at eBay. You can't sell a prohibited item under any circumstance. Take a look at the following list. A little common sense tells you there's good reason for not selling these items, including liability issues for the seller (what if you sold alcohol to a minor? — that's against the law).

The following is a list of items prohibited as of this writing, so don't try to sell 'em at eBay.

Alcohol (Alcohol may be allowed if the value of the item lies in the collectible container (bottle) exceeding the alcohol's retail price. The item should not be currently available at a retail outlet. The auction should state that the container has not been opened, and the seller should be sure that the buyer is over 21.)

Animals and wildlife products

Catalogs (current issues) and Web sales

Counterfeit currency or stamps

Counterfeit items

Credit cards

Drugs and drug paraphernalia

Firearms, ammunition, replicas, and militaria

Fireworks

Government IDs and licenses

Human parts and remains (Skulls, skeletons, and items that may contain human hair are permissible as long as they're used for educational purposes.)

Lockpicking devices

Lottery tickets

Mailing lists and personal information

USDA prohibited plants and seeds

Postage meters

Prescription drugs and devices

Recalled items

Satellite and cable TV descramblers

Stocks and other securities (Old or collectible stock certificates may be sold provided that they're cancelled or are from a company that no longer exists.)

Stolen property

Surveillance equipment

Tobacco

Travel (All sellers listing airline tickets, cruises, vacation packages, or lodging must be verified by Square Trade.)

Check the following address for updates:

`http://pages.ebay.com/help/sell/questions/prohibited-items.html`

Questionable items

A *questionable item* is iffy — determining whether or not you can sell it is tricky. Under certain circumstances, you may be able to list the item for sale at eBay. To fully understand when and if you can list a questionable item, visit the links that I highlight in Table 4-1. *Note:* All URLs listed in Table 4-1 begin with `http://pages.ebay.com/help/policies`

Table 4-1	Questionable Items and Where to Find the Rules Regulating Them
Can I Sell This?	*Go Here to Find Out**
Alcohol	`/alcohol.html`
Artifacts	`/artifacts.html`
Autographed Items	`/autographs.html`
Batteries	`/batteries.html`
Contracts and tickets	`/contracts.html`
Electronics equipment	`/electronics.html`
Event tickets	`/event-tickets.html`
Food	`/food.html`
Freon and other refrigerants	`/freon.html`
Hazardous materials	`/hazardous-materials.html`
International trading — sellers	`/international-sellers.html`
Mature audiences	`/mature-audiences.html`
Offensive material	`/offensive.html`
Pesticides	`/pesticides.html`
Police-related items	`/police.html`
Pre-sale listings	`/pre-sale.html`
Slot machines	`/slot-machines.html`
Used clothing	`/used-clothing.html`
Used medical devices	`/medical-devices.html`
United States embargoed goods from prohibited countries	`/embargo.html`
Weapons and knives	`/weapons.html`

* All URLs begin with `http://pages.ebay.com/help/policies`

The Chanel-style purse

I once listed a quilted leather women's purse that had a gold chain strap, which I described as a Chanel-style purse. Within two hours, I received an Informational alert from the eBay listing police. I described the item to the best of my ability, but found that it became a potentially infringing item. My use of the brand name *Chanel* caused my auction to come under the violation of keyword spamming (more on that in the section "Potentially Infringing items").

In its informational alert, eBay described my violation:

"Keyword spamming is the practice of adding words, including brand names, which do not directly describe the item you are selling. The addition of these words may not have

been intentional, but including them in this manner diverts members to your listing inappropriately."

Ooops! You can see how my ingenuous listing was actually a violation of policy. Think twice before you add brand names to your auction description. Thankfully, the eBay police judge each violation on a case-by-case basis. Because my record is clear, I merely got a reprimand. Had my violation been more deliberate, I might have been suspended.

To see the Chanel USA statement on violations, visit its About Me page. The violations apply to many items that may be listed at eBay:

```
http://members.ebay.com/aboutme/
    chanelusa/
```

Potentially infringing items

Potentially infringing items follow a slippery slope. If you list a potentially infringing item, you may infringe on existing copyrights, trademarks, registrations, or the like. Get the idea? These items are prohibited for your own protection.

Items falling under the potentially infringing category are generally copyrighted or trademarked items, such as software, promotional items, and games. Even using a brand name in your auction as part of a description (known as keyword spamming) may get you into trouble.

Keyword spamming manipulates the eBay search engine by including an unrelated item in the listing for a copyrighted or trademarked item, and then diverting bidders to an auction of other merchandise. This is frustrating to the person trying to use the search engine to find a particular item and unfair to members who've properly listed their items.

Keyword spamming can take many forms. Some merely mislead the prospective bidder while others are legal infringements. A few of the most common are

- ✔ Superfluous brand names in the title or item description
- ✔ Using something like "not brand X" in the title or item description
- ✔ Improper trademark usage
- ✔ Lists of keywords
- ✔ Hidden text — white text on a white background or hidden text in HTML code. The white text resides in the auction HTML, so it shows up in the search but is not visible to the naked eye. Sneaky, eh?
- ✔ Drop-down boxes

To get the latest on eBay's keyword spamming policy, go to

```
http://pages.ebay.com/help/policies/listing-keywords.html
```

The eBay Verified Rights Owners program

eBay can't possibly check every auction for authenticity. But to help protect trademarked items, it formed the Verified Rights Owners (VeRO) program.

Trademark and copyright owners expend large amounts of energy to develop and maintain control over the quality of their products. If you buy a "designer" purse from a guy on the street for $20, it's probably counterfeit, so don't go selling it on eBay.

eBay works with VeRO program members to educate the community about such items. They work also with verified owners of trademarks and copyrights to remove auctions that infringe on their products. If eBay doesn't close a suspicious or blatantly infringing auction, both you and eBay are liable for the violation.

To become a member of the VeRO program, the owners of copyrights and trademarks must supply eBay with proof of ownership. To view the VeRO program information and download the application for membership, go to

```
http://pages.ebay.com/help/community/notice-infringe2.pdf
```

Note: eBay cooperates with law enforcement and may give your name and street address to a VeRO program member.

To view a list of other VeRO members' About Me pages, go to

```
http://pages.ebay.com/help/community/vero-aboutme.html
```

Repeating various un-trademarked keywords can get you in trouble as well. eBay permits the use of as many as five synonyms when listing an item for sale. A permissible example of this might be: purse, handbag, pocketbook, satchel, and bag. Adding many un-trademarked keywords would cause the auction to come up in more searches.

Trading Violations

Both buyers and sellers can commit trading violations by attempting to manipulate the outcome of an auction or sale. Many of the violations aren't necessarily buyer- or seller-exclusive but apply to both. Regardless of the nature of a violation, such behavior violates everyone who's part of the eBay community.

As a valued member of the community, it's partially your responsibility to look out for such violations — so that eBay continues to be a safe community in which to do business. Should you see a violation, report it immediately to the eBay Security Center (see "eBay's Security Center," later in this chapter). In this section, I detail many common violations so that you can be on the outlook for them — and I'll just assume that you won't be committing any yourself.

 We need to be watchdogs because we need to protect the other users in our community. Don't feel like a squealer if you make a report. Remember that it takes just one rotten apple to spoil the basket, so if you see a violation, do your duty and report it.

When the competition doesn't play fair

Unfortunately, you may sometimes encounter non-community-minded sellers who interfere with your auctions or sales. This interference can take on several forms, such as sellers who illegally drive up bids or "steal" bidders.

 Again, should you fall victim to bad deeds, be sure to report the bad-deed-doer's actions immediately. (Check out "Taking Action: What to Do When Someone Breaks the Rules," later in this chapter). eBay will take some sort of disciplinary action. Penalties range from formal warnings and temporary suspension to indefinite suspension. eBay reviews each incident on a case-by-case basis before passing judgment.

Shill bidding

Shill bidding is the practice of placing a bid on an item to artificially inflate the final value. It's the bane of every eBay user (whether buyer or seller) and undermines community trust. Shill bidding is a violation of the Federal wire-fraud statute, which encompasses the practice of entering into interstate commerce to defraud — it's a felony and not something to be toyed with!

The practice of shill bidding has been a part of auctions from their beginnings. To prevent the suspicion of shill bidding, people in the same family, those who share the same computer, and folks who work or live together should not bid on each other's items.

Should you ever even dream of participating in any sort of auction manipulation, I urge you to think twice. You might think you're smart by using another e-mail address and username, but that doesn't work. Every time you log onto your ISP, your connection carries an IP address. So no matter what name or computer you use, your connection will identify you. eBay can use this number to track you through its site.

Shill bidders are fairly easy to recognize, even for the eBay user who isn't privy to things such as IP addresses. By checking a bidder's auction history, you can easily determine a user's bidding pattern. A bidder who constantly bids up items and never wins is suspicious.

Spurious sellers often employ shill bidding to increase the number of bids on an item to more quickly make it a hot item. This doesn't mean that all hot auctions are products of shill bidding, it means that hot auctions are desirable and pull in lots of extra bids (due to the herd mentality). Rogues would like all their auctions to be hot and may take any road to ensure that they are.

Transaction interference

Have you ever received an e-mail from an eBay seller offering you an item that you're currently bidding on for a lower price? This is called *transaction interference,* and it can prevent sellers from gaining the highest bid possible.

Transaction interference occurs also when a troublemaker who has it "in" for a particular seller e-mails bidders participating in the seller's current auctions to warn them away from completing the auction. Tales of woe and much bitterness usually accompany such e-mails. If a bidder has a problem with a seller, that bidder can — and should — file a report with eBay and leave negative feedback for that seller. This sort of e-mail barrage can potentially fall under the category of libel and isn't a safe thing to practice. If you receive an e-mail like this, ignore its message but report it to eBay.

Transaction interception

They say the criminal mind is complex; when it comes to transaction interception, it certainly is! *Transaction interception* occurs when an eBay scalawag keeps track of closing auctions and then, when the auction is finished, e-mails the winner as if the scalawag were the seller. The e-mail often looks official and is congratulatory, politely asking for payment. Interceptors usually use a post office box for such mischief. This behavior goes beyond being a trading violation — it's stealing.

The best way to protect yourself from such miscreants is to accept payments through a payment service, such as PayPal, by using a <u>Pay Now</u> link. For more about setting up a payment service account, see Chapter 13.

Fee avoidance

Basically, *fee avoidance* is the practice of evading paying eBay fees by going around the eBay system. There are many ways to commit fee avoidance — sometimes without even realizing it. Read this section carefully so that you don't fall into this violation by mistake.

You're guilty of fee avoidance if you

- ✔ Use information that you've received from an eBay member's contact information in an attempt to sell a listed item off the system

- ✔ Close your auction early because a user e-mailed you to offer to buy an item you were auctioning, and you accepted the offer

- ✔ End your auction before it legally closes by canceling bids, to sell the item to someone who has e-mailed you with an offer of a higher price

- ✔ Use an eBay member's contact information to sell an item from one of your closed auctions off the eBay site in which the reserve wasn't met

- ✔ Offer duplicates of your item to the unsuccessful bidders in your auction, unless you use the Second Chance option.

Take a look at the discussion on listing policies in Chapter 2 for listing violations that also might fall into this category.

Non-selling seller

Refusing to accept payment from the winning bidder and refusing to complete the transaction is simply wrong. Very, very bad form! You are legally and morally bound to complete any transaction in which you enter.

Baaad bidders

Nothing can ruin a seller's day like a difficult bidder, such as someone who asks questions that are clearly answered already in your auction description or someone who asks you to close the auction so that he or she can buy the item offline. Sheesh — you'd think no one read the rules. From the non-paying bidder to the unwelcome and shady, you might encounter the buyers I describe here.

Bid shielding

When two or more eBay members work together to defraud you out of real auction profits, they're guilty of *bid shielding*. One member, lets call him Joe, places an early bid on your item, with a proxy bid. Immediately, the accomplice, (we'll call her Sharon), places a very high proxy bid to drive it to the max or beyond. If legitimate bidders bid, they only ratchet up the second bidder's bid — they don't outbid the high bidder's proxy. When the auction is coming to a close, the high bidder (Sharon) retracts her bid, thereby granting the winning bid to her buddy (Joe), the original low bidder. The ultimate point of bid shielding is that it increases the bid to such a high level that normal bidding by authentic bidders is discouraged.

This illegal bidding process is used not only to get bargain-priced merchandise but also to drive bidders away from competitors' auctions by artificially inflating the high bid level.

Unwelcome bidder

In this business, you might think that you couldn't possibly regard anyone as an *unwelcome bidder,* but you just might. Remember how you painstakingly explain your terms in your auction description? That's lost on people who don't take the time to read those descriptions or choose to ignore them. Consider the following points:

- ✔ You state in your description that you ship only within the United States, but you see a bidder with an e-mail address that ends in .jp (Japan), .au (Australia), .uk (United Kingdom), or whatever. You should e-mail that bidder immediately to emphasize your domestic-only shipping policy.

- ✔ You state in your description that you don't want bidders who have a negative feedback rating or more than one negative in a six-month time span, but someone fitting that description bids on your auction. You may want to contact this bidder, who might be new to the eBay system and might not understand the legal connotations of making a bid.

- ✔ You decide to cancel a bid for one of the previous two reasons, but the bidder continues to bid on your auction.

- ✔ You've blocked a particular bidder (see Chapter 3) who's now using a secondary account to bid on your auctions.

If you encounter any of the previous situations, contact eBay immediately to report the unwelcome bidder; see "eBay's Security Center," later in this chapter.

Non-paying buyers

If there's one thing that just ain't tolerated at eBay, it's a non-paying buyer (NPB). eBay reminds all bidders, before they place a bid, that "If you are the winning bidder, you will enter into a legally binding contract to purchase the item from the seller." You'd think that was clear enough, but sadly, many people out there think bidding and buying on eBay is a game. If you see a high bidder on your auction who has a very low or negative feedback, dropping a line reiterating eBay policy never hurts.

How you, as a seller, communicate with the high bidder is also important. Many times a well-written, congenial, businesslike e-mail can cajole the basically good person into sending payment. To see some samples that get the job done, drop by Chapter 12.

I've been selling and buying at eBay for more than five years. During that time, I've had to file only five non-paying buyer alerts (see the steps a bit later in this section). I think that non-paying buyers tend to bid on certain types of items. After you've seen some NPBs, you'll get an idea of which items to stay away from. My NPB items? A gas-powered scooter, a video game, and some Beanie Babies. Serious collector or business items have never been an issue.

To reduce the number of non-paying buyers, eBay has established that all eBay users are indefinitely suspended if they have three non-paying buyer alerts filed against them. An *indefinite suspension* is a suspension of members' privileges to use the eBay site for more than 60 days, with no definite reinstatement date. If users attempt to re-register at eBay and use the system under new IDs, they risk being referred to the United States Attorney's Office for the Northern District of California for criminal prosecution.

Before filing a non-paying buyer alert, give the winner a second chance to send payment. If you still don't receive payment, follow these steps to recoup your Final Value fees and be eligible for the non-paying buyer relist credit:

1. **As soon as you have a winner, contact him or her.**

2. **If you don't hear from the winner within three days of the auction's end time, send a payment reminder:**

    a. **Go to the My eBay Views area on the My eBay page. Under Selling, click the <u>Sold</u> link.**

    b. **Click the <u>View Payment Status</u> link next to the pertinent auction.**

    c. **Click the <u>Send a Payment Reminder</u> link**

    You may send a reminder between 3 and 30 days after the auction closes.

If you still don't hear from or receive money from your high bidder, it's time to swing into action by filing an alert.

You must file the alert no earlier than 7 days and no later than 45 days after the auction has ended.

Follow these steps to file a non-paying buyer alert:

1. **In the My eBay Views area of the My eBay page, click the <u>Selling Manager</u> link. In the Selling links box that appears (on the left), click the <u>Non-Paying Buyer Policy</u> link.**

   Alternately, go to the following address:

   ```
   http://cgi3.ebay.com/aw-cgi/eBayISAPI.dll?NPB
           ComplaintForm
   ```

2. **Log into eBay and file the alert.**

   Even if you're permanently logged into eBay, you have to sign in with your password again, for security reasons. Then type in the item number in question, and press Send Request. Your alert will be filed with eBay.

Seven days after filing a non-paying buyer alert, you may apply for a final value fee credit (see Figure 4-2). Use the link on the My eBay: All Selling page or go to

```
http://cgi3.ebay.com/aw-cgi/eBayISAPI.dll?CreditRequest
```

You must file for your final value fee credit within 45 days of the auction's close.

When you file for the final value fee credit, you also have the option of blocking that buyer from your auctions.

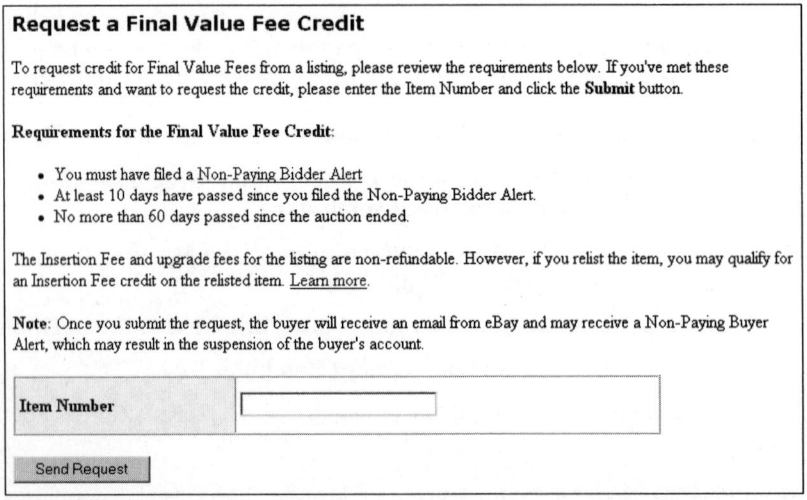

Request a Final Value Fee Credit

To request credit for Final Value Fees from a listing, please review the requirements below. If you've met these requirements and want to request the credit, please enter the Item Number and click the **Submit** button.

Requirements for the Final Value Fee Credit:

- You must have filed a <u>Non-Paying Bidder Alert</u>
- At least 10 days have passed since you filed the Non-Paying Bidder Alert.
- No more than 60 days passed since the auction ended.

The Insertion Fee and upgrade fees for the listing are non-refundable. However, if you relist the item, you may qualify for an Insertion Fee credit on the relisted item. <u>Learn more</u>.

Note: Once you submit the request, the buyer will receive an email from eBay and may receive a Non-Paying Buyer Alert, which may result in the suspension of the buyer's account.

Item Number	

Send Request

Figure 4-2:
Credits for
the final
value fee.

Don't be lured by phishing

Fraudulent e-mail has become a common occurrence. Without warning, a request for confirmation of your personal details arrives allegedly from your bank, Internet ISP, credit card company, PayPal, or even eBay. These e-mails are *phishing* for your personal information and passwords to defraud you of your money or your identity.

These e-mails look just like a legitimate e-mail from the company that holds your data. If you follow the links in the e-mail to "update" your information, you'll be brought to a Web page that duplicates a legitimate Web page.

How can you protect yourself from these scammers?

✔ **Look for personalization.** Your bank, eBay, or PayPal will address the e-mail to your proper name, not, for example, to *Dear PayPal Member*.

✔ **Never go to the Web site in question from the link in the e-mail.** Open up a new browser and type the URL that you normally use to enter the site. After you log in, you'll know whether there's a problem with any of your information.

✔ **Always look for secure Web site information.** If you're logged onto a secure Web site, the URL will begin with `https://` rather than the standard `http://`. You'll also see a lock symbol in the status bar at the bottom of your browser window.

✔ **Regularly log onto your Internet accounts.** By keeping in regular contact with your providers, you'll know about issues with your accounts before they have a chance to cause a problem.

✔ **Report the e-mail.** If you receive an e-mail supposedly from PayPal, forward the e-mail to `spoof@paypal.com`. Forward an e-mail purportedly from eBay to `spoof@ebay.com`.

I take things into my own hands by checking the suspicious e-mail's underlying code. You can do this if you use Internet Explorer and Outlook, by opening the e-mail, right-clicking it, and choosing View Source. When you view the HTML code, you'll be able to see the actual URL of the site that would get your response if you click the link, as shown in the figure.

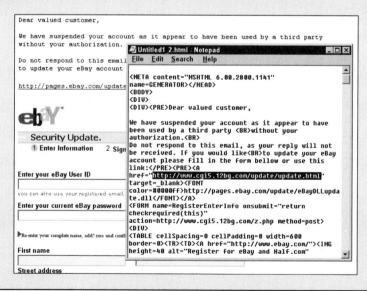

If you work things out with the winner, you may remove the non-paying buyer alert within 90 days of the close of the auction. eBay sends an e-mail to notify the winner that the alert has been removed at your request. You'll find the link to remove the warning from your buyer's record at

```
http://cgi3.ebay.com/aw-cgi/eBayISAPI.dll?RemoveNPB
          WarningShow
```

In the case of Dutch auctions or eBay Storefront items, you may file a non-paying buyer alert only *once* per listing. You may file against as many bidders as necessary in that one alert, but you can't go back and file more alerts later. You may remove a non-paying buyer warning at any time.

Not knowing who's who

Most eBay users use user IDs rather than expose their e-mail addresses for all to see. However, you must supply eBay with your contact information. When you register at eBay, its software immediately checks your primary phone number area code against your zip code to verify that the two numbers are from the same city. If you've supplied incompatible codes, the eBay servers will recognize that and ask you to reinput the correct codes.

An eBay member who's involved in a transaction with you can get your phone number by clicking Search on the eBay navigation bar and then clicking the Find Members button that appears below the bar. You can also get to eBay Member search at the following address:

```
http://cgi3.ebay.com/aw-cgi/eBayISAPI.dll?MemberSearchShow
```

When you arrive at the page, scroll to the form that requests Contact Info, as shown in Figure 4-3.

To be on the up-and-up at eBay (and to keep others honest, too), make sure that you

✔ **Have your current phone number on file at eBay:** If a bidder can't reach you, you're in violation of the False Contact Information policy and you *can* be disciplined.

✔ **Have your current e-mail address on file:** If your bidder continually gets e-mail bounced back from your e-mail address, you could get in big trouble.

✔ **Report all underage bidders:** If you suspect that a bidder in one of your auctions is underage (eBay requires that all users be over 18), eBay may close the account. Underage bidders may be using their parent's credit card without permission, or perhaps even a stolen card, for registration.

✔ **Verify e-mail purportedly coming from an eBay employee:** If someone e-mails you claiming to work for eBay, be sure to check it out before replying. When eBay employees conduct personal business on the site, company policy requires that they use a personal, non-company e-mail address for their user registration. If you suspect someone is impersonating an eBay employee for harmful purposes, contact the Security Center.

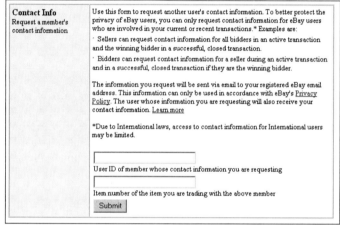

Figure 4-3:
eBay's
Contact
Info form.

Taking Action: What to Do When Someone Breaks the Rules

You need to take a business-like approach to problems at eBay, whatever those problems may be. In previous sections of this chapter, I outline eBay's many rules, as well as the bad deeds and bad seeds you're likely to encounter while doing business at eBay.

As a member of the eBay community, you have the responsibility of knowing and abiding by eBay's rules and regulations. This responsibility includes notifying eBay when someone tries to sell an illegal item (see "Is What You Want to Sell Legal?," earlier in this chapter), an integral part of keeping eBay a safe and lucrative place to do business. In this section, I discuss who to call when someone breaks the rules and what to do when a third-party is necessary.

Here are the basic steps you can follow:

- **Contact the buyer:** If you're involved in a transaction, get the buyer's contact information by using the following:

  ```
  http://cgi3.ebay.com/aw-cgi/eBayISAPI.dll?
        MemberSearchShow
  ```

  Call the buyer to see whether you can diplomatically resolve the situation.

- **Seek out eBay security:** Use the Security Center to report any shady actions, policy violations, or possible fraud, such as a community member impersonating an employee or a suspicious auction. Likened to the front desk at your local police station, eBay's Security Center report form gets results. Click the Security Center link, which appears at the bottom of most eBay pages, and then click the bright green Report a Problem link. Alternatively, you can go directly to

  ```
  http://pages.ebay.com/help/contact_inline
  ```

  You'll find an all-purpose security form on this page to help you in your eBay transactions. These forms will be routed to the right department for action.

- **Apply for online resolution:** SquareTrade offers online dispute resolution services and mediation for eBay members. See the following section on how to involve SquareTrade.

- **Contact the National Fraud Information Center (NFIC):** If you feel you've become a victim of fraud, be sure to file a report through eBay channels. To really bring down wrath on your nemesis, report them to the NFIC by calling 1-800-876-7060.

- **Contact local law enforcement:** If you become the target of a check-bouncer, contact the local law enforcement in your bidder's home town. eBay will supply any information necessary to help law enforcement clear the world of fraud. Provide eBay with the name of the local law enforcement officer, agency, telephone number, and case number or police report number. Also include the offending user's ID and the auction item's number. For a state-by-state list of the possible criminal penalties, visit

  ```
  www.ckfraud.org/penalties.html#criminal
  ```

SquareTrade to the rescue

Threats of suing each other, filing fraud charges, and screaming back and forth don't really accomplish anything when you're in the middle of a dispute at eBay. Back in the olden days of eBay, when you weren't able to respond to feedback, users threw negative feedback back and forth willy-nilly, which resulted in some vile flame wars.

These days you have SquareTrade, one of the best services that you can use as a seller. When you're selling regularly at eBay, you will undoubtedly run into a disgruntled buyer or two. SquareTrade, a Web-based dispute resolution company, waits in the wings to pull you out of the most difficult situations.

Should you find yourself in an inexorably difficult situation with one of your bidders, and you'd like to take the situation up a notch, go to the following page, shown in Figure 4-4:

```
http://www.squaretrade.com/cnt/jsp/odr/overview_odr.jsp?
          marketplace_name=ebay
```

After you click the <u>File a Case</u> link on this page and answer a few questions regarding the situation, SquareTrade generates and sends an e-mail to the other party, giving instructions on how to respond. From this point, the case information and all related responses appear on a private, password-protected page on the SquareTrade site.

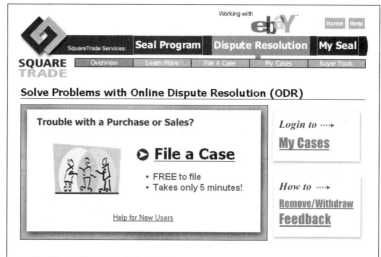

Figure 4-4:
SquareTrade
Dispute
Resolution
start page.

SquareTrade offers three main services to eBay members, which I discuss in this section:

- ✔ Online dispute resolution through direct negotiation
- ✔ Professional mediation
- ✔ SquareTrade Seal

Online dispute resolution

Online dispute resolution is a fast, private, and convenient way to resolve your auction disputes — and it's *free*. Both you and the buyer work together through the SquareTrade Web-based system. Online dispute resolution (ODR) works whether your transaction is in the United States or another country. Every day, more than 400 buyers file cases with the ODR service.

The SquareTrade Web-based negotiation tool is automated, and you and the other party get to communicate on neutral ground. When (and if) the buyer responds, the two of you can work out the situation online and without human interaction. If you're unable to reach a solution, you need to move on to professional mediation (see the following section).

SquareTrade states that problems are usually solved in 10 to 14 days and 85 percent of all cases are resolved without going to mediation. The process will run a quicker course if both people in the transaction are at their computers and answer e-mail during the day.

Participation in ODR is voluntary. If a buyer is set on defrauding you, he or she probably isn't going to engage in a resolution process. If you get no response to your ODR, report your situation to the Security Center.

Professional mediation

If push comes to shove, and in auction disputes it certainly may, you might have to resort to professional mediation. A *mediator,* who is neither a lawyer nor a judge but an impartial professional, works with both parties to bring the situation to a convivial conclusion. This service is available for a reasonable fee of $20 per issue.

If both parties participating in dispute resolution agree to mediation, each party communicates with only the assigned mediator, who communicates with both parties through the same case page. Your case page shows only your communications with the mediator. The mediator reviews both sides of the story to find a mutually acceptable solution to the problem. He or she tries to understand the interests, perspectives, and preferred solutions of both parties, and tries to help both parties understand the other's position.

The mediator is there to disperse highly charged emotions commonly associated with disputes and recommends a resolution only if both parties agree to have the mediator do so. By using the mediation service, you do not lose your right to go to court if things aren't worked out.

SquareTrade seal

A SquareTrade seal lets prospective bidders know that you deal with customers promptly and honestly. Should you choose to get a SquareTrade seal, SquareTrade inserts it into your auctions automatically. (Each seal icon contains a digital watermark with an encrypted expiration date.) You can use the seal in your auctions only if SquareTrade approves you.

Your Square Trade seal approval is based on several points:

- ✓ **Identity verification.** SquareTrade will verify your identity using the information you provide through a third party.

- ✓ **Superior selling record.** SquareTrade runs your eBay feedback history through five individual checks. It has an advanced system based on its extensive experience of dispute resolution that allows it to evaluate the quality and quantity of eBay feedback.

- ✓ **Dispute resolution.** They check whether you have a history of resolving disputes.

- ✓ **Commitment to standards.** You pledge to meet the SquareTrade standards regarding selling and to respond to disputes within two business days.

After you have a seal, you must continue to uphold SquareTrade standards and maintain an acceptable feedback rating. If approved, the nifty little personalized seal icon will appear on each of your auctions. Users can click the icon to access your own Seal Display page on the SquareTrade site.

Recently, SquareTrade did a study of 623 SquareTrade seal members, comparing their feedback for the four months after they became a seal member to their feedback in the prior four months. They found that once a seller became a SquareTrade seal member, negative feedback was reduced by 43 percent. The ratio of negative to positive feedback went from 1 in 60 before to 1 in 280 after.

The SquareTrade seal (shown in Figure 4-5) currently costs around $7 per month — an affordable and good idea if you're in this business for the long run. The seal tells prospective buyers that you care about good customer service and don't tolerate fraudulent activity. It also says that you abide by the SquareTrade selling and customer service standards, which dictate that you will

- ✓ Disclose contact information and credentials
- ✓ Provide clear and accurate descriptions of goods and services in your auctions
- ✓ Clearly disclose pricing, including all applicable fees
- ✓ List clear policies on after-sales services, such as refunds and warranties
- ✓ Maintain privacy policies
- ✓ Conduct transactions on only secure sites
- ✓ Respond to any disputeis filed against you within two business days

To provide an additional security feature for your buyers, you can bond your auctions. Doing so also protects you. See Chapter 10 for more information.

Figure 4-5:
The Square-
Trade Seal.

eBay's Security Center

The Security Center is the eBay version of the FBI. By rooting out evil-doers, it serves and protects — and puts up with an immense amount of e-mail from users.

If you see an item on eBay that isn't allowed (see "Is What You Want to Sell Legal?"), be sure to make eBay aware of the auction. The Community Watch team will then take over and investigate the item and, when necessary, end the auction and warn the seller.

When you click the Security Center link, which is at the bottom of most eBay pages, you'll see the page shown in Figure 4-6. Click the Report a Problem button to get action.

You then fill out a step-by-step customer service report, which is shown in Figure 4-7.

Figure 4-6:
The eBay
Security
Center.

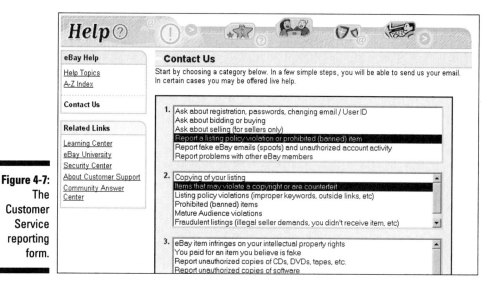

Figure 4-7:
The
Customer
Service
reporting
form.

Alternatively, you can get to the Security Center customer service reporting form at

```
pages.ebay.com/help/contact_inline/index.html
```

Chapter 5

Your Very Own eBay Store

In This Chapter

▶ Figuring out the lure of the online shop

▶ Choosing a name

▶ Setting up your eBay store

▶ Managing your eBay store

▶ Selling your stuff

▶ Closing your sales

*I*f you're doing well selling your items on eBay auctions, why open a store? Have you used the eBay Buy It Now feature in one of your listings? Did it work? In an eBay store, all items are set at a fixed price and online until cancelled (or listed at least 30 days), so it's kind of like a giant collection of Buy It Now featured items. Get the idea?

When you're opening a store, you have just three main rules to remember and apply: location, location, location. If you were going to open a brick-and-mortar store, you could open it in the corner strip mall, a shopping center, or even somewhere downtown. You'd have to decide in what location your store would do best; that goes for an online store as well. You'll find tons of locations to open an online store, including online malls (when you can find them) and sites such as Amazon.com, Yahoo!, and, of course, eBay.

You have to pay rent for your online store, but opening and running an online store isn't nearly as expensive as a store in the real world (where you also have to pay electrical bills, maintenance bills, and more). Plus, the ratio of rent to sales makes an online store a much easier financial decision, and your exposure can be huge.

In this chapter, I show you step-by-step how to hang out your virtual shingle and get business booming by opening your own eBay store.

Online Stores Galore

Amazon.com, Yahoo!, and eBay make up the big three of online stores. They're the top locations and get the most visitors. According to comScore Media Metrix, in April 2004 these sites garnered an astounding number of *unique* visitors (that counts *all* of one person's visits to the sites just *once* a month):

- Yahoo!: 113,190,000 (it's a search engine; I must hit it ten times a day — but I rarely visit the auctions)
- eBay: 60,016,000
- Amazon.com: 39,083,000 (it sells books, CDs, DVDs, and lots of other merchandise, but how many of these people are going to the zShops?)

No doubt feeling competition from Yahoo! and Amazon.com, eBay decided to open its doors (in July 2001) to sellers who wanted to open their own stores. The fixed price stores were a normal progression for eBay in its quest to continue as the world's marketplace. And eBay Stores make sense: They're a benefit to all current eBay sellers and open doors to new shoppers who don't want to deal with auctions.

eBay is an online store that specializes in selling *your* stuff, not *theirs*. It doesn't stock a stick of merchandise, and it isn't in competition with you. In addition to its staggering number of visitors, eBay offers you the most reasonable store rent. To see what I mean, check out the sample rents in Table 5-1.

Table 5-1	Online Starter Store Monthly Costs		
	eBay	*Yahoo Shopping*	*Amazon zShops*
Basic rent	$15.95	$39.95	$39.99
Listing fee	$.02	0	$.10 after 40,000 items
High final value fee	5.25%	1.5%	5%

For more information on current rankings, go to the comScore Web site at www.comscore.com and search for *eBay*. This site keeps a monthly scorecard of unique visitors to the top 50 Internet sites. It's worth a visit now and then to see where the industry is going.

I don't think it's going to take a rocket scientist to convince you that having a space in eBay Stores (see Figure 5-1) is a way better bargain than setting up shop anywhere else. I know the stores aren't based on auctions, but Buy It Now items are as easy to handle as auctions. To review prices and rules before opening your store, go to

```
pages.ebay.com/storefronts/seller-landing.html
```

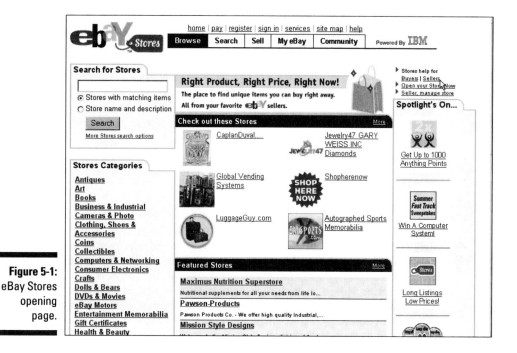

Figure 5-1:
eBay Stores
opening
page.

Your eBay Store Name

You've decided to take the plunge and open an eBay store. Do you have an eBay user ID? Have you thought of a good name for your store? Your store name doesn't have to match your eBay user ID, but they're more recognizable if they relate to each other. You can use your company name, your business name, or a name that describes your business. I recommend that you

TIP

Mind your underscores and hyphens

If you want to use your eBay user ID for your store name, you can — unless it contains a hyphen (-) or an underscore (_). Remember how eBay recommends that you break up words in your user ID with a dash or an underscore? Uh oh, that's no good for an eBay store name. I'm in that situation. My user ID is marsha_c; without the underscore, it translates into a user ID that someone else has already taken! Even though it hasn't been used since 1999, someone else has it, which means I can't use it. (marsha_c is probably a crummy name for a store anyway!)

A favorite seller of mine — mrswarren — realized that mrswarren isn't a good name for a store either. So she named her store *Pretty Girlie Things,* which suits her merchandise to a T.

use the same name for your eBay store that you plan to use in all your online businesses. By doing so, you'll begin to create an identity (or as the pros call it, a *brand*) that customers will come to recognize and trust.

Your online eBay store should not replace your Web site (see Chapter 8); it should be an extension of it. When people shop at your eBay store, you must take the opportunity to make them customers of your Web site through your store's About the Seller page (which is also your About Me page on eBay). Good deal!

Setting up Shop

It's time to get down to business. Go to the eBay Stores hub and click the Sellers link in the upper-right corner of the screen (refer to Figure 5-1). This takes you to the Seller's hub of eBay Stores, as shown in Figure 5-2. If you click all the links you see here, you get the eBay company line about how good an eBay store can be for your business. You already know how good an eBay store can be for your business, so skip the propaganda and get right down to business (but don't forget to check for any policy changes that may affect your store's operations).

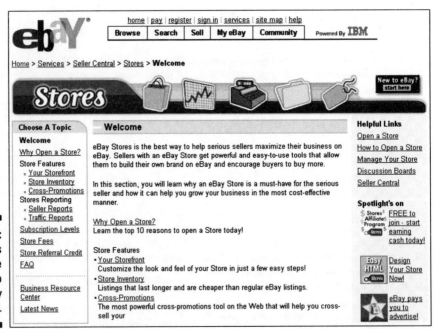

Figure 5-2:
The Seller's welcome page to eBay Stores.

Before you click that link to open your store, ask yourself two questions:

✔ **Can I make a serious commitment to my eBay store?** A store is a commitment. It won't work for you unless you work for it. You have to have the merchandise to fill it and the discipline to continue listing store and auction items. Your store is a daily, monthly, and yearly obligation. When you go on vacation, you need someone else to ship your items or your customers may go elsewhere. You can close your store for a vacation, but eBay will reserve your store name for only 30 days. After that, you have to come up with a new name (and your competition may have taken over your famous store name).

✔ **Will I work for my eBay store even when I don't feel like it?** You have to be prepared for the times when you're sick or just don't feel like shipping, but orders are waiting to be shipped. You have to do the work anyway; it's all part of the commitment.

eBay gives you the venue, but it's in your own hands to make your mercantile efforts a success. If you can handle these two responsibilities, read on!

If you're serious and ready to move on, click the Open a Store link in the upper-right corner of the page (refer to Figure 5-2). Because you're always signed in on your home computer, you're escorted to a page reminding you that eBay stores fall under the same User Agreement that you agreed to when you began selling on eBay. Click the Continue button to access the Build Your Store pages (see Figure 5-3).

You need to make a few decisions to create a good store. So before building your store, read the following sections.

Next, follow these steps:

1. **Choose a color theme.**

   eBay provides some elegant color and graphics themes. You can change the color scheme or layout later, so until you have time to go hog-wild and design a custom masterpiece, choose one of the fourteen clearly organized layouts, either predesigned or with easily customizable themes. Don't select something overly bright and vibrant; you want something that's easy on the eyes, which is more conducive to a comfortable selling environment.

   You have the option of selecting a store theme that doesn't require you to insert a custom logo or banner. I highly recommend against it. You need to establish a unifying brand for your online business.

2. **Click Continue.**

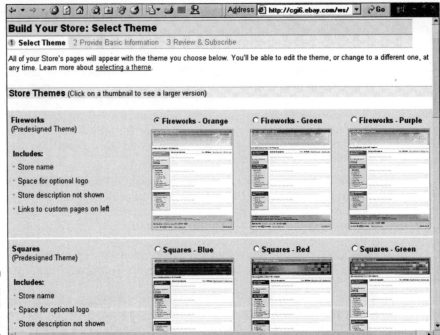

Figure 5-3:
Select the
store theme.

3. **Type your new store's name (see Figure 5-4).**

    You've decided on a store name, right? Your eBay store name can't exceed 35 characters. Before you type it, double-check that you aren't infringing on anyone's copyrights or trademarks. You also can't use any permutation of eBay trademarks in your store's name.

4. **Type a short description of your store.**

    When I say short, I mean *short.* This paragraph is 248 characters, and you have only *300* characters to give a whiz-bang, electric description of your store and merchandise. You can't use HTML coding to doll up the description, and you can't use links. Just the facts please, and a little bit of dazzle.

    The importance of this description is huge. When people search eBay stores and descriptions, the keyword information you put here is referenced. Also, if the store header contains your description (as in the Classic style themes), search engines such as Google and Yahoo! will look in this description for the keywords to classify and list your store.

    Write your copy ahead of time in Word. Then, still in Word, highlight the text and choose Tools➪Word Count. Word gives you the word count of the highlighted text. Check the character count with spaces, to be sure your text fits.

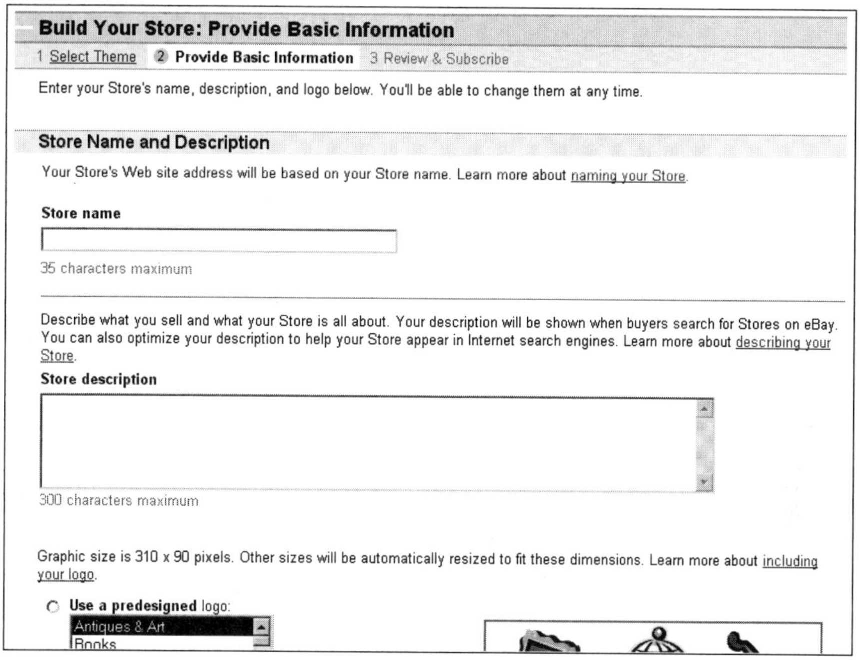

Build Your Store: Provide Basic Information

1 Select Theme   ② **Provide Basic Information**   3 Review & Subscribe

Enter your Store's name, description, and logo below. You'll be able to change them at any time.

Store Name and Description

Your Store's Web site address will be based on your Store name. Learn more about naming your Store.

Store name

35 characters maximum

Describe what you sell and what your Store is all about. Your description will be shown when buyers search for Stores on eBay. You can also optimize your description to help your Store appear in Internet search engines. Learn more about describing your Store.

Store description

300 characters maximum

Graphic size is 310 x 90 pixels. Other sizes will be automatically resized to fit these dimensions. Learn more about including your logo.

○ **Use a predesigned** logo:

Antiques & Art
Books

Figure 5-4:
Type your
store's
name and
description.

5. **Select a graphic to jazz up the look of your store.**

   You can use one of eBay's clip-art style banners or create a custom 310 x 90 pixel size one. If you use one of eBay's graphics, you must promise (hand over heart) that you won't keep it there for long (See the text after this set of steps for info on designing your own graphics — or hiring someone to do it.)

6. **Click Continue.**

   Now you're getting somewhere. At this point, your eBay store will look something like what you see in Figure 5-5. You are about to open an eBay storefront (drum-roll, please).

7. **Sign up for the basic store ($9.95 a month), and click the Start My Subscription Now button.**

   Your store is now LIVE on the Internet with nothing up for sale — yet.

8. **Click the supplied link to get in the trenches and customize your store further.**

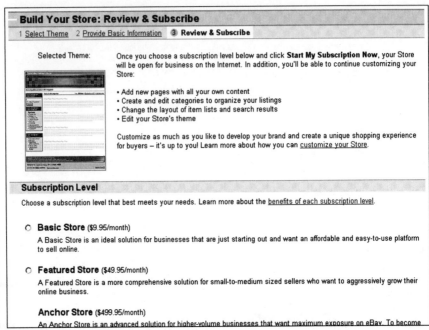

Build Your Store: Review & Subscribe

1 Select Theme 2 Provide Basic Information ③ **Review & Subscribe**

Selected Theme:

Once you choose a subscription level below and click **Start My Subscription Now**, your Store will be open for business on the Internet. In addition, you'll be able to continue customizing your Store:

• Add new pages with all your own content
• Create and edit categories to organize your listings
• Change the layout of item lists and search results
• Edit your Store's theme

Customize as much as you like to develop your brand and create a unique shopping experience for buyers — it's up to you! Learn more about how you can customize your Store.

Subscription Level

Choose a subscription level that best meets your needs. Learn more about the benefits of each subscription level.

○ **Basic Store** ($9.95/month)

A Basic Store is an ideal solution for businesses that are just starting out and want an affordable and easy-to-use platform to sell online.

○ **Featured Store** ($49.95/month)

A Featured Store is a more comprehensive solution for small-to-medium sized sellers who want to aggressively grow their online business.

Anchor Store ($499.95/month)

An Anchor Store is an advanced solution for higher-volume businesses that want maximum exposure on eBay. To become

Figure 5-5:
Verify your choices and become a store owner.

If you're wondering in which category your store will be listed on the eBay Stores home page, it's all up to you. eBay checks the items as you list them in the standard eBay category format. For example, if you have six books listed in the Books: Fiction and Nonfiction category and five items in the Cameras & Photo category, you'll be in the listings for both of those categories. Your custom store categories (read on) will be used to classify items only in your store.

If you use one of eBay's prefab graphics, people shopping your eBay store will know that you aren't serious enough about your business to design a simple and basic logo. I've had many years of experience in advertising and marketing, and I must tell you that a custom look will beat out clipart any day. Your store is special — put forth the effort to make it shine.

If you have a graphics program, design a graphic with your store's name. Start with something simple; you can always change it later when you have more time. Save the image as a GIF or a JPG, and upload it to the site where you host your images (your own Web site, your ISP, or a hosting service).

A bunch of talented graphic artists make their living selling custom Web graphics on eBay. If you aren't comfortable designing, search eBay for *web banner* or *banner design*. Graphic banners on eBay sell for about $10 to $20 — certainly worth the price in the time you'll save.

Running Your Store

You can customize your store at any time by clicking the Seller Manage Store link, which is at the bottom of your Store's page and in the upper-right corner of the eBay Store's hub page. The page shown in Figure 5-6 appears, with headings describing important tasks for your store.

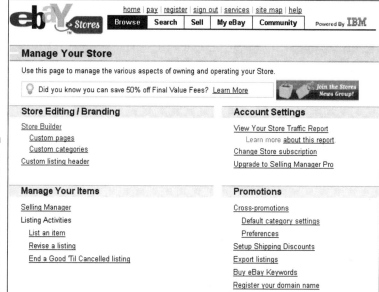

Figure 5-6:
Here's where you can perform all the necessary tasks for running a store.

Store design and marketing

In the Store Editing/Branding list, you can perform the major tasks required for your store:

✔ **Store Builder:** You can go back to Store Builder (the original store setup area) to change the name of your store or the theme of your pages. You can also change the way your items are displayed: gallery view (as in Figure 5-7) or list view (as in Figure 5-8). Neither view is inherently better, but I like the gallery view because it shows the thumbnails of my items.

You should also select the order in which your items will sort. Highest priced first, Lowest priced first, Items ending first, or Newly listed first. I like Ending first as my sort, so that buyers can get the chance to swoop in on items closing soon.

Home > eBay Stores > Marsha Collier's Fabulous Finds > **All Categories**   Add to My Favorite Stores

Marsha Collier's Fabulous Finds

Maintained by: marsha_c (2805 ★) 🏆 **Power Seller** me 🔲

I'm the author of the Dummies series of books on eBay, including "eBay for Dummies" & "Starting an eBay Business for Dummies." In my store you'll find lots of items to help you sell on eBay, take great pictures, and absolutely fabulous gifts during holiday seasons!

Marsha Collier's Fabulous Finds Search	28 items found in **All Categories** View: **All Items** | Buy It Now only | Auction only

Sort by items: **ending first** \| newly listed \| lowest priced \| highest priced

Store Categories

Store home
- Seller's Tools (20)
- Girly Things (4)
- Fun Stuff (3)
- Fancy Food (1)

Display
- Hide Gallery View
- View ending times (Ends PDT)

Store Pages
- Store Policies

Item Title

NEW eBay Bargain Shopping for Dummies SIGNED Author 2U 🖼🔲
$13.99
$14.99 *Buy It Now*
Time Left: 1d 05h 11m

TRUE COLOR Task Lamp LIGHT 13w 5000K Cloud Dome w Bulb 🖼🔲
$33.95
$34.95 *Buy It Now*
Time Left: 1d 21h 38m

New CLOUD DOME Digital Lighting Kit 7" Ext LOW SHIPPING 🖼🔲
$162.99
Time Left: 1d 21h 39m

2004 EBAY FOR DUMMIES 4th Ed Signed Marsha Collier 2U 🖼🔲
$19.99
$20.99 *Buy It Now*
Time Left: 3d 02h 57m

2004 EBAY FOR DUMMIES 4th Ed Marsha Collier Signed 2U 🖼🔲

TRUE COLOR Task Lamp LIGHT 13w 5000K Cloud Dome w Bulb 🖼🔲

Figure 5-7: My eBay store in gallery view.

Home > eBay Stores > ... > **Noblespirit**

Noblespirit

Maintained by: noblespirit (10120 ☆) 🏆 **Power Seller** me 🔲

J. CORTESE NEARLY 50 YEARS IN THE BUSINESS OF RARE COINS AND STAMPS AT YOUR SERVICE. J. Cortese is a major wholesale supplier of coins, stamps and paper money to dealers throughout the world.

Noblespirit Search

	745 items found in **All Categories** View: **All Items** | Buy It Now only | Auction only

Sort by items: ending first \| newly listed \| lowest priced \| **highest priced**

Store Categories

Store home
- Other Items (745)

Display
- Gallery view
- View ending times (Ends PDT)

Store Pages
- Store Policies
- About the Seller

Picture hide	Item Title	Price ▼	Bids	Time Left
NO RESERVE	NobleSpirit~ VALUABLE Bank Safe Deposit BOX!! 🖼🔲	$2,350.00	33	3d 03h 44m
NO RESERVE	VERY RARE Vintage Japan Solid BRONZE Hand Carved Statue 🖼🔲	$2,000.00	-	3d 05h 10m
NO RESERVE	NobleSpirit~ GOLD 1875 CC $20 NGC XF 40$1000. Coin!! 🖼🔲	$735.00	13	3d 03h 37m
NO RESERVE	NS~STAGGERING Coin, Stamp, & Collectible INHERITANCE! 🖼🔲	$565.75	13	6d 03h 40m
NO RESERVE	ENORMOUS GERMAN dealer STAMP Stock HUGE	$456.00	6	4d 02h 56m

Figure 5-8: Noblespirit's eBay store in list view.

✔ **Custom pages:** Most successful eBay sellers have a store policies page. Figure 5-9 shows you the one for my store. When you set up a policies page, eBay supplies you with a choice of layouts. Just click <u>Create New Page</u> link to see the template that you want to use, as shown in Figure 5-10. Don't freak out if you don't know HTML, eBay helps you out with an easy-to-use HTML generator as in the Sell Your Item form.

Figure 5-9: My eBay store policies page.

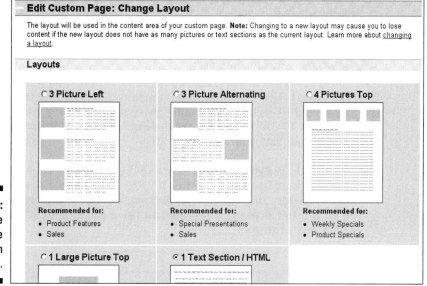

Figure 5-10: eBay Store page custom templates.

Following are some important policies to include:

- Indicate to what locations you'll ship.

- Specify the sales tax you plan to collect. If your state doesn't require you to collect sales tax, leave the area blank. If it does, select your state and indicate the proper sales tax. Most states won't require you to collect sales tax unless the sale is shipped to your home state. Check the links in Chapter 15 to verify your state's sales tax regulations.

- State your customer service and return policy. Fill in the information regarding how you handle refunds, exchanges, and so on. If you're a member of SquareTrade (see Chapter 4), mention here that you subscribe to its policies. Be sure to include whatever additional store information you think is pertinent.

You can also set up a custom home page for your store, but it's not a popular option. It's best to let your visitors go right to the page listing what you're selling, don't you think?

✔ **Custom categories:** Here's where you really make your store your own. You may name up to 19 custom categories that relate to the items you sell for your store.

✔ **Custom listing header:** Do this. Don't ask questions, just do it. The custom listing header display is one of the best tools you can use to bring people into your store. Click the link and select the option to Show your custom listing header on all your eBay auctions and fixed-price sales. This will encourage shoppers to visit your eBay store when they browse your eBay listings.

When customizing, be sure to include your store logo as well as a store search box. In Figure 5-11, you can see how the store header looks at the top of an eBay listing.

Manage your items

We've all listed items on eBay, so I don't plan on boring you with a tutorial on how to list your items here (although I give you some listing and photo image tips in Chapter 11). Following are the main differences between listing an item in your store and listing an auction on eBay:

✔ You have to assign your item to one of the prescribed store categories that you designated while setting up your store. If your new item falls into a category that you haven't defined, you can always go back to your store and add a category (as many as 19) or put it in the eBay-generated Other Items category.

✔ You don't place a minimum bid or a reserve price on your store items because everything you list in your eBay store is a Buy It Now item.

✔ Listings in an eBay store can be put up for sale for 30, 60, 90, or 120 days or GTC (good till cancelled). The listing fees are shown in Table 5-2. Finally, you can buy something for 2 cents!

Figure 5-11:
Super
promotion
on your
auctions:
add a link to
your eBay
store
and the
capability to
search the
store.

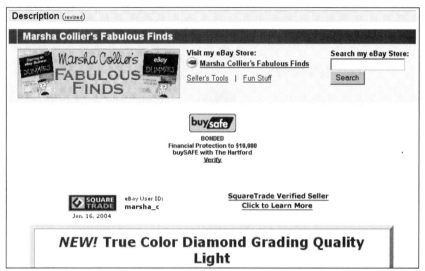

Table 5-2	Store Inventory Insertion (Listing) Fees		
Listing Time	*Insertion Fee*	*Surcharge*	*Total*
30 days	$.02	$0	$.02
60 days	$.02	$.02	$.04
90 days	$.02	$.04	$.06
120 days	$.02	$.06	$.08
Good Till Cancelled	$.02 per 30 days	N/A	$.02 per 30 days

The items you list in your eBay store *will not* appear in the regular eBay site title search. Your items *will* be seen if one of your buyers does a Seller or Stores search from the eBay Search page. That's why you pay only 2 cents per listing for 30 days. You *must* put a link in your auctions to your eBay store (see the next section) — and tell the auction browsers that you have more stuff for them that they "can't find in a regular eBay search."

Create an About the Seller page

If you haven't already created an eBay About Me page, do it now! The About Me page becomes the About the Seller page in your store. This page is a primary tool for promoting sales. (See Chapter 3 regarding About Me pages). You can put this page together in about ten minutes — max — with eBay's handy and easy-to-use templates!

Promotions

eBay has added some excellent ways to promote your store. As an eBay store owner, you have access to promotional tools that other sellers can't use. The most valuable of these is cross promotions — there's no charge to use it either! The cross-promotion box appears after a buyer places a bid on or purchases an item from an eBay seller.

The beauty of having a store is that the cross-promotion box appears *twice*: once with your regular listings and again with a different assortment of items (if you want), after someone buys an item. Best of all? You get to select which items are shown with your individual auctions.

Figure 5-12 shows you a cross-promotion box that appears when someone views one of my auctions.

Figure 5-12:
A cross promotion in one of my eBay auctions.

You can set up the promotions so that they default to show other items from related store categories, or you can go in and set them up yourself for individual auctions. Again, every listing has two sets of options: one for when a user views your listings, and the other for when someone bids or wins your item.

Marketing Your Wares

eBay has more tempting options that you can use to spruce up your store items. These options work exactly like the ones eBay offers for your auctions (see Chapter 10). When choosing whether to use these options, remember that your eBay store items only appear when someone searches in the eBay stores. eBay store items don't appear in a regular eBay search, so the Gallery option may be the most beneficial option at this time. Check out Table 5-3 for a rundown of optional feature fees.

Table 5-3	eBay Optional Store Features			
	Price			
Feature	*30 days*	*60 days*	*90 days*	*120 days*
Feature item in store search	$19.95	$24.95	$29.95	$34.95
Item subtitle	$0.02	$0.04	$0.06	$0.08
Gallery	$0.01	$0.01	$0.01	$0.01
Listing Designer	$0.10	$0.10	$0.10	$0.10
Highlight title	$5.00	$7.00	$9.00	$11.00
Boldface title	$1.00	$2.00	$3.00	$4.00

Making a Sale

From the buyer's point of view, shopping at an eBay store is much different than winning an auction. eBay stores feature fixed-price sales; the buyer will get the merchandise as soon as you can ship it (instead of waiting for the auction to run its course). Even though your auctions show up on your store's home page, all regular listings in your eBay store are Buy It Now items.

When a buyer makes a purchase from an eBay store, here's what happens:

1. The buyer clicks the Buy It Now button on the listing page. The Review Payments page appears, where the buyer can review the purchase. This page contains the shipping amount that you specified when you listed the item.

2. **The buyer provides shipping information (required).** When eBay notifies you that a sale has been made, you have all the information you need. You don't have to scurry around looking for the return address on the envelope when the payment arrives.

3. **The buyer reviews the transaction and then clicks the confirm button.** The information about the sale is e-mailed to you, and the buyer receives confirmation of the sale.

Your eBay store will be an essential backup to your auctions. It's a great place to put out-of-season items, accessories for the items you sell actively, and even consignment items between relisting. Considering the price of an eBay store, you have to make only a few sales per month to pay for it — and when your sales start to build, your efforts will be greatly rewarded!

Part II
Setting Up Shop

The 5th Wave   By Rich Tennant

©RICHTENNANT

Did I mention that I ran across a balloon animal storefront on eBay recently?

In this part . . .

Your hobby is what you love, and I'm betting you have a houseful of duplicate items — the perfect stuff to sell on eBay! Or why not buy from other collectors locally and become a specialist on eBay? Or perhaps you'd like to sell inventory from an existing business or from others on consignment. Or maybe you want to start buying wholesale merchandise like the big boys.

As you can see, the options are countless. In this part, I talk about how to find merchandise to sell, the best way to sell it, and your ever-important Web site.

Chapter 6

Stocking the Store

In This Chapter

▶ Going to dollar stores

▶ Joining discount club stores

▶ Prowling garage sales

▶ Researching going-out-of-business sales

▶ Going, going, gone

▶ Visiting resale shops

▶ Finding freebies

▶ Selling salvage

▶ Buying by the case

▶ Searching eBay

▶ Selling by consignment

*Y*ou're probably wondering just how you can possibly get enough merchandise to list as many as twenty items a day. You're thinking that there aren't possibly enough sources out there to fulfill that kind of volume. Success on eBay isn't easy. Many hours and a good deal of perspiration — along with loads of inspiration — are necessary to make a good living selling online. You *can* do it — if you apply the same amount of effort in acquiring merchandise.

One of my mottoes is "Buy off-season, sell on-season." You can get great bargains on winter merchandise in the heat of summer. January's a great time to stock up on Christmas decorations, and the value of those trendy vintage aluminum trees doubles in November and December. Cashmere sweaters, too! In the winter, you can get great deals on closeout summer sports merchandise. It's all in the timing.

How are you going to acquire the products you need? I've spent hours, days, weeks, okay, even months trying to work out the best ways to stock an eBay business. Ultimately this depends on you, your personality, and the type of merchandise you plan to sell. I've tried many of the tactics that I discuss in this chapter, as have some eBay sellers that I know, so here I pass on all the secrets and caveats that each of us discovered along the way.

Dollar Stores

Dollar stores come in all shapes and sizes. They can be filled with junk or treasure, and it takes a practiced eye to separate the wheat from the chaff. Try going in with a teenager, and see whether he or she reacts to any of the items for sale. Sometimes only one in five visits works out, but you'll know when you see the item — and at these prices you can afford to go deep! Stock at these stores doesn't stay on the shelf for too long; if you pass on an item, it may not be there when you return for it the next day. Maybe another savvy eBay seller picked up the values.

99¢ Only Stores

The crème de la crème of the dollar-type stores on the West Coast are the 99¢ Only stores. (Okay, $.99 isn't $1.00, but I still think it qualifies as a dollar store!) You can find these stores in California, Nevada, Arizona, and Texas. The highest price in the store is 99¢, and some items can be bought for as little as 29¢.

The bulk of the items sold at 99¢ Only stores are closeouts or special opportunity buys. When a company changes its labels, for example, it might sell all remaining stock with the old labels to 99¢ Only. I've found some profitable books, Olympics memorabilia, and pop culture items at this store. The chain is expanding rapidly, so visit its Web site at www.99only.com to see whether a store is opening near you. Other dollar stores are probably in your area. Pull out the phone book (or bother the 411 operators) and see what you can find.

It's not unusual for dollar store warehouses to sell direct to a retailer (that's you!). Find out where the distribution warehouse is for your local dollar store chain and make contact. The 99¢ Only stores have a wholesale unit called Bargain Wholesale that runs out of their City of Commerce California offices. They sell directly to retailers, distributors, and exporters. You can go a long way here by being nice. Befriend the office manager or warehouse manager, who might then call you when merchandise that matches your specialty comes in.

Big Lots

Another super selling chain is the Big Lots company, which encompasses the Pic N Save, Mac Frugal's, Big Lots, and Odd Lots stores. They may have items priced at more than a dollar, but they specialize in closeout merchandise. All their merchandise sells for well under most discounters and at deep discounts to retailers. This is a great place to find toys, household goods — almost anything. Troll their aisles at least once a month to find items that you can resell on eBay. The Big Lots company has stores in 46 states; check its Web site at www.biglots.com for store locations near you.

When you get your state's seller's permit (see Chapter 15), you can take advantage of the Big Lots Wholesale Web site, at www.biglotswholesale. com. If you think that Big Lots regular prices are low, you should see their wholesale prices! The minimum order from the Web site is $500, which will get you a lot of merchandise. Before placing an order, be sure to check and see whether the item is selling on eBay. If many eBay sellers are trying to sell the item now, why not place an order and sell when the other sellers have exhausted their stock? When fewer sellers are selling, the price usually goes up. Supply and demand is the name of the game.

Tuesday Morning

One of my editors is going to kill me for mentioning one of her favorite eBay merchandise sources — but here it is. Tuesday Morning has more than 500 stores scattered over the United States. They sell first-quality designer and brand-name closeout merchandise at deep-deep discounts, 50% to 80% below retail.

The key here is that the store sells recognizable brand names, the kind of items that eBay shoppers look for. I've seem items at their store from Samsonite, Thomas Kincade, Limoges, Wedgwood, Royal Doulton, Madame Alexander, and even Barbie!

Find your local store at their web site, www.tuesdaymorning.com. If you sign up for their eTreasures newsletter, you'll get advance notice of when the really good stuff arrives at the store. (Sometimes they have only a dozen of a particular item per store, so you have to be there when the doors open.)

Discount Club Stores

Warehouse stores made their mark by selling items in bulk to large families, clubs, and small businesses. In case you haven't noticed, these stores have recently upscaled and sell just about anything you could want. Their shelves are brimming with current merchandise ripe for the picking.

Sam's Club

In addition to shopping for bargains at the Sam's Club in your neighborhood, you can now visit their auctions at auctions.samsclub.com. What a fantastic place to find merchandise to sell on eBay. The closeouts on the auction site can sell at a fraction of retail price.

Costco

Believe it or not, one day I was wheeling my cart around Costco (to buy my monthly ration of meat) and right in front of me was a huge display with women jumping and grabbing at the merchandise. I glanced above to read the sign: Fendi Baugette Handbags $199.99. My daughter and I elbowed our way (in not too ladylike fashion, I might add) through the crowd and saw the regularly $450 priced purses, stacked like lunchmeat. In those days, the Baugette was new and sold on eBay for around $350. Needless to say, we bought all that our credit cards could handle.

In the first edition of this book, I talked about a special on the Costco Web site, www.costco.com, for a new *Snow White & the Seven Dwarfs* DVD. For $18.49, you could pre-order the Snow White DVD and get a second Disney DVD for *free*. When there's an offer like this, you can sell two items on eBay for the price of one. If I had followed my own advice and bought a case of this deal and held some for future sales, I'd be in the money today. It seems that Disney movies are released for a limited time only. Now, that original DVD set sells on eBay for around $40.

When an item is new but has some collectibility, I suggest you buy in bulk, sell some of the item off to make up your investment, and save the balance for later. This has paid off for me a good many times with Disney films, Barbies, and Andy Warhol dinnerware.

Garage Sales

What can be better than getting up at 6 a.m. to troll the local garage sales? I say nothing — if you're motivated to find lots of good eBay merchandise and prepared for the garage sales. Buy the newspaper or check your local news-paper's classified ads online (just run a Google search for your local newspaper's name), and print maps of the sale locations from MapQuest or Yahoo! You know the neighborhoods, so you can make a route from one sale to the next that makes sense — and figure in bathroom stops and coffee breaks.

Neighbors often take advantage of an advertised sale and put out some stuff of their own. Bring a friend; you can cover more ground faster if two of you are attacking the sales.

A few tips on shopping garage sales:

✔ Fancier neighborhoods have better stuff than poor or middle class ones. I know that sounds unfair, but I know for sure that rich folks' trash is better than mine.

✔ Look for sales that say "Early Birds Welcome," and make them the first on your list so you can get them out of the way. It seems like a universal bell goes off somewhere and all garage sales start at 8 a.m. *sharp!*

✔ The stuff you find at estate sales is often of a higher quality. These sales feature things that have been collected over many, many years.

✔ Keep an eye out for "moving to a smaller house" sales. These are usually people who have raised children, accumulated a houseful of stuff (collectibles? old toys? designer vintage clothes?), and want to shed it all so that they can move to a condo in Palm Springs.

Any toys people are selling while downsizing are usually good ones.

✔ I usually put sales that feature "kids' items and toys" on the end of my list, and I go only if I'm not too tired. These are generally young couples (with young children) who are trying to raise money or are moving. More often than not, they're keeping the good stuff and are simply shedding the excess.

Going-Out-of-Business Sales

Going-out-of-business sales can be a bonanza, but be careful and don't be misled. Many states require businesses that are putting on a going-out-of-business sale to purchase a special license that identifies the business as *really* going out of business. Some store ads may read "Going Out for Business" or some similar play on words, so you need to be sure that you're going to the real thing. When a retailer is liquidating its own stock, you're going to get the best buys. A retailer will often run the sale week by week, offering bigger discounts as time goes by. If a company is really going out of business, don't be afraid to make an offer on a quantity of items.

A chain of children's wear went out of business here in southern California a while back. This chain also carried a smattering of popular dolls. A seller I know made an offer for all remaining dolls and subsequently purchased the dolls at a great price. Throughout the following year, she then sold them on eBay for three to four times what she had paid.

Auctions

Two types of auctions where you can pick up bargains are liquidation and estate auctions. (I also discuss charity auctions, where you may be able to find bargains while donating to a good cause.) You'll find perfectly salable and profitable items, but each type of auction has its idiosyncrasies. Before you go to any auction, double-check payment terms and find out whether you must bring cash or can pay by credit card. Also, before you bid on anything, find out the *hammer fee,* or *buyer's premium.* These fees are a percentage that auction houses add to the winner's bids; the buyer has the responsibility of paying these fees.

Liquidation auctions

When a company gets into serious financial trouble, its debtors (the people to whom the company owes money) obtain a court order to liquidate the company to pay the bills. The liquidated company then sells its stock, fixtures, and even real estate. Items sell for just cents on the dollar, and you can easily resell many of these items on eBay. A special kind of auctioneer handles these auctions. Look in the phone book under Auctioneers: Liquidators and call local auctioneer's offices to get on mailing lists. This way, you'll always know when something good comes up for sale.

Estate auctions

Estate auctions are the higher level of estate garage sales. Here you can find fine art, antiques, paper ephemera, rare books, and collectibles of all kinds. Aside from the large estate auctions, most auction houses have monthly estate auctions in which they put together groups of merchandise from various small estates. Find out when these auctions are being held and mark them on your calendar.

These auctions are attended mostly by dealers, who know the local going prices for the items they bid on. But because they're buying to sell in a retail environment, their high bids will generally be the wholesale price for your area. If a particular item is flooding your market, the high bid may be low. I've seen some incredible bargains at Butterfield's estate auctions here in Los Angeles. When you're in a room full of local dealers, they're buying what's hot to resell in your city — not what's going to sell across the country. That entire market will be yours.

Charity silent auctions

I'm sure you've been to your share of silent auctions for charity. A school or an organization will get everyone from major corporations to the local gift shop to donate items. The items are then auctioned off to the highest bidder, usually in a silent format.

Have you seen this headline before?

"Make Hundred$ of thou$ands in profits by reselling items from Government Foreclosure auctions!" Yes, I've seen this headline too. You send someone money, and they let you in on the big "secret."

Here's the secret. You can find out about many government auctions at these sites:

✔ www.ustreas.gov/auctions/customs. This site gives information on seized Department of the Treasury property auctions held in New Jersey, California, Florida, Texas, Arizona, and other locations. The lists of the lots for sale are posted about a month before the auctions. You can also call the hot line at 703-273-7373 for up-to-date information. They also post the bid results for previous auctions, so you can get an idea about the selling price of various lots.

✔ www.ustreas.gov/auctions/irs/. Our buddies at the Internal Revenue Service have their own auction site. Here you can find a wide assortment of real property: patents, livestock, vehicles, planes, boats, business equipment, household goods, and real estate. They sell just about everything. (These guys are serious about collecting their tax money!)

✔ gsaauctions.gov/gsaauctions/gsaauctions. This is the official link to the General Services Administrations surplus, seized, and forfeited property auctions. These are electronic bidding online auctions that are held daily. You can even find used crash test vehicles here (good for selling the undamaged parts on eBay).

✔ http://www.usps.com/surplus vechicles/. Got a hankering to be tooling around town in a modified postal truck? Well, here's your chance! This site sells all kinds of vehicles and will provide the links to phone numbers for every vehicle maintenance center, sorted by state. They even sell vehicles on eBay under the seller ID usps-al-pmsc.

✔ www.stealitback.com. Gotta love this site! It's the auction site for Propertybureau.com, a business started to help local police departments use the Internet to sell their seized items rather than hold individual sales. You'll find lots of varied and constantly changing merchandise here. If you've been the victim of theft, they also have a registry where you can list the serial numbers of your stolen goods. If the items ever come up for sale, they'll see that the items are returned to you.

✔ www.usps.com/auctions. Ever wonder where all the post office's lost packages go? Check this site for auction locations and times. Also search Google for *mail recovery centers*.

✔ www.govliquidation.com. This is a private company specializing in government liquidation auctions.

For other sites, run a Google search for *state surplus* (results include tons of links to individual state-seized property auctions), *seized property*, *tax sales*, *confiscated property*, and *state auction*. Remember, if you're asked for payment to get the information, it's not an official site.

You can find many a great item at these auctions. Aside from new merchandise, collectors may feel good about donating some collection overflow to a charity. I purchased the keystone of my Star Trek action figure collection at a charity auction: the very rare tri-fold Borg (one of perhaps only fifty in existence). This figure has sold as high as $1000 on eBay, and I paid just $60, all while donating to a charity. (Okay, now it's selling for only about $400 on eBay — but heck, it was *still* a deal!)

Goodwill, Salvation Army, and Resale Shops

Participating in a charity such as Goodwill or the Salvation Army is a powerful thing with many benefits. You don't have to worry about having a garage sale to get rid of unwanted stuff (no need to have strangers trodding all over the lawn, crunching the daisy borders while sniffing around at the stuff for sale), and you can pretty much write-off many items as a charity tax deduction. And it's simple: You just load the goods into your car and take 'em to the store. It's a win-win-win situation. The extra win is you acquiring valuable pieces at bargain-basement prices.

At resale stores, such as Goodwill and the Salvation Army, you'll sometimes uncover treasures while other times you'll find only junk. I recommend befriending the manager who sees the merchandise as it comes in, will know just what you're looking for (because you said so in a friendly conversation), and will call you before the items hit the floor. This type of relationship can save you from making fruitless trips.

Some stores receive merchandise from a central warehouse, where donations are first sent for minor rehabilitation and cleaning. Other, smaller operations process items in-house, with the store manager supervising. The resale store is a business that runs on a schedule. Ask the manager (whom you've befriended) when the truck regularly comes in. Being there when the truck arrives enables you to view items before the general public.

A sharp seller I know is always at his local Salvation Army when the trucks come in. One day as workers unloaded the truck, he saw a plaque-mounted baseball bat. Withholding his excitement, he picked it up and found that it was a signed Ty Cobb bat with a presentation plaque. Although he didn't know exactly what it was, he took a gamble and brought it to the cash register, where he paid $33 minus the senior citizen discount. He took the bat to his office and made a few phone calls, later discovering that the bat was indeed a rare Louisville Slugger bat that had been presented to the Georgia Peach, Ty

Cobb. But he'll never sell it because it's his good luck bat, which now hangs above the desk in his warehouse.

Goodwill Industries is definitely gearing up for the 21st century. You can shop at its online auctions and get super values on the best of their merchandise. Don't forget to check the going prices on eBay before you buy. Have fun at `www.shopgoodwill.com`.

Freebies

Freebies come in all shapes and sizes and — best of all — they're free, of course. Freebies are usually samples or promotion pieces that companies give away to introduce a new product, service, or, best of all, a media event. Even carefully trimmed ads from magazines can fetch high prices from collectors.

 When you go to the cosmetic counter and buy a way-too-expensive item, be sure to ask for tester-sized samples. Name brand cosmetic and perfume samples of high-priced items sell very well on eBay. Also, look for *gift with purchase* deals. If it's a specialty item, you can usually sell it on its own to someone who'd like to try a sample themselves rather than plunge headlong into a large purchase. Less special items can be grouped together as lots. Be sure to put the brand names in the title.

Remember the talking Taco Bell Chihuahua giveaway? Those cute little dogs were all the rage and sold for big money on eBay. It almost seems foolish to remind you of the McDonald's Teenie Beanie Baby giveaways; moms, dads, and dealers were driving in circles through the drive-thru, purchasing as many of the Happy Meals as each store would allow. They'd then drive to the next McDonald's to purchase a different toy. In my house alone, we had frozen hamburgers for three months!

When *Return of the Jedi* was re-released in 1997, the first 100 people to enter each theater got a Special Edition Luke Skywalker figure. These figures are still highly prized by collectors and when the next part of the Star Wars saga is released, you can bet the prices on this figure will rise yet again.

In 1995, Paramount network premiered a new show, *Star Trek Voyager.* In selected markets, Paramount sent a promotional microwave popcorn packet as a Sunday newspaper insert. These are still selling well (when you can find them), although the value rises and falls according to current interest in Star Trek.

Before you pass by a freebie, reconsider its possible future resale value.

Salvage: Liquidation Items, Unclaimed Freight, and Returns

The easiest buys of all, *salvage merchandise* is retail merchandise that has been returned, exchanged, or shelf-pulled for some reason. Generally, this merchandise is sold as-is and where-is and may be in new condition. To buy this merchandise, you must have your resale (sales tax number) permit and be prepared to pay the shipping to your location — unless you're buying it on eBay.

Available all over the country, the liquidation business has been thriving as a well-kept secret for years. As long as you have space to store salvage merchandise and a way to sell it, you can acquire it for as low as 10 cents on the dollar. When I say you need storage space, I mean lots of space. To buy this type of merchandise at bottom-of-the-barrel prices, you must be willing to accept truckloads — full 40–53 foot eighteen wheelers, loaded with approximately 22–24 4' x 4' x 6' (or 7') pallets — of merchandise at a time. Often these truckloads have manifests listing the retail and wholesale price of each item on the truck. If you have access to the more than 10,000 square feet of warehouse that you'll need to unpack and process this amount of merchandise, you're in business.

Several types of salvage merchandise are available:

- ✔ **Unclaimed freight:** When a trucking company delivers merchandise, a *manifest* (a document containing the contents of the shipment) accompanies the freight. If, for some reason, a portion of the shipment arrives incomplete, contains the wrong items, or is damaged, the entire shipment may be refused by the merchant. The trucking company is now stuck with as much as a truckload of freight. The original seller may not want to pay the freight charges to return the merchandise to his or her warehouse (or accept blame for an incorrect shipment), and so the freight becomes the trucker's problem. The trucking companies arrive at agreements with liquidators to buy this freight in the various areas that the liquidators serve. This way, truckers are never far from a location where they can dump, er, drop off merchandise.

- ✔ **Returns:** Did you know that after you buy something and decide that you don't want it and return it to the store or mail-order house, it can never be sold as new again (in most states anyway)? The merchandise is generally sent to a liquidator who agrees in advance to pay a flat percentage for goods. The liquidator must move the merchandise to someone else. All major retailers liquidate returns, and much of this merchandise ends up on eBay or in closeout stores.

If you're handy at repairing electronics or computers, you'd probably do very well with a specialized lot. You may easily be able to revitalize damaged merchandise, often using parts from two unsalable items to come up with one that you can sell in like-new working condition.

✔ **Liquidations:** Similar to the liquidation auctions that I mention in a previous section on auctions, these liquidators buy liquidation merchandise by truckloads and sell it in smaller lots. The merchandise comes from financially stressed or bankrupt companies that need to raise cash quickly.

✔ **Seasonal overstocks:** Remember my motto? "Buy off-season, sell on-season"? At the end of the season, a store may find its shelves overloaded with seasonal merchandise (such as swimsuits in August) that it must get rid of to make room for the fall and winter stock. These brand-new items become salvage merchandise because they're seasonal overstocks.

✔ **Shelf-pulls:** Have you ever passed up one item in the store for the one behind it in the display because its box was in better condition? Sometimes the plastic bubble or the package is dented, and you'd rather have a pristine one. That box you just passed up may be destined to become a *shelf-pull.* The item inside may be in perfect condition, but it's cosmetically unsalable in the retail store environment.

I scoured the Internet and found tons of liquidators. The following are some sites that stood out and offered a wide variety of deals:

www.wholesalecentral.com

www.mywebwholesaler.com

www.salvagecloseouts.com

www.amerisurplus.com

www.closeouts.digiscape.net

www.amlinc.com

www.tdwcloseouts.com

Be careful before signing up for a newsletter on some of these sites. My spam woes grew to massive proportions after I did so. To preserve your privacy, sign up for a free Yahoo! or Hotmail account and use it for this type of promotional offer.

A proportion of liquidation items, unclaimed freight, and returns may not be salable for the reasons that I discuss in the rest of this section. Although you'll acquire many gems that stand to bring you profit, you'll also be left with a varying percentage of useless items. Read on carefully.

Drop shipping to your customers

Some middlemen, wholesalers, and liquidators specialize in selling to online auctioneers through a *drop-ship service*. Some crafty eBay sellers make lots of money selling lists of drop shipping sources to eBay sellers — I hope not to you. Dealing with a drop shipper means that you don't ever have to take possession of (or pay for) the merchandise. You're given a photo and, after you sell the item, you give the vendor the address of the buyer. They charge your credit card for the item plus shipping, and they'll ship the item to your customer for you.

This way of doing business costs *you* more and lowers your profits. If you're in business, your goal is to make as much money as you can. Because the drop shipper is in business too,

they'll mark up the merchandise they sell to you (and the shipping cost) so they can make their profit.

Be careful when using a drop shipper. Ask for references. See whether a zillion sellers are selling the same merchandise on eBay — and not getting any bites. Also, what happens if they run out of an item that you've just sold? You can't just say oops to your buyer without getting some nasty feedback. It's your online reputation at stake. If you find a solid source and believe in the product, order a quantity and have it shipped to your door. Don't pay for someone else's mark-up for the privilege of shipping to your customers.

Items by the pallet

Some suppliers take the risk and purchase salvaged merchandise by the truckload. They then break up each truckload and sell the merchandise to you a pallet at a time. You'll probably find some local liquidators who offer this service, or you can go online to find one. Here's the rub: finding the right person to buy from.

As in any business, you'll find both good-guy liquidators and bad-guy liquidators. As you know, the world is full of e-mail scammers and multi-level marketers who are in business to take your money. No one trying to sell you merchandise can possibly *guarantee* that you'll make money, so beware of liquidators who offer this kind of promise. I don't care who they are or what they say. Carefully research whomever you choose to buy from. Use an Internet search engine and search for the words *salvage, liquidation,* and *pallet merchandise.*

Some liquidation sellers sell their merchandise in the same condition that it ships in to their location, so what you get is a crapshoot. You may lose money on some items while making back your money on others. Other sellers who charge a bit more will remove less desirable merchandise from the pallets. Some may even make up deluxe pallets with better quality merchandise. These loads cost more, but if they're filled with the type of merchandise that you're interested in selling, you'll probably write better descriptions and subsequently do a better job selling them.

Getting a pallet of merchandise shipped to you can cost a bundle, so finding a source for your liquidation merchandise that's close to your base of operations is a good idea. You'll notice that many liquidation sites have several warehouses, which translates to lower shipping costs for the buyer. (They can then also accept merchandise from places close to the various warehouses.) You might see FOB (freight on board) and a city name listed, which means that when you buy the merchandise, you own it in the city listed. You're responsible for whatever it costs to ship the merchandise to your door. Search around; you may have to go through many sources before you find the right one for you.

When you find a source from which you want to buy merchandise by the pallet, check out a few things before spending your hard-earned cash:

- ✔ Do they sell mostly to flea marketers (you might not want that kind of merchandise because you're looking for *quality* at a low price) or close-out stores (more retail-oriented)?
- ✔ Did you get a reply within 24 hours after calling or e-mailing?
- ✔ Does anyone you speak to appear to care about what you want to sell?
- ✔ Are the available lots within your budget?
- ✔ Are the lots general or have they been sorted to include only the type of merchandise that you want to sell?
- ✔ How long has this liquidator been in business and where does its merchandise come from?
- ✔ Does the source guarantee that you *will* make money or that you *can* make money by buying the right merchandise? Remember: No one can guarantee that you'll make money.
- ✔ Does the supplier offer on its Web site references that you can contact to find out some usable information on this seller's items and the percentage of unsalable goods in a box or pallet?
- ✔ Is a hard sell involved? Or is it a matter-of-fact deal?

Before you get dazzled by a low, low price on a lot and click the Buy It Now button, check the shipping cost. Many so-called wholesalers will lure you in with bargain-basement prices, only to charge you three times the normal shipping costs. Do your homework before you buy!

Job lots

Manufacturers often have to get rid of merchandise, too. Perhaps a particular manufacturer made five million bobbing-head dolls and then sold only four million to retailers. It has to quickly unload this merchandise (known as *job lots*) so that it'll have the cash to invest in next season's array of items. Job lots often consist of hundreds or thousands of a single item. You'd best enjoy what you're selling because you'll be looking at the stuff for a while.

Remember supply and demand — don't ever flood the eBay market. Otherwise, your item will become valueless.

Many Web sites specialize in job lots, but you have to visit them often because the deals are constantly changing. One worth checking out is Liquidation.com, shown in Figure 6-1. Visit them at `www.liquidation.com`.

Figure 6-1: Liquidation.com constantly has desirable lots of liquidation merchandise.

Wholesale Merchandise by the Case

Purchasing wholesale merchandise may require that you have your state's resale license, which identifies you as being in the business. Be sure that you have one before you try to purchase merchandise direct from another business. Also, when you have a resale number and purchase merchandise from another business — known as a business to business (B2B) transaction — you probably won't be charged tax when you purchase your stock because you'll be paying sales tax when you sell the items. Go to Chapter 15 to find out how to get that magic resale number.

When you have your resale number, you can go anywhere you want to buy merchandise. If you want to buy direct from a manufacturer, you can. Unfortunately, manufacturers often have a monetary minimum for the amount of your order, which may be more than you want to spend (and you'd get more of a particular item than you'd ever want at once). To remedy that, see whether you can find some independent retailers who buy in quantity and who perhaps will let you in on some quantity buys with manufacturers.

Sometimes the liquidators that I discuss in the preceding section get cases of perfectly salable goods in their loads. Pallets break up into many cases, and liquidators will often sell these cases individually on eBay. What a great way to acquire goods for your eBay business; I know of several eBay sellers who buy their merchandise this way.

Resale Items on eBay

I'll keep this eBay buying technique short and sweet: Use the magic search engine! But be careful; many a get-rich-quick schemer will use boldface keywords in their auctions to attract your attention. Look only for good quality merchandise to resell. Remember that the only way to make a living on eBay is to sell quality items to happy customers so that they'll come back and buy from you again. Be sure to search eBay auction titles for the following keywords: **resale**, **resell**, **"case of"** (see Figure 6-2), **"case quantity"**, **"lot of"**, **"pallet of"** (see Figure 6-3), **closeout**, and **surplus**. Be sure to use the quotes anywhere that I've included them here because this forces the search engine to find the words in the exact order you write them inside the quotes.

Also be sure you check out the wholesale categories on eBay. After noticing how many sellers were buying from other sellers, eBay set up wholesale subcategories for almost every type of item. You can find the wholesale items in the category list on the left side of the page after performing a search, or just got to the eBay home page, scroll down the list of categories, and click Wholesale. You'll be brought to the Wholesale hub page, as shown in Figure 6-4. Just click the category of your choice to find some great deals.

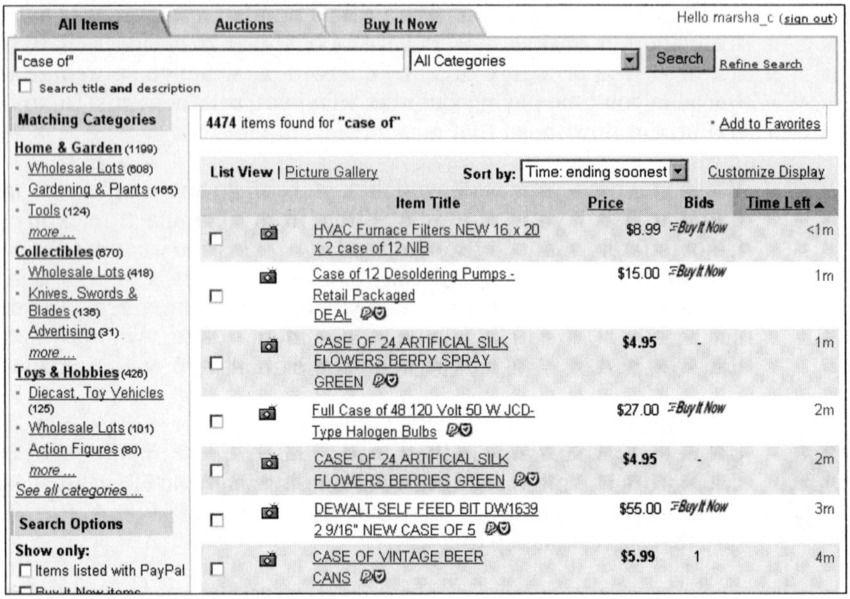

Figure 6-2: Results of a "case of" search on eBay.

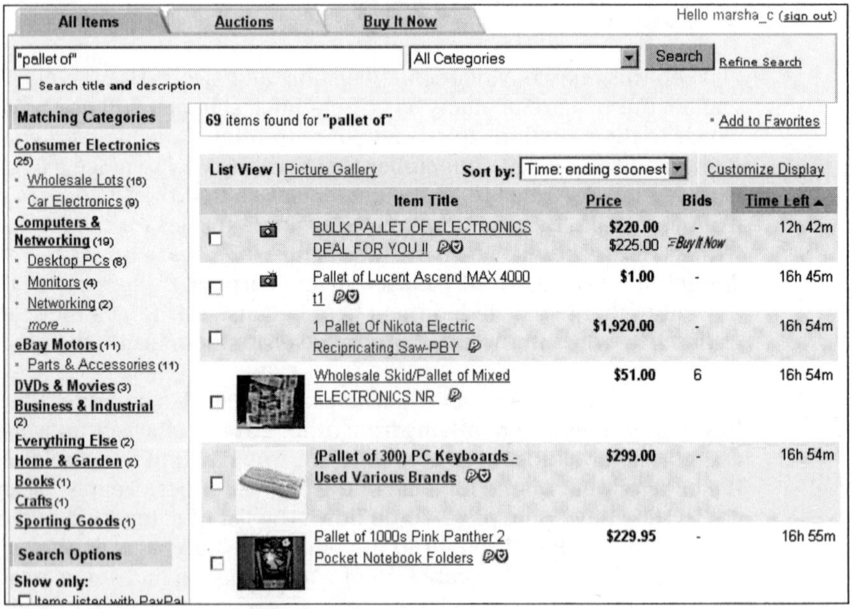

Figure 6-3: Results of "pallet of" search.

Consignment Selling

Consignment sales are the up-and-coming way for you to help newbies by selling their items on eBay. Lots of sellers do it, and several retail locations base their business on it. You take property of the item from the owner and sell it on eBay. You're responsible for taking photos and marketing the auction on eBay — for a fee. In addition to the money you earn selling on consignment, you also get excellent experience for future auctions of your own merchandise.

To set up your business for consignment sales, you should follow a few guidelines:

1. Design a consignment agreement (a contract), and send it to the owners of the merchandise before they send you their items. Doing so ensures that all policies are set up in advance and that no questions will arise after the transaction has begun.

2. Have the owners sign and send the agreement to you (the consignor) along with the item.

Become an eBay Trading Assistant

After you have fifty feedbacks under your belt on eBay (and have sold at least four items in the past 30 days), you can become a registered eBay Trading Assistant. Check out `pages.ebay.com/tradingassistants` (shown in the figure) to get all the details.

eBay publishes a directory of consignment sellers that you can search by telephone area code, Zip code, or country. Check out who in your area is a registered Trading Assistant. Read their terms and fees. Consignment sellers charge varied amounts based on their geographic location (some areas can bear higher fees than others).

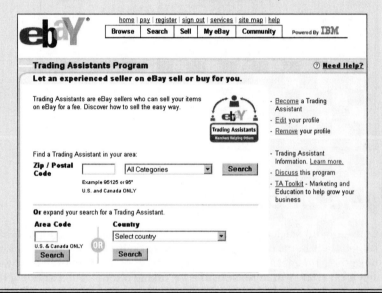

3. Research the item based on past sales so that you can give the owners an estimated price range of what the item might sell for on eBay.

4. Photograph the item carefully (see Chapter 11 for some hints) and write a thoughtful, selling description.

5. Handle all e-mail inquiries as though the item were your own; after all, your fee is generally based on a percentage of the final sale.

What do you charge for all your work? I can't give you a stock answer for that one. Many sellers charge a flat fee for photographing, listing, and shipping that ranges from $5–$10 plus as much as a 30 percent commission on the final auction total (to absorb eBay fees). Other sellers base their fees solely on the final sale amount and charge on a sliding scale, beginning at 50 per-cent of the total sale, less eBay and payment service fees. You must decide how much you think you can make on an item.

Traditional auction houses handle consignment sales in a similar fashion.

When you've reached the next level of your eBay enterprise and are looking to spend some serious money on your merchandise, check out *eBay Timesaving Techniques For Dummies*. In that book I delve into the type of wholesale-buying secrets normally reserved for the big-time retailers.

Chapter 7

Knowing the Value of What You're Selling

In This Chapter

▶ Searching eBay

▶ Finding publications in your area of interest

▶ Using online appraisal services

▶ Authenticating your merchandise

*I*f you don't know what your item is worth, you may not get the highest price in any market. If you don't know how to make your item easy to find, it may not be noticed by even the hardiest of collectors. If you don't know the facts or what to say, your well-written title and detailed description (combined with a fabulous picture) may still not be enough to get the highest price for your item.

Knowing your item is a crucial part of successful selling at eBay. This is why I suggest in Chapter 1 that you specialize in a small group of items so that you can stay on top of ever-changing trends. An item may be appraised or listed in a book for a high value, but what you care about is the price at which the item will actually sell. Imagine someone uncovering a hoard of your item and, not knowing the value of it, dumping them on eBay with low Buy It Now prices. This scenario would drive down the value of the item within a couple of weeks.

The values of collectibles go up and down. Star Wars items are a perfect example; values skyrocketed during the release of the latest movie, but now prices have settled to a considerably lower level. A published book of value listings is valid only for the *moment* the book is written. If you stay on top of your market in a few specialties, you'll be aware of these market fluctuations. If you're looking for the highest price instead of looking to liquidate excess inventory, I'd hold any special Star Wars items until the next film is released.

You no doubt *will* purchase the occasional gem and will want to make the most money possible, so in this chapter I examine the different ways you can find out just how much something is worth. I start with the easiest and most accurate method to the most laborious. I hope you can get your answer the easy way.

The Easy Way: eBay Search

Who woulda thunk it? The best tool for evaluating your items is right under your nose. The eBay search tool is the best and quickest link to finding your pricing information. To see how items like yours have been selling, search the completed auctions. You can search these results also to see in which categories to list your item and at what time of day the high bidders for your type of item jumped in and won.

Every type of item has a different type of bidder. This makes sense, right? Would a person searching for collectible dolls have the same shopping habits as a coin collector? Probably not; coins tend to be more expensive than collectible dolls. Although generalities can be dangerous, *profiling* your item's buyer is worthwhile. After you check out the completed auctions for items like yours, you'll be amazed at how the buying patterns of shoppers in different categories become crystal clear. After you arm yourself with this knowledge, you'll know not only how much your items should go for but also the best time to end the auction.

If you're selling a common item, it's also important to check to see how many other sellers are selling the same item — and when their auctions close. Nothing can kill your profits like being the second or third auction closing with the same piece of merchandise. You have to space your auctions apart from the others, or the law of supply and demand will kick in — and kick you in the wallet.

The way the search system works has changed drastically over the years, so be sure that you know how to use this valuable tool. Almost every eBay page has a small box for searching. Initially you may find it easier to go to the search page, but if you know the search engine *syntax,* or shorthand, you can pinpoint your items with amazing accuracy.

Here are some pointers to help you get the most out of the eBay search engine:

✔ The search engine isn't case sensitive, so you don't have to worry about using capitalization in your search.

✔ To find more needles in the haystack, be sure to select the Search Titles and Descriptions option.

✔ To find historical pricing (what the item has sold for in the past), be sure to check the box to search Completed listings as well as current.

✔ If you're looking for a popular item, don't search only auction titles and descriptions; search by category, too. For example, suppose that you're searching for a Winnie the Pooh baby outfit. Type *Pooh outfit* and you'll get a ton of results. Look to the left of the page, and see the category that more closely matches your search. In Figure 7-1, the matching category is Clothing, Shoes & Accessories. Click the link below for the Infants & Toddlers subcategory. Now you'll see the search results in the appropriate category — I guarantee you'll find exactly what you're looking for.

✔ Don't use conjunctions (*or, and*) or articles (*a, an, the*) in your search; the search engine might misconstrue these *noise* words as part of your search. Some sellers use the ampersand (&) in place of the word *and*, so if you include *and* in your search, you won't find auctions that use the ampersand. In addition, some sellers, due to the 55-character limit, may not place *the* in their title; the same goes for *a, or,* and *and*.

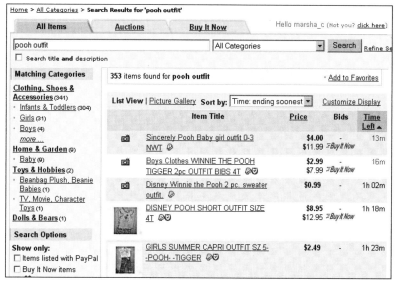

Figure 7-1:
The eBay search results with the Matching Categories refinement box.

Advanced searching methods

If you need to pinpoint a particular item or just want to weed out bogus responses, you can try a variety of advanced search methods, shown in Table 7-1. You can use these shortcuts in any of eBay's search windows.

Table 7-1	Advanced Search Syntax	
Symbol	*Effect*	*Example*
Quotes (","")	Limits search to the exact phrase in the quotes	**"American Staffordshire"** yields auctions relating only to this breed of dog
Asterisk (*)	Works like a wild card in poker	**196* fashion** displays auctions that relate to 1960s fashion
Parentheses (()) and comma (,)	Finds items related to either word	**(shipperke,schipperke)** finds items spelled both ways
Minus sign (-)	Excludes words	**watch -digital** gets you a lovely analog watch
Minus sign (-), parentheses (()), and comma (,)	Excludes more than one word	**Packard -(hewlett,bell)** finds those rare Packard auto collectibles
At (@) and number 1	Searches two out of three words	**@1 new purse shoes dress** gets you a nice new outfit

Now that you know how to finesse the search engine, head to the search page and see if you can work some magic.

If you have the item number, you can type or paste it into any of the eBay search boxes to get to that item.

Using eBay Advanced Search

By clicking More Search Options at the bottom of the Search>Find Items page, you can access eBay's advanced search options. With the advanced search, you can narrow your search to check out the competition (who's selling your items). In the basic search, you also have few options:

✔ **View results:** You can choose whether you want to see a mini gallery of photos. Although this may not ordinarily help when you're doing research, information is key; you might just see a variation of the item in photos that you didn't know about.

✔ **Search in categories:** You can narrow your search to one of the 23 major categories at eBay. If your product is made for men, women, or children, you may get more efficient results by looking in the category that applies directly to your item. Strangely, when searching for a ladies watch, I found the following synonyms and abbreviations for *ladies: lady's, ladys, lds,* and *femmes.*

✔ **Completed listings only:** Check this box to go directly to completed listings for your item research.

✔ **Sort by:** You can find items by auctions that end first (default), newly listed items first, lowest prices first, or highest prices first.

When you click the More Search Options link, you can narrow your search even further:

✔ **Payment:** You can isolate your search to only those sellers who accept PayPal. This may enlighten you as to whether buyers of this product pay higher prices if they have the option to pay with credit cards. (Although the PayPal exclusion will not include other methods of credit card payments, it still speaks strongly for credit card users.)

✔ **Locate items near you:** If you're selling something big that you can't (or don't want to) ship, you want to deliver it or have the buyer pick it up. This option allows you to check out the competition only in your closest major metropolitan eBay trading area.

✔ **Multiple item listings:** This option allows you to search by quantity or lot.

So how can you search completed auctions to find bidding patterns on items like yours? Here's a way to dig out all the details you need:

Perform a search on the item for which you want information on the Basic Search Options page. When the results appear (see Figure 7-2), you'll see how many other sellers are selling your same item. That way, you can determine whether it's the right time to sell. (If all active auctions for your items have high bids, its time to sell — just be sure not to list your auction to end at a similar time as another one.)

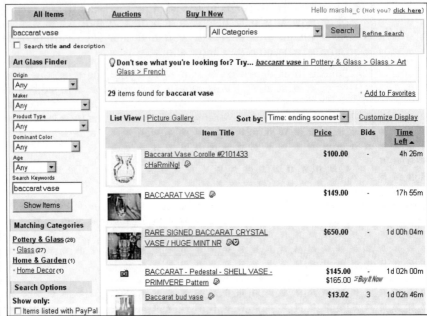

Figure 7-2:
Results of an
investigatory
search.

To dig into the details for historic pricing, also perform the completed items search from the advanced search options page:

1. **Click the link on the basic Search page to expand the advanced options.**

2. **Click the Completed_listings only option box in the options area on the top.**

3. **To sort by price, go to the Sort By drop down menu at the bottom of the page and click the <u>highest prices first</u> option.**

4. **Click Search.**

   The results of completed auctions of your particular item for the last 14 days appear sorted by highest prices first. Now you're at the heart of the matter (see Figure 7-3). Pull out your calendar and make note of what days your item landed the highest bids. More often than not, you'll find that a pattern appears. Your item may see more action on Sunday or Monday or Thursday or whenever. After you figure out the days that your item gets the highest bids, pull out a copy of the eBay time chart that appears on the Cheat Sheet (at the front of the book) and evaluate what time of day your high bidders like to bid.

Matching Categories

Pottery & Glass (58)
· Glass (58)
Antiques (9)
· Decorative Arts (9)
Live Auctions (7)
· Antiques & Decorative Arts (7)
Home & Garden (3)
Art (1)
Books (1)

Search Options

Show only:
☐ Items listed with PayPal
☐ Buy It Now items
☐ 🎁 Gift items
☑ Completed listings
☐ Items priced
[____] to [____]
Show Items
Customize options displayed above.

More on eBay

Shop eBay Stores 🔵
· Ponkel's Store (4)
· Randy Esada Designs Inc

💡 **Don't see what you're looking for?** Try... *baccarat vase* in Pottery & Glass > Glass > Art Glass > French

69 items found for baccarat vase
☑ Show only: Completed listings   · Add to Favorites

List View | Picture Gallery   Sort by: Price: highest first ▼   Customize Display

Item Title	Price ▼	Bids	End Date
ERTE & BACCARAT Bronze and Crystal Vase 🔲 " SEA MAIDENS " Edition 128/199 S/N RARE!!!	$15,000.00	-	May-02 23:19
BACCARAT - TWIST Vase - MIB 🔲	$3,289.99	-	Apr-25 12:56
BACCARAT - ARCHITECTURE Vase 🔲	$3,099.00	-	Apr-25 12:47
Baccarat large "Edwige Vase"	$1,500.00	15	Apr-25 13:56
BACCARAT - OCEANIE Vase red 🔲	$916.00	-	Apr-25 12:48
BACCARAT FRENCH CRYSTAL LARGE VASE	$650.00	-	Apr-26 17:06
RARE SIGNED BACCARAT CRYSTAL VASE / HUGE MINT NR 🔲	$650.00	-	May-02 10:00
Baccarat Architect Vase 🔲	$560.55	12	May-02 15:12

Figure 7-3:
The Completed Auctions search results, sorted by highest prices first.

There you have it: the method that will get you the most information that eBay can give you on the sales trends on your item. It's money in the bank. Use it!

If you can't find any auctions for your item, you have a few more options. You're not gonna believe I'm saying this, but try searching `auctions.yahoo.com` or go to `auctions.amazon.com`. At least you'll see whether someone else in the world is selling one. None of the cool search features that I previously discuss will work — hey, they ain't eBay.

eBay also has a superior tool for checking your competitor's auctions. After a while, you will identify the sellers that frequently sell items similar to yours. Aside from keeping them in your favorite sellers list on your My eBay page (for more on that, see Chapter 3), here's a way to see whether one of your competing sellers has an item like yours up for sale:

1. **Go to the Search area, and click the <u>Items By Seller</u> link on the left.**

2. **Enter the seller's user ID in the box provided.**

   To search their completed listings, select the time frame in which you want to search. To search their current listings, just go to the bottom and click the Search button.

Useful Publications

So what if your item isn't for sale on eBay and hasn't been for 30 days? What's the first thing to do? Check out your local newsstand for one of the many publications devoted to collecting. Go over to Yahoo Yellow Pages at yp.yahoo.com. Type your zip code to limit the search to your part of the country and type a search for **newsstand** and **news stand**. You can also search for **Magazines — Dealers** in your area. Let your fingers do the walking and call the newsstands in your area and ask whether they have publications in your area of interest. If no newsstands are listed in your area, visit the local bookstore.

Here's a list of some popular reference publications:

- ✔ ***Action Figure Digest:*** Find out who's hot in the action figure biz in this monthly magazine. Its Web site sells back issues; go to www.tomart.com.

- ✔ ***Antique Trader:*** This magazine has been the bible of the antique collecting industry for more than 40 years. Visit its online home on the Collect.com Web site at www.collect.com/interest/periodical.asp?Pub=AT for more articles and subscription information.

- ✔ ***Autograph Collector:*** This magazine gives the lowdown on the autograph business as well as samples of many autographs for identification. Its Web site, www.autographcollector.com, features links to price guides it publishes.

- ✔ ***Barbie Bazaar:*** The official Mattel magazine packed with everything Barbie! Here you'll find news on what's hot in Barbie collecting and see all the new dolls put out by the Barbie team at Mattel. Visit the site at www.barbiebazaar.com for subscriptions and news.

- ✔ ***Collector Editions:*** You'll find information on plates, figurines, glass, prints, cottages, ornaments, and dozens of other contemporary decorative collectibles in this monthly magazine.

- ✔ ***Doll Reader:*** The Ultimate Authority Doll Reader has been dishing out the scoop on collectible dolls of all sorts for more than 25 years. It's the place to go to catch the trends on the latest in doll collecting. At www.dollreader.com, you'll get an idea of what's in the very informative magazine.

- ✔ ***Goldmine:*** The magazine for CD and record collecting. The Web site, www.collect.com/interest/periodical.asp?Pub=GM, has many sample articles and information from its issues.

- ✔ ***Numismatic News:*** Another standard, *Numismatic News* has been around for more than 50 years. The first issue each month includes a pull-out guide to retail U.S. coin prices. Every three months, it also includes a U.S. paper money price guide. Check out *Numismatic News* on the Web at www.collect.com/interest/periodical.asp?Pub=NN.

- *Sports Collectors Digest*: Takes sports collectibles to the highest level. Visit its Web site at `www.collect.com/interest/periodical.asp?Pub=SD` and sign up for a free e-mail newsletter.

- *Stamp Collector*: I subscribed to this magazine when I was in grade school, and it's still around. Actually it's been around a lot longer, since 1931. (Hey, I'm not that old!) They too have an informative Web site; go to `www.collect.com/interest/periodical.asp?Pub=SC`.

- *Teddy Bear Review*: Since 1986, this review has offered pages of information on bear collecting. For a free sample issue, go to `www.jonespublishing.com/index-teddybear.htm`.

It seems that every leading magazine has its own Web site. In the next section, I mention some useful Web sites for pricing references.

Online Sources of Information

Because you're all so Internet savvy (what's better than getting the information you want at a millisecond's notice?), I assume you plan to visit the magazine Web sites that I mention in the preceding section. In this section, I give you a few more fun online sources where you might be able to get more insight about your items.

Web sites

Many Web sites devoted to different collectible areas list prices at recently completed auctions. These auctions are the best evaluation of an item's value because they're usually directed towards specialists in the specific collectible category. Most of the participants in these auctions *really* know their stuff.

You may have to poke around the following Web sites to find the prices realized at auction, but once you do, you'll have the holy grail of estimated values. Look for links that point to auction archives. Many of these sites will consign your item from you as well and sell it to their audience:

- Antiques, art, all kinds of rare stuff: `www.sothebys.com`

- Art auctions: `www.artprice.com` charges for its searches by artist, but has an immense database

- Autographs, movie posters, and comic books: `www.autographs.com`

- Coins and sports memorabilia: `www.collectors.com`

- Collectible advertising glasses: `www.pgcaglassclub.com` (you've got to see this stuff!)

✔ United States coin price guide: www.pcgs.com/prices/

✔ Currency auctions: www.lynknight.com

✔ Rock and roll memorabilia (home of the world's rarest records): www.goodrockintonight.com

✔ Rare coins: www.bowersandmerena.com

✔ Sports memorabilia and cards: www.superiorsports.com

Online appraisals

I've had a bit of personal experience with online appraisals, which seem quite tempting at first glance. At second glance, though, I realized that unless the person doing the appraisal could actually *see* and *feel* the item, an accurate appraisal couldn't be performed. Also, you have no guarantee that the person at the other end is really an expert in the field that relates to your item.

I had a few items *e-appraised* by a very prestigious (now defunct) online appraisal company, and the appraisals seemed a bit off. Then I took one, a painting, to Butterfields (now Bonhams) in Los Angeles and found that the value of the painting was ten times what my e-appraisal read.

The bottom line here is that if it's an item of real value and it's worth appraising, it's worth getting appraised in person. Most large cities have auction houses, and many of those auction houses have monthly *consignment clinics* (a way for auction houses to get merchandise for their future auctions). If you bring an item to the auction house, you aren't legally bound to have it sell your item for you, but it may not be a bad idea. All you'll get is a free verbal appraisal; the auction house won't fill out any official paperwork or anything, but at least you'll get an idea of what your item is worth. Real appraisals are expensive, are performed by licensed professionals, and come with a formal appraisal document.

Authentication Services

Some companies provide the service of *authenticating* (verifying that it's the real deal) or authenticating and *grading* (determining a value based on the item's condition and legitimacy). To have these services performed on your items, you'll have to send them to the service and pay a fee.

Following are a few excellent sites for grading coins:

- Professional Coin Grading Service (PCGS): www.pcgs.com.

- American Numismatic Association Certification Service (AMNACS) — sold to Amos Press in 1990: www.anacs.com.

- Numismatic Guaranty Corporation of America (NGCA): www.ngccoin. com/ebay_ngcvalue.cfm. The site offers eBay users a discount and features a mail-in grading and certification service for your coins.

- PCI Coin Grading Service (PCI): www.pcicoins.com.

Stamp collectors (or those who have just inherited a collection from Uncle Steve) can get their stamps "expertized" (authenticated) by the American Philatelic Society. Visit www.stamps.org/services/ser_aboutexpertizing. htm for more information.

For comic books, Comics Guaranty, LLC (CGC) https://www.cgccomics. com/ebay_comic_book_grading.cfm will seal (enclose in plastic to preserve the quality) and grade at a discount for eBay users.

You can find the links to authentication discounts for eBay users at pages. ebay.com/help/community/auth-overview.html.

Sports cards and sports memorabilia have a bunch of authentication services. If you got your autograph or memorabilia direct from the player or team, you can assure its authenticity. Having the item authenticated may or may not get you a higher price at eBay. Try these sites:

- **Professional Sports Authenticator (PSA):** Offers eBay users a discount at www.psacard.com/cobrands/submit.chtml?cobrandid=23.

- **Sportscard Guarantee (SCG):** Has an eBay discount on card authenticating at www.sgccard.com/new/grading.html.

- **Online Authentics:** Reviews autographs by scans online or by physical review. Look at its services at www.onlineauthentics.com.

The best way to find a good authenticator in your field is to search the items at eBay and who is the most prominent authenticator listed in the descriptions. For example, note in the coins area that certain grading services' coins get higher bids than other services. You can also go to an Internet search engine (Google or Yahoo) and type the keywords **coin grading** (for coins). You'll come up with a host of choices; use your good sense to see which one suits your needs.

Remember that not all items need to be officially authenticated. Official authentication does add value to the item, but if you're an expert on your items, you can comfortably rate them on your own in your auctions. People will know from your description whether you're a specialist. Your feedback will also work for you by letting the prospective bidder or buyer know that your merchandise from past sales has been top-drawer.

Chapter 8

Establishing a Base of Operations: Your Web Site

In This Chapter

▶ Finding free Web space

▶ Choosing a host

▶ Deciding on the perfect name

▶ Registering the perfect name

▶ Marketing your piece of the Web

*Y*our eBay store is important to your business, but it doesn't replace an e-commerce Web site. Yes, eBay is an important site (duh) for your sales and store, but so is your own business Web site. You should establish your own presence on the Web. And although you can — and should — link your site to eBay, don't miss out on the rest of the Internet population.

You don't have a Web site yet? The Web has so many sites with pictures of people's dogs and kids that I just assumed you had your own site, too. The space for a Web site comes *free* from your ISP (I even have an embarrassing one with family pictures). One of these sites can be the practice site for your business. Take down pictures of the baby, and post pictures of items you're selling — or at the very least, install the eBay Merchant Kit (see Chapter 2).

You do have a Web site? Have you taken a good look at it lately to see whether it's up to date? (I just looked at mine — ugh.) Does it link to your eBay auctions, eBay store, and the gallery that I discuss in Chapter 5?

Most small and medium businesses are increasing their online revenue. In spring 2004, Interland, one of the leading Web hosting providers, took a survey of some of their shared hosting customers to measure the barometer of online activities. They found that 63% of respondents have 5 or fewer employees — does that sound like you? Figure 8-1 shows how important a Web site is to their business.

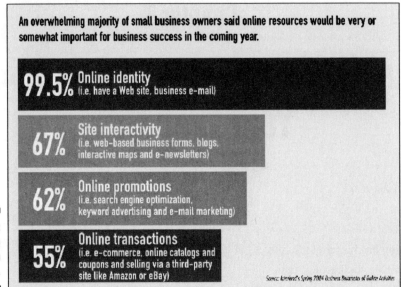

An overwhelming majority of small business owners said online resources would be very or somewhat important for business success in the coming year.

99.5% Online identity
(i.e. have a Web site, business e-mail)

67% Site interactivity
(i.e. web-based business forms, blogs, interactive maps and e-newsletters)

62% Online promotions
(i.e. search engine optimization, keyword advertising and e-mail marketing)

55% Online transactions
(i.e. e-commerce, online catalogs and coupons and selling via a third-party site like Amazon or eBay)

Source: Interland's Spring 2004 Business Barometer of Online Activities

Figure 8-1:
A revealing
graph from
Interland.

Whether or not you have a Web site, this chapter has something for you. I provide a lot of detail about Web sites, from thinking up a name to choosing a host. If you don't have a site, I get you started on launching one. If you already have a site, I give you some pointers about finding the best host. For the serious-minded Web-based entrepreneur (that's you), I also include some ever-important marketing tips.

Free Web Space — a Good Place to Start

Although I love the word *free,* in real life it seems like nothing is *really* free. *Free* generally means something won't cost you too much money — but may cost you a bit more in time. When your site is free, you aren't able to have your own direct URL (Universal Resource Locator) or domain name. Most likely, a free Web site has an address such as one of the following:

```
www.netcom.com/~marshac
home.socal.rr.com/marshac
members.aol.com/membername
```

Having some kind of site at least gives you the experience in setting one up. When you're ready to jump in for real, you can always use your free site as an extension of your main business site.

To access the Internet, you had to sign on with an Internet Service Provider (ISP), which means you more than likely already have your own Web space. Most ISPs allow you to have more than one e-mail address per account. Each e-mail address is entitled to a certain amount of free Web space. Through the use of *hyperlinks* (small pieces of HTML code that, when clicked, route the clicker from one place to another on the page or on other Web site), you can combine all the free Web space from each e-mail address into one giant Web site. Take a look at Table 8-1, where I compare some popular ISPs.

Table 8-1	ISPs Who Give You Free Web Space	
ISP	*Number of E-Mail Addresses*	*Total Space per Account*
America Online (AOL)	7	2MB per e-mail address (14MB)
AT&T WorldNet	6	10MB per e-mail address (60MB)
Earthlink	8	10MB
MSN (using Explorer 6.1)	10	30MB
Pacific Bell DSL	3	3MB
Road Runner	5	5MB/$.99 per extra MB per month
msnTV	6	3MB
Yahoo GeoCities*	1	15MB

*Yahoo GeoCities isn't an ISP, but it is a reliable online community that gives each member online Web space. Membership is free. Extra megabyte space is available for purchase.

Why learn HTML when Web page editors can do it for you?

If you need some help designing those first pages (I *never* became proficient in HTML and still depend on software to design my site), try looking for inexpensive HTML Web software. I just checked eBay, and an older version of Corel Web Designer was selling for $9.99. Another program, Web Easy 5 Professional edition, is selling for less than $50.00. Lots of Web page editors are available; the key is to find one that includes a graphical (WYSIWYG, or what-you-see-is-what-you-get) interface that allows you to preview your pages as you design them. You can also use an older version of Microsoft FrontPage (without the extensions) to design simple Web pages.

If America Online (AOL) is your Internet provider, you may already know that AOL often has some serious issues regarding its users getting e-mail from the rest of the Internet. You can't afford to run a business in an area that has e-mail issues. Your AOL account gives each of your seven screen names 2MB of online storage space (refer to Table 8-1). You can best utilize this space by using it to store images for eBay, not to run a business site. Each screen name, at 2MB, can store fifty 40K images. (For more information on how to use this space for your extra images, see Chapter 11.)

Many ISPs have their own page-builder (HTML-generating) program that's free to their users.

Poke around your ISP's home page for a <u>Community</u> or <u>Your Web space</u> link. For example, after poking around the Road Runner ISP's home page (www.rr.com), I found and clicked the <u>Member Services</u> link, which led me to a page offering various options. I finally found a <u>Personal Home Page</u> link, which took me to a page that would walk me through setting up my own home page. After agreeing to the Terms of Service, I can simply log on and set up my home page. Road Runner offered me the option of using Microsoft FrontPage, which is one of the best and easiest Web-building programs around.

I highly recommend FrontPage, but if you want all its benefits, you'll need a site that uses FrontPage *extensions* (portions of the FrontPage program that reside on the server and enable all the HTML magic to happen automatically — and you don't have to write in the code). Save FrontPage extensions for *hosted* Web sites (the ones you pay for) when you have a good deal of allotted space. Installing Microsoft FrontPage extensions on a small Web site like the one that Road Runner provides will take up too many of your precious megabytes. (Yahoo!, however, has them installed for the GeoCities sites, and doesn't count them as part of your allotted megabyte count.)

In lieu of getting involved in a huge (and expensive) program such as FrontPage, you might want to consider using a quick and easy HTML generator such as CuteHTML. If you're not looking to get extra fancy, this is the program for you. I often use CuteHTML to put together my eBay auctions when I use tables (to put pictures next to my text). You can download a free trial; the price to buy the program is only $19.99. You can find it on the GlobalSCAPE Web site at

www.globalscape.com/o/914

If it's offered, use FTP (File Transfer Protocol) to upload your pages and images. You can still design pages in Microsoft FrontPage — just don't use the fancy features. If your ISP doesn't supply an FTP program for you, go to the following and download a free trial of CuteFTP:

www.globalscape.com/o/912

Cute FTP is a small, simple program that will help you get your pages and images to your site. Your first Web pages may be simple, and that's okay. You have to get used to having a Web site before you can really use it for commerce. Put up a home page that links to a few product-related pages and your eBay auctions and, voila, you're in business. If you're feeling more adventurous about your Web site, check out the next section, where I describe a handful of Web site hosts.

Paying for Your Web Space

If you've been on the Internet for any length of time, you've been bombarded by hosting offers through your daily spam. A Web hosting company houses your Web site code and electronically doles out your pages and images to Web page visitors.

If you take advantage of PayPal's free Pay Now buttons or Shopping Cart, you can turn a basic-level hosted site into a full-on e-commerce store without paying additional fees to your hosting company. The PayPal tools are easily inserted into your pages with a snippet of code provided by PayPal. See information later in this chapter.

Before deciding to spend good money on a Web hosting company, thoroughly check it out. Go to that company's site to find a list of features they offer. If you still have questions after perusing the Web site, look for an 800 number to call. You won't find any feedback ratings like you find on eBay, but the following are a few questions to ask (don't hang up until you're satisfied with the answers):

- **How long have they been in business?** You don't want a Web host that has been in business only a few months and operates out of their basement. Deal with someone who's been around the Internet for a while and, hence, knows what they're doing. Is the company's Web site professional looking? Or does it look like your neighbor's kid designed it? Does the company look like it has enough money to stay in business? You wouldn't want it disappearing mysteriously with your money.

- **Who are some of their other clients?** Poke around to see whether you can find links to sites of other clients. Take a look at who else is doing business with them and analyze the sites. Visit several of their client sites. Do the pages and links come up quickly? Do all the images appear in a timely manner? Web sites that load quickly are a good sign.

- **What is their downtime-to-uptime ratio?** Does the Web host guarantee *uptime* (the span of time its servers stay operational without going down and denying access to your site)? Expecting a 99 percent uptime guarantee is not unreasonable; you're open for business — and your Web host needs to keep it that way.

✔ **How much Web space do you get for my money?** MSN (Microsoft Network Internet access service) gives you 30MB for free; you'd better be getting a whole lot more if you're paying for it!

✔ **What's their data transfer limit?** *Data transfer* is a measurement of the amount of bytes transferred from your site on the server to the Internet. In July 2001, my site had 93,000 hits; in July 2004, it had more than 500,000. Each hit transfers a certain amount of bytes (kilobytes, megabytes) from your host's servers to the viewer's computer.

✔ **Do they offer toll-free technical support?** When something goes wrong with your Web site, you need it fixed immediately. You must be able to reach tech support quickly without hanging around on the phone for hours. Does the Web host have a technical support area on its Web site where you can troubleshoot your own problems (in the middle of the night)?

Whenever you're deciding on any kind of provider for your business, take a moment to call their tech support team with a question about the services. Take note of how long you had to hold and how courteous the techs were. Before plunking down your hard-earned money, you should be sure that the provider's customer service claims aren't merely that — just claims.

✔ **What's the policy on shopping carts?** In time you're probably going to need a shopping cart interface on your site. Does your provider charge extra for that? If so, how much? In the beginning, a convenient and professional-looking way to sell items on your site is to set up a PayPal shopping cart or PayPal Pay Now buttons. When you're running your business full-time, however, a shopping cart or a way to accept credit cards is a must.

✔ **What kind of statistics will you get?** Visitors who go to your Web site leave a bread-crumb trail. Your host collects these statistics, so you'll be able to know which are your most and least popular pages. You can know how long people linger on each page, where they come from, and what browsers they're using. How your host supplies these stats to you is important. One of the best reporting formats is provided from a company called WebTrends (www.webtrends.com).

✔ **Are there any hidden fees?** Are they charging exorbitant fees for setup? Charging extra for statistics? Imposing high charges if your bandwidth suddenly increases?

✔ **How often will the Web host back up your site?** No matter how redundant a host's servers are, a disaster may strike and you need to know that your Web site won't vaporize. *Redundancy* is the safety net for your site. You may be interested in how many power backups a company has for the main system. Perhaps it has generators (more than one is good) and more.

If you have a Web site and you're like me, you're always looking for other hosts that offer more bang for your buck. It takes time to look behind the glitzy promotional statements and find out the facts behind each company. Go to `www.tophosts.com` and click the link to their current Top 25 Web hosts. You might want to also check out `www.webhostdir.com/webhostawards`. They check out Web hosting companies monthly. Take a look at who's listed and then go to check out the host's own Web site.

Table 8-2 provides a comparison of some host service costs. In the rest of this section, I fill you in on the details about the four Web hosting companies listed in Table 8-2: ReadyHosting.com, Interland, Microsoft Small Business Center, and Yahoo! Web Hosting. Make sure you check out their Web sites, however, to get the most current information.

Table 8-2	Comparing Entry-Level Hosting Costs			
Feature	*Ready Hosting.com*	*Interland*	*Microsoft*	*Yahoo! Web Hosting*
Monthly plan cost	$8.25	$9.95	$29.95	$11.95
Yearly discount rate	$99	$107.40	$274	N/A
Disk Space storage	500MB	200MB	200MB	50MB
Data transfer/month	Unlimited	5GB	10GB	20GB
24/7 Toll-free tech support	No	Yes	Yes	Yes
E-mail aliases	Unlimited	50	30	10
FrontPage Capability	Yes	Yes	Yes	No

Keep in mind that 200MB disk storage space can host as many as 6000 HTML pages.

ReadyHosting.com

Here's a little guy who's worked hard: ReadyHosting.com (see Figure 8-2) has been hosting Web space since June 2000 and is a C-net Certified Award Winner. More than 150 new sites sign up with the service each day. Sites are hosted on servers running state-of-the-art software, and each site comes with a Cart32 e-commerce Shopping Cart. (Cart32 integrates directly into Microsoft FrontPage, holds inventory, validates credit cards, and more.) For details, check out

`www.readyhosting.com`

Figure 8-2:
The Ready
Hosting.com
home page.

Interland.com

Interland is a big company with big sophisticated equipment, and it hosts a bunch of the big guys on their own private servers. They've been in the hosting business since 1995 and host sites for more than 4 million small and medium-sized businesses.

For little guys, Interland (see Figure 8-3) offers *shared hosting,* and that's probably what you'll be using for quite a while. With shared hosting, your site resides with others on a single server, sharing all resources.

If your Internet sales gross more than a hundred thousand a year, you might have to look into *dedicated hosting,* in which your site is on a server of its own and is managed by the technical experts at your hosting company.

One of the best features of the company is its 24/7 toll-free technical support: Its online support gives intensive advice on how to solve problems on your own. Check out this site at the following address:

```
www.interland.com
```

Figure 8-3:
The
Interland.
com home
page.

Microsoft Small Business Center

If Interland is big, Microsoft is gargantuan; it's the leader in everything related to personal computing (as if you didn't know that). To grab a piece of the e-commerce market, Microsoft is making a strong push with its improved Small Business Center site (see Figure 8-4), which has always been a home for business Internet utilities and has now come full circle to hosting Web sites and promoting e-commerce.

Availing yourself of their Web hosting is an easy procedure. You can find out the details of their current offerings at

```
http://www.microsoft.com/smallbusiness/default.mspx
```

Microsoft Small Business Center FTPs your pages through the use of Microsoft FrontPage (must be purchased separately). Design your own pages in FrontPage and take advantage of the many promotional and commerce-enabled options offered on the site.

Figure 8-4:
The
Microsoft
Small
Business
Center
home page.

Microsoft Small Business Center also has a Traffic Builder program for banner advertising on the LinkExchange network. Banner ad campaign prices range from $50–$500. Rates rise as you target your advertising and specify where you want the ad to appear. See the section "Marketing Your Web Site (More Visitors = More Business)," later in this chapter, for more about getting the word out about your Web site.

Yahoo! Web site services

Yahoo! is trying to do a little bit of everything these days. I'm never sure which direction it's going. Yahoo! took over GeoCities (one of the original free Web site hosts) a few years back, so my family Web site became a free Yahoo! site. Considering that I have a free site, I must admit that the services that Yahoo! offers have been top-drawer, disproving the notion that you get what you pay for. But then again, I'm not running a business from the site; it's just a bunch of family pictures.

When you subscribe to one of Yahoo!'s Web hosting plans, you can download their free SiteBuilder software, which allows you to be up and running with the basic site quickly. Thank goodness, you don't have to know any HTML to use it. The download includes access to more than 300 stock templates that you can customize any way you want. If you don't want to use SiteBuilder, you can use good old Microsoft FrontPage to design your site.

Design help *and* hosting

Interland offers many levels of entry. There's the basic do-it-yourself package listed in Table 8-2, but they also offer the services of their crack team of professional Web designers to help you get up and running. It always helps to have the assistance of a professional when you're just starting out.

They give you the use of their own FTP service and an online easy-to-use WYSIWYG Website Content Manager (so you don't have to invest in extra software). You can add all the pages you want to your professionally formatted site.

Check out the more than 300 Web sites they've designed at www.youreallycan.com

You'll get a clear idea of the type of custom designs they've produced for small businesses.

Their beginning Website Express package includes online training with one of their experts and a three-page custom-designed starter site. (You can build an unlimited number of your own pages from there.) The package costs only $19.95 a month with a $299.99 one-time setup fee. This is an economical and professional way to get your online empire started.

If you're looking for a store solution, you can subscribe to a do-it-yourself, e-commerce, full-featured site for $39.95 a month. This site includes product merchandising templates, order management systems, and more. Check out their award-winning offerings at

smallbusiness.yahoo.com

What's in a Web Site Name: Naming Your Baby

What to name the baby, er, Web site? It's almost as much of a dilemma as deciding on your eBay user ID or eBay store name. If you don't have an existing company name that you want to use, why not use the same name as your eBay store? (Check out Chapter 5 for details about eBay stores.) Lock it up now so that you can keep your brand forever.

Name your site with a name that identifies what you do, what you sell, or who you are. And be sure you like it, because once its yours and you begin operating under it and establishing a reputation, it'll be with you 20 years from now when you're still selling online! (I know, it should only happen!)

A few Web sites offer wizards to help you decide your domain name. A particularly intuitive one can be found at the following:

```
www.namesarecheap.com/wizard.shtml
```

In a small, Web-based form, you input your primary business type and keywords that describe your business. The wizard then displays a large number of options and also lets you know whether the options are available. Very convenient.

Before you attempt to register a name, you should check to be sure it isn't anyone else's trademark. To search an updated list of registered United States trademarks, go to the following and use the electronic trademark search system:

```
www.trademarksearchforfree.com
```

After a search, you may want to trademark your site name. NameProtect.com is an online service that can help you with that. It offers online trademark applications and also refers you to an attorney if you'd like to use one; just go to their site for further information.

Registering Your Domain Name (Before Someone Else Takes It)

Talk about your junk e-mail. I get daily e-mails advising me to Lose 40 pounds in 40 days, accept credit cards now, and of course REGISTER MY NAME NOW! The last scam seems to be geared to obtaining my e-mail address for other junk mail lists rather than trying to help me register my Web site. Choosing a select *registrar* (the company that handles the registering of your site name) is as important as choosing the right Web host. You must remember that the Internet is still a little like the wild west, and that the James gang might be waiting to relieve you of your hard-earned cash. One of the ways to protect yourself is to understand how the registry works (knowledge *is* power), so read on.

In October of 1998, U.S. government officials decided to expand the domain registration business by breaking up the Network Solutions site (previously the only place that you could register your Web site). This opened up the Web to all kinds of people selling domain names.

Before you decide on a registrar for your domain name, take a minute to see whether the registrar is accredited by ICANN (Internet Corporation for Assigned Names and Numbers — the international governing body for domain names) or is reselling for an official ICANN-accredited registrar. (You'll have to ask who they register with.) The Accredited Registrar Directory is updated constantly, so check the following for the most recent list:

```
www.internic.com/regist.html
```

For a comparison of registration fees, see Table 8-3.

Table 8-3   Comparing Yearly Domain Name Registration Fees

Registrar	Registration Fee	URL Forwarding
e-names.org	$16.99	Free
inexpensivedomains.com	$15.00	included
namesarecheap.com	$14.00	included
networksolutions.com	$34.99	$12.00

You'll usually get a substantial discount from the more expensive registrars when you register your domain name for multiple years — a good idea if you plan on staying in business. Also, if you register your name through your hosting service, you might be able to cut the prices in Table 8-3 in half! The only drawback is that your prepaid registration might go out the window if you choose to change hosting companies.

If you're registering a new domain name but already have a site set up with your ISP, you need a feature called URL, or Web address, forwarding. This feature directs any hits to your new domain name from your existing long URL address. Some registrars offer this service, but watch out for hidden surprises, such as a free offer of the service, which means they will probably smack a big fat banner at the bottom of your home page. Your registrar should also have some available tech support. Trying to troubleshoot DNS issues is a job for those who know what they're doing! Remember, sometimes you get what you pay for.

Domain parking

Suppose that you've come up with a brilliant name for your site and you get really big and famous. Then someone else uses your Web site name but registers it as a .net — while yours is a .com. To avoid this situation, when you're ready to register your site, make sure you register both domains (.com and .net) and park them with your registrar. For example, www.ebay.net and ebay.org are registered to (guess who?) ebay.com. You can check the owner of any domain name at any of the Web hosting or registrar sites.

Making your personal information private

ICANN requires every registrar to maintain a publicly accessible WHOIS database displaying all contact information for all domain names registered. Interested parties (or fraudsters) can find out the name, street address, e-mail address, and phone number of the owner of the site by running a *whois* search on the domain name. You can run a whois search by going to www.whois.net and typing in the domain name in question.

This information can be very useful to spammers who spoof your e-mail address as their return address to cloak their identity, identity thieves, stalkers, and just about anyone up to no good. To see the difference between private and public registrations, run a whois search on my Web site, www.coolebaytools.com, and www.ebay.com.

Registrars such as Network Solutions offer private registration for an additional $9 a year. Check to see whether your registrar offers this service. For updated information on private registration, visit my Web site.

Marketing Your Web Site (More Visitors = More Business)

After you set up your Web site, it's time to let the world know about it. Having spent many years in the advertising business, I can spot businesses that *want* to fail. They open their doors and expect the world to beat a path to them and make them rich. This doesn't happen — ever.

You must take an active approach to letting the world in on the goodies you have for sale. This means spending a good deal of time promoting your site by running banner ads and getting your URL into a search engine. There are no shortcuts.

About a trillion people out there want to take your money for advertising your Web site. As with all transactions regarding your Web site, knowing who you're dealing with is key. If you want to run your banner on someone else's site, don't spend money; ask to do an exchange. The more advertising that you can get for free, the better. If you decide that you want to pay for advertising, I recommend that you wait until after you've made a profit selling merchandise from your site.

A simple link to your Web site from your eBay About Me page will draw people to your site initially. You'll be pleasantly surprised.

Banner ad exchanges

The way banner ad exchange services work is simple. You design a banner ad in your graphics program to a designated size following certain standards (see the following list), and the service displays the banner on other sites. When Web surfers click your banner, they're taken to your site, where they'll see all the great stuff you have for sale. You can even target what type of sites you want your banner to appear on as well. Remember that this is an *exchange*. Someone else's banner will appear on your pages in exchange for showing yours on other sites.

Here are the standard specs for a banner ad:

   468 pixels wide by 60 pixels high

   GIF format (no JPEGs)

   Nontransparent

   File size less than 10K (10240 bytes)

   If animated, the animation stops at seven seconds and doesn't include loops

Banner design

If you think that designing an eye-catching banner ad (see the one I used for my company in Figure 8-5) is beyond your graphic talents, you'll be happy to know that many excellent graphic artists on the Internet can produce one for you. Type *banner design* into any search engine, and you'll come up with a ton of listings. To find a designer who matches your needs, look at samples (and pricing) on their Web sites.

Figure 8-5:
One of my
animated
banner ads.

On eBay, search for *web banner* or *banner design*. I found 77 listings of banner ad designers with reasonable prices; I'm sure you'll find one who meets your needs.

Microsoft Banner Advertising

Microsoft Banner Advertising is one of the largest and most effective networks on the Net. They rotate your banner throughout their 400,000 sites and give you great stats on how often your banner is viewed, your page visits, and your clickthrough ratio (the number of times people click your banner and visit your site to the number of times your banner is displayed).

Getting your URL into a search engine

For people to find your site (and what you're selling), they must be able to locate you. A popular way that people do this is by searching with a search engine. So you should submit your site to search engines. Go to the search engines that interest you and look for a link or a help area that will enable you to submit your site. Be sure to follow any specific instructions on the site; some may limit the amount of keywords and the characters allowed in your description.

To submit your URL to search engines, you need to do a little work (nothing's easy, is it?). Write down 25–50 words or phrases that describe your Web site; these are your *keywords*. Now, using as many of the words you came up with, write a description of your site. With the remaining words, create a list of keywords, separating each word or short phrase by a comma. You can use these keywords to add meta tags to the header in your HTML document for your home page. *Meta tags* are identifiers used by search engine *spiders,* robots that troll the Internet looking for new sites to classify on search engines. Meta tags are used like this:

```
<META NAME = "insert your keywords here separated by commas"
       CONTENT = "short description of your site">
```

If you have a problem coming up with keywords, check out Yahoo! GeoCities handy meta tag generator, which you can use for free:

```
http://geocities.yahoo.com/v/res/meg.html
```

Submit It!

Submit It! (see Figure 8-6), part of Microsoft's Small Business Center, handles your site submissions to hundreds of online search engines automatically, saving you the trouble of going from site to site. For $49 a year, the service will submit as many as 10 URLs as often as you'd like. They even send you a regular report letting you know of their progress. Your site will be listed also in the Microsoft Small Business Directory as part of your subscription. This is money well spent.

Figure 8-6:
Submit It!

Google

Google crawls the Internet regularly with its spider, Googlebot, looking for new sites to index on Google Search. If Googlebot has missed your site, go to the following and let Google know that you're site is ready for listing:

```
www.google.com/addurl.html
```

Google doesn't guarantee that your site will be listed, but the process takes less than a minute. What could it hurt?

Yahoo!

Yahoo! is one of the more difficult sites to list with, although you *can* get a free listing if you fill out all the forms correctly and wait six to eight weeks. Instructions for the free listing are at the following:

```
http://docs.yahoo.com/info/suggest/
```

If you pay Yahoo! Express $299, you'll be listed immediately (funny how that works). Go to the following for more details:

```
http://smallbusiness.yahoo.com/bzinfo/prod/marketserv/
        yexpress.php
```

Yahoo! guarantees that you'll be reviewed in just seven business days.

Part III
Business Is Business — No Foolin' Around!

In this part . . .

Now it's time to delve into the dollars and sense of your eBay business. In this part, I discuss automating your business by using online and offline tools, jazzing up your auctions, setting up your home photo studio, and handling shipping (the bane of most businesses). I also give you the lowdown on two other important aspects of your business: working with customers and collecting payments.

Chapter 9

Software Built for Online Auctions

● ●

In This Chapter

▶ Figuring out what tasks you can automate

▶ Finding online auction management services

▶ Exploring auction management software

● ●

*N*ow that eBay has become a world marketplace, a single-page auction or item listing is becoming an increasingly valuable piece of real estate. Millions view your sale, and the more auctions and fixed-price items that you can list, the better your chance to make a good living. Time is money: You need to post your auctions quickly and accurately.

Auction posting, record keeping, inventory cataloging, photo managing, and statistic gathering are all tasks that you can automate. The more your business grows, the more confusing things can become. Automated tools can help you keep it all straight. But remember that the more tools you use, the more expense you may be adding to your business. Always keep your bottom line in mind when evaluating whether to use fee-based software and services.

In this chapter, I discuss how to automate different tasks, software that you can use to automate, and Web sites that offer services to make your daily chores considerably more bearable. After you read this chapter, you'll be well-equipped to decide whether or not you want to automate your business.

Considering Tasks for Automation

You'll have to perform certain office tasks, no matter how few or how many auctions you're running. Depending on your personal business style, you may want to automate any or all of the following tasks. You may choose to use a single program, a manual method, or some features from one program and some from others. For those who aren't ready for the automated plunge,

I offer alternatives. Where appropriate, I insert references guiding you to where in this book or on the Web you can find more information about the automated services I discuss.

Setting up images for automatic FTP upload

You have several ways to store the display images in your auctions. If you're using an auction management service or software (such as MarketWorks.com or Auction Wizard, both of which I discuss later in this chapter), an *uploader* is usually included as a part of the software. Many online services merely fetch the photos from your hard drive without the need for additional FTP software. To accomplish this, you use a screen similar to eBay's Sell Your Item Page, shown in Figure 9-1.

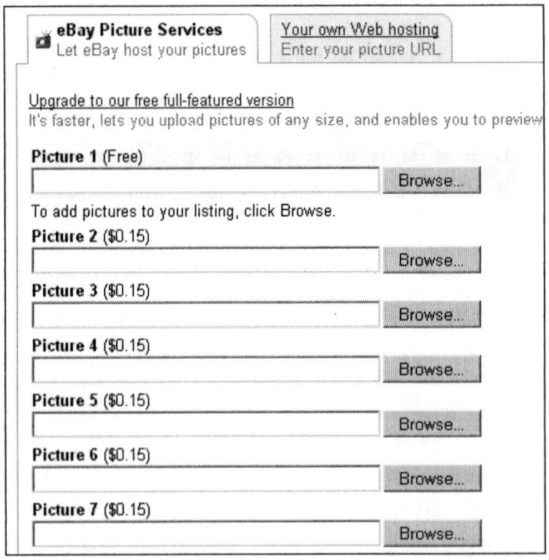

Figure 9-1:
Uploading images from your hard drive.

With this format, you merely click the Browse button to access the Open File window, and then find the location of the image on your hard drive. When you've located the images that you want to upload (one per line), click the Upload button and the images will be on their way to the service's servers.

If you choose to keep images on your own Web site (which makes the images available for your Web site, too), you'll have to use some sort of FTP software. You probably aren't using close to the total space that your hosting service allots to you for your Web site, making for plenty of room to store a separate folder of eBay images. ISPs often also give you several megabytes of storage space (see Chapter 8).

A straightforward, standalone FTP software program should be part of your auction arsenal, even if you use a service or other software. (I like to have a backup method.) My personal favorite is CuteFTP from GlobalSCAPE, shown in Figure 9-2.

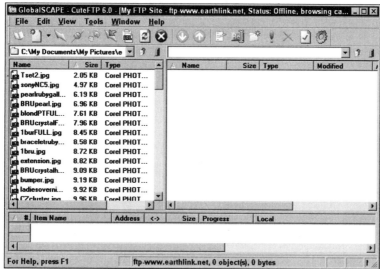

Figure 9-2:
CuteFTP
Home
Edition.

CuteFTP is so simple to use, I've never read the instructions. To send files to a site, type the location and your username and password. Click Connect, and CuteFTP automatically connects to the site. From this point, you merely drag and drop to move a file from the screen on the left (your hard drive) to the screen on the right (your Web site). A 30-day free trial is downloadable from

```
www.globalscape.com/o/912
```

You can register the program for only $39.95.

Setting up an auction photo gallery

Until you get your own eBay store, setting up a photo gallery is a great alternative. If your customers have a high-speed connection, they're able to browse your auctions through photographs. Some auction management sites host your gallery. Some charge for this service; others do not. The best part is that you can produce your own gallery without any fancy programs or auction management software at no additional cost to you.

To make your own gallery on eBay without installing fancy scripts in your listings, you need to do three things. You must include eBay gallery photos with all your listings. (You're doing that anyway, right?) Next, test the following URL in your browser, substituting your own user ID where indicated in *bold*:

```
http://search-desc.ebay.com/search/search.dll?
        MfcISAPICommand=GetResult&query=youreBayuserID&ht=
        1&srchdesc=y&SortProperty=MetaEndSort&st=1
```

Figure 9-3 shows you a sample of what you'll see.

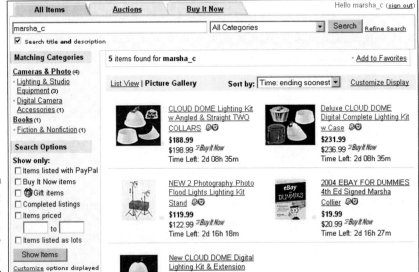

Now that you have seen a sample of your gallery, insert the following HTML into your auction to include a link to your gallery.

```
<a href="  search-desc.ebay.com/search/search.dll?
        MfcISAPICommand=GetResult&query=youreBayuserID&ht=
        1&srchdesc=y&SortProperty=MetaEndSort&st=1">
        <B>Click <I>here</I> to view yourebayuserID
        Gallery</B> <img
        src="http://pics.ebay.com/aw/pics/ebay_my_button.g
        if" alt="My Gallery on eBay"></a >
```

As you can see in Figure 9-4, this HTML sniplet also inserts the custom eBay button.

Figure 9-4:
A link
from your
auctions to
your own
gallery.

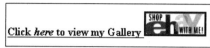

Sorting auction e-mail

A vital function of any auction software or system is the ability to customize and send e-mails to your winners. Many sellers use the default letters in these programs, which tend to be a bit — no, incredibly — impersonal and uncaring. (To see some examples of customer-friendly e-mails and tips on drafting your own, head to Chapter 12.) You must decide whether you want the program to receive e-mail as well.

Most computer-resident auction management programs have their own built-in e-mail software as part of the program. When you download your winner information from eBay, the program automatically generates invoices and congratulatory e-mails.

How to handle your auction-related e-mail is a personal choice. Although I currently use eBay's Selling Manager to send auction related e-mails, I receive auction e-mail through Outlook, using a separate folder titled Auctions that contains subfolders for eBay Buy and eBay Sell.

Automating end-of-auction e-mail

If you want to set up e-mails to be sent automatically after an auction ends, you must use a software application to do so. The software should download your final auction results, generate the e-mail, and let you preview the e-mail before sending it out. Many of the online sites that I discuss later in this chapter (see the section "Online auction management sites") send out winner confirmation e-mails automatically when an auction is over; be sure that you set your preferences to Preview the e-mail before sending if you want to use this option.

Keeping inventory

Many eBay power sellers depend on the old clipboard or notebook method — crossing off items as they sell them. If that works for you, great. Others prefer to use an Excel spreadsheet to keep track of inventory.

Most of the auction management packages that I detail later in this chapter (see the section "Auction management software") handle inventory for you. Some automatically deduct an item from inventory when you launch an auction. You have your choice of handling inventory directly on your computer or keeping your inventory online with a service that's accessible from any computer, wherever you are.

I handle my inventory on my desktop through QuickBooks. When I buy merchandise to sell and post the bill to QuickBooks, it automatically puts the merchandise into inventory. When I input my sale, it deducts the items sold from the standing inventory. I can print a status report whenever I want to see how much I have left — or have to order.

Generating HTML

Fancy auctions are nice, but fancy doesn't make the item sell any better. Competitive pricing and low shipping rates work in your favor — especially with eBay's Compare Items feature in Search. Also, a clean listing with as many photos as necessary goes a long way to sell your product. Some software and services offer a large selection of templates to gussy up your auctions. But you must think of your customers; many of them are still logging on with dial-up connections, which are notoriously slow. The use of simple HTML doesn't slow the loading of your page, but the addition of miscellaneous images (decorative backgrounds and animations) definitely makes viewing your auction a chore for those dialing up. And forget the background music — it *really* slows things down!

Don't fret; you can make do by repeatedly incorporating two or three simple HTML templates, cutting and pasting new text as necessary. Most auction management programs offer you several choices of templates. I recommend that you stick with a couple that are similar, giving a standardized look to your listings, just the way major companies give a standardized look to their advertising and identity. Your customers will get used to the look of your auctions and feel comfortable each time they open one.

I use CuteHTML to generate much of my code for auction descriptions. An important line of code that everyone seems to forget is the one that inserts a picture into your auction description. On the Sell Your Item page, click the tab to view in HTML mode, and insert the following line below where you'd like your image to appear in your description:

```
<img src="http://www.yourserver.com/imagename.jpg">
```

Be sure to substitute your own server and image name. If you want to put one picture on top of another, just type `<P>` between the lines of code — repeat the HTML line with a different image name for each image that you want to display.

If you're in a rush and need a quick and easy HTML generator, go to my Web site at `www.coolebaytools.com` and click Tools. My book, *eBay Timesaving Techniques For Dummies* has sample HTML code for auction descriptions as well as a chart of all the code you'll ever need for an eBay auction.

One-click relisting and selling similar items

Using an auction software or service speeds up the process of posting or relisting items. After you input your inventory into the software, posting or relisting your auctions is a mouse click away. All the auction management software packages that I detail later in this chapter include this feature.

If you buy your items in bulk, you might want to take advantage of eBay's free relisting tool. By clicking the <u>Sell Similar</u> link (see Figure 9-5) on any successful listing, you can automatically relist your items. Sell Similar starts the listing as new, so if it doesn't sell you can avail yourself of the Relist feature. This way, if the item sells the second time, your listing (insertion fees) for the first listing will be credited.

Although eBay says that Sell Similar is for relisting items, it works also when listing a duplicate of an item that has sold successfully. The only difference is that you aren't credited for the unsold auction listing fee.

One savvy seller I know uses the eBay Sell Similar feature to post new auctions. She merely clicks the <u>Sell Similar</u> link, and then cuts and pastes her new information into the existing HTML format. That's why her auctions all have the same feel and flavor.

Click here to relist an unsold item

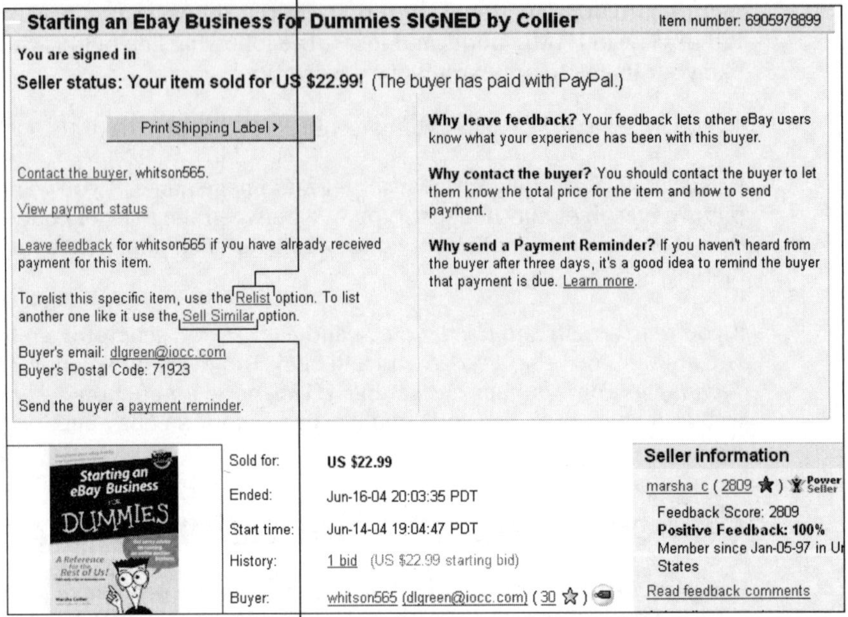

Starting an Ebay Business for Dummies SIGNED by Collier		Item number: 6905978899

You are signed in

Seller status: Your item sold for US $22.99! (The buyer has paid with PayPal.)

Print Shipping Label >

Why leave feedback? Your feedback lets other eBay users know what your experience has been with this buyer.

Contact the buyer, whitson565.

View payment status

Why contact the buyer? You should contact the buyer to let them know the total price for the item and how to send payment.

Leave feedback for whitson565 if you have already received payment for this item.

To relist this specific item, use the Relist option. To list another one like it use the Sell Similar option.

Why send a Payment Reminder? If you haven't heard from the buyer after three days, it's a good idea to remind the buyer that payment is due. Learn more.

Buyer's email: dlgreen@iocc.com
Buyer's Postal Code: 71923

Send the buyer a payment reminder.

Figure 9-5:
The Relist and Sell Similar links on a completed auction page.

			Seller information
Sold for:	US $22.99		marsha_c (2809 ⭐) 👑 Power Seller
Ended:	Jun-16-04 20:03:35 PDT		Feedback Score: 2809
Start time:	Jun-14-04 19:04:47 PDT		**Positive Feedback: 100%**
History:	1 bid (US $22.99 starting bid)		Member since Jan-05-97 in Ur States
Buyer:	whitson565 (dlgreen@iocc.com) (30 ☆) ✉		Read feedback comments

Click here to use the Sell Similar option

Scheduling your listings for bulk upload

If you want to schedule the unattended launch of your auctions without incurring eBay's 10-cent fee, you must use an online management service (check out the "Online auction management site" section, later in this chapter). If you can be at your computer to send your auctions to eBay singly or in bulk, you can use the Turbo Lister application, which eBay offers at no charge. (For details, see the "Turbo Lister" section, later in the chapter.)

Researching your statistics

There are so many questions when you're selling on eBay. What is the best time to end my auction? What day should I start my listing? Is it better to run a 5-day or a 7-day auction? Now an online service can help you separate the rumors from the facts.

Lots of eBay *experts* out there will give you hard-and-fast rules to guarantee success with your listings. It's a lot of bunk. Every category and every type of item may draw shoppers at different times of the day and different days of the week.

The best experts are those who are selling every day on eBay, day in and day out. They are usually PowerSellers and do their own research for their list-ings. They don't have the time to spout off and give you secrets. I'm a regular seller on eBay (a PowerSeller too), and I've noticed distinct variations in my sales through a fantastic online service called ViewTracker from Sellathon. It's really one-of-a-kind.

Sellathon tracks your listings using a small piece of code that you insert in your auctions. The site gives you loads of information about your visitors, without violating anyone's privacy. Here are some of the things you can find out:

- ✔ How many times someone has visited your auction
- ✔ The date and time the visitor arrived at your auction and what city, state, and country your visitor is from
- ✔ Whether the reserve price was met when the visitor arrived
- ✔ When the item receives a bid (and how many bids have been placed up to that moment)
- ✔ Whether the visitor has chosen to watch this listing in his or her My eBay page
- ✔ Whether the visitor browsed a category, searched a category, searched all of eBay, used eBay's Product Finder utility, and came from "See Seller's Other Items" or some other page and what category they were browsing
- ✔ If they were searching, what search terms they used to find your item and did they search Titles Only or Titles and Descriptions
- ✔ Whether the user elected to view Auctions Only, Buy it Now, or both

You get all this information and more. Sellathon offers a 30-day free trial at www.sellathon.com. After that, the service is $4.95 a month or $49.00 a year.

To end an old wives tale about what days your auctions get the highest hits, Figure 9-6 shows you a chart from my Sellathon account, showing how many visits 26 listings got each day. Verrry interesting.

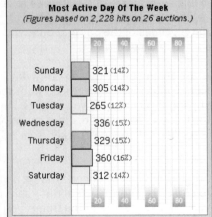

Figure 9-6:
That's 2,228
hits on
26 auctions
in 7 days!

Photo hosting

If all you need is photo hosting, and you've checked out your ISP and they don't give you any free Web space to use (please check Chapter 8 for a list of ISPs and the amount of Web storage space they give to their customers), you can always use eBay's picture services to host an additional picture in each auction at $.15 an image.

However, if you run more than 40 auctions a month, here's a better alternative. Pair Networks offers a reasonably priced package, the FTP Account, which seems to be tailored for eBay sellers. For $5.95 a month you get 100MB of storage space to hold your eBay images, an e-mail address, and e-mail forwarding (which forwards any mail coming to this address to your private address). For more information, visit

```
www.pair.com/services/web_hosting/ftp.html
```

Automating other tasks

That's not all! You can automate a few more tasks. Having so many options is like being in a candy store: You may want it all, but that might not be good for you. For example, if you use online postage, you may not want to print your labels because that would be doubling your work. Take a serious look at the options you're offered and see whether they fit into your particular work style.

Checking out

When someone wins or buys an item, eBay's checkout integrates directly with PayPal and will also indicate your other preferred forms of payment. If you're closing less than a hundred auctions a day, that's all you need. eBay and PayPal will also send an e-mail to you and the buyer so that you can arrange for payment.

Some online auction management services offer your own private checkout area, which will cost you a percentage of your sale, so you must decide whether your business warrants this option. A personalized winner's notification e-mail can easily contain a link to your PayPal payment area, making a checkout service unnecessary.

Printing shipping labels

Printing shipping labels without printing postage can be the beginning of a laborious two-step process. Two companies, endicia.com and.stamps.com, print your labels and postage all in one step. Check out Chapter 17 for information on how this works.

Some sites print your winner's address labels without postage, as does eBay's Selling Manager. That works well if you don't mind carrying your packages to the post office for postage. (Why would you do that? A burning need to stand in line, I guess!)

Tracking buyer information

Keeping track of your winners isn't rocket science. You can do it in an Excel spreadsheet or a Word document, both of which are exportable to almost any program for follow-up mailings promoting future sales. If you choose to have an online management service do this for you, be sure that you can download the information to your computer (in case you and the online service part ways someday).

Generating customized reports

Sales reports, ledgers, and tax information are all important reports that you should have in your business. Online services and software supply different flavors of these reports.

PayPal allows you to download your sales data into a format compatible with QuickBooks, a highly respected and popular bookkeeping program. You can also choose to download your data in Excel spreadsheet format (the downloads work also in Microsoft Works). PayPal reports are chock full of intensely detailed information about your sales and deposits. Putting this information in a standard accounting software program on a regular basis makes your year-end calculations easier to bear. (In Chapter 16, I detail what else you might need for this task.)

Submitting feedback

If you're running a lot of auctions, leaving feedback can be a chore. One solution is to automate the submission of feedback through an online service or software. But timing the automation of this task can be tricky.

Don't leave feedback for an eBay transaction until after you've heard from the buyer that the purchase is satisfactory. Leaving positive feedback immediately after you've received payment from the buyer is too soon. After you receive an e-mail assuring you that the customer is satisfied, manually leaving feedback by going to the feedback forum (or the item page) can be just as easy — if not easier — as bulk-loading feedback.

Managing Your Business with Online Resources and Software

If you searched the Internet for auction management services and software, you'd come up with a bunch. For simplicity's sake, I've chosen to examine just a few of these services in this chapter. After speaking to many sellers, I've found online services that offer uptime reliability (uptime is key here; you don't want the server that holds your photos going down or mislaunching your auctions) and software that's continually updated to match eBay changes.

Using a site or software to run your auctions takes practice, so I suggest that you try any that appeal to you and offer free preview trials. As I describe these different applications, I include a link so that you can check them out further. Table 9-1 compares the costs of many auction management and online services.

Some software and services work on a monthly fee, whereas others work on a one-time purchase fee. For a one-time-purchase software application to truly benefit you, it *must* have the reputation for updating its software each time eBay makes a change in its system. The programs that I discuss in this chapter have been upgraded continually to date.

Most services have a free trial period. Be sure that you don't spend a bunch of your precious time inputting your entire inventory, only to discover you don't like the way the service works. Instead, input a few items to give the service a whirl.

Table 9-1	Cost Comparisons for Auction Management Services and Software
Site Services or Software	*Cost*
AAASeller.com	$9.95/month
AuctionHelper.com	1.5% of sales ($.15–$.70); $10.00/month (minimum)
Auction Wizard 2000 (`auction wizard2000.com`)	$75.00 (first year) $50.00 renewal
ChannelAdvisor.com	$29.95/month ($299.00/year)
eBay Seller's Assistant	$9.99/month
eBay Seller's Assistant Pro	$24.99/month
eBay's Selling Manager	$4.99/month
eBay's Selling Manager Pro	$15.99/month
InkFrog.com	$12.95/month
MarketWorks.com	2% of sales ($.10–$3.00); $14.95/month (minimum)
Meridian (`www.noblespirit.com`)	$9.95 /month
Shooting Star (`www.foodogsoftware.com`)	$49.95 flat fee
SpareDollar.com	$4.95 /month
Spoonfeeder.com	$49.95 + $4.99/month
Vendio (`www.vendio.com`)	$.10 per listing
Zoovy.com	$49.95 ($399.95 setup fee)

Online auction management sites

Auction management Web sites handle almost everything, from inventory management to label printing. Some sellers prefer online (or hosted) management sites because you can access your information from any computer. You might use every feature a site offers, or you might choose a bit from column A and a bit from column B and perform the more personalized tasks manually. Read on to determine what service might best suit your needs.

Although quite a few excellent online services for automating sales are available, I have room here to show you only a few. Remember that by using an online service, your information resides on a server out there in cyberspace; if you're a control freak, it may be a bit much to bear. Many services are similar in format, so in the following sections I point out some of the highlights of a few representative systems.

When selecting a service, look for a logo or text indicating that the service is an eBay Certified Developer, Preferred Solution Provider, or API licensee. These people have first access to eBay's system changes and can implement them immediately. Others may have a day or so lag time to update their software.

Following are some of the popular ones in the online auction management arena:

AAASeller (www.aaaseller.com)

ándale (andale.com)

AuctionHawk (www.auctionhawk.com)

AuctionHelper (www.auctionhelper.com)

Auctiva (www.auctiva.com)

Inkfrog (www.inkfrog.com)

Zoovy.com (www.zoovy.com)

ChannelAdvisor

ChannelAdvisor's founder Scot Wingo got into the auction business around the turn of the century. His first foray into the eBay world was AuctionRover, a site that had tools to perform an extensive eBay search, list auctions, and check pricing trends. The company's cute Rover logo was fashioned after Wingo's Border Collie, Mack.

Fast forward to today. ChannelAdvisor is a highly popular management service for all levels of eBay sellers. They supply listing and management services to everyone from Fortune 1000 companies to the little old lady next door.

How? They offer three levels of software: Enterprise for large businesses who want to outsource their online business, Merchant for midsized businesses and higher-level PowerSellers, and Pro for small businesses and individuals. The powerful software suites help eBay sellers successfully manage and automate the sale of their merchandise.

Starting at the entry level, you can get the Pro version of ChannelAdvisor for $29.95 a month. Here's what they offer the beginning level seller:

- ✔ **Listing design and launching:** Create your listings with their standard templates or use your own HTML to design auction descriptions. List your items immediately or schedule a listing. ChannelAdvisor will launch the auction when you tell them to.

- ✔ **Item and inventory management:** If you want to keep your inventory online, you can create it on their system. If you want to input your inventory offline, you can import it from their Excel template. You can also import open auctions or store listings to your ChannelAdvisor account for relisting or servicing.

- ✔ **Image hosting:** You get 250MB of space to host your images. You can upload them to the site four at a time, or use FTP to upload a large quantity.

- ✔ **Post-auction management:** This function merges your winning auction information and generates customized e-mail and invoices to your buyers. You can print mailing labels too.

To tour the various offerings of ChannelAdvisor and find out about their free trial period, visit

```
www.channeladvisor.com
```

MarketWorks (previously AuctionWorks)

A group of collectors who saw the need for power tools for power sellers developed this highly graphical site (www.MarketWorks.com). I think they've succeeded. (They were known in the eBay community as AuctionWorks but changed their name in June 2004.) A high percentage of eBay power sellers use the site. They launch approximately two million listings on eBay every month. MarketWorks offers help links at every turn, a first-rate online tutorial, free toll-free support (that's a free phone call and free support), and free interactive training classes for registered users. The site integration is broad, here are just a few of their features:

- ✔ **Item and inventory management:** Features the ClickLaunch Single Step Launcher, which launches individual items to auction while adding them to inventory. (The site also has a bulk item launching capability.) LaunchBots provides automated launching of your listings. You can import existing auctions from eBay and import with their Bulk Inventory Upload form in Excel and MS Access.

- ✔ **Image hosting:** Enables you to bulk upload 15 images at a time to their servers. The basic account allows 100MB of storage. If your images average 30K each, you should be able to upload almost 3500 images into the 100MB image hosting space.

✔ **Auction reporting:** Generates accounts receivable, item history, and post-sales reports from the Reports area. MarketWorks has its own Traction System for sales and item tracking. The reporting feature offers customizable views of your sales data, item and auction data, accounts receivable, and sales tax by state!

✔ **Templates and listing:** MarketWorks uses their own trademarked Ballista template listing system. You can use their predefined color templates or use their macros with your own predefined HTML template, substituting the macros for stock areas in your template. By using their custom ad template option and well-thought-out macros, you can take your own HTML and make a MarketWorks template.

✔ **Post-auction management:** Sends out automated e-mail to your winners, linking them back to your own branded checkout page. If customers want to pay with PayPal or your own Merchant Account, they have to link from there. MarketWorks combines multiple wins for shipping and invoicing. You have the option to set six different feedback comments, which you choose at the time of posting.

MarketWorks offers all their users a StoreFront with its own URL at no additional charge. If an item sells from your StoreFront, you pay the usual 2% commission. When you load items into inventory, you have the choice of immediately listing them in your StoreFront. All your items are seamlessly integrated. To get current information and sign up for a free trial, go to

```
www.MarketWorks.com
```

Meridian

Meridian Software was developed by eBay Shooting Star PowerSeller Joe Cortese. Through his own experience on eBay, he developed this service to fulfill all the needs of an eBay seller, at a very reasonable price of $9.95 a month.

As a high-volume eBay seller, he was looking for an easier way to handle his 3000 unique auctions a month. You can apply the same technology to yours. Meridian features hands-free, enterprise-level listing and more:

✔ **Item and inventory management:** Includes calendar- and time-based (dates and times for launching) auction scheduling, automated auction launching and relisting, the ability to import past or current auctions, and the ability to import auction data from a spreadsheet or database.

✔ **Image hosting:** Offers space for storing pictures. You can upload bulk images to its Web site or FTP your images directly.

✔ **Auction reporting:** Generates current running auction statistics — the total number and dollars of current and past auctions — and an itemized report of each auction.

✔ **Post-auction management:** Allows you to send (manually or automatically) a variety of customized e-mails to winners and non-paying bidders. Your invoices can link directly to PayPal.

✔ **Consignment tools:** For sellers who sell for others (see information on eBay's Trading Assistants program in Chapter 6), Meridian offers complete tracking and inventory by consignor married to their auction management system.

The post-auction management features also include the ability to send automatic feedback and to create mailing labels for each sale. So that feedback isn't posted until you're sure the transaction is successfully completed, you have the option of disabling the automatic feedback feature.

Auction management software

Many sellers prefer to run their auction businesses from their own computers. I happen to like the option of being able to reference my old auctions on my backups. Luckily, some valuable auction software programs are available to perform all the same tasks you get from the online services.

To those who would rather have the software at home, there are some solid choices other than the ones I examine in the next section. You might also want to visit these other sites for their quality auction management software:

Auction Tamer (auctiontamer.com)

DEK Auction Manager (dekauctionmanager.com)

Shooting Star (foodogsoftware.com)

SpoonFeeder (www.spoonfeeder.com)

You can accomplish almost all the same tasks on your own computer as you can with online services — except online auction checkout. You can always use eBay's checkout as your final stop or include a link in your end-of-auction e-mails. And if you want, you can set up a checkout page on your own Web site that gathers your auction information.

eBay's Selling Manager

eBay recently replaced the All Selling tab of your My eBay page with Selling Manager, which displays a summary of your current transactions (see the figure). Many sellers (even some Power Sellers) rely on Selling Manager to handle their eBay management chores.

From Selling Manager, you can:

✔ **View listing status:** You can see which sales activities you've completed and what you still have to do.

✔ **Send custom e-mail and post feedback:** Customize your e-mail templates and set up stored feedback comments to help you run through the post-sales process quickly.

✔ **Relist in bulk:** Relist multiple sold and unsold listings at once.

✔ **Maintain sales records:** See individual sales records for every transaction, including a history of the transaction status.

✔ **Print invoices and shipping labels:** Print labels and invoices directly from sales records.

✔ **Download sales history:** Export your sales records to keep files on your computer.

✔ **Keep track of NPB and FVF:** File non-paying bidder alerts and final value fee requests.

The fee to use Selling Manager is $4.99 a month. They also offer a Pro version that incorporates inventory management and more for $15.99 a month.

Summary

Last updated on Jun-21-04 01:16:12 PDT

Quick Stats	GMS	# of listings
Scheduled Listings		**0**
Starting within the next hour		0
Starting today		0
Active Listings	$11.75	**30**
Closing within the next hour		0
Closing today		1
Sold Listings	$2,001.03	**27**
Awaiting Payment		1
Awaiting Payment, eligible for Non-Paying Buyer Alert		0
Paid and ready to ship		2
Paid and waiting for feedback		16
Paid and shipped		24
Unpaid and eligible for Final Value Fee credit		0

* Updates every 10 mins.

Most of the software packages will perform the following operations:

✔ Maintain inventory

✔ Prepare and list auctions

✔ Manage e-mail

✔ Automate feedback

✔ Provide HTML templates

✔ Track income and expenses

Auction Wizard 2000

Way back in 1999, Standing Wave Software developed a product that would handle large inventories and meet the needs of the growing eBay population. Enter Auction Wizard. In 2000, the company introduced a more robust version, Auction Wizard 2000, to meet the challenges presented by changes on eBay.

This software is a tour de force of auction management whose pieces are integrated into one program. Aside from the processes just described, you can also

✔ Handle consignment sales. Keep track of consignment sales by consignees, including all fees.

✔ Edit your images before uploading. The software allows you to import your images, and crop, rotate, or resize images for your auctions.

✔ Upload your pictures with built-in FTP software while you're working on your auctions, eliminating the need for another piece of auction business software.

The program interface is straightforward. I always plunge into new programs without reading the instructions, and I was able to use the program right off the bat. I'm still not a whiz at it, but that's probably because Auction Wizard 2000 has so many features that I haven't had the time to study them all.

To begin using the software, simply download your current eBay auctions directly into the program. When your auctions close, send customized e-mails (the program fills in the auction information) and manage all your end-of-auction business. Some sellers launch their auctions by using TurboLister (see the "Turbo Lister" section at the end of this chapter), and then retrieve them and handle the end-of-auction management with Auction Wizard 2000. For a 60-day free trial, go to their site at

```
www.auctionwizard2000.com
```

Seller's Assistant Basic and Pro

Of the two versions of Seller's Assistant, Basic and Pro, the professional version is what you're going to need for your eBay business. Because the software is owned by eBay, it's the first to have updates for eBay's latest changes.

The setup, as with other management programs, takes a while. With this program, you have the option of using eBay Picture Services for your photos if your Web site goes down for any reason.

eBay's Seller's Assistant Basic is a solid listing program, offering a variety of templates. Seller's Assistant automatically inputs your standard shipping information and auction messages into your auctions so you don't have to retype them every time. You can customize your e-mail correspondence, and Seller's Assistant will generate the appropriate e-mail messages after retrieving your completed auction information from the site. The program is available as a monthly subscription fee charged to your regular eBay bill.

The Pro version (which supports multiple user IDs) takes things up a notch, handling your auction listings as well as automating bulk listing and end-of-auction business. The Pro version will

- ✔ Spell check your auction listings
- ✔ Schedule your auction launches for a later posting (see the following tip)
- ✔ Keep track of your inventory
- ✔ Launch items directly from stock at hand
- ✔ Automating bulk-feedback posting
- ✔ Print shipping labels
- ✔ Create sales reports and lots more

SAPro's Template studio can be a bit of a challenge until you're used to it. Seller's Assistant Pro comes with a gaggle (yes, a gaggle) of various themes. The good thing about the themes is that you can put your picture anywhere you want in the description. The bad part is that you have no control of the spacing of the lines of text. Luckily, you can edit the themes to customize a look for your auctions.

One of the finer points of the Pro edition is that you can schedule your auction listings for a particular time and space out your auctions (within a group of items to be listed) by a set number of minutes. This is valuable because so many bidders bid during the last few minutes of the auction, when the highest bidding takes place.

To check out the latest changes and upgrades, and to compare the two program versions, visit

```
pages.ebay.com/sellers_assistant/compare.html
```

Turbo Lister

I like Turbo Lister because it's simple and easy to use. It has a built-in WYSI-WYG (what you see is what you get) HTML editor and makes preparing my listings offline easy. When I'm ready, I just click a button and they're all listed at once. You can also stagger listings and schedule them for a later date for a fee.

Using Turbo Lister is as simple and straightforward as posting a listing using the Sell Your Item page on the eBay site. One of its benefits is that it allows you to prepare auctions while offline and group them for launching all at once to eBay. Using the program is a two-step process. First, you download the application from eBay at

```
pages.ebay.com/turbo_lister/download.html
```

Next, install Turbo Lister on your computer, you can list auctions on the easy-to-use form (see Figure 9-7) and send them all to eBay in a group. You can also keep the listings in the program for relisting in the future. What could be simpler?

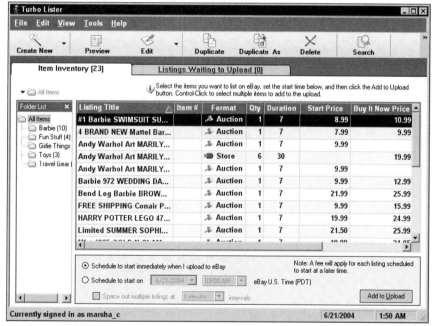

Figure 9-7:
The Turbo Lister program, ready to go on your home computer.

Chapter 10

Dollars and Sense: Budgeting and Marketing Your Auctions

....

In This Chapter

▶ Marketing your listings by choosing the right category
▶ Using promotional options to your advantage
▶ Paying eBay: The lowdown on basic fees

....

*Y*our entire online business is just that: a business. In every business, decisions are made regarding how much money is spent for each division of the company. Because you're the head of your company, you must make these decisions. Even if you're running auctions on a part-time basis, you still have to consider budget concerns. The one area in which you don't have to set aside money is shipping and fulfillment; in the eBay model, the buyer pays your shipping and handling costs. (See Chapter 14 for more on shipping.)

When you list an item for sale on eBay, you must consider what the item will sell for, in what category to list it, and whether to add any eBay listing options. Establish a minimum percentage that you assign as your profit so that you can determine how much to spend on your advertising budget. If your item has a considerable amount of competition in its category, you may want to add some of the options eBay offers to make folks notice it and want to buy it. The cost of these options (or advertising) needs to fit into your established advertising budget for the particular item.

In this chapter, I give you a preview of the various options eBay offers its users, highlighting the cost of these options along the way. I also detail the basic eBay fees. When you've finished reading this chapter, you should be well on your way to establishing a working budget and have a handle on marketing your items.

Listing Your Items

With tens of thousands of categories, finding the right place for your item can be daunting. (For more on eBay categories, see Chapter 2.) You need to apply some marketing techniques when deciding where to place your auctions. You should also be thinking about your budget; you can list an item in two separate categories, but you have to pay double for that. Does your budget allow for it?

To find where other sellers have listed items that are similar to yours, perform a completed item search for your item in the More Search Options page. In the Search box, type your item keywords, click the option to search Completed Listings Only, and indicate that you want your results sorted by highest prices first. Figure 10-1 illustrates the results of this kind of search.

Figure 10-1:
Results of
the category
item search,
showing the
categories
in which the
item is listed
(on the left).

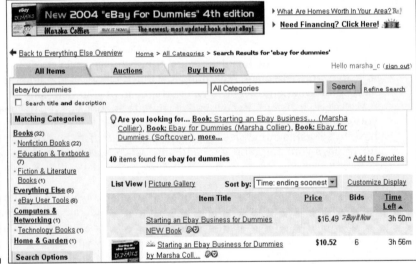

After you have your results, click the completed listings with the highest priced bids. At the top of the auction page, you'll see the listed category. You may find that your item is listed successfully in more than one category.

Check the active listings; are lots of people selling your item? If you see that you're one of forty or fifty selling the item, you need to get creative as to where to list your item. Evaluate the item and its potential buyers. In what categories would someone shopping for your item search?

Suppose you've found two perfect categories in which to list your item. eBay allows you to list an item in two categories (see Figure 10-2), but does that mean it's the best marketing decision for your auction? That depends. When you list an item in two categories, you must pay two listing fees. Depending on the time, the season, the availability of your item, and how much you paid for it, you may or may not have the money to budget for listing an item twice. In addition, many eBay buyers are quite savvy in using the search engine. If they search for your item using the search engine rather than by browsing the categories, listing the item in two categories might be a needless expense.

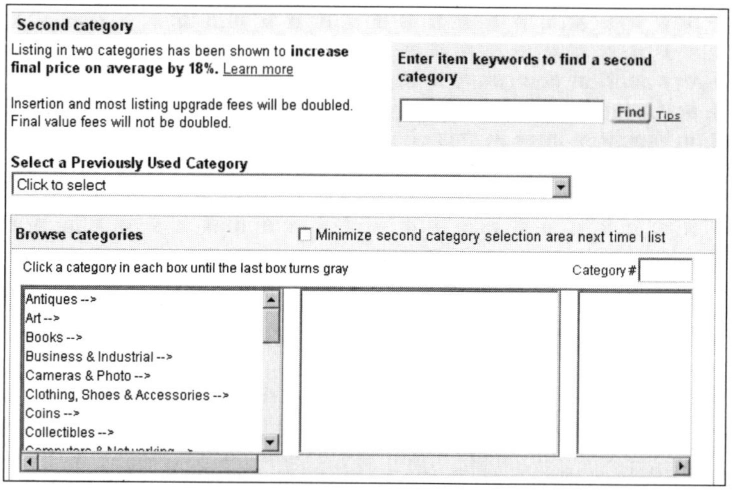

Second category

Listing in two categories has been shown to **increase final price on average by 18%.** Learn more

Insertion and most listing upgrade fees will be doubled. Final value fees will not be doubled.

Enter item keywords to find a second category

[ ] Find Tips

Select a Previously Used Category

Click to select ▼

Browse categories — [ ] Minimize second category selection area next time I list

Click a category in each box until the last box turns gray   Category # [ ]

Antiques -->
Art -->
Books -->
Business & Industrial -->
Cameras & Photo -->
Clothing, Shoes & Accessories -->
Coins -->
Collectibles -->
Computers & Networking

Figure 10-2: List your item in two categories in the Sell your item form.

You can change your category mid-auction, starting it in one category and ending it in another. And at the end of an auction in which your item doesn't sell, you can use the relisting feature to run the auction again in another category.

eBay's Optional Listing Features

When you come to the point in listing your item that brings you to eBay's optional listing features, you see the headline, "Get more bids with these optional features! Make your item stand out from the crowd!" Sounds pretty good, doesn't it? But getting carried away by these options is easy and can lead to spending all your expected profits before you earn them.

In the eBay University Advanced Selling class, instructors quote auction success rates for the features, but in the real life of your business, success varies from auction to auction and category to category. If you take the boldface option and then your auction appears in a category full of boldface auction titles, the bold just doesn't have the punch you paid for. Your auction would stand out more without the bold option. It's the same with highlighting. Certain categories are loaded with sellers that go overboard in the use of this feature — all the auction titles appear in a big lavender blur.

You must weigh the pros and cons in terms of how these options affect your eBay business. Will spending a little extra money enhance your item enough to justify the cost? Will you be able to make the money back in auction profits? You must have a good understanding of what the options are and when and how you can use them to their fullest advantage.

In every auction you run, you have to pay an insertion fee for listing your auction and a final value fee. (I discuss these two fees in the "eBay's Cut of the Action" section, later in this chapter.) If you accept credit card payments, you must also pay a fee to the payment service. Estimate your expenses from these basics before you consider spending money for advertising. (See Chapter 9 for fee calculator software that can help you make up your auction budgets.)

Home-page featured auctions

A user who goes to www.eBay.com first arrives at the eBay home page. A Featured Items area appears in the middle of the home page; below this area are links to six home-page featured auctions. When you click the <u>all featured items</u> link (see Figure 10-3), the home-page featured items page appears (see Figure 10-4). Most of these items are fixed-price listings that feature hundreds of items at a time. Many also feature items that list for more than $1000.

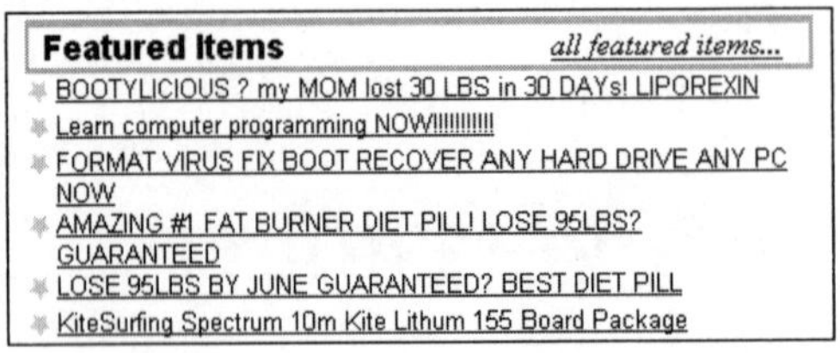

Figure 10-3:
The <u>all featured items</u> link on the eBay home page.

Featured Items	*all featured items...*
✴ BOOTYLICIOUS ? my MOM lost 30 LBS in 30 DAYs! LIPOREXIN	
✴ Learn computer programming NOW!!!!!!!!!!	
✴ FORMAT VIRUS FIX BOOT RECOVER ANY HARD DRIVE ANY PC NOW	
✴ AMAZING #1 FAT BURNER DIET PILL! LOSE 95LBS? GUARANTEED	
✴ LOSE 95LBS BY JUNE GUARANTEED? BEST DIET PILL	
✴ KiteSurfing Spectrum 10m Kite Lithum 155 Board Package	

The home-page featured auction option will set you back $39.95 for a single item. If you have two or hundreds of widgets to sell, it'll cost $79.95. For big-ticket items, you've found the perfect location to draw an audience that may easily earn back your $39.95. People who are new to eBay come in through the front page; this is prime real estate. The six auctions featured on the home page rotate randomly throughout the day. There's no guarantee that your item will be featured as one of the six home page links — but it will appear in the home page Featured category linked from the home page.

Another benefit of this option is that if someone searches your keywords or browses through your category, auctions featured on the front page appear at the top of the page (along with Featured Plus auctions, which I describe next). But you must keep in mind how much you're paying for this option. Unless your auction will bring you more than a few hundred dollars, this feature probably isn't worth the additional cost.

Featured Plus

Featured Plus is an option I've used with much success. When you choose the Featured Plus option, your auction is listed at the top of the page when a shopper searches for keywords or browses category listings. Although your auction doesn't appear on the eBay home page (see the preceding section), it will appear at the top of your selected *category* home page (see Figure 10-5).

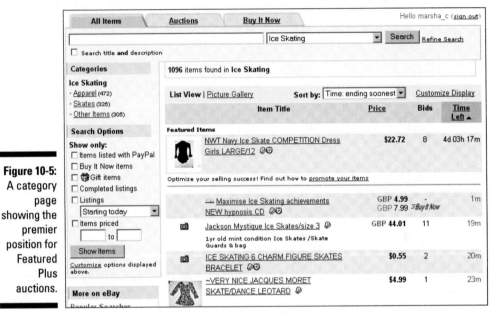

Figure 10-5:
A category page showing the premier position for Featured Plus auctions.

You get extra exposure for just $19.95, but you must still consider your auction budget. How much do you expect your item to sell for? Will the $19.95 expense benefit your auction enough to justify the expenditure? Be sure that your item will bring you more than a few hundred dollars before choosing this option.

Subtitle

You may use 55 characters for you item's title. Title search is the de facto search on eBay. From the statistics I've seen of my own auctions, 90% of searches were made for title only, versus title and description. But how can you make your item stand out when it shows up with hundreds of other items that look the same? Use the subtitle option!

When your item has something special about it or could use some extra description, the subtitle option allows you more space to give vital information to the browsing shopper. Take a look at the examples in Figure 10-6.

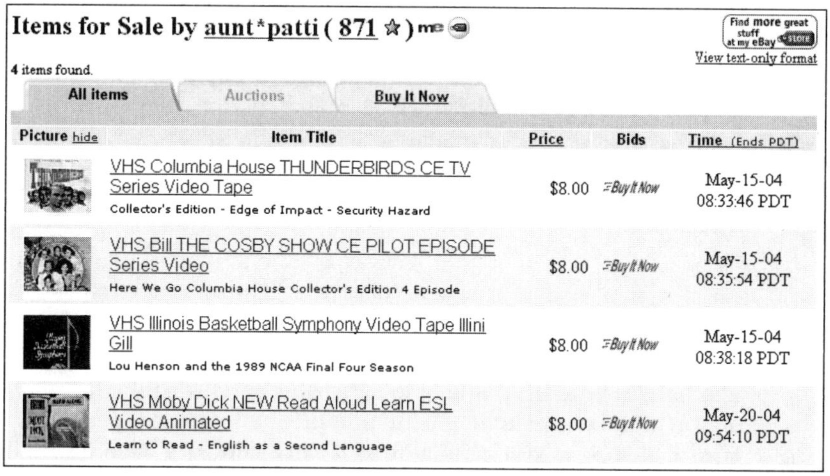

Figure 10-6:
eBay seller
aunt*patti
makes good
use of the
subtitle
option by
adding
pertinent
additional
information.

Highlight option

I was excited when eBay announced the highlight option. I'm a big fan of high-lighting books, reports, and the like. Ever since college, I can't read a book without my trusty neon-yellow highlighter. Highlighting makes anything stand out on a white page of text. This works just as well on eBay as it does on paper — except eBay uses a lavender colored highlighter — ick!

Unfortunately, as with anything in life, less is more. If you choose to list your auction in a category where all the sellers decide to use the highlight option, the only listings that will stand out will be the ones *without* highlighting.

The highlight feature will set you back just $5. Does your budget allow for that? To give your auction title a punch for a smaller amount of money, con-sider the bold option, described later in this section.

Listing Designer

eBay comes up with options to fill the needs (or wants in this case) of users. Sellers enjoy putting colorful graphics around their descriptions. It will also help you design your description, placing pictures in different places on the page. But if you have a good description (creatively done with HTML color and emphasis) plus a good picture (inserted with the HTML code I gave you), your item will draw bids just the same as if you spent $.10 extra (per listing) for the Listing Designer option.

If you want your descriptions surrounded by graphics, make sure they aren't too intensive. Otherwise, the pages will load too slowly for dial-up users. Also, you can develop your own template or buy your own from savvy eBay graphics gurus (see Chapter 9).

You can use a graphics template to "brand" your listings on eBay, giving them a uniform look. If you want to use a template, decide on one and make it your trademark.

Boldface option

The boldface option is one of my favorites and probably the most used option in the eBay stable. An auction title in boldface type stands out in a crowd, unless . . . you got it, unless it's in a category loaded with boldface auction titles. If the $1 that eBay charges for this benefit is in your auction budget, odds are it will get you a good deal more views than if you didn't use it. Boldface is an exceptional buy; I suggest going for it whenever you can.

To recap your title option costs, see the "Listing fees" section later in this chapter.

View counter

Counters have become a popular free option in the online world. Placed on your auction by an outside service at your request, the numeric view counter ticks up each time someone loads your page from eBay. This can add up to numbers that impress bidders (convincing them they're viewing a hot deal) or impress other sellers to run out and sell the identical item at eBay.

A counter is a terrific tool for marketing your auctions — sometimes. If you have an auction with no bids and a counter that reads a high number, newbie bidders may be dissuaded from taking a flyer and bidding on your auction. Their thinking is, if that many people looked at this auction and didn't bid, something must be wrong with the item. They'll tend to doubt their own instincts as to what is and isn't a good deal. In a situation such as this, however, what might be going on is that savvy bidders are just watching your auction, waiting to bid at the last minute.

A *private counter* shields the numbers from the eyes of casual lookie-loos. The figures are available to only you through a password-protected login page.

Private counters come in different flavors. Some of the most helpful private counters are smart counters that offer a breakdown of visitors hour-by-hour.

This type of counter is available from several online vendors (see Figure 10-7). eBay offers you a free counter, but it's not a smart counter.

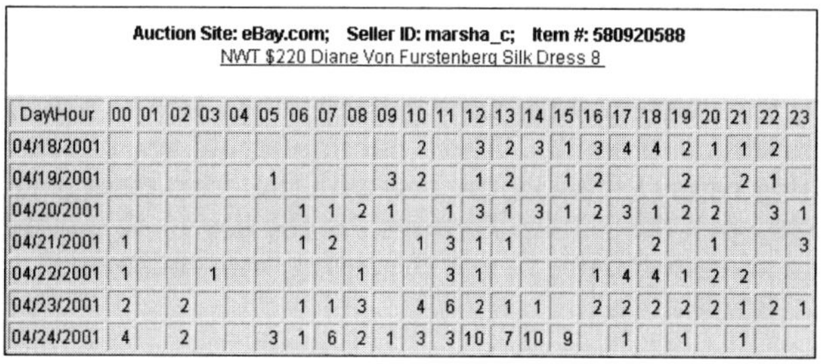

Figure 10-7: A Manage Auctions. com private counter.

Auction Site: eBay.com;   Seller ID: marsha_c;   Item #: 580920588
NWT $220 Diane Von Furstenberg Silk Dress 8

Day\Hour	00	01	02	03	04	05	06	07	08	09	10	11	12	13	14	15	16	17	18	19	20	21	22	23
04/18/2001										2		3	2	3	1	3	4	4	2	1	1	2		
04/19/2001					1				3	2		1	2		1	2			2		2	1		
04/20/2001				1	1	2	1		1	3	1	3	1	2	3	1	2	2			3	1		
04/21/2001	1				1	2		1	3	1	1				2	1								3
04/22/2001	1		1					1		3	1			1	4	4	1	2	2					
04/23/2001	2		2			1	1	3		4	6	2	1	1		2	2	2	2	1	2	1		
04/24/2001	4		2		3	1	6	2	1	3	3	10	7	10	9		1			1				

The gallery

eBay bills the gallery as its "miniature picture showcase," and indeed it is. By adding a gallery photo, a thumbnail image (96 x 96 pixels) of your item appears next to your listing when the user browses the category view or search results, which can reap you many benefits. When someone runs an auction search, eBay defaults to showing all items, and that includes a gallery preview, as shown in Figure 10-8.

Figure 10-8: Note how the gallery photos draw your attention.

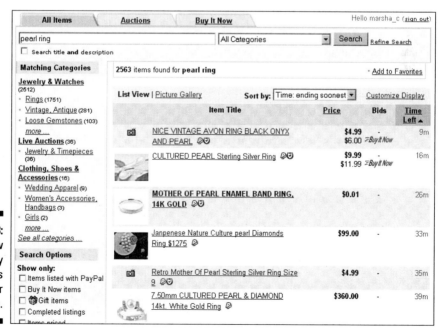

If you don't use the gallery image, but still have a picture in your description, your listing features only a lowly camera icon when searched. This makes choosing the 35-cent option a worthwhile expenditure. If your item will sell for less than $10, however, I recommend that you reconsider the extra charge.

Nothing draws the eye better than the gallery photo next to a listing in a search with hundreds of results. Which auction would you check out? The one with the tiny camera icon, or the one with the crisp clear gallery picture tempting you to open the listing? Pictures are the key to all quality advertising. Don't miss an opportunity to add this extra little "billboard" to your listings.

Don't get carried away with the idea that a large percentage of bidders are going to view their search results in the picture gallery option, which results in pages featuring only gallery photos and titles. Those who know what they're doing — and who are searching for a deal — aren't going to dismiss auctions without gallery photos. The newbies — or anyone for that matter — with dial-up connections may not have the patience to wade through pages of images.

eBay also offers to feature your gallery photo on the top of gallery-only pages for $19.95. These photos run three across the top of the page, as shown in Figure 10-9, rather than the five across for the regular gallery pictures. These featured gallery pictures are also larger (140 x 140 pixels) than the regular gallery pictures.

When you take advantage of the gallery, be sure to crop your photo tight to the subject. For more help with your images, see Chapter 11.

Buy It Now

The Buy It Now feature, shown in Figure 10-10, has a few significant benefits. If you have a target price for the item you're listing, make that your Buy It Now price. You can also use this option during frenzied holiday shopping times or with very hot items. Try posting a slightly higher than normal price and perhaps you'll get a bite, er, sale.

The Buy It Now feature disappears when someone bids on the item or, if you've placed a reserve on the auction, when a bidder meets your reserve price. You can't use Buy It Now with a Dutch auction.

To use this feature, you must have a feedback rating of at least 10, or be ID verified. (ID Verify is eBay's secondary form of identification, permitting you to participate in the site without submitting a credit card. See Chapter 3 for more info.)

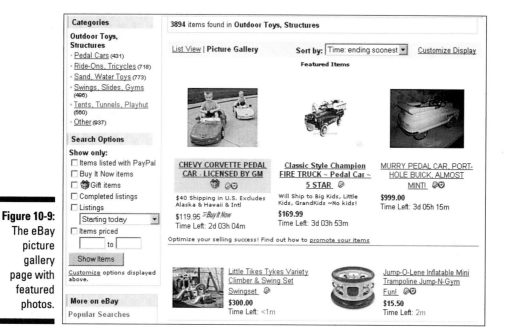

Figure 10-9:
The eBay
picture
gallery
page with
featured
photos.

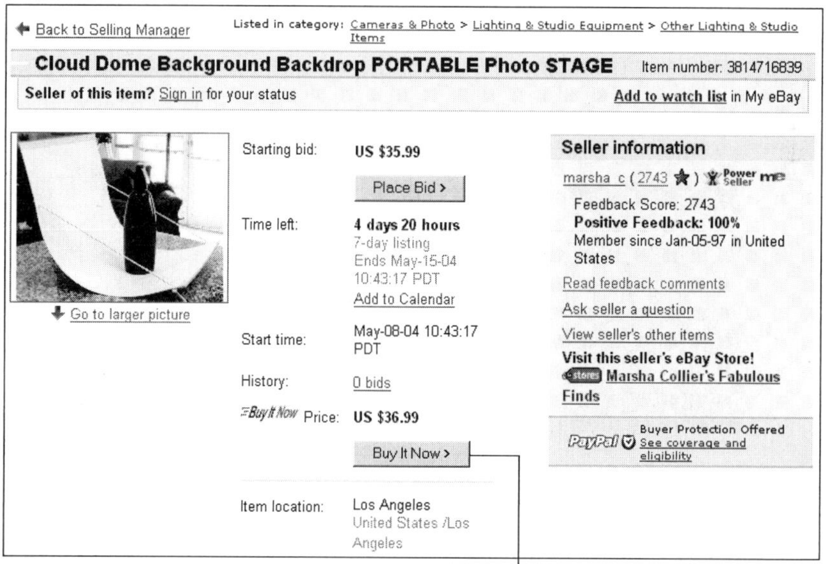

Figure 10-10:
The Buy
It Now
feature.

Buy It Now button

Buy It Now adds a sliding fee based on your listing price. See the following table for prices. If your item will sell for a low price, remember my golden rule: Before paying for a feature, ask yourself whether it's in your listing budget.

List Price	Buy It Now Fee
$0.01-9.99	$0.05
$10-24.99	$0.10
$25-49.99	$0.20
$50+	$0.25

eBay's Cut of the Action

Becoming complacent and blithely ignoring your eBay costs as you list items for sale is easy to do. As a person in business for yourself, you must always take into account outgoing costs as well as incoming profits. The cost of your initial listing is just the beginning of your advertising budget for that item; you have to factor in the cost of all the options and features you use as well. Then, when the item sells, you pay eBay a final value fee. (For fees regarding your eBay store, check out Chapter 5.) In this section, I review the costs for listing an auction and for a fixed-price listing on eBay.

The fees I detail here aren't the end of your fees. If you use a credit card payment service, they will also charge you a fee. In Chapter 13, I examine the costs of the most popular credit card payment services.

Insertion (listing) fees

Your insertion fee is based on the highest dollar amount of two things: your minimum opening bid or the dollar amount of your reserve price. If you start your auction at $.99 and have no reserve, the listing fee is $.30. But if you start your auction at $.99 and set an undisclosed reserve price of $50.00, your auction costs $4.40 to post. When you place a reserve on your item, you're charged an insertion fee based on the amount of the reserve — plus the reserve auction charge.

The reserve auction charge is automatically refunded if the reserve price is met.

For a summary of eBay insertion fees, see Table 10-1. (The fees for eBay Motors are in Chapter 2.)

If your item doesn't sell, don't think you can get your insertion fees back. They are non-refundable. You do have the option of relisting your unsuccessful auction without being charged a second listing fee, but *only* if your item sells with the second listing. If it doesn't sell the second time, you *will* be charged again. Writing a better title, starting with a lower opening bid, or adding a snappier description will help in selling the item. Maybe you should think about changing the category as well.

Table 10-1   eBay Listing Fees for Fixed-Price Single Item or Auction

Opening Bid or Reserve Price	Insertion Fee
$.01 to $.99	$.30
$1.00 to $9.99	$.35
$10.00 to $24.99	$.60
$25.00 to $49.99	$1.20
$50.00 to $199.99	$2.40
$200.00 to $499.00	$3.60
$500.00 and more	$4.80

Whether you're listing one item with a starting bid of $1000.00 or 100 items for $5.00 each in a Dutch auction, your insertion cost per auction is never more than $4.80.

I recap the cost of the various eBay listing options in Table 10-2.

Table 10-2   Fees for eBay Listing Options

Option	Listing Fee
Home page featured	$39.95 (single item); $79.95 (multiple items)
Featured Plus	$19.95
Highlight	$5.00
Subtitle	$.50
Bold	$1.00
Listing Designer	$.10
Gallery	$.35
Gallery featured	$19.95
Buy It Now	$.05
Scheduled listing	$.10
List in two categories	Double insertion fee
Ten-day auction	$.40

eBay Final Value Fees

eBay's version of the Hollywood back-end deal is the final value fee. Big stars get a bonus when their movies do well at the box office; eBay gets a cut when your auction sells. After your auction ends, eBay charges the final value fee to your account in a matter of minutes.

An auction in the Real Estate category is *not* charged a final value fee. Successful auctions in the eBay Motors category, however, are charged a flat final value fee. (See Chapter 2 for information on fees in both categories.)

Even a rocket scientist would have trouble figuring out exactly how much eBay receives at the end of your auction. To help you calculate how much you'll owe eBay, see Table 10-3.

Table 10-3	Final Value Fees
If Your Item Sells For	*You Pay a Final Value Fee Of*
$.01 to $25.00	5.25% of the selling price
$25.01 to $1000.00	5.25% on the first $25.00 plus 2.75% of the remainder of the selling price from $25.01 to $1000.00
$1000.00 and up	5.25% on the first $25.00 plus 2.75% of the next $975.00 plus 1.5% of the remainder on selling prices over $1000.00

Here are some sample prices and commissions:

Closing bid	*What you owe eBay*
$10.00	5.25% of $10.00 = $.53
$256.00	5.25% of $25.00 plus 2.75% of $231.00 = $7.66
$1284.53	5.25% of $25.00 plus 2.75% of $975.00 plus 1.5% of $284.53 = $32.39
$1,000,000.00	5.25% of $25 plus 2.75% of $975.00 plus 1.5% of $999,000.00 = $15,013.12

To save yourself brain-drain, use an eBay fee calculator to check your fees before you set prices. See Chapter 9 for software that will do this for you.

Chapter 11

Jazzing Up Your Auctions

- -

In This Chapter

▶ Writing a great description

▶ Setting up a photo studio

▶ Shooting great pics

▶ Scanning your items

▶ Kicking it up with imaging software

▶ Hosting your pics

▶ Finding HTML templates

- -

Rule #1: A good photograph and a concisely written description should be the goal for all your auctions. My years of advertising experience have proved this to me repeatedly in almost every type of media. If you're trying to fetch the highest possible bid for an item, keep your auction listings simple and professional: no dancing clowns (unless you're selling clowns), no overdone graphics, and no difficult-to-read typefaces. Less is more.

In this chapter, you find out how to write eye-catching descriptions and improve the visual elements of your auction listings. From there, you can make decisions regarding what you want to do and how to best accomplish your goals.

Writing Winning Text

When you write descriptions for your auctions, be sure that you describe your items clearly and completely. Mention everything about the article, including flaws or damage. When you're honest up front, you'll have a happy bidder. Remember to include your terms of sale and specify what type of payments and credit cards you accept. Be sure to include your shipping charges, too. Following is a checklist of things to mention:

- ✔ Size, style, color (garment measurements are also valuable because sizes aren't always universal)
- ✔ Condition (new, new with tags, used, gently used, well-worn)
- ✔ Manufacturer's name
- ✔ Year of manufacture (if important)
- ✔ Fabric or material (if important)
- ✔ Any damage to the item
- ✔ Special features
- ✔ That you've stored it in a clean, dry place (if you have)

After you list all the facts, get excited and add a little flowery text in your description. Think infomercial! Think Shopping Channel! Whoopee! They make things sound so good that you feel that you *must* have whatever item they're selling. You can do the same, if you take the time. In Chapter 12, I give you some more pointers on writing the best auction descriptions possible.

Your eBay Photo Studio

Taking pictures? No problem! You have a digital camera, and you know how to use it. Just snap away and upload that picture, right? Sorry, but no. There's a good way and a bad way to take photos for eBay and, believe it or not, the professional way isn't necessarily the most expensive way.

I recommend that you set up a mini photo studio for taking your eBay auction pictures. That way, you won't have to clean off your kitchen counter every time you want to take pictures.

If you must use the kitchen counter or a desktop, be sure to use an inexpensive photo stage, which you can find on — where else — eBay.

You need several basic things in your photo studio; the extras you should have are based on the type of merchandise you're selling. An eBay *generalist*, someone who will sell almost anything online — like me! — should have quite a few extras for taking quality photos. Check out a portion of my home photo studio in Figure 11-1.

Figure 11-1:
My eBay
photo setup,
which I'm
featuring
here in an
eBay
auction.

What you find in this section might be more than you thought you'd need to take good pictures. But your photographs can help sell your merchandise, so you need to take this part of your business seriously. Of course, if you sell only one type of item, you won't need such a varied selection of stuff, but you should have the basic photo setup. Go into it slowly, spending only as much as is prudent at the time. Also, check my Web site (www.coolebaytools.com) for more ideas.

Digital camera

Digital cameras are mysterious things. You may read about *mega pixels* (a million pixels) and think that more is supposed to be better, but that doesn't apply to eBay applications or to Web images. Mega pixels measure the image resolution that the camera is capable of recording. For online use, all you need from a camera is 640 x 480 pixels (or at most 800 x 600) because computer monitors are incapable of taking advantage of more pixels. If you use a higher resolution picture, all you'll do is produce a pixel-bloated picture that takes a looooong time to load online.

You don't need a million pixels, but you do need the following:

- ✔ **Quality lens:** I'm sure anyone who has worn glasses can tell the difference between a good lens and a cheap one. Really cheap cameras have plastic lenses, and the quality of the resulting pictures is accordingly lousy. Your camera will be your workhorse, so be sure to buy one from a company known for making quality products.

- ✔ **Removable media:** Taking the camera to your computer and using cables and extra software to download pictures to your hard drive is annoying. Removable media eliminates this annoyance. The most popular are Smart Media cards (black wafer-thin cards), Compact Flash cards (in a plastic shell), and Sony Media Sticks; all are no larger than a matchbook. Insert these cards into your computer, if your computer has ports for them, or you can get an adapter that connects to your computer through a USB or parallel port. You can get either device on eBay for about $30.

Some cameras (specifically the Sony Mavica FD series) use a regular 3½-inch floppy disc as a convenient storage method. These cameras are hugely popular with eBay sellers for just that reason.

- ✔ **Tripod and tripod mount:** Have you ever had a camera hanging around your neck while you're trying to repackage some eBay merchandise that you've just photographed? Or perhaps you've set down the camera for a minute and then can't find it? Avoid this hassle by using a tripod to hold your camera. Tripods also help you avoid blurry pictures from shaking hands. To use a tripod, you need a tripod mount, the little screw hole that you see in the bottom of some cameras. In the following section, I give you some tips on finding the right tripod.

- ✔ **Macro setting capability or threading for a lens adapter:** If you're ever going to photograph coins, jewelry, or small detailed items, these tools will come in handy. A camera's macro setting enables you to get in really close to items while keeping them in focus. A threaded lens mount enables you to add different types of lenses to the camera for super macro focus or other uses.

- ✔ **Autofocus and zoom:** These options just make life easier when you want to take pictures. The ability to zoom in and keep things in focus should be standard features.

The bottom line here is to buy a brand name camera. I use a Sony Mavica FD92. It's outdated, but it's also loaded with all the bells and whistles I need for eBay photos. It stores images on a Sony Memory stick or on a floppy disk, which I just pop out and insert in my computer. The camera's floppy disk convenience makes the Mavica FD series a favorite of eBay sellers.

I bet you could find a camera that fits your needs right now on eBay for less than $150. Remember that many digital camera users buy the newest camera available and sell their older, low-megapixel cameras on eBay for a pittance. Many professional camera stores also sell used equipment.

Other studio equipment

Certain endeavors seem to be open pits that you throw money into. I promise that your eBay photo studio will not be one of these pits — now or later.

Tripod

A tripod is an extendable aluminum stand that holds your camera. You should look for one that has a quick release so that if you want to take the camera off the tripod for a close-up, you don't have to unscrew it from the base and then screw it back on for the next picture.

The legs should extend to your desired height, should lock in place with clamp-type locks, and should have a crank-style geared center column so that you can raise your camera up and down for different shots. Most tripods also have a panning head for shooting from different angles. You can purchase a tripod from a camera store or on eBay for as low as $25.

Power supplies

If you've ever used digital cameras, you know that they can blast through batteries faster than sugar through a five year old. A reliable power supply is a must. You can accomplish this in a couple of ways:

- **Rechargeable batteries:** Many specialists on eBay sell rechargeable batteries and chargers. Pick up quality Ni-MH (nickel metal hydride) batteries because this kind, unlike Ni-Cad (nickel cadmium) batteries, has no memory effect. That means you don't have to totally discharge them.

- **CR-V3 lithium ion batteries:** This is a new kind of battery that takes the place of two standard AA batteries. Lithium batteries are the longest lasting and lightest batteries available, but they're also expensive. Then some smart guy figured out a way to put two batteries into one unit; considerably cutting the price. This new battery can average 650 photos before you have to change it. The CR-V3 is available also in a rechargeable form, thereby extending the life even further (and reducing your battery budget significantly).

If your eBay photo studio includes a camera on a tripod (and it should), you can use a good, old-fashioned AC adapter (you know, it's the one that plugs into the wall).

Lighting

Trying to take good pictures of your merchandise can be frustrating. If you don't have enough light and use the camera's flash, the image might be washed out. If you take the item outside, the sun might cast a shadow.

I've seen some eBay sellers use a flash and instruct their children to shine a flashlight on the item as they photograph it from different angles — all the while hoping that the color isn't wiped out. The autofocus feature on most digital cameras doesn't work well in low light.

After consulting specialists in the photo business to solve the digital camera lighting problem, I put together an inexpensive studio lighting set for online auction photography. Please check my Web site (www.coolebaytools.com) for information on how to obtain this package. It's the same one that I successfully use in my home photo studio (refer to Figure 11-1).

Professional studio lights can be expensive, but you might also be able to find a set for around $150. (You need at least two lights, one for either side of the item, to eliminate shadows.) Search eBay for used studio lighting; I'm sure you'll find a good deal.

Cloud Dome

If you're going to attempt to photograph a lot of jewelry, collectible coins, or other metallic items, you'll become frustrated at the quality of your pictures. Metallic objects seem to pick up random color from any kind of light you shine on them for picture taking. Gold jewelry will photograph with a silver tone and silver will look goldish!

After conferring with lots of eBay photo gurus, I was told the secret of getting crisp, clear, close-up pictures: use a Cloud Dome. It stabilizes your camera (just as if you were using a tripod) and filters out all unwanted color tones, resulting in image colors that actually look like your item.

The Cloud Dome is a large plastic bowl that you mount your camera on. You take pictures through the dome. The translucent white plastic diffuses the light so that your item is lit evenly from all sides, eliminating glare and bad shadows. Check out the manufacturer's web site at www.clouddome.com to see some amazing before and after pictures.

The Cloud Dome also manages to get the best images from gems. You can actually capture the light in the facets! Pearls too will show their luster. Several eBay members (including yours truly) sell the Cloud Dome; I highly recommend it!

Props

To take good photos, you need some props. Although you may think it strange that a line item in your accounting program will read "Props," they do qualify as a business expense. (Okay, you can put it under photography expense; *props* just sounds so Hollywood!)

How often have you seen some clothing on eBay from a quality manufacturer, but you just couldn't bring yourself to bid more than $10 because it looked like it had been dragged behind a car and then hung on a hanger before it was photographed? Could you see how the fabric would hang on a body? Of course not. Take a look at Figure 11-2; that dress looks simply fantastic, darling!

Figure 11-2: Midge, the mannequin, modeling one of my eBay successes.

Diane Von Furstenberg BRAND NEW with tags!
100% Silk Jersey dress
Fits Size 6 or 8

This lovely silk number is THE sexiest dress! It's by hot designer Diane Von Furstenberg (who is featured in the new issue of Vogue). It's a fabulous silk jersey spaghetti strap dress, with a sexy cowl neckline. The original price of the dress is $220, and it can be yours for the highest bid. Draping beautifully on the body, it's got a sexy below the knee length and a very flattering cut.

Bid with confidence and bid whatever you feel this great dress is worth to you as it is selling with NO RESERVE! Winning bidder to pay shipping & handling of $5.25, and must submit payment within a week of winning the auction. Credit cards are accepted through Billpoint and PayPal.

GOOD LUCK, HAPPY BIDDING!

Click below to...
View my other auctions - Win more than one and $AVE on shipping!

Mannequin

I hate to even say it, but if you're selling clothing, you'd better photograph it on a mannequin. If you don't want to dive right in and buy a mannequin, at least get a body form to wear the outfit. Just search eBay for *mannequin* to find hundreds of hollow forms selling for less than $20. If you sell children's clothing, get a child's mannequin form as well. The same goes for men's clothes. If worse comes to worst, find a friend to model the clothes. There's just no excuse for hanger-displayed merchandise in your auctions.

I got my mannequin (Midge) at a department store liquidation sale here in Los Angeles. I paid $25 for her. Her face is a little creepy, so I often crop her head out of the photos. She has a great body and everything she wears sells at a profit. Many stores upgrade their mannequins every few years or so. If you know people who work at a retail store, ask when they plan to sell their old mannequins; you may be able to pick one up at a reasonable price.

Steamer

Clothing is fairly crumpled when it comes out of a shipping box. It may also get crumpled lying around, waiting for you to photograph it and sell it on eBay. If the clothing isn't new but is clean, run it through your dryer with Dryel (the home dry-cleaning product) to take out any musty smells. There's nothing like old, musty-smelling clothes to sour a potentially happy customer.

The clothes you want to sell may be wrinkled, but ironing is a bear (and may damage the fabric), so do what the retail professionals do: Use steamers to take the wrinkles out of freshly unpacked clothing. Get the type of steamer that you use while the article of clothing is hanging up, so you can just run the steamer up and down and get the wrinkles out. The gold standard of steamers is the Jiffy Steamer. It holds a large bottle of water (distilled only), rolls on the floor, and steams from a hose wand. Some models sell on eBay for under $100. Until you're ready to make an investment that big, at least get a small handheld version that removes wrinkles; search eBay for *(garment,clothes) steamer* to find some deals.

Display stands, risers, and more

Jewelry does not photograph well on most people's hands and actually looks a lot better when you display it on a stand (see Figure 11-3) or a velvet pad. If you're selling a necklace, display it on a necklace stand, not on a person. I bought my display stands from a manufacturer but had to wait several months to receive them. Apparently, this type of quality display stand is made to order, so I recommend searching for them on eBay (you'll get them sooner).

Risers can be almost anything that you use to prop up your item to make it more attractive in a picture. Put riser pieces that aren't attractive under the cloth that you use as a background. (You can find risers on eBay.)

You wouldn't believe what the back of some professional photo setups look like. Photographers and photo stylists think resourcefully when it comes to making the merchandise look good — from the front of the picture, anyway! Throughout my years of working with professional photographers, I've seen the most creative things used to prop up items for photography:

Figure 11-3:
An eBay
listing
featuring a
professional
jewelry
display.

✔ **Bottles of mercury:** Mercury is a heavy liquid metal. A photographer I once worked with used little bottles of this stuff to prop up small boxes and other items in a picture. But mercury is a poison, so I suggest you do the same with small bottles (prescription bottles work well) filled with sand.

✔ **Beeswax and clay:** To set up photos for catalogs, I've seen photographers prop up fine jewelry and collectible porcelain with beeswax (the kind you can get from the orthodontist works great) or clay. Beeswax is a neutral color and doesn't usually show up in the photo. However, you must dispose of beeswax often because it picks up dirt from your hands and fuzz from fabric.

✔ **Museum Gel and Quake Hold:** These two products are invaluable when you want to hold a small object at an unnatural angle for a photograph. (They're like beeswax and clay, but cleaner.) I discovered them after losing everything breakable in my home in the Northridge earthquake. Museums use these putty-like products to securely keep breakables in one place — even during an earthquake!

✔ **un-du:** Un-du is a clear liquid that will get sticky residue off of almost anything. If your item has sticker residue on it, it's bound to show up in the picture. Squirt on a little un-du and use its patented scraper to remove the goo and bring back the shine.

✔ **Metal clamps and duct tape:** These multipurpose items are used in many photo shoots in some of the strangest places. Your mannequin may be a few sizes too small for the dress you want to photograph. How do you fix that? Don't pad the mannequin; simply fold over the dress in the back and clamp the excess material with a metal clamp, or use a small piece of duct tape to hold the fabric taut.

Keep a collection of risers and propping materials in your photo area so they're always close at hand.

Backgrounds for your images

Backgrounds come in many shapes and sizes. You can use paper, fabric, or one of the portable photo stages for smallish items.

In professional photo-talk, *seamless* is a large roll of 3-foot (and wider) paper that comes in various colors and is suspended and draped behind the model and over the floor. (Ever wonder why you never see the floor and wall come together in professional photos?) Photographers also drape the seamless over tabletop shots. Some people use fabrics such as muslin instead of seamless.

I keep satin and velvet on hand. (Be sure to clean black velvet with sticky tape before you use it in a picture — lint appears huge in pictures.) I recommend using neutral fabrics (such as white, light gray, natural, and black) for photographing your merchandise so that the color of the fabric doesn't clash with or distract from your items.

The Cloud Dome people have also invented a cool photo stage. I like it because it's portable (easy to store), nonbreakable, simple to clean, and inexpensive. It's sold on eBay and is pictured in Figure 11-4.

Figure 11-4:
Cloud
Dome's
photo stage
(seltzer
bottle not
included).

Taking Good Pictures

If you have a small home photo studio setup (see the preceding section) with a quality camera, a tripod, props, and lights, you're well on your way to taking some quality shots for your auctions. A few things to remember:

- ✔ **Zoom in on your item:** Don't leave a bunch of extraneous background in your pictures. Crop extra background in your photo-editing program (see the "Image-Editing Software" section, a bit later in this chapter) before you upload the images to your image-hosting service.

- ✔ **Watch out for distracting backgrounds:** If you don't have a studio table-top, or if the item is something that won't fit on a table, try to make the background of the photo as simple as possible. If you're shooting the picture outside, shoot away from chairs, tables, hoses — you get the idea. If you're shooting in your home, move the laundry basket out of the picture.

One of my favorite eBay pictures featured a piece of fine silver taken by the husband of the lady selling the piece on eBay. Silver and reflective items are hard to photograph because they pick up everything in the room in their reflection. In her description, the lady explained that the man reflected in the silver coffeepot was her husband and not part of the final deal. She handled that very well!

- ✔ **Be sure the items are clean:** Cellophane on boxes can get nasty looking, clothing can get linty, and all merchandise can get dirt smudges. Not only will your items photograph better if they're clean, they'll sell better, too.

Clean plastic or cellophane with WD-40 (no kidding); it will take off any sticker residue and icky smudges. Un-Du is the best adhesive remover for paper, cardboard, clothing, and more, plus it comes with a handy plastic scraper. I also keep a kneaded rubber art eraser around to clean off small dirt smudges on paper items. Any cleaning solution helps your items (even a little 409), but use these chemicals with care so that you don't destroy the item while cleaning it.

- ✔ **Check the camera's focus:** Just because a camera has an autofocus feature doesn't mean that pictures automatically come out crisp and clear. Low light, high moisture, and other things can contribute to a blurred image. Double-check the picture before you use it.

Using a Scanner

Scanners have come a long way in the past few years. A once expensive item can now be purchased new for a little more than a hundred dollars. If you sell books, autographs, stamps, or documents, a scanner may be all you need to shoot your images for eBay.

When shopping for a scanner, don't pay too much attention to the resolution. As with digital cameras, images for the Internet (JPEGs) needn't be any higher than 72 ppi (pixels per inch). Any quality scanner can get that resolution these days. Quality makes a difference in the manufacture of the scanner, so stick with brand names.

You should use a *flatbed* scanner, on which you lay out your items and scan away. I replaced my old scanner with an HP OfficeJet, which is not only a scanner but also a printer and reducing/enlarging color copier — some even come with a fax! These nifty flatbed units are available brand new on eBay. I've seen the HP models, new in box, sell for as low as $100.

A few tips on scanning images for eBay:

- ✔ If you're taking traditionally processed photographs and scanning them on a scanner, have them printed on glossy paper because they'll scan much better than those with a matte finish.

- ✔ You can scan 3-D items, such as a doll, on your flatbed scanner and get some respectable-looking images. To eliminate harsh shadows, lay a black or white t-shirt over the doll or her box so that it completely covers the glass. This way you'll have a clean background and you'll get good light reflection from the scanner's light.

- ✔ If you want to scan an item that's too big for your scanner's glass, simply scan the item in pieces, and then reassemble it to a single image in your photo-editing program (see the following section).

- ✔ Boxed items are a natural for a flatbed scanner. Just set them on top of the glass, and scan away. You can crop the shadowed background with your photo-editing software (see the following section).

Image-Editing Software

Lose the idea that the software that comes with your scanner is good enough. It may be just fine for some uses, but the kind of control that you need is only available in *real* image-editing software, not a mere e-mail picture generator.

I've always been happy using Photoshop, but it's a large and expensive program. It's also a bit of overkill for eBay images. Recently I started using Paint Shop Pro by Jasc software. It's a robust professional program at a fraction of the price of Photoshop. It's also one of the easiest-to-learn programs on the market. I've seen new packages of Paint Shop Pro 8.1 sell for as low as $50 (if you're a good shopper, I know you *can* find these deals). Hint: Look for sellers putting *Paint Shop* as one word (*Paintshop*) in the title.

Paint Shop Pro offers features that enable you to make a good picture out of a bad one. It also has an awesome export-to-Web feature that compresses the images so that they hold their quality while becoming smaller. Images compressed in this fashion download a lot faster for dial-up customers. You can also touch up your family photos in this easy-to-use (okay, low learning curve) program.

And don't forget that you'll be working with images not only for eBay items but also for your Web site. (Check out Chapter 8 for more about putting together a Web site.) The manufacturer, Jasc Software, runs an eBay store, and sells their software at a discount. You can also go to the manufacturer's Web site www.jasc.com and download a free trial

A Home for Your Images

You need a professional and safe place to store your pictures for eBay. If your images don't appear when someone clicks your auction, or if your images take too long to load, a user might click off your auction and go to the next one. If you have more than one option, test each with a few pictures because you want one that's reliable.

If you use auction management software, you may not need an FTP program to upload your images. Most complete management programs integrate their own FTP program as part of the package and may also include image storage space on their server. Check out Chapter 9 for more about auction management software packages.

You should always put your eBay images in a separate directory — not in an active part of your Web site. You may think that using your business Web site is a good place to store your images, but it isn't. If you want to keep track of your site statistics, such as the number of visitors, hits, and the like, hosting your own images will ruin the data. A call for one of your eBay images counts as a hit on your site, and you'll never get accurate Web site stats.

Free ISP space

Most ISPs (Internet Service Providers) give you at least 5MB of storage space for your personal home page. Although this space isn't appropriate for your final business site, it's a perfect place to host your pictures. Everyone has an ISP, and all ISPs give you space. You may have to use an FTP program to upload to your Web space, or your ISP may supply its own uploader. Go to the home pages for your ISP (the member area), and check out what it offers. Visit Chapter 8 for more information on ISP space.

AOL will try to get you to build some kind of hometown page, but here's what to do instead: Go to the top of the AOL page frame and click the Internet tab. Then click FTP. When another screen appears, click the <u>Go to FTP</u> link. Whew, you're almost there. Now click the `members.aol.com` FTP site, and you're taken to your FTP area. From there you can upload all your files, up to a maximum of 2MB per screen name. Remember which photos are stored in each screen name FTP space because the URL locator for each screen name is different.

Auction management sites

If you're using one of the auction management Web sites that I discuss in Chapter 9, you're covered for most of your back office tasks. These Web sites supply enough Web space to hold all your eBay images. They also have a convenient one-click upload from your hard drive.

If you find that you truly have no place to host your images, take a look at some of the less expensive auction management sites. As of this writing, you can get image hosting *and* other auction utilities for around $10 a month at

```
AAASeller.com, AuctionHawk.com, Inkfrog.com, and
              manageauctions.com
```

eBay Picture Services

You can also use eBay Picture Services to host your photos for eBay, but the quality of your photos is better if you host them directly from a site. Really clear pictures on Picture Services are few and far between. Picture Services reformats your photo to fit in a layout 400 pixels wide by 300 pixels tall and then compresses the file for quick viewing. This process can destroy the quality of your carefully photographed images if you haven't saved them in a compatible size. You're running a business, so be businesslike and use the method that presents your photos in their best light.

To get the free top-of-page image that you see on many auctions, you must use eBay Picture Services. I suggest that you use eBay Picture Services for your primary image and also use secondary images of your items hosted elsewhere. If one of the picture servers goes down, at least your listing will have pictures. The first picture is free; all you have to do is click the box on the Sell Your Item page's Picture Services area, next to Add picture. This picture will also be the default picture for use as your all-important gallery image. (See Chapter 10 for more on using the gallery.)

eBay offers two versions of Picture Services. The basic version (see Figure 11-5) allows you to upload eBay-ready images as they appear on your computer.

Add pictures   ⊘ Live help

| eBay Picture Services | Your own Web hosting |
| Let eBay host your pictures | Enter your picture URL |

Upgrade to our free full-featured version
It's faster, lets you upload pictures of any size, and enables you to preview, crop, and rotate your pictures

Picture 1 (Free)
[   ] Browse...
To add pictures to your listing, click Browse.
Picture 2 ($0.15)
[   ] Browse...
Picture 3 ($0.15)
[   ] Browse...
Picture 4 ($0.15)
[   ] Browse...
Picture 5 ($0.15)
[   ] Browse...
Picture 6 ($0.15)
[   ] Browse...

Figure 11-5: The basic Picture Services photo-hosting page.

If you want to rotate or crop the picture, you need the advanced picture service. Click the <u>Upgrade</u> link, and a screen similar to Figure 11-6 appears.

To upload your pictures using the advanced version, follow these steps:

1. **Click the Add Picture button, which appears in the picture frame.**

   A browsing window appears.

2. **Locate the directory that holds your eBay images on your computer.**

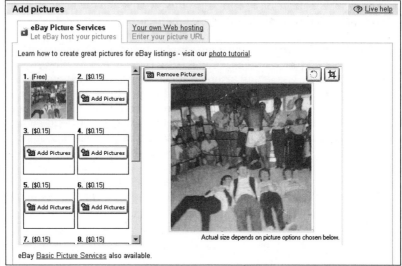

Figure 11-6:
eBay's
advanced
Picture
Services.

3. **Click the image in the browsing window.**

   The image name appears in the filename box.

4. **Click the Open box.**

   The selected image appears in the picture frame.

5. **To rotate the image, click the circular arrow (at the upper left of the main image box).**

6. **To crop the image:**

   a. **Click the crop box in the right corner of the larger image.**

      Two squares appear at opposite corners of your main image.

   b. **Click the frame on the outside of your image, and move the bar until the offensive area is cropped out.**

      You can do this from the sides, top, and bottom of the picture.

Sometimes Picture Service will shrink your image to a too-small size, but you can't do much about it. Just be sure to reload the image anytime you relist the item; otherwise, the gallery image may just get smaller and smaller. eBay continues to improve Picture Services, so don't give up on it. Use it for the free image, and be sure to upload secondary images from an outside site.

HTML and You

My small grasp of HTML gets me only so far. I usually use a program such as CuteHTML to produce code for my Web site or eBay listings. Luckily, you don't have to know a lot of code to produce eBay auctions.

The Sell Your Item form has an excellent, basic HTML generator that has a toolbar similar to the one in a word processor. As you can see in Figure 11-7, you can use the toolbar to change the size, font, or color of the text. You can also insert coding by switching to the "Enter your own HTML" view of the description to include your own hosted images in the listing description. (Check out Chapter 9 for some sample coding to use in your own listings.)

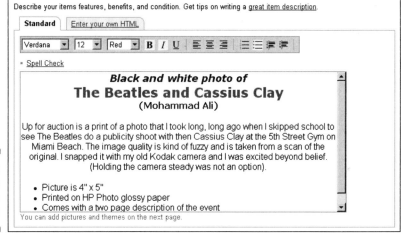

Figure 11-7: eBay's HTML code generator.

For a quick and easy HTML fix, go to my Web site at

`www.coolebaytools.com`

Then go to the Tolls area and click <u>Cool free ad tool</u>. You'll get a quick HTML generator; feel free to use it as often as you like. There's no charge. You can select border colors and include an image in your description area. Nothing fancy, mind you, just nice clean HTML. You type your information as indicated and select colors, as shown in Figure 11-8. When you're finished, click the View Ad button. On the next page, you'll see HTML code for your auction description that you can cut and paste into the auction description area of the Sell Your Item page.

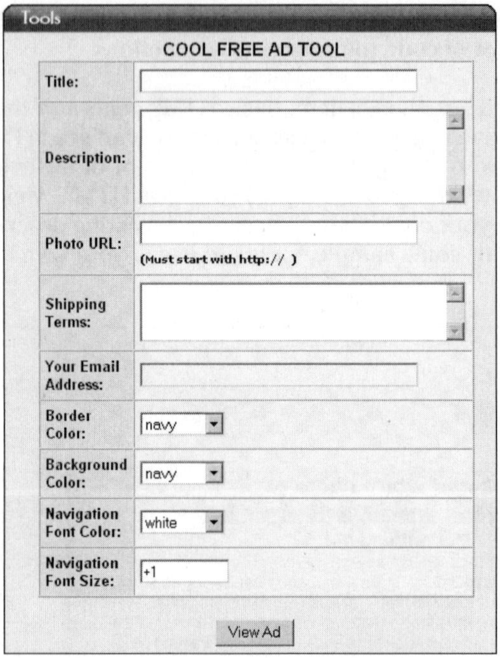

Figure 11-8:
The Cool
Free Ad
Tool page.

Chapter 12

Providing Excellent Customer Service

In This Chapter

▶ Making a good first impression

▶ Writing the perfect e-mail

*B*usiness, bah! eBay's supposed to be fun! But business is business and if you're in business, you must remember that your customers are number one. Businesses become successful by providing fantastic customer service and selling quality merchandise. You have to move in the same direction. The image that you project through your e-mails and ads identifies you to the bidders as a good guy or a bad guy. No kidding. Your e-mails should be polite and professional. Your ads shouldn't make prospective buyers feel like you're hustling them, sneaking in hidden fees, or being pushy with several rules for bidding.

You don't have to have the most beautiful auctions on eBay to succeed. You need products that sell, and you need to take the time to build good customer relations! In this chapter, I cover some ways — from writing effective auction descriptions to sending cordial e-mails — to let your customers know that they're number one in your book.

Meeting Your Customers

eBay is a person-to-person marketplace. Although many sellers are businesses (like you), the perception is that sellers on eBay are individuals (versus businesses) earning a living. The homespun personal approach goes a long way to being successful when selling on eBay. One of the reasons many buyers come to eBay is that they want to support the individuals who had the gumption to start their own small enterprise on the site.

After you've written a brilliant title for your auction, prospective buyers click your listing and scroll down to your description. Do they have to dodge through pointless verbiage, losing interest along the way? Or do you get right down to business and state the facts about your item?

Here are a few things to remember when writing your auction description:

- ✔ **Write a factual description.** Do you carefully describe the item, stating every fact you know about it? Are you clear in your description and careful not to use any jargon? Finally, does it answer almost any question a potential buyer might ask? If not, do some revising.

- ✔ **Include some friendly banter.** You want to make the customer feel comfortable shopping with you. Don't be afraid to let your personality show!

- ✔ **Update your My eBay page.** Let people know a little about you and who they're dealing with. When customers have to decide between two sellers selling the same item and all else is equal, they will place their bid with the seller who makes them feel secure.

- ✔ **Limit the number of auction rules (or terms of sale).** Some sellers include a list of rules that's longer than the item's description. Nothing will turn off a prospective buyer like paragraph after paragraph of rules and regulations. If you really *must* put in a litany of rules, use the following bit of HTML to make the size of the text smaller: `<font size=-1>`

- ✔ **Choose a reasonable typeface size.** Many users are still looking at eBay on an 800 x 600 display. If you design your auctions at 1024 x 768, your typefaces may be way too large for the average user. Forcing a user to scroll and scroll to find the details only leads to frustrated customers.

- ✔ **Quote a shipping amount.** Many bidders pass up auctions that don't disclose the shipping charges. Make use of eBay's shipping calculator to give your customers a fair shake at the shipping costs. If many others are selling the same item you're selling, quoting reasonable shipping costs will help you reel in a buyer.

It's just plain bad taste to overcharge on shipping. eBay buyers expect that you'll pad up to a dollar for packing and shipping costs, but adding more than that can make you look like you're trying to squeeze every penny out of your bidder . . . not a good feeling when you're on the other end!

- ✔ **Keep photos a practical size.** Most users still connect with a dial-up Internet connection, and if they have to wait for your large pictures to load, they may go elsewhere for the item. If your listing doesn't fully open within a few seconds, the person will back out and go on to another listing.

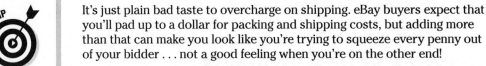
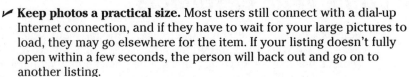

Telling your story

Being honest and forthright encourages customers to consider your offerings on eBay. Also, if you go the extra mile and give some bonus information, the customer will feel more at ease.

An excellent example comes from a Power Seller, e.vehicles. John Rickmon, the seller, throws in a few special touches to draw in the customer. As you may gather by his user ID, John sells vehicles on eBay — and does very well at it!

When you participate in eBay Motors, the prospective buyer has the option of ordering a CarFax report on the vehicle's history from the listing page. This costs the buyer a special eBay price of $19.99 just to view the report. John orders the CarFax report himself and puts a link to a PDF version of it right in the auction description. Saving the buyer $19.99 doesn't seem like much, but its one of those simple touches that makes the customer at ease.

John also posts his business philosophy at the end of his auctions, here's part of it:

"My dealership is entirely focused on the sales of vehicles via the eBay format. I make all purchasing and sales decisions and am 100% responsible for the content of my auctions, including all text and photography. I personally answer every email and conduct all business regarding the sale of this vehicle.

I buy and list approximately 10-15 units per month; I look at hundreds of vehicles each week that do not make the cut...

This is my living. *I do this full time. I do not have a "car lot." EBay has been my dealership for years and all operations are focused towards bringing you the best vehicle possible at the best price you will find. I am committed to this format and take your vehicle purchase very seriously. You are dealing with a secure seller."*

Wow, don't you just want to buy a car from this guy?

Communicating with Your Customers

Perhaps English class wasn't your favorite, but when it comes to being a professional, incorporating good grammar, proper spelling, and punctuation in your communications portrays you as a pro. Before writing this book, even I hooked up with some grammar and punctuation sites to brush up on my writing skills. (Okay, I also have brilliant editors covering up my transgressions. . . .)

Throughout the rest of this section, I provide some examples of effective e-mails. Study these and also check out a few of business letter books (for example, *Writing Business Letters For Dummies,* by Sheryl Lindsell-Roberts and published by Wiley). And don't forget good manners. You don't want to be too formal, but you do want to be personable and polite.

The initial inquiry

The first written communication you have with a prospective buyer is an inquiry e-mail. A bidder can ask you a question about your item by clicking the <u>Ask the seller a question</u> link on the auction or sale page, which automatically generates an e-mail addressed to you. Often these questions are brief.

At least 20 percent of the time that I send an inquiry to a seller, I don't get a response — guaranteeing that I won't be buying that product. I refuse to buy from someone who doesn't even care to respond to a question. When I do get responses, more often than not it's a terse, brusquely written note. Many people choose not to use punctuation or capitalization in their e-mails. How professional looking is that? Not very. Sellers who take the time to write a short, considerate reply that includes a greeting and a thank you for writing get my money.

You should respond quickly, clearly, and politely — and with a sales pitch. Remind the soon-to-be bidder that you can combine several wins to save on shipping costs. And by all means, use this opportunity to point out other auctions you have that may also interest the writer. Now that's customer service.

The letter can be brief and straightforward. For example, I wrote the following note in response to a question regarding the condition of the Christmas tree in one of my auctions:

Hello,

Yes, the aluminum Christmas tree in my auction is in excellent condition. The 58 branches are full and lush and will look great for the holidays. Please write again if you have any more questions or concerns.

Don't forget to check my other auctions for a color wheel and a revolving tree turner. They would look great with this tree, and I can combine them for shipping.

Thank you for writing,

Marsha
www.coolebaytools.com

Isn't that nice? The note addresses the question in a respectful and personable manner. Writing a note like this doesn't take long. You should be doing it.

Also, putting your Web site or eBay store URL in your signature is a great way to get new customers to view your other merchandise.

The winner's notification letter

Have you ever received a bulk-generated boilerplate winner's confirmation letter? The seller hasn't bothered to fill in half the blanks, and you're almost insulted just by reading it? Receiving a note like this after you've requested that the seller combine purchases (and the letter pays no attention to your request) is especially annoying. E-mails can cross, but a personal approach goes a long way with customers.

I'm not saying you shouldn't automate your eBay business. I'm merely suggesting — strongly recommending — that you take the time to personalize even your canned e-mail responses. If you decide to send automated responses, choose a program that allows you to combine multiple wins in one letter and to apply the correct shipping costs the first time.

Here's the tried and true winner's notice that I send out:

Congratulations!

Yours was the winning bid on eBay item #122342911 for the Emilio Pucci book. You got a great deal! I am looking forward to a pleasant transaction and positive feedback for both of us.

Please include a copy of this e-mail with your name and shipping address along with your payment:

> *Winning Bid Amount $14.95*
>
> *Shipping and Handling $2.50*
>
> *TOTAL Amount Due $17.45*

You may pay by money order, with a personal check, or with a credit card through PayPal. If you are not set up with them, just e-mail me and I'll send you a PayPal invoice.

A money order or online payment assures immediate shipping upon receipt of payment! If you pay by check, I will ship your item after a 14-day clearing period; be sure to include the item name and your e-mail address with payment. Please send your payment to the address shown below:

> *Marsha Collier*
> *1234 Anywhere Street*
> *Los Angeles, CA 91352*

Your payment is expected on or before Saturday, April 2, 2005. I look forward to receiving it. I will ship on receipt of payment in full, via U.S. priority mail with delivery confirmation.

Thank you for your Winning Bid! I am delighted to be dealing with you and know you will enjoy your purchase.

Marsha_c
Marsha Collier
www.coolebaytools.com

At the end of a winner's notice letter, offer your winner some special discounts or other offers from your Web site. Include a few items this particular winner may be interested in (based on the current win) and include a link to your site. Also include the reminder that you can combine postage and that you look forward to a response.

The payment reminder

Writing a payment reminder can get sticky. You don't want to aggravate the buyer, but time is wasting and you could spend this time reposting your item. When writing a payment reminder, you need to be firm but pleasant. Real things can happen in people's lives. Family members get sick, and people just plain forget. Perhaps your payment fell between the seat of the winner's car on the way to the post office. (That's the excuse I used when I forgot to mail a payment — feel free to use it.)

When you honestly forget to send a payment, nothing is more humiliating than someone debasing you through e-mail. So remember that people do make mistakes, and check the winner's feedback before you send the letter. If you can garner from the feedback that this winner has a habit of not following through on bids, you can definitely be a bit firmer in your wording. Always set a clear deadline for receiving payment, as shown in the following letter:

Hello,

You won an auction of mine on eBay last week for the Emilio Pucci book. Your payment was due yesterday and it still has not arrived. Perhaps sending payment has slipped your mind considering your busy schedule. I know it can easily happen.

Please e-mail back within 48 hours and let me know whether you want to go through with our transaction. I'd like to put the item back up for sale if you don't want it.

Thank you for your bid,

Marsha Collier

Leaving feedback for buyers

After you leave feedback, you can't take it back and you can't repost to correct an erroneous evaluation of another user. I know that it's easier to leave feedback after you receive payment, but waiting to see how the transaction evolves afterwards is prudent — especially if the package gets lost in the mail, turning a previously kind and sweet buyer into a screaming nutcase. Same thing if the item is damaged. You should evaluate a buyer based on more than whether the person pays for an item. (Buyers are supposed to do that — it's a contract, remember?) When leaving feedback for buyers, consider the following:

✔ Did they return your communications quickly?

✔ Did they pay in a timely manner?

✔ If a problem occurred with the item or in shipping, did they handle it in a decent manner or did they try to make your life a living hell?

Remember that sellers are judged on communication, shipping time, the quality of packaging, and friendliness. As a seller, you have the duty of leaving quality feedback to set guidelines that all sellers use to rate buyers.

How firm you choose to get with a non-paying bidder is up to you. I've dealt with a few non-paying bidders on eBay, but I've left only two negative feedbacks. Some people who tend to overbid are indeed violating the contract to buy, but legitimate reasons might explain why someone hasn't followed through on an auction. You must decide which method to take and how far you want to stretch your karma (what goes around comes around). Assess each case individually, and don't be hasty in leaving negative feedback until you know the whole story.

The payment received and shipping notice

I know that you probably aren't going to send out a payment received letter for every transaction, but it would surely be nice if you did. Staying in constant communication with your buyers will make them feel more secure with you and with buying on eBay. You want them to come back, don't you?

When you receive payment and are ready to ship, sending a short note like the following helps to instill loyalty in your customer:

Hi there (insert name of winner),

Your payment was received and your item will ship tomorrow. Please e-mail me when it arrives so that I can hear how pleased you are with your purchase.

When the transaction is over, I hope you will leave positive feedback for me because building a good reputation on eBay is very important. I'd really appreciate it, and I'll be glad to do the same for you.

Thank you for bidding & winning,

Marsha Collier
Marsha_c
www.coolebaytools.com

If you haven't heard from the buyer within a week, send another note.

The "Your item is on the way" e-mail

I always send out the automatic e-mail from UPS or FedEx announcing the shipment tracking number. You can also send out an e-mail from PayPal by inserting the tracking number into the PayPal payment record. These e-mails aren't very personalized, so I follow up with another, more personal note:

Subject: Your book is on the way!

Hi (insert buyer's name)!

You will be receiving another e-mail with the package's delivery confirmation number and information on the mode of shipment.

Thank you for buying my item. If there is any question when the package arrives, PLEASE e-mail me immediately. Your satisfaction is my goal, and I'm sure any problem can be easily taken care of. Please let me know when the package arrives so that we can exchange some very positive feedback!

Marsha Collier
www.coolebaytools.com

Good customer service will get you many repeat customers and buckets of positive feedback. Good communication will head off problems before they start. If your customers have received communication from your all during your transactions, they'll be more likely to discuss a glitch with you rather than make a knee-jerk reaction and leave negative feedback.

Chapter 13

When the Money Comes Rolling In

· ·

In This Chapter

▶ Finding the payment method that suits your needs

▶ Discovering the ins and outs of payment services

▶ Exploring merchant accounts

· ·

The hours spent selecting your items, photographing them, touching up the pictures, and writing brilliant auction copy all come down to one thing: getting paid. At first thought, you might be happy to take any form of negotiable paper, bonds, and stocks (okay, no dotcom stock). As you become more experienced and collect for more auctions, however, you'll decide which payment methods you prefer and which are more heartache than they're worth.

Receiving and processing payments takes time and patience. The more payment methods that you accept, the more you have to keep track of. Throughout this chapter, I detail the various payment options (including how to handle payment from international buyers) and how each affects your business.

It Doesn't Get Any Simpler: Money Orders

I begin my discussion of payments with money orders and cashier's checks because I think they're the greatest way to receive payment. Money orders and cashier's checks are fast, cheap, and negotiable (just like cash). Cashier's checks are purchased at a bank and are generally debited immediately from the winner's checking account at purchase. For some unknown reason, banks take it upon themselves to charge a minimum of $5 to issue a cashier's check. This is a pretty steep charge to the winner, which is why I suggest money orders.

Money orders are available almost anywhere and cost less than $1.00. In my neighborhood, the stores I called charge $.99 for a money order up to $500. In this section, I detail just four vendors (both online and off) that offer money order services. Table 13-1 shows a cost comparison of these vendors.

Table 13-1	Money Order Cost Comparison	
Vendor	*$25 Money Order*	*$110 Money Order*
7-Eleven	$.99	$.99
United States Post Office (domestic)	$.90	$.90
United States Post Office (international)	$3.25	$3.25
Canada Post (in U.S. currency)	$4.00 CDN	$4.00 CDN
BidPay.com (Western Union Auction Payments)	$2.95	$7.42

If you want money orders, you should familiarize yourself with the various charges so that you can recommend to your auction winners the service with the most reasonable cost. Saving your customers money (especially when it's not going to you) is a sign of good customer service. Asking buyers to pay a large additional fee is unfair — unless the buyers are international. In that case, the best way for them to pay you is by money order through an issuer such as American Express (with offices in most countries). International buyers deal in the currency of their own countries; when they purchase a money order and send it in dollars, you're paid with cash in good old American greenbacks.

7-Eleven (and other convenience stores)

There are more than 21,000 7-Eleven stores in the world. I'll bet there's one within driving distance of your house. For your customer, the best part about 7-Eleven is that each has an ATM to draw cash from credit cards with which to purchase a money order. At only $.99, money orders from 7-Eleven are a bargain! If you don't know where the closest 7-Eleven is, go to the following

```
go.vicinity.com/7eleven/prxStart.dsp
```

You can also buy money orders from several other convenience store chains, such as Circle K, Dairy Mart, and AM/PM.

United States Postal Service

Most sellers especially love USPS money orders, which have all the benefits of a regular money order — plus, because the post office issues these money orders, the nice clerks at the post office will graciously cash them for you with proper identification. Postal money orders are safe, too, and acceptable everywhere. The post office goes to great pains to ensure authenticity by including a Benjamin Franklin watermark, a metal security thread, and a double imprint of the dollar amount on the money order. (No more fears that you've received a color copy of a money order.)

Both domestic and international (for sending U.S. dollars to foreign countries) money orders are available at post offices in amounts up to $700 for $.90 each. If the money order is lost or stolen (in eBay-speak, that usually means the buyer hasn't sent it to you yet), buyers must present the receipt for a trace on a lost money order. For a small fee, buyers can also get a copy of a paid money order (as long as they have the receipt), for as long as two years after the date it has been paid.

Many sellers bring their money orders to the post office when they ship their packages and cash them for their petty cash fund — or to pay for outgoing postage.

Western Union

AuctionPayments.com (formerly called BidPay) is an affiliate of Western Union and the most popular money order seller, probably because it was the first or maybe because it promotes better than anyone else. AuctionPayments. com accepts Visa, MasterCard, or Discover payments from your buyers and sends payment to you through the mail (both in the United States and internationally). Luckily, the United States has a good postal system, so you receive your money orders from AuctionPayments.com swiftly and ship out the item quickly as well. They don't handle most international currencies, but if you're a seller in the United Kingdom, they will send your buyer's funds to you in pound sterling for an additional $5.00 USD (United States Dollars) fee.

AuctionPayments.com charges your customers from $1.95 up to $4.95 plus 2.25% of any amount more than $100.00. See Table 13-2 for the fee schedule. 7-Eleven is sounding better all the time.

Table 13-2	Western Union AuctionPayments.com Money Order Fees
Money Order Amount	_Fee_
$10.00 and under	$1.95
$10.01–$30.00	$2.95
$30.01–$50.00	$3.95
$50.01–$100.00	$4.95
$100.01–$700.00	$4.95 + 2.25%

To register with AuctionPayments.com so that you can begin to accept them as a payment method for your auctions, go to www.auctionpayments.com. Click Sign In/Register (in the top-right corner of the page, as shown in Figure 13-1) and provide some basic information. After AuctionPayments. com processes your application, you will receive a confirmation.

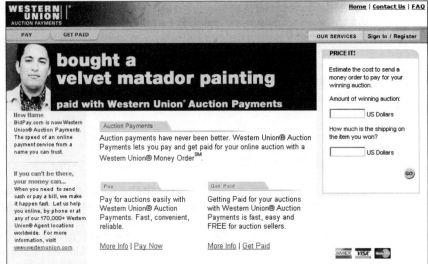

Figure 13-1: The Auction Payments. com home page.

Pay Me When You Get This: Cash On Delivery

I can't say enough to discourage you from using C.O.D. as a payment method. But I'm gonna try! You give your package to the post office, UPS, or FedEx, which collects the payment after delivering the package. Sound straightforward and easy? What happens when the carrier tries to deliver the package and the recipient isn't home? Your items can sit for a week or two, during which time buyers may decide that they don't want to pick up the items from the shipper. If you're lucky, you'll get your items back in two to three weeks.

The cash on delivery service is also expensive. In addition to postage, the post office charges $5.50 for C.O.D. service.

Another bad part of C.O.D.? You might wait a month to receive payment, even when the addressee is home the first time and accepts delivery. Do yourself a favor and don't offer it as a payment option. You're only asking for trouble. You're not a bank, and you're not in the finance business. Get your money up front.

Accepting cash payments

I'm sure you've received cash from some of your winners. I don't like cash. If the buyer doesn't send the exact amount due, you have to call the buyer, who may claim that the correct amount should be there. Mail can be stolen. We had a rash of mail thievery where I live; people were stealing envelopes right out of mailboxes. All of a sudden, *you* must have lost the difference — and you have no recourse with cash.

Postal inspectors are constantly battling this problem, but you won't know your mail is being stolen until you've missed enough mail — usually bills and outgoing checks. Explaining to a buyer that the money never arrived is difficult. The thief has the cash while your reputation may be shot. You can e-mail, phone, and talk and discuss, but the bottom line is that you haven't received your money and they insist you have it.

The Check's in the Mail: Personal Checks

Personal checks are the easiest way for buyers to make payments. They can just dash off a check, put it in the mail, and bam, you're paid. But it's not always as easy for the seller. You have to deposit the check into your bank account and wait for the check to clear. Believe it or not, in these days of electronic transfers, wiring funds, and international money transfers, you might wait more than two weeks for a check to clear.

Paper checks

After you deposit a check, your bank sends it to a central clearinghouse, which then sends it to the signatory's bank clearinghouse. Then the individual bank decides whether the check can be paid. You may think that a way around the system is to call the bank and see whether the account currently has sufficient money in it. The account may have sufficient funds when you call, but the depositor can withdraw money before the check gets through the system — and then the check bounces. And don't forget the 24-hour turnaround rule: Even if the bank has the money and you're standing there with the check, the bank can deny payment within 24 hours, leaving you with a bad check.

Even though everything seems to be electronic these days, the paper routing of old-fashioned checks can take two weeks or longer. I've received only one bad check as an eBay payment. I deposited the check, waited ten business days, and then shipped the item. On the eleventh business day, the bank sent me the bounced check. The buyer clearly knew that the check had bounced but didn't notify me. Luckily the buyer made good on the check.

If you find yourself with a check that's bouncing higher than a superball and an uncooperative buyer, remember that it's against the law to pass bad checks. To see a list of penalties, state by state, visit the National Check Fraud Center at the following address:

```
www.ckfraud.org/penalties.html#civil
```

In many states, if a resident passes a bad check, you are legally able to collect three times the amount of the bad check!

Bottom line? I warn all my winners that I may hold the item for more than two weeks before I ship. I make exceptions for buyers who have an excellent feedback rating or who I've successfully done business with before. Dealing with personal checks isn't worth the potential grief they can cause. Try to get an e-check or an instant transfer through PayPal (see the following section) or have your winners pay with credit cards through a payment service. For more on payment services, see the "I Take Plastic: Credit Cards" section, later in this chapter.

Bank debits (e-checks and instant transfers)

Despite the attached fees and a *short* waiting period, accepting a PayPal e-check or an instant transfer is a nice, clean transaction because it's immediate cash in your account. After indicating that they want to pay with an e-check, buyers must register their bank account with PayPal and give them the information required as shown in Figure 13-2.

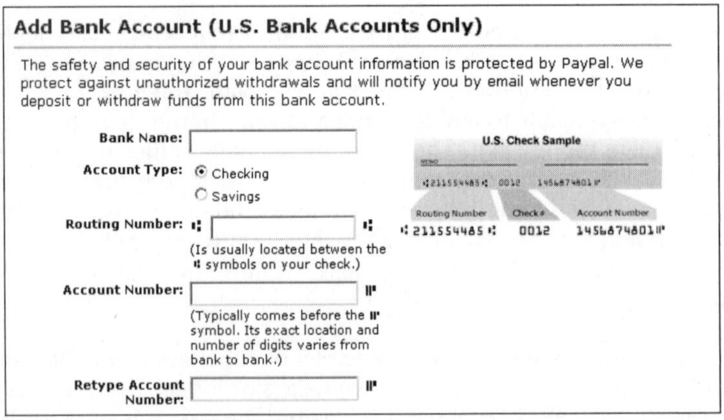

Add Bank Account (U.S. Bank Accounts Only)

The safety and security of your bank account information is protected by PayPal. We protect against unauthorized withdrawals and will notify you by email whenever you deposit or withdraw funds from this bank account.

Bank Name: _____

Account Type: ⦿ Checking
            ○ Savings

Routing Number: ⑆ _____ ⑆
(Is usually located between the ⑆ symbols on your check.)

Account Number: _____ ⑈
(Typically comes before the ⑈ symbol. Its exact location and number of digits varies from bank to bank.)

Retype Account Number: _____ ⑈

U.S. Check Sample

⑆211554485⑆ 0012 1456874801⑈

Routing Number   Check#   Account Number
⑆ 211554485 ⑆ 0012 1456874801⑈

Figure 13-2: The information required to register your bank account with PayPal.

When a buyer pays with an electronic check, it will take as many as four days to clear. An instant transfer (on the other hand) credits your account immediately as long as the buyer has a credit card (or bank debit card) as a backup funding source — should your instant transfer fail. PayPal allows you to accept e-checks for up to $10,000 but will charge you the same fees as those for a credit card.

You can accept e-checks also from Yahoo PayDirect, but the maximum transaction amount is $400.

Hold This for Me: Escrow Service

Escrow.com (eBay's official escrow service) makes it more comfortable for a buyer to proceed with transactions of more than $500 (the upper limit for eBay and PayPal fraud protection). By using escrow, buyers gain peace of mind because they know the transaction will be completed securely and easily.

Another way to assure your buyer when participating in high-dollar transactions is to run a bonded auction. This type of service, described in the "Helping your buyers buy safely" sidebar, cost you less than an escrow service and doesn't hold up your money.

You or your buyer must register to use the Escrow.com service. When you want to offer escrow as a payment option in one of your auctions, be sure to indicate such on the Sell Your Item form so that it appears on the auction page. After the auction, the seller should initiate the escrow by going to www.escrow.com or to the eBay services page by clicking the Services link in the eBay navigation bar. After you arrive at the Services page, scroll down and click the Escrow Services link under Payments. On the resulting page, shown in Figure 13-3, click the Start New Transaction button. You start the process by typing the eBay item number. To proceed with escrow, the buyer must send payment to Escrow.com. Escrow.com accepts all credit cards (including American Express and Discover), cashier's checks, money orders, wire transfers, and personal or business checks. A check is subject to a 10-day delay.

After the buyer makes the payment, Escrow.com asks the seller to ship the item to the buyer. When the buyer receives the merchandise, the inspection period begins promptly at 12:01 a.m. the next weekday and continues for a time previously set by the buyer and seller.

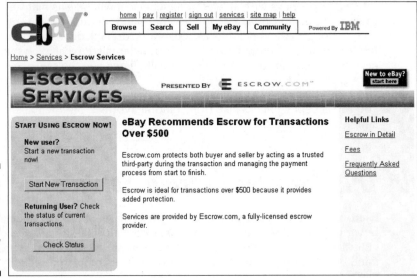

Figure 13-3:
Starting an
escrow with
Escrow.com
at eBay
services.

The buyer notifies Escrow.com that the merchandise is approved, and then Escrow.com releases payment to the seller. If the buyer doesn't feel that the merchandise is what he or she ordered, the buyer must return the item to the seller in its original condition, adhering to the Escrow.com shipping requirements. The buyer also must log on to the Web site to input return shipping information.

In the event of a return, the seller has the same inspection period to ensure that the item was returned in its original condition. After that is confirmed, Escrow.com will refund the buyer (less the escrow fee and, if agreed on ahead of time, the shipping fee). Either the buyer or the seller can pay the escrow fee; the two can even split the cost. But you need to decide who will pay the fee up front and indicate this in your auction listing. The buyer is responsible for paying the escrow fee for all returns, no matter who had initially agreed to pay the fees.

In Table 13-3, I include a listing of the escrow fees. (Credit cards are not accepted for payments of more than $7,500.00.)

Table 13-3	Escrow.com Escrow Fees		
Transaction Amount	**Check or Money Order**	**Credit Card**	**Wire Transfer**
Up to $1500.00	$22.00 + 0.5%	$22.00 + 3.0%	$37.00 + 0.5%
$1500.01–$7,500.00	2%	4.5%	$15.00 + 2.0%
$7,500.01–$20,000.00	1.75%	n/a	$15.00 + 1.75%
$20,0000.01 and up	1.5%	n/a	$15.00 + 1.5%

Helping your buyers buy safely

To boost sales and avoid having to deal with escrow delays, why not bond your eBay sales? Surety bonding has been used for about 5000 years to guarantee business transactions between buyers and sellers who don't know each other. A new service, buySAFE, bonds select sellers (through the Hartford insurance company) to guarantee their eBay transactions up to $10,000. Shoppers like seeing a guarantee; when they see a BuySAFE seal on your listings, they get just what they want.

To be eligible for the buySAFE seal, you must pass a rigorous check, which proves to buySAFE that you're a solid seller. After you get your seal and bond your transactions, you'll be charged 1% of your final selling price for the bonding. I've found that the seal easily boosts my bids by 1%, so it works for me. For more details and an introductory offer for readers of this book, check out their site at www.buysafe.com/coolebaytools.

Sadly, escrow service has become one of the most highly publicized scams on the Internet. Unscrupulous sellers set up fake escrow sites, sell a bunch of high dollar items on eBay to unsuspecting buyers, and then direct the buyers to the faux escrow Web site to set up their escrow. The buyers send their money (thinking the transaction is safe). After the fraudulent seller collects a bunch of money, they shut down the Web site and abscond with the money! Many buyers are gun-shy of using escrow to pay for expensive items. Consider bonding your transactions to lure higher bids and confer a guarantee to the buyer. (Read the details in the "Helping your buyers buy safely" sidebar.)

I Take Plastic: Credit Cards

As people become more comfortable with using credit cards on the Internet, credit cards become more popular for eBay payments. Plus, major credit card payment services have insured eBay payments to registered users, making credit cards safe for the buyer and easy for you. Credit card transactions are instantaneous; you don't have to wait for a piece of paper to travel cross-country.

For all this instantaneous money transfer, however, you pay a price. Whether you have your own *merchant account* (a credit card acceptance account in the name of your business) or take credit cards through a payment service (more on this in a minute), you pay a fee. Your fees can range from 2% to 7%, depending on how you plan to accept cards and which ones you accept. Unfortunately, many states have made it illegal to charge a credit card surcharge to make up this difference. You have to write off the expense of accepting credit cards as part of your business budget.

The fees brick and mortar stores pay for accepting credit cards are much less than those paid by online, mail, or phone orders. In most promotional material, the vendor usually quotes the "swiped card" rates. Because you won't have the buyer's card in hand to swipe, be sure to inquire with your provider for the proper rate before signing any papers.

I have to explain the downside of accepting credit cards for your online sales. To protect yourself, please be sure to check the feedback — both feedback they've received and feedback they've left — of all bidders before accepting any form of credit card payment for a high-ticket item. Some buyers are chronic complainers and are rarely pleased with their purchases. They may not be satisfied with your item after it ships. In that case, they can simply call their credit card company and get credit for the payment; you'll be charged back (your account will be debited) the amount of the sale. (See the "Forget the buyer: Seller beware!" sidebar in this chapter.)

Credit card payment services

Person-to-person payment systems, such as eBay's PayPal and Yahoo PayDirect, allow buyers to authorize payments from their credit cards or checking accounts directly to the seller. These services make money by charging percentages and fees for each transaction. It all happens electronically through an automated clearinghouse — no fuss, no muss. The payment service releases to the seller only the buyer's shipping information; all personal credit card information is kept private. This speeds up the time it takes the buyer to get merchandise because sellers are free to ship as soon as the service lets them know that the buyer has made payment and the payment has been processed.

From the seller's point of view, person-to-person payment service transaction fees are lower than the 2.5 to 3.5 percent (per transaction) that traditional credit card companies charge for merchant accounts.(Get the details in the "Your very own merchant account" section, coming up.) Even traditional retailers may switch their online business to these services to save money. In this section, I discuss the top payment services and how each works.

Before you decide which credit card payment service to use, get out your calculator and check their Web sites for current rates. Calculate your own estimates; don't rely on a site's advertised samples. I've found that the charts on the Web tend to leave out certain minor fees. I've found also that comparison charts quoting the competition's prices tend to include optional fees. Beware — and do your own math.

When you pay the fee to your payment service, realize that the total amount of your transaction — including shipping fees, handling charges, and any sales tax that you charge — incurs a fee. The payment service charges a percentage based on the total dollar amount that's run through its system.

Forget the buyer: Seller beware!

When buyers dispute a sale, they can simply call PayPal or their credit card company and refuse to pay for the item. You lose the sale and possibly won't be able to retrieve your merchandise. A payment service or merchant account will then *chargeback* your account without contacting you and without negotiating. Technically, the buyer has made the purchase from the payment service — not from you — and the payment service won't defend you. I've heard of chargebacks occurring as long as six months after the transaction, although eBay says they can occur no later than 60 days after they sent you the first bill on which the transaction or error appeared. No one is forcing the buyer to ship the merchandise back to you. Just like eBay Fraud Protection (see Chapter 3), the credit card companies skew the rules to defend the consumer. As the seller, you have to fend for yourself. See Chapter 4 on how to report fraudulent buyers. You usually have no way to verify that the shipping address is the one the credit card bills to. So, to add to your problems, the card may actually be stolen.

PayPal confirms through AVS (Address Verification Service) that the buyer's credit card billing address matches the shipping address and gives you the option to not accept payments from buyers whose addresses don't match. PayPal offers seller protection against spurious chargebacks under the following circumstances:

✔ Fraudulent card use

✔ False claims of non-delivery

✔ False claims of non-delivery

See the section on PayPal for more details on how to be covered by seller protection.

If the issuing bank resolves a chargeback in the buyer's favor, PayPal charges you $10 if you're determined to be at fault but will waive the fee if you meet all of the requirements of the PayPal Seller Protection policy.

Here's some good news: Major credit card companies are trying to curb online fraud for their merchant accounts. Visa has the new Verified by Visa acceptance, which takes buyers to a Visa screen (through software installed on the merchant's server) and verifies their identity through a Visa-only password. MasterCard uses SET (Secure Electronic Transactions), a similar encrypted transaction verification scheme. These systems are expected to substantially reduce fraud and chargebacks.

PayPal

PayPal is the largest of the online person-to-person payment services. Thankfully, eBay had the presence of mind to acquire this previously independent service, so it has now become the de facto standard for eBay payments.

PayPal (see Figure 13-4) allows buyers to safely click and pay with a credit card or e-check directly from eBay after they've won an auction or made a purchase. It's conveniently integrated into all eBay transactions. If your auction uses the Buy It Now feature or is a fixed-price listing, buyers can pay for their purchases immediately with PayPal payments.

Figure 13-4:
The PayPal
home page.

To accept credit card payments, you must have a premier or business level
account. Buyers may join when they win their first auction and want to pay
with PayPal, or they can go to www.PayPal.com and sign up. The story's
slightly different for the seller. You need to set up your PayPal account *before*
you choose to accept it in your auctions or sales.

Here are more than a few particulars about PayPal accounts:

- ✔ Auction payments are deposited into your PayPal account. Choose one
  of several ways to get your money:
- ✔ Have the money transferred directly into your registered checking account.
- ✔ Receive payment by check (PayPal charges $1.50 for the check).
- ✔ Keep the money in your PayPal account for making payments to other
  sellers.
- ✔ Withdraw the cash from an ATM with a PayPal debit card and get back
  1.5% of the money spent on purchases.
- ✔ Shop online with a virtual MasterCard that carries your balance to any
  Web site that accepts MasterCard.
- ✔ PayPal has its own feedback system, the Buyer Community Participation
  Number. The number after a user's name reflects the number of unique
  PayPal Verified users with whom this user has done business. The higher
  the number, the more likely the user is experienced and trustworthy.
  Clicking the number produces a report like the one shown in Figure 13-5.

Member Information

About **The Collier Company, Inc:**

To protect your security, PayPal offers information on the status of this member.

Seller Reputation:	(1020) Verified Buyers
Account Status:	Verified
Account Type:	U.S. Business
Account Creation Date:	Feb. 2, 2000
PayPal Member For:	4 years 3 months

• Member may choose to deny payments without a Confirmed Address

Business URL: http://www.coolebaytools.com

Cust. Service Email:

Seller Reputation
The Seller Reputation Number measures how many Verified PayPal members have paid that seller. New transactions are added 30 days after they occur, to ensure that the Reputation Number reflects successful exchanges.

Account Status
U.S. Users are considered "Verified" if they have confirmed the bank account they have added to their PayPal account. Verification is a positive signal to the Community that a user has complied with Community security measures.

Account Type
Accounts can be Personal, Premier, or Business. Active sellers are required to have a Premier or Business account.

Figure 13-5:
My PayPal Member Information box.

✔ As a seller with a premier or business account, you can choose to accept or deny a payment without a confirmed address. A confirmed address means that the ship to address indicated by the buyer is the same as the billing address on the credit card the buyer chose to register with PayPal. On the accept or deny page, information about the buyer is shown, including verification status, account creation date, and participation number.

✔ PayPal assesses your account $10 for any chargeback. The fee is waived if you've fulfilled the requirements in the PayPal Seller Protection policy (see next point). To specify whether you want to accept a credit card payment from a buyer without a confirmed address, log on, go to your account, and then click the Profile tab. Next, scroll down Selling Preferences and click Payment Receiving Preferences. If you accept payment from a non-confirmed address, that transaction will not be covered by the PayPal Seller Protection policy.

✔ The PayPal Seller Protection policy protects you against chargebacks, unauthorized card use, and non-shipments. To comply with this policy, you must do the following:

• Be a verified member of PayPal: Allow PayPal to confirm with your bank that your checking account and address is your own.

• Ship only to a confirmed address: PayPal confirms that the buyer's ship to address coincides with the address to which the credit company sends monthly bills. Fraudulent shoppers often ask you to ship to another address — don't do it.

- Keep proof of shipping that can be tracked online: Here's where those delivery confirmation things come in handy. See Chapter 14 to see how you can get them for free.

- Ship tangible goods: PayPal doesn't cover goods that are transmitted electronically.

- Accept only single payments from a single account: Don't let a buyer try to pay portions of a purchase from different e-mail addresses. Someone who's trying to pay using several accounts may be attempting to defraud you.

- Ship PayPal purchases only to United States buyers at United States addresses: Seller protection isn't extended to international shipments.

In June 2004, PayPal changed the tiers for seller's fees. Seller's fee tiers are now adjusted based on the prior month's transaction volume. Look at Table 13-4 for the updated PayPal fee tiers. However, if you were receiving the 2.2% merchant rate (pus $.30 per transaction) on your PayPal transactions before June 15, 2004, your fees are grandfathered through August 6, 2005.

Table 13-4	PayPal Domestic (U.S.) Fees		
Standard Rate	*Merchant Account Tiers*		
$0.00–$3000.00	*$3,000.01–$10,000.00*	*$10,000.01–$100,000.00*	*> $100,000.00*
2.9%+$0.30	2.5%+$0.30	2.2%+$0.30	1.9%+$0.30

A brilliant feature of PayPal is the ability to download your sales and deposit history to your computer. Although PayPal also offer files that integrate with QuickBooks, (more on QuickBooks in Chapter 16), the standard downloads are feature-rich. Rather than importing just sales figures, you see each and every detail of your transaction — dates, names, addresses, phone numbers, amounts, and more. Even fees and taxes (if you charge sales tax) are broken down separately, making bookkeeping a breeze. The download imports into Microsoft Works and Excel. Downloading you history will help you calculate income taxes and sales taxes, reconcile your accounts, predict sales trends, calculate total revenues, and perform other financial reporting tasks. It will also give you an excellent customer data base.

The deposits download will give you detailed information for all the deposits that you receive: payments, PayPal transaction and deposit fees, refunds, rebates, and any adjustments made to your account.

Follow these steps to download your sales and deposit histories:

1. On your PayPal Main Overview page, click to the History tab.

2. **Click the <u>Download My History</u> link, on the right side of the page.**

3. **Enter the time span and the file format for the information that you want to view.**

4. **Click the Download History button.**

    The information appears on the screen. Or if the servers are busy, you'll receive an e-mail (usually in a minute or two) when the reports are ready.

5. **Save the file in a directory that you can conveniently access for bookkeeping.**

You can just double-click the file to open it in Excel or Works. You now have all the information you could possibly need to apply to your bookkeeping program.

Registering with PayPal

If you aren't registered with PayPal yet (what's holding you up?), use the convenient <u>Selling</u> link on the All Selling page, which you reach from your My eBay page. To get more information, just click the <u>PayPal</u> link to arrive at the PayPal Seller Overview page (see Figure 13-6), and then click the Sign Up button to begin registration. The registration form in Figure 13-7 appears. Tell them what country you're from, fill in the basic required information, and you're in.

Figure 13-6:
The PayPal
Seller
Overview
page.

Figure 13-7:
The new
seller
registration
page.

The convenience of PayPal integration into the eBay site shines when your item is purchased. Winners just click a Pay Now button that pops up on your auction page immediately after the listing closes. When you list auctions, you pre-set the shipping and handling charges that appear in the shipping box at the bottom of the page. When winners click the Pay Now button (see Figure 13-8), they're taken directly to a payment page set up with your information. The process is as easy as purchasing something through Buy It Now.

Figure 13-8:
The Pay
Now button
appears
when the
buyer wins.

When a purchase is made and the payment is deposited in your PayPal account, the system holds the money until you choose how you want to withdraw it.

PayPal accepts payments from 38 foreign countries. For a current list of countries from which PayPal accepts payments, sign on to your PayPal account and go to

```
www.paypal.com/us/cgi-bin/webscr?cmd=_display-approved-
              signup-countries
```

Because credit card and identity theft is so prevalent on the Internet — and an expensive burden to e-commerce — PayPal uses the extra security measure provided by Visa and MasterCard called CVV2. Most credit cards have three additional numbers listed on the back, immediately following the regular 16-digit number. Merchants use these numbers for security or verification but aren't allowed to store them, so they're presumably protected from hackers. However, in the unlikely event your credit card doesn't have these numbers yet, PayPal still allows you to use your card by verifying it through a procedure known as *random charge*. PayPal charges about $1 or so to your card and asks you to disclose the pin number printed on your statement. Then PayPal knows that you control the card and didn't steal it.

Withdraw your funds from the PayPal account on a regular basis; you need that money to operate your business. Don't let it become a temporary savings account — unless you choose the PayPal interest-bearing account (check out www.PayPal.com for more details). Also, any money you have in your account can be extricated for a chargeback — and chargebacks can be applied as many as 60 days after the transaction. For more about chargebacks, see the "Forget the buyer: Seller beware!" sidebar, in this chapter.

Yahoo! PayDirect

A joint venture between Yahoo! and HSBC Bank USA, Yahoo! PayDirect is a payment service with a twist: You can receive payment for any of your auctions whether they're on Yahoo! or eBay. To sign up, go to www.yahoo.com and click the PayDirect link. To pay for auction winnings, your buyers simply click an HTML link that you insert in your auctions.

Yahoo! PayDirect charges transaction fees, just like PayPal, as shown in Table 13-5. But they also charge a monthly account fee (see the next paragraph).

Table 13-5	Yahoo! PayDirect Transaction Fees
Premier or Business	*Fee*
Standard rate	2.4% + $.30
Preferred rate	2.2% + $.30

Yahoo! PayDirect charges a $5.00 monthly service fee for the privilege of having an account. If your monthly account balance is $5.00 or more, they will deduct the fee from your account. If your balance is less than $5.00, the fee is deducted from your linked and verified bank account. If your balance is less than $5.00 and you don't have a verified bank account linked to your PayDirect account, the fee will be charged to your linked credit card.

Yahoo! also offers a logo that you can insert into your auctions. Just copy the supplied HTML coding into your eBay auction description, as shown in Figure 13-9, if you want to offer your buyers the option of paying through PayDirect.

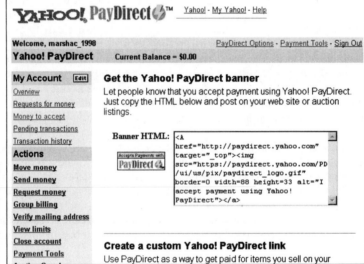

Figure 13-9: Yahoo! PayDirect auction logo generator.

Your very own merchant account

If your eBay business is bringing in more than $20,000 a month, a credit card merchant account may be for you. At that level of sales, discounts kick in and your credit card processing becomes a savings to your business rather than an expense. Before setting up a merchant account, however, I recommend that you look at the costs carefully. I get at least one e-mail each week begging me to set up my own merchant account, and each one offers lower fees than the last. But charges buried in the small print make fees hard to calculate and even harder to compare. Even those who advertise low fees often don't deliver. Be sure to look at the entire picture before you sign a contract.

The best place to begin looking for a merchant account may be your own bank, where they know you, your credit history, and your business reputation and have a stake in the success of your business. If your credit isn't up to snuff, I recommend building good credit before pursuing a merchant account because your credit rating is your feedback to the offline world.

If your bank doesn't offer merchant accounts for Internet-based businesses, find a broker to evaluate your credit history and hook you up with a bank that fits your needs and business style (or join Costco as a last resort; see the following section). These brokers make their money from your application fee, from a finder's fee from the bank that you finally choose, or both.

After you get a bank, you'll be connected to a *processor,* or transaction clearinghouse. Your bank merely handles the banking; the clearinghouse is on the other end of your Internet connection when you're processing transactions, checking whether the credit card you're taking is valid and not stolen or maxed out.

The next step is setting up your *gateway,* the software (ICVerify or PCAuthorize, for example) with which you transmit charges to the clearinghouse. Some gateways use HTML Web sites and take the transactions directly on Web-based forms (Cybercash or VeriFone, among others). Web-based gateways connect your Web forms to real-time credit card processing.

In Table 13-6, I highlight various possible costs associated with setting up and maintaining a merchant account.

Table 13-6	Possible Internet Merchant Account Fees
Fee	*Average Amount*
Setup fee	$25.00–$250.00
Monthly processing fee to bank	2.5% (1.5%–5%)
Fee per transaction	$.20–$.50
Processor's fee per transaction	$.35–$.50
Internet discount rate	2%–4%
Monthly statement fees	$9.00–$15.00
Monthly minimum processing fee	$15.00–$30.00
Gateway processing monthly fee	$20.00–$40.00
Application fees	$50.00–$500.00
Software purchase	$350.00–$1000.00
Software lease	$25.00 per month
Chargeback fee	$15.00

Remember that some merchant accounts will charge you some of these fees and others may have a bunch of little snipes at your wallet. In the following list, I define some of the fees in Table 13-6:

- ✔ **Setup fee:** A one-time cost that you pay to either your bank or to your broker.

- ✔ **Discount rate:** A percentage of the transaction amount (a discount from your earnings), taken off the top along with the transaction fee before the money is deposited into your account.

- ✔ **Transaction fee:** A fee per transaction that's paid to the bank or to your gateway for the network.

- ✔ **Gateway or processing fee:** Your fee for processing credit cards in real time that's paid to the Internet gateway.

- ✔ **Application fee:** A one-time fee that goes to the broker or perhaps to the bank.

- ✔ **Monthly minimum processing fee:** If your bank's cut of your purchases doesn't add up to this amount, the bank takes it anyway. For example, if your bank charges a minimum monthly fee of $20 and you don't hit $20 in fees because your sales aren't high enough, the bank charges you the difference.

If you're comfortable with all the information in the preceding list and in Table 13-6, and you're looking for a broker, heed my advice and read everything a broker offers carefully. Be sure you aren't missing any hidden costs.

Costco member's credit card processing

Here's some true discount credit card processing: a one-stop merchant account and gateway! You can not only buy tuna fish in bulk with a Costco membership but also obtain a reasonably priced way to handle a merchant account (check out Table 13-7) through the NOVA Network. Costco got together with Nova Information Systems, one of the nation's largest processors of credit card transactions, to offer Costco Executive members a discounted Internet credit card processing service. Costco Executive Membership brings the cost of a Costco membership up from $45 to $100, but you get the benefit of receiving 2% back for most purchases (not including tobacco, gas, food, and some other purchases).

Table 13-7	Fees for Costco Executive Member Internet Credit Card Processing*	
Fee	**Amount**	
Discount rate per transaction to NOVA	2.10%	
Transaction fee to NOVA per transaction	$.28	
NOVA monthly fee minimum	$20.00	

* You also need a gateway, in the form of software (such as PC Transact It) or a relationship with a gateway service.

To get any Internet commerce account, you should already have the following in place:

✔ Products and pricing

✔ A return and refund policy

✔ An active customer service phone number

✔ Posted delivery methods and shipment time

✔ A privacy policy stating that you will not share your customer's information with any other entity

✔ A registered domain in your name or the name of your business

✔ A secure order page with https and lock

To begin the application process, follow these steps:

1. **Go to** www.costco.com.

2. **At the top of the home page, click the <u>services</u> link.**

3. **Scroll to the Services for your Business area and click the <u>Merchant Credit Card Processing</u> link.**

   The page shown in Figure 13-10 appears.

4. **Read the information and Click the <u>Apply Now</u> link.**

5. **Type your Executive Membership number, and fill out the secure form.**

   Filling out the form speeds up the application process.

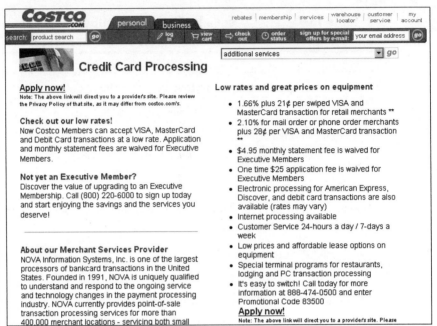

Figure 13-10:
The Costco merchant credit card processing service.

After sending your form, you'll receive a full application package by two-day air. A Costco representative will also contact you by telephone. For further information or to apply by phone, call Costco Member Services at 888-474-0500 and mention promotion code 83500.

The VeriSign Payflow link service

If you have less than 1000 transactions a month through eBay and your Web site, you may want to check out some of the services from VeriSign, a publicly traded company and the world's largest Internet trust service. A respected world-class company and the leader in its field, VeriSign offers gateway services at a reasonable price.

To participate, you must first sign up for a merchant account from your bank, from Costco, or by applying through the Payflow preferred Merchant Account providers. The VeriSign Payflow service picks it up from there. You can integrate the Payflow service directly into your Web site. When you send out your winner's congratulatory letter, include a link to the page on your site that links to VeriSign. When your orders are submitted to VeriSign for processing, both you and your customer receive a transaction receipt acknowledgement through e-mail when the transaction has been processed. VeriSign processes your transactions while you're online.

VeriSign changes a $179 setup fee as well as $19.95 a month for up to 500 transactions. Additional transactions cost $.10 each. For more information, go to the following:

```
www.verisign.com/products/payflow/link/index.html
```

Chapter 14

Getting It from Your Place to Theirs

. . . .

In This Chapter

▶ Examining shipping options and costs

▶ Exploring private insurance

. . . .

I think the best part of eBay is making the sale and receiving payment. After that comes the depressing and tedious process of fulfilling your orders. You shouldn't feel bad if this is the point that makes you take pause and sigh. Order fulfillment is one of the biggest problems (and yuckiest chores) that face any mail order or online enterprise. The onerous task of packing and mailing is the bane of almost all businesses.

But as an eBay businessperson, you *must* attend to these tasks, however much you'd rather not. So in Chapter 17, I detail what you need for packing (boxes, bubble pack, and so on) and some options for purchasing online postage. And in this chapter, I explain just how your items will get to their destinations, exploring your shipping options, costs, and insurance coverage along the way.

Finding the Perfect Shipping Carrier: The Big Three

When you're considering shipping options, you must first determine what types of packages you'll generally be sending (small packages that weigh less than two pounds or large and bulky packages) and then decide how you'll send your items. Planning this before listing the item is a good idea.

Deciding on your carrier can be the most important decision in your eBay business. You need to decide which one is more convenient for you (close to your home base, provides pick up service, gives better customer service) and which is the most economical (leverages your bottom line). Most eBay sellers send packages using ground service rather than airmail or overnight, but a shipper who can give you both options may be offering you a good deal because you don't have to deal with more than one vendor.

Settling on one main shipper to meet most of your needs is important because all your records will be on one statement or in one area. You might also need a secondary shipper for special types of packages. One shipper can't be everything to every business, so having an account with more than one can be to your advantage. Also, shippers may not sign up new accounts as readily in the middle of a strike or work slowdown.

In this section, I give you the lowdown on the three major carriers — FedEx Ground, UPS, and the US Postal Service (USPS) — so you can see who fits your requirements. For a summary of shipping costs from these three, see Table 14-1. Note that FedEx and UPS include tracking numbers for delivery confirmation. The USPS charges extra; delivery confirmation is $.45 for Priority Mail and $.55 for Media Mail and Parcel Post. For info on eliminating these fees, see the "Free delivery confirmation" section, later in this chapter. Also check out Chapter 17 for more information.

Table 14-1	Shipping Costs from Coast to Coast (Residence Delivery)			
Delivery Service	*2 lbs.*	*5 lbs.*	*10 lbs.*	*15 lbs.*
FedEx Home Delivery (4 days)	$6.36	$7.61	$9.59	$12.71
UPS Residential (5 days)	$8.35	$10.10	$12.85	$17.25
USPS Priority Mail (2 days)	$5.75	$12.15	$19.20	$27.80
USPS Media Mail (7 days)	$1.84	$3.10	$4.84	$6.34
USPS Parcel Post (7 days)	$4.49	$9.43	$18.14	$22.64

You can now prepare UPS or USPS shipping documents online through PayPal. See Chapter 17 for the ins and outs (and pros and cons) of shipping through PayPal.

When you start shipping a few dozen packages a week, you might want to check out *eBay Timesaving Techniques For Dummies*, by yours truly, for an in-depth analysis of the big three and their variable shipping rates.

Shipping the BIG stuff!

When it comes to shipping heavy or big stuff, you have a couple of options. Because I like using FedEx, I check FedEx Freight first. My husband once purchased four large heavy equipment tires on eBay, and there was no way they could go with a regular carrier. We called FedEx Freight and told the seller to place the tires on a pallet and secure them. FedEx Freight picked them up. Shipping was reasonable, but the only caveat was that the shipment had to be delivered to a place of business, not a residential location.

A Web site called www.freightquote.com negotiates rates with several major freight forwarders. Before attempting to sell a heavy item, you can sign onto their Web site with the weight and dimensions of your shipment, and they'll give you a free quote on the spot.

Federal Express

Federal Express (FedEx) is world famous for its reliable service. It's the number-one choice for all major companies who "Absolutely, positively have to get it there on time." FedEx also has a reputation for some of the highest costs in the business — but only to the untrained eye. FedEx acquired Roadway Package Service (RPS) and formed FedEx Ground, which has a separate division called FedEx Home Delivery that delivers to residences. For the services they provide, you'll be happy to pay what you do. Read on.

FedEx Ground and Home Delivery

When Home Delivery began, their slogan was "The neighborhood friendly service that fits the way we live, work, and shop today." Although I rarely get warm fuzzies from my package delivery, this slogan brought meaning to the philosophy behind their service: to bring professional shipping to your home residence. FedEx Home Delivery offers low rates and a high-quality service. They're the only shipper that offers a money-back guarantee on home service. They deliver until 8 p.m. *and* on Saturdays, but not on Monday.

To open an account, visit the FedEx Home Delivery Web site, shown in Figure 14-1, at

```
www.fedex.com/us/services/ground/us/homedelivery
```

Even if you have a current Federal Express account, you need to sign on to add the Ground service (which includes Home Delivery). Registering for Ground service is even easier than registering on eBay, so give it a shot.

Figure 14-1:
The FedEx
Home
Delivery
home page.

I opened my FedEx Home Delivery account through a link on the main FedEx home page, and got the skinny on how to use the service. The online calculator allows you to choose the option of Home Delivery, so you don't even have to look up alternative rates and charts. And just as other shippers do, FedEx Home Delivery gives you a service schedule to let you know how long it will take your package to arrive at its destination (see Figure 14-2).

Figure 14-2:
The FedEx
Home
Delivery
service
schedule
from Los
Angeles to
New York.

Here are a few fast facts about FedEx Ground and Home Delivery services:

- ✔ You print out your own labels and barcodes for your packages and track them online.

- ✔ FedEx Home Delivery works on a zone system based on your zip code and how far the package is going. Refer to the FedEx Home Delivery zone chart or get the cost online through the online calculator.

- ✔ Each shipment is covered for $100.00 in declared value. Additional insurance is $.35 per $100.00 or a fraction thereof.

- ✔ Residential deliveries are limited to 70-pound packages.

- ✔ Daily pick-up service adds an additional weekly charge of $10.00 to your account.

- ✔ Dropping off packages at Federal Express counters incurs no additional charge.

- ✔ FedEx Home Delivery delivers Tuesday through Saturday till 8 p.m.

If FedEx Ground shipping charges seem to be a great deal, they are! But you can get an even better deal if you charge your FedEx shipping to an American Express Business card (one that gives you access to the American Express Open Network). You save an additional 5% on all FedEx Ground shipments when you use online shipping and place your orders online. If you have such a card, be sure it is officially linked so you get the discount. Call the FedEx/ Open Network desk at 1-800-231-8636.

FedEx Online

FedEx has one of the most intuitive online applications for shipping. The FedEx Ship Manager interface will turn your computer into a one-person shipping shop. You can generate labels for all forms of FedEx in one place. The site allows you to search for rate quotes and track packages, and it includes a shipping notification option to send tracking information e-mail to your recipients.

Larger businesses can get the Ship Manager workstation, complete with PC and printers. The workstation has the unique ability to choose from other carriers. Aside from FedEx Express and FedEx Ground, you can also access UPS shipping services, which allow you to rate, track, report, and ship for multiple carriers on one system.

United Parcel Service

Everyone's familiar with the big brown trucks that tool around town delivering packages hither and yon. Those trucks belong to the United Parcel Service, or UPS, whose home page is shown in Figure 14-3.

Figure 14-3:
The UPS
hub.

UPS offers three levels of service based on your shipping needs:

- ✔ **Internet account:** Print your own bar-coded labels so that you can drop off packages at the UPS counter (you can also do that without an account) or give packages to a UPS driver. You can also use Internet account rates when shipping through PayPal.

- ✔ **Occasional shipper account:** Use UPS for the rare large box or heavy shipment. An occasional shipper can call UPS for a next-day pick-up. You have to pay an additional $4 per package for the driver to pick up from you if you don't feel like bringing the package to the UPS local counter.

- ✔ **Pick-up account:** When you hit the big time, you're able to get the lowest UPS rates and have a driver make daily stops to pick up your packages. Fees for a pick-up account run from $7 to $16 per week (based on the amount of packages you ship each week) over the cost of your package shipping.

For big shippers, UPS offers its Application Program Interface (API), which can be integrated into a company's home servers.

To register for UPS online, go to

```
www.ups.com/content/us/en/index.jsx
```

After typing your personal or business information and answering a few basic questions, *UPS* will decide what account is right for you. By registering, you can also track packages and ship online. You can sign up for an account also through PayPal.

Here are some quick facts about UPS:

- ✔ Shipping with UPS requires that you pay a different rate for different zones in the country (zones 1–8). The cost of your package is based on its weight, your zip code (where the package ships from), and the addressee's zip code (where the package is going). To figure out your cost, use the handy UPS cost calculator shown in Figure 14-4.

- ✔ UPS offers a chart that defines the shipping time for your ground shipments.

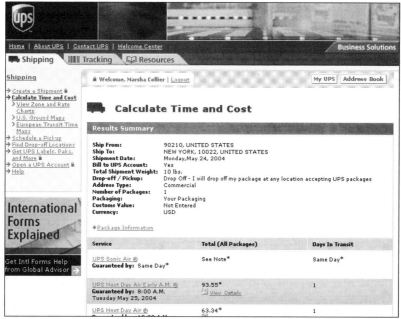

Figure 14-4: The UPS cost calculator.

✔ Each package has a tracking number that you can input online to verify location and time of delivery.

✔ Delivery to a residence costs over $1.00 per pound more than delivery to a commercial location.

✔ UPS delivers packages Monday through Friday.

✔ $100.00 in insurance is included with every shipment. For valuations over $100.00, insurance costs an additional $.35 cents per $100.00.

United States Postal Service

Whether you call it snail mail, pops (plain old postal service), or whatever nickname you like, the United States Postal Service has been delivering the mail since 1775, when our first postmaster (Benjamin Franklin) took the reins. The USPS has attempted to get every piece of mail delivered to every part of our country. Check out its Web site in Figure 14-5.

The USPS is open to everyone. You don't have to set up an account to use its services. To get a basic idea of what you'll pay to send a package, you can access a rate calculator on the USPS Web site (`www.usps.gov`). The post office provides many services; in this section, I go over the most popular forms of mail used by eBay sellers.

Figure 14-5: The United States Postal Service Web site.

Priority Mail

The two-to-three-day Priority Mail service is the most popular form of shipping for eBay packages. You can get free cartons, mailing tape, and labels from the post office. (See Chapter 17 for a complete list of what the USPS supplies for your mailing needs.) You can also print postage online through endicia.com or stamps.com (see Chapter 17 again).

The Priority Mail rates are perfect for one-pound packages ($3.85 flat rate cross-country) and two-pound packages (from $3.95, based on distance). They also have a flat-rate Priority envelope in which you can jam as much as possible (regardless of the package's final weight) for $3.85.

The Priority Mail rates (including free shipping materials) are attractive until you get into heavier packages (refer to Table 14-1). Also, if you don't print your postage online, delivery confirmation costs you an additional $.45 for Priority Mail ($.55 for Parcel Post and Media Mail). Delivery confirmation tells you only *if* the package was delivered; it doesn't trace the package along its route.

Media Mail

To stay new and hip, the post office has renamed its old Book Rate to Media Mail, causing many eBay sellers to mistakenly miss out on this valuable mailing tool. The savings are immense (refer to Table 14-1). The drawback is that you must mail only books, cassettes, videos, or computer-readable media. Transit time on Media Mail is seven days, but the cost savings on heavy packages are worth it.

Parcel Post

If you want to use USPS and have a heavy package (up to 70 pounds) that doesn't fit the requirements for Media Mail, use Parcel Post. However, USPS Parcel Post rates don't cut it when you compare them to the UPS or FedEx Ground rates.

USPS Application Program Interface

If you want to print your own postage, you can use USPS Click-N-Ship, endicia. com, or stamps.com — that is, unless you're a large corporation and you'd like to incorporate the Post Office tools into your own Web site. USPS has an application program interface (API) that allows your Web site to interact with the USPS servers, as shown in Figure 14-6. With this software, big businesses can get delivery confirmation (among other services) at no charge and print their own barcodes.

The integration of USPS APIs isn't for the meek and small (like me — and maybe you?), but you can go to a reliable independent source for the little guy. See the following section on Shippertools.com.

Figure 14-6:
USPS
Web Tools
Documenta-
tion Center.

Free delivery confirmation

A couple of pros that understand APIs and delivery confirmation stuff have
licensed the post office API (see the preceding section) and are offering its
use through a simple Web interface. Shippertools.com has developed a site
where you can get *free* (that's right — *free*) delivery confirmations on all of
your USPS Priority Mail shipments. In addition, its system verifies shipping
addresses through the post office servers, tracks your shipments in a handy
online worksheet, and keeps an online address book for you. It even works
when you're shipping from more than one location.

The best part of the service is the convenient interface, which allows you to
store all your shipping information and check the delivery of shipped packages with a click of your mouse.

The nice folks at Shippertools.com do need a little something to cover server
costs and their fine work, so you have to fork over $6.95 a month for unlim-
ited delivery confirmations. You have to ship more than 16 packages per
month for the service to pay for itself — but reaching that goal won't be a
problem after you're through with this book.

You don't have to purchase any fancy software or labels. After you sign up
with Shippertools.com (see Figure 14-7), your computer receives a barcode

and delivery confirmation number direct from the USPS servers. Just print it on plain white paper and tape it to your package with clear packing tape. It's that easy!

Figure 14-7:
The Shippertools .com sign-in home page.

Look at Table 14-2 to see how much this service can save you — not counting the time you save not waiting in post office lines.

Table 14-2	Shippertools.com Delivery Confirmation Savings per Month	
Priority Mail Packages Shipped per Month (at $.45 Each)	*Total USPS Charge*	*Shippertools.com (at $6.95 Monthly) Saves You*
25	$11.25	$4.30
50	$22.50	$15.55
100	$45.00	$38.05
200	$90.00	$83.05
300	$135.00	$128.05

Protecting Packages with Universal Parcel Insurance Coverage

If you think that printing your own postage is slick, you're gonna love the Universal Parcel Insurance Coverage (U-PIC), a service that automates the post office insurance hassle. U-PIC has been in the package insurance business since 1989, mainly insuring packages for large shippers. U-PIC has expanded its business to the online auction arena, and you can insure packages that you send through USPS, UPS, FedEx, and other major carriers. If you use its insurance on USPS-shipped packages, you can save as much as 80 percent on insurance rates. If you use U-PIC, you can stop purchasing insurance for your packages with your carriers.

The U-PIC service also enables you to print your postage through an online postage service, and, if you have just a few packages, give them directly to your USPS mail carrier. (You don't have to stand in line to get your insurance form stamped.) If you have a ton of boxes, you'll need to drive them to the post office and shove them over the counter. No waiting in line, no hassle!

To apply for the U-PIC service, you must fill out a Request to Provide (RTP) form. Go to their Web site at www.u-pic.com and click the Apply link (see Figure 14-8). You must answer questions about who you are, how many packages you send, how many insurance claims you've filed in the past two years, and your average value per package.

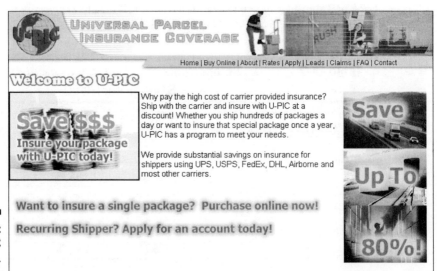

Figure 14-8: The U-PIC home page.

After you fill out the online form and agree to the policy (Evidence of Insurance), a U-PIC representative will contact you within 48 hours. The representative will answer your questions and help you decide which of their programs will work best for your eBay business. (I give you some details about these in just a bit.)

Your U-PIC sales representative will explain to you exactly how to declare value with U-PIC based on your present system. At the end of each shipping month, you fax, e-mail, or snail mail your shipping reports to U-PIC.

To place a claim with U-PIC on a USPS shipment, you must do so no sooner than 30 days after the date of mailing, and you must supply the following:

✔ A signed letter, stating the loss or damage from the consignee

✔ A copy of the monthly insurance report you turned in to U-PIC reflecting the insured value

✔ A completed U-PIC claim form (one claim form per claim)

✔ A copy of the original invoice or the end of auction form

Because you're paying for private insurance, U-PIC suggests that you include in the package a copy of your insurance policy (or at the very least a note explaining that you have an insurance policy covering your shipments) so that your buyer doesn't think you're overcharging (which makes some folks a bit cranky).

Table 14-3 compares U-PIC and USPS insurance rates. UPS charges $.35 per $100.00 package value (after the initial $100) — U-PIC charges only $.14 per $100.00 UPS shipment value. FedEx charges $.50 per $100 value with a $2.50 minimum. By using U-PIC, you can insure your FedEx packages for $.20 per $100.00 value.

Table 14-3	USPS and U-PIC Domestic Insurance Coverage Rate Comparison		
Coverage	*USPS*	*U-PIC Standard*	*U-PIC with USPS Delivery Confirmation*
$.01–$50.00	$1.10	$.75	$.50
$50.01–$100	$2.00	$.75	$.50
$100.01 to $200.00	$3.00	$1.50	$1.00
$200.01 to $300.00	$4.00	$2.25	$1.50
$300.01 to $400.00	$5.00	$3.00	$2.00

U-PIC will also insure international shipments. The cost to insure international USPS parcels is only $1.00 per $100.00, with no deductible.

If you're a high-volume shipper, you can negotiate an even lower rate with U-PIC. To reach U-PIC, call toll-free at 800-955-4623 or visit their Web site at www.u-pic.com.

Occasional shipper program

The occasional shipper program is for the person who ships one to five packages per month. You can pay for your insurance online using a credit card, but the rates are not as attractive as those for the standard program.

Offline standard program

The offline standard program is the service for eBay businesspeople who ship a large amount of packages per month. At the end of each shipping month, you generate an insurance report and use it to calculate your premium. You can pay the premium by check or through PayPal. You can get a discount when shipping with the post office when you use a delivery confirmation.

Part IV

Your eBay Back Office

The 5th Wave   By Rich Tennant

"I think we ought to check first to see if eBay has a category for 'Fertility gods: Ancient'."

In this part . . .

Setting up your eBay business as a real business entity involves some unpleasant paperwork, applying for licenses, organizing, and record keeping. Even though you should discuss your issues with a professional, I fill in the blanks and get you started on the right track. I also provide a handy checklist of the items you need to run your business online, such as your legal status, bookkeeping requirements, and software to automate shipping.

Chapter 15

Going Legit

In This Chapter

▶ Deciding your business format

▶ Covering the legalities

*B*usiness format? You ask, "What's a business format?" I hate to be the one to tell you: You can't just say, "I'm in business," and be in business. When you started selling on eBay, maybe you were happy just adding a few dollars to your income. Now that the money is coming in faster, you have a few more details to attend to. Depending how far you're going to take your business, you have to worry about taxes, bookkeeping, and possible ramifications down the line.

I want to remind you that I am *not* a lawyer or an accountant. The facts I give you in this chapter are from what I've learned over the years. When you begin a formal business, it's best to involve an attorney and an accountant or a CPA. At the very least, visit www.nolo.com, a great Web site that offers some excellent business startup advice and forms.

One of the first rules in the eBay User Agreement reads ". . . your eBay account (including feedback) and User Id may not be transferred or sold to another party." This means if you begin your business on eBay with another person, you'd better have some kind of agreement up front about who gets the user ID in case of a sale. And if you sell your business, the person with the original ID had better be involved actively with the new company — as the rules say, your feedback can never be transferred or sold. A new owner would have to start a new account on eBay with a new name — unless the principal from the old company was contractually involved and was the actual eBay seller.

To my knowledge, no one has tested this rule in court, and I'll bet you don't want to be the first to face eBay's top-notch lawyers. Know that this is the rule and plan for it.

Types of Businesses

Businesses come in several forms, from a sole proprietorship all the way to a corporation. A corporation designation isn't as scary as it sounds. Yes, Microsoft, IBM, and eBay are corporations, but so are many individuals running businesses. Each form of business has its plusses and minuses — and costs. I go over some of the fees involved in incorporating later in this chapter. For now, I detail the most common types of businesses, which I encourage you to weigh carefully.

Before embarking on any new business format, be sure to consult with a professional in the legal and financial fields.

Sole proprietorship

If you're running your business by yourself part-time or full-time, your business is a *sole proprietorship.* Yep, doesn't that sound official? A sole proprietorship is the simplest form of business. Nothing is easier or cheaper. Most people use this form of business when they're starting out. Many then graduate to a more formal type of business as things get bigger.

If a husband and wife file a joint tax return, they *can* run a business as a sole proprietorship (but only one of you can be the proprietor). However, if both you and your spouse work equally in the business, running it as a partnership — with a written partnership agreement — is a much better idea. (See the next section, "Partnership," for more information.) A partnership protects you in case of your partner's death. In a sole proprietorship, the business ends with the death of the proprietor. If the business has been a sole proprietorship in your late spouse's name, you may be left out in the cold.

Being in business adds a few expenses, but you can deduct from your state and federal taxes many of those expenses (relating to your business). A sole proprietorship *can* be run out of your personal checking account (although I don't advise it). The profits of your business are taxed directly as part of your own income tax, and the profits and expenses are reported on Schedule C of your tax package. As a sole proprietor, you're at risk for the business liabilities. All outstanding debts are yours, and you could lose personal assets if you default.

Also, you must consider the liability of the products you sell on eBay. If you sell foodstuff, vitamins, or neutraceuticals (new age food supplements) that make someone ill, you may be personally liable for any court-awarded damages. If someone is hurt by something you sell, you may also be personally liable as the seller of the product.

Partnership

When two or more people are involved in a business, it can be a *partnership*. A general partnership can be formed by an oral agreement. Each person in the partnership contributes capital or services and both share in the partnership's profits and losses. The income of a partnership is taxed to both partners, based on the percentage of the business that they own or upon the terms of a written agreement.

You'd better be sure that you can have a good working relationship with your partner: This type of business relationship has broken up many a friendship. Writing up a formal agreement when forming your eBay business partnership is an excellent idea. This agreement is useful in solving any disputes that may occur over time.

In your agreement, be sure to outline things such as

- ✔ How to divide the profits and losses
- ✔ Compensation to each of you
- ✔ Duties and responsibilities of each partner
- ✔ Restrictions of authority and spending
- ✔ How disputes should be settled
- ✔ What happens if the partnership dissolves
- ✔ What happens to the partnership in case of death or disability

One more important thing to remember: As a partner, you're jointly and severally responsible for the business liabilities and actions of the other person or people in your partnership — as well as your own. Again, this is a personal liability arrangement. You are both personally open to any lawsuits that come your way through the business.

The partnership has to file an informational return with the IRS and the state, but the profits of the partnership are taxed to the partners on their personal individual returns.

LLC (Limited Liability Company)

A *limited liability company,* or LLC, is similar to a partnership, but also has many of the characteristics of a corporation. An LLC differs from a partnership mainly in that the liabilities of the company are not passed on to the members (owners). Unless you sign a personal guarantee for debt incurred, the members are responsible only to the total amount they have invested into the company. But all members *do* have liability for the company's taxes.

You'll need to put together an operating agreement, similar to the partnership agreement. This also will help establish which members own what percentage of the company for tax purposes. Most states will require you to file Articles of Organization forms to start this type of business.

An LLC is taxed like a sole proprietorship, with the profits and losses passed on to the members' personal tax returns. An LLC may opt to pay taxes like a corporation and keep some of the profits in the company, thereby reducing the tax burden to the individual members. Although members pay the LLC's taxes, it must still file Form 1065 with the IRS at the end of the year. This gives the IRS extra data to be sure that the individual members properly report their income.

Corporation

A *corporation* has a life of its own: its own name, its own bank account, and its own tax return. A corporation is a legal entity created for the sole purpose of doing business. One of the main problems a sole proprietor faces when incorporating is realizing that he or she can't help themselves to the assets of the business. Yes, a corporation can have only one owner: the shareholder(s). If you can understand that you can't write yourself a check from your corporation, unless it's for salary or for reimbursement of legitimate expenses, you may be able to face the responsibility of running your own corporation.

The state in which you run your business sets up the rules for the corporations operating in its borders. You must apply to the Secretary of State of the state in which you want to incorporate. Federal taxes for corporations presently range from 15 to 35 percent, and they're generally based on your net profits. Often employee owners of corporations use the company to shelter income from tax by dividing the income between their personal and corporate tax returns. This is frequently called *income splitting* and involves setting salaries and bonuses so that any profits left in the company at the end of its tax year will be taxed at only the 15 percent rate. It's kind of fun to see how much the big guys pay and how much you'll pay in taxes if you leave profits in a small corporation, so check out Table 15-1 for the rates.

Getting your legal documents prepared online

You just *knew* legal services would go online eventually, didn't you? If you're thinking of setting up one of the business formats described in this chapter, you might be interested in putting things together online. Real lawyers are there to help you. A new venture, www.legalzoom.com, will handle legal document preparation for business incorporation, partnerships, and more for incredibly low prices. This online venture was developed by a group of experienced attorneys, co-founded by Robert Shapiro (yes, *that* Robert Shapiro — of O.J. fame).

They feature an amazing online law library that can answer many of your questions and help you make informed decisions. Documents are prepared according to how you answer online questionnaires, which are designed to cover most legal transactions. LegalZoom checks your work, and e-mails your documents or mails them printed on quality acid-free paper for your signature.

You may want to also do at least a phone consultation with an attorney in your area, perhaps one who is a member of the local Chamber of Commerce.

Table 15-1	Federal Tax Rates for Corporations
Taxable Income	*Tax Rate*
$0–$50,000	15%
$50,001–$75,000	25%
$75,001–$100,000	34%
$100,001–$335,000	39%
$335,001–$10,000,000	34%
$10,000,001–$15,000,000	35%
$15,000,001–$18,333,333	38%
$18,333,334 and more	35%

Often in small corporations, most of the profits are paid out in tax-deductible salaries and benefits. The most important benefit for a business is that any liabilities belong to the corporation. Your personal assets remain your own, because they have no part in the corporation.

Taking Care of Regulatory Details

Let me give you some important words to make your life easier in the long run: Don't ignore city, county, state, and federal regulatory details. Doing so may make life easier at the get-go, but if your business is successful, one day your casual attitude will catch up with you. Ignorance is no excuse. To do business in this great country, you must comply with all the rules and regulations that are set up for your protection and benefit.

Fictitious business name statement

If you plan on running your business under a name different from your own, you may have to file a *fictitious name statement* regardless of the legal format of your business. In most states, every person who regularly transacts business for profit under a fictitious business name must file. Depending on where you live, you generally file this form with the county clerk. After a certain length of time after you file, your fictitious name will be published in a newspaper that has a section of fictitious names in its classified section. Usually the newspaper files with county agencies and publishes for you in one procedure.

If you have a small community or neighborhood newspaper, check with it to see whether it files fictitious name statements. These newspapers also have the lowdown on all the licenses and certificates that you'll need for your locality. Choosing small newspapers to handle these issues for you is a smart idea because they tend to charge a lot less than big-city dailies. Plus, you get to help another small business in your area.

Business license or city tax certificate

Business licenses are the official-looking pieces of paper you see behind the register at local stores. Every business must have one, and depending on your local laws, you may have to have a *city license* or a *city tax registration certificate*. Yes, even if you're running a business out of your home and have no one coming to do business at your home, you may still need this. If you don't have one, the authorities may charge you a bunch of penalties if they ever find out. Avoiding this step isn't worth the risk.

To save you hanging on the phone, listening to elevator music, and being transferred and disconnected ad nauseam, I'm supplying you with the direct links to apply for your licenses. See Table 15-2. These URLs are accurate at the time of this writing, but as everybody knows, URLs change frequently. Check the following for updates:

```
www.sba.gov/hotlist/license.html
```

Table 15-2	Web Sites for Business License Information
State	*URL*
Alabama	www.alabama.gov/business/startbusiness.html
Alaska	www.dced.state.ak.us/occ/home.htm
Arizona	www.commerce.state.az.us/SmallBus/Default.asp
Arkansas	www.state.ar.us/business_res.php
California	www.calgold.ca.gov/
Colorado	www.colorado.gov/business.htm
Connecticut	www.ct-clic.com/business/business.htm
Delaware	www.state.de.us/dedo/small_business.html
District of Columbia	brc.dc.gov/whattodo/business/
Florida	sun6.dms.state.fl.us/dor/businesses/
Georgia	www.sos.state.ga.us/firststop
Guam	www.admin.gov.gu
Hawaii	www.hawaii.gov/dbedt/start/index.html
Idaho	www.idoc.state.id.us/business/idahoworks/substartbusiness.htm
Illinois	www.illinoisbiz.biz/bus/step_by_step.html
Indiana	www.state.in.us/sic/owners/ia.html
Iowa	www.iowasmart.com/blic/
Kansas	www.accesskansas.org/operating/

(continued)

Table 15-2 *(continued)*

State	URL
Kentucky	www.sos.ky.gov/ONESTOP/PROGRAM/onestop.asp
Louisiana	www.sec.state.la.us/comm/fss/fss-index.htm
Maine	www.econdevmaine.com/doing-biz.htm
Maryland	www.blis.state.md.us/BusinessStartup.aspx
Massachusetts	www.dor.state.ma.us/business/doingbus.htm
Michigan	www.michigan.gov/businessstartup
Minnesota	www.dted.state.mn.us/01x00f.asp
Mississippi	www.olemiss.edu/depts/mssbdc/going_intobus.html
Missouri	www.ded.mo.gov/business/startabusiness/
Montana	bizmt.com/bizassist/start.asp
Nebraska	www.nebraska.gov/business/html/337/index.phtml
Nevada	tax.state.nv.us/taxnew/forms.htm
New Hampshire	www.nhsbdc.org/startup.htm
New Jersey	www.state.nj.us/Business.shtml
New Mexico	www.edd.state.nm.us/nmbusiness/newbusiness/
New York	www.gorr.state.ny.us/gorr/Startbus.html
North Carolina	www.secretary.state.nc.us/blio/startbus.asp
North Dakota	www.growingnd.com/toolkit/
Ohio	www.sos.state.oh.us/sos/busiserv/index.html
Oklahoma	www.oktax.state.ok.us/oktax/busreg.html

State	URL
Oregon	www.filinginoregon.com/obg/index.htm
Pennsylvania	www.paopenforbusiness.state.pa.us
Rhode Island	www2.sec.state.ri.us/faststart/
South Carolina	www.myscgov.com/SCSGPortal/static/business_tem1.html
South Dakota	www.state.sd.us/drr2/newbusiness.htm
Tennessee	www.scoreknox.org/library/numbers.htm
Texas	www.tded.state.tx.us/guide/
Utah	www.utah.gov/business/starting.html
Vermont	www.thinkvermont.com/start/
Virgin Islands	www.usvi.org/dlca/index.html
Virginia	www.yesvirginia.org/corporate_location/vedpstart_a_business.aspx
Washington	www.dol.wa.gov/mls/startbus.htm
West Virginia	www.state.wv.us/taxrev/busreg.html
Wisconsin	www.wisconsin.gov/state/byb/
Wyoming	/uwadmnweb.uwyo.edu/SBDC/starting.htm

Sales tax number

If your state has a sales tax, a _sales tax number_ (the number you use when you file your sales tax statement with your state) is required before you officially sell anything. If sales tax applies, you may have to collect the appropriate sales tax for every sale that ships within the state that your business is in.

Some people also call this a _resale certificate_ because when you want to purchase goods from a wholesaler within your state, you must produce this number (thereby certifying your legitimacy) so that the dealer can sell you the merchandise without charging you sales tax.

To find the regulations for your state, try a couple of terrific sites that supply links to every state's tax board, which should have the answers to your questions:

- ✔ www.mtc.gov/txpyrsvs/actualpage.htm
- ✔ www.taxadmin.org/fta/link/forms.html

Don't withhold the withholding forms

Aye, caramba. I swear it feels like the rules and regulations are never going to end, but if you have regular employees, you need to file *withholding forms* to collect the necessary taxes that you must send to the state and the IRS on behalf of your employees. You're also expected to deposit those tax dollars with the IRS and your state on the date required, which may vary from business to business. Many enterprises go down because the owners just can't seem to keep their fingers out of withheld taxes, which means the money isn't available to turn in when the taxes are due (another reason why you should have a separate bank account for your business).

If you have employees, you probably need to get the following:

- ✔ **Federal Employee Tax ID number:** File IRS form SS-4. You can apply for this number online, by going to the following:

  www.irs.gov/businesses/small/article/0,,id=102767,00.html

  For more information, call 1-800-829-1040. For forms to fill out the old-fashioned way, call 1-800-829-3676.

- ✔ **State Employer number:** You need this for withholding taxes if your state has an income tax. Check the following site for more information:

  www.taxadmin.org/fta/forms.ssi

Chapter 16

Practicing Safe and Smart Record-Keeping

. . . .

In This Chapter

▶ Understanding first things first: bookkeeping basics

▶ Saving your records to save your bacon

▶ Finding bookkeeping software

▶ Using QuickBooks for your bookkeeping needs

. . . .

*B*ookkeeping, *bah!* You'll get no argument from me that bookkeeping can be the most boring and time-consuming part of your job. You may feel that you just need to add your product costs, add your gross sales, and bada-bing, you know where your business is. Sorry, not true. Did you add that roll of tape you picked up at the supermarket today? Although it cost only $1.29, it's a business expense. How about the mileage driving back and forth from garage sales and flea markets? Those are expenses, too. I suspect that you're also not counting quite a few other "small" items just like these in your expense column.

Once I actually get into the task, I must confess that I enjoy posting my expenses and sales. It gives me the opportunity to know exactly where my business is at any given moment. Of course, I'm not using a pencil-entered ledger system; I use a software program that's easy and fun. In this chapter, I give you the lowdown on the basics of bookkeeping, emphasize the impor-tance of keeping records in case Uncle Sam comes calling, and explain why using QuickBooks is the smart software choice. Keep reading: This chapter is *required*.

Keeping the Books: Basics That Get You Started

Although posting bookkeeping can be boring, clicking a button to generate your tax information is a lot easier than manually going over pages of sales information on a pad of paper. That's why I like to use a software program, particularly QuickBooks (more about that in the section titled "QuickBooks: Making Bookkeeping Uncomplicated").

I suppose that you *could* use plain ol' paper and a pencil to keep your books; if that works for you, great. But even though that might work for you now, it definitely won't in the future. Entering all your information into a software program now — while your books may still be fairly simple to handle — can save you a lot of time and frustration in the future, when your eBay business has grown beyond your wildest dreams and no amount of paper can keep it all straight and organized. I discuss alternative methods of bookkeeping in the "Bookkeeping Software" section. For now, I focus on the basics of bookkeeping.

Hiring a professional to do your year-end taxes

When I say that you must hire a professional to prepare your taxes, I mean a certified public accountant (CPA) if your business format is a corporation or an enrolled agent (EA) for a sole proprietorship or partnership. An *enrolled agent* is a tax professional who's licensed by the Federal Government and specializes solely in taxation and current tax laws. Enrolled agents must pass an annual two-day exam (less than a third of the people who take the test pass it) and are required to fulfill continuing education requirements to maintain their standing. Just like a CPA or a tax attorney, EAs are authorized to appear before the IRS on your behalf in the event of an audit. Unlike a CPA or an attorney, however, EAs don't charge an arm and a leg. They're a valuable addition to your business arsenal.

Although the folks at your local "We Do Your Taxes in a Hurry Store" may be well meaning and pleasant, the people doing your taxes may have gone through only a six-week course in the current tax laws. This does not make them tax professionals. When business taxes are at stake, a professional with whom you have a standing relationship is the best choice. If you don't know one, ask around or call your local Chamber of Commerce.

Posting bookkeeping can be boring. At the end of the year when you have a professional do your taxes, however, you'll be a lot happier — and your tax preparation will cost you less — if you've posted your information cleanly and in the proper order. That's why using QuickBooks (see the "QuickBooks: Making Bookkeeping Uncomplicated" section) is essential to running your business.

To effectively manage your business, you must keep track of *all* your expenses — down to the last roll of tape. You need to keep track of your inventory, how much you paid for the items, how much you paid in shipping, and how much you profited from your sales. If you use a van or the family car to pick up or deliver merchandise to the post office (I can load eight of the light kits that I sell on eBay in our car), you should keep track of this mileage as well. When you're running a business, you should account for every penny that goes in and out.

Bookkeeping has irrefutable standards called GAAP (Generally Accepted Accounting Procedures) that are set by the Financial Accounting Standards Board. (It sounds scary to me too.) Assets, liabilities, owner's equity, income, and expenses are standard terms used in all forms of accounting to define profit, loss, and the fiscal health of your business.

Every time you process a transaction, two things happen: One account is credited while another receives a debit (kind of like yin and yang). To get more familiar with these terms (and those in the following list), see the definitions in the chart of accounts later in this chapter (in Table 16-2) and in Appendix A (a mini glossary I've included for your convenience). Depending on the type of account, the account's balance either increases or decreases. One account that increases while another decreases is called *double-entry accounting*:

- ✔ When you post an expense, the debit *increases* your expenses and *decreases* your bank account.

- ✔ When you purchase furniture or other assets, it *increases* your asset account and *decreases* your bank account.

- ✔ When you make a sale and make the deposit, it *increases* your bank account and *decreases* your accounts receivable.

- ✔ When you purchase inventory, it *increases* your inventory and *decreases* your bank account.

- ✔ When a portion of a sale includes sales tax, it *decreases* your sales, and *increases* your sales tax account.

Manually performing double-entry accounting can be a bit taxing (no pun intended). A software program automatically adjusts the accounts when you input a transaction.

As a business owner, even if you're a sole proprietor (see Chapter 15 for information on business types), you should keep your business books separate from your personal expenses. (I recommend using a program such as Quicken to keep track of your *personal* expenses for tax time.) By isolating the business records from the personal records, you can get a snapshot of what areas of your sales are doing well and which ones aren't carrying their weight. But that isn't the only reason keeping accurate records is smart; there's the IRS to think about, too. In the next section, I explain Uncle Sam's interest in your books.

Records Uncle Sam May Want to See

One of the reasons we can have a great business environment in the United States is because we all have a partner, Uncle Sam. Our government regulates business and sets the rules for us to transact our operations. To help you get started with your business, the IRS maintains a small-business Web site (shown in Figure 16-1) at the following address:

```
www.irs.gov/businesses/small
```

In this section, I highlight what information you need to keep and how long you should keep it (just in case you're chosen for an audit).

Figure 16-1:
IRS home
page for
small
businesses.

Supporting information

Aside from needing to know how your business is going (which is really important), the main reason to keep clear and concise records is because Uncle Sam may come knocking one day. You never know when the IRS will choose *your* number and want to examine *your* records. In the following list, I highlight some of the important pieces of *supporting information* (things that support your expenses on your end-of-year tax return):

- ✔ **Receipts:** Dear reader, heed this advice: Save every receipt that you get. If you're out of town on a buying trip and have coffee at the airport, save that receipt — it's a deduction from your profits. Everything related to your business may be deductible, so you must save airport parking receipts, taxi receipts, receipts for a pen that you picked up on your way to a meeting, *everything.* If you don't have a receipt, you can't prove the write-off.

- ✔ **Merchandise invoices:** Saving all merchandise invoices is as important as saving all your receipts. If you want to prove that you paid $400 and not the $299 retail price for that PlayStation 2 that you sold on eBay for $500, you'd *better* have an invoice of some kind. The same idea applies to most collectibles, in which case a retail price can't be fixed. Save all invoices!

- ✔ **Outside contractor invoices:** If you use outside contractors — even if you pay the college kid next door to go to the post office and bank for you — you should also get an invoice from them to document exactly what service you paid for and how much you paid. This is supporting information that will save your bacon, should it ever need saving.

- ✔ **Business cards:** It may sound like I'm stretching things a bit, but if you use your car to look at some merchandise, pick up a business card from the vendor. If you're out of town and have a meeting with someone, take a card. Having these business cards can help substantiate your deductible comings and goings.

- ✔ **A daily calendar:** This is where your Palm Handheld comes in. Every time you leave your house or office on a business-related task, make note of it in your Palm. Keep as much minutia as you can stand. Your Palm Desktop can print a monthly calendar. At the end of the year, staple the pages together and include them in your files with your substantiating information.

- ✔ **Credit card statements:** You're already collecting credit card receipts (although mine always seem to slip through the holes in my purse). If you have your statements, you have monthly proof of expenses. When you get your statement each month, post it into your bookkeeping program and itemize each and every charge, detailing where you spent the money and what for. (QuickBooks has a split feature that accommodates all your categories.) File these statements with your tax return at the end of the year in your year-end envelope (shoe box?).

I know that all this stuff will pile up, but that's when you go to the store and buy some plastic file storage containers to organize it all. To check for new information and the lowdown on what you can and can't do, ask an accountant or a CPA. Also visit the IRS Tax Information for Business site, shown in Figure 16-2, at

```
www.irs.ustreas.gov/businesses/index.html
```

Figure 16-2: Get tax information from the horse's mouth here.

How long should you keep your records?

How long do you have to keep all this supporting information? I hate to tell you, but I think I've saved it all. I must have at least ten years of paperwork in big plastic boxes and old files in the garage. But you know, I'm not too extreme; the period in which you can amend a return or in which the IRS can assess more tax is never less than three years from the date of filing — and can even be longer. As of my last visit to the IRS Web site, the information in Table 16-1 applied.

Table 16-1	How Long to Keep Your Tax Records
Circumstance	*Keep Records This Long*
You owe additional tax (if the following three points don't apply)	3 years
You didn't report all your income and what you didn't report is more than 25% of the gross income shown on your return	6 years
You file a fraudulent tax return	No limit
You don't bother to file a return	No limit
You file a claim of refund or credit after you've filed	3 years or 2 years after tax was paid (whichever is longer)
Your claim is due to a bad debt deduction	7 years
Your claim is from worthless stock	7 years
You have information on assets	Life of the asset

Even though I got this information directly from the IRS Web site and literature (Publication 583, "Starting a Business and Keeping Records"), it may change in the future. You can download a PDF copy of the booklet by going to the following address:

```
www.irs.gov/pub/irs-pdf/p583.pdf
```

If Adobe Acrobat Reader isn't installed on your computer, you can download the software (it's free) from the IRS Web site. It doesn't hurt to store your information for as long as you can stand it and stay on top of any changes the IRS may implement.

Bookkeeping Software

Keeping track of your auctions is hard without software, but keeping track of the money you make without software is even harder (and more time consuming). If using software to automate your auctions makes sense, so does using software to automate your bookkeeping. You can afford to make a mistake here and there in your own office, and no one will ever know. But if you make a mistake in the books, your partner (Uncle Sam) will notice — and be quite miffed. He may even charge you a penalty or two so that you'll remember not to make those mistakes again.

Those penalties aren't small either. A three-day-late tax deposit will cost you and additional 10% tax penalty. That can be quite an expensive lesson.

When I started my business, I used accounting ledger pads (which had just replaced the chisel and stone format). I soon found that I had way too many ledgers to keep track of and cross reference. A calculator was useful, based on the assumption that I typed the correct figures to start with.

Spreadsheet software can be a boon when you're just starting out. A program such as Microsoft Works (comes free on most new computers) or Excel is an excellent way to begin posting your business expenses and profits. The program can be set up to calculate your expenses, profits, and (I hope not too many) losses. Microsoft Works comes with several free financial worksheet templates that you can easily adapt for an eBay small business. Also, you can find current Excel templates to get you started at `office.microsoft.com`. There's no need to spend any extra money on templates when you're first starting!

With official bookkeeping software, reconciling a checkbook is a breeze. You merely click off the deposits and checks when the statement comes in. If I made a mistake originally when inputting the data, the software (comparing my balance and my bank's) lets me know that I made an error. This kind of efficiency would have put Bob Cratchit out of a job!

I researched various Web sites to find which software was the best selling and easiest to use. I had many discussions with CPAs, enrolled agents, and bookkeepers. The software that these professionals most recommend for business is Intuit's QuickBooks. (Thank goodness that's the one I use.) QuickBooks is considered the best, which is why I devote so much of this chapter to it. Some people begin with Quicken and later move to QuickBooks when their business gets big or incorporates. My theory? Start with the best. It's not that much more expensive — on eBay, I've seen new, sealed QuickBooks Pro 2004 software for as low as $135 and QuickBooks for as low as $65 — and it will see you directly to the big time.

QuickBooks: Making Bookkeeping Uncomplicated

QuickBooks offers several versions, from basic to enterprise solutions tailored to different types of businesses. QuickBooks Basic and QuickBooks Pro have a few significant differences. QuickBooks Pro adds job costing and expensing features and the ability to design your own forms. QuickBooks Basic does a darn good job too, so check out the comparison at `quickbooks.intuit.com` and see which version is best for you. I use (and highly recommend) QuickBooks Pro, so that's the version I describe in the rest of this section.

Stephen L. Nelson wrote *QuickBooks 2004 For Dummies* (published by Wiley). His book is amazingly easy to understand. I swear that neither Steve nor my publisher gave me a nickel for recommending his book. (Heck, I even had to pay for my copy.) I recommend it simply because it answers — in plain English — just about any question you'll have about using the program for your bookkeeping needs. Spend the money and get the book. Any money spent on increasing your knowledge is money well spent (and may be a tax write-off).

I update my QuickBooks software yearly, and every year it takes me less time to perform my bookkeeping tasks (because of product improvements). If you find that you don't have time to input your bookkeeping data, you may have to hire a bookkeeper. The bonus is that professional bookkeepers probably already know QuickBooks, and the best part is that they can print daily reports for you that keep you apprised of your business condition. Also, at the end of each year, QuickBooks will supply you with all the official reports your enrolled agent or certified public accountant will need to do your taxes. (Yes, you really do need an EA or a CPA; see the "Hiring a professional to do your year-end taxes" sidebar elsewhere in this chapter.) You can even send them a backup on a zip disk or a CD-ROM. See how simple bookkeeping can be?

QuickBooks Pro

When you first fire up QuickBooks Pro, you must first answer a few questions to set up your account. Among the few things you need to have ready before you even begin to mess with the software are the following starting figures:

- ✔ **Cash balance:** This may be the amount in your checking account (no personal money, please!) or the amount of money deposited from your eBay profits. Put these profits into a separate checking account to use for your business.

- ✔ **Accounts receivable balance:** Does anyone owe you money for some auctions? Outstanding payments make up this total.

- ✔ **Account liability balance:** Do you owe some money? Are you being invoiced for some merchandise that you haven't paid for? Total it and enter it when QuickBooks asks you.

If you're starting your business in the middle of the year, gather any previous profits and expenses that you want to include because you'll have to input this information for a complete annual set of diligently recorded books. I can guarantee that this is going to take a while. But after you've gathered together your finances, even if it takes a little sweat to set it up initially, you'll be thanking me for insisting you get organized. It just makes everything work smoother in the long run.

QuickBooks EasyStep Interview

After you've organized your finances, you can proceed with the QuickBooks EasyStep Interview, which is shown in Figure 16-3. The EasyStep interview is designed to give those with accounting-phobia and those using a bookkeeping program for the first time a comfort level. If you mess things up, you can always use the back arrow and change what you've input. If you need help, simply click the Help button and the program will answer many of your questions. Hey, if worse comes to worst, you can always delete the file from the QuickBooks directory and start over.

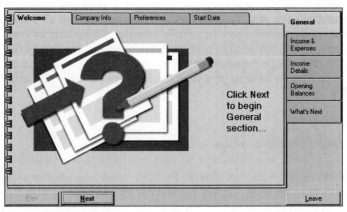

Figure 16-3:
The
QuickBooks
Pro
EasyStep
Interview
start page.

For the whirlwind tour through the QuickBooks EasyStep Interview, just follow these steps (which are only a general guideline):

1. **Start QuickBooks, and choose the Create a New Company option.**

   You're now at the EasyStep interview.

2. **On the first page of the interactive portion of the interview, type your company name (this becomes the filename in your computer) and the legal name of your company.**

   If you've filed a fictitious name statement (see Chapter 15), the fictitious name is the legal name of your company.

3. **Continue to follow the steps, answering other questions about your business, such as the address and the type of tax form you use.**

4. When QuickBooks asks what type of business you want to use, choose Retail: General.

(If you have another business than just your eBay sales, perhaps consulting or teaching others, you may way to just accept the QuickBooks with No Business option and build your chart of accounts from the one they give you — that's what I did.)

QuickBooks doesn't offer an online sales business choice, so Retail: General is the closest to what you need (see Figure 16-4). With the chart of accounts that I feature in the following section, you can make the appropriate changes to your accounts to adapt to your eBay business.

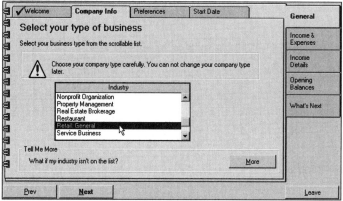

Figure 16-4:
Selecting
your
company
type.

5. When QuickBooks asks whether you want to use its chosen chart of accounts, choose Yes.

See Figure 16-5. You can always change the accounts later. If you want to spend the time, you can also input your entire custom chart of accounts manually (but I *really, really* don't recommend it).

6. Answer some more general questions, which I'm sure you can handle with the aid of the incredibly intuitive QuickBooks help area.

7. When the preferences pages appear, I recommend that you select the "Enter the bills first and then enter the payments later" option.

That way, if you input your bills as they come in, you can get an exact idea of how much money you owe at any time by just starting the program.

8. Click the box to indicate that you collect Sales Tax.

9. On the Sales Tax preferences page, indicate the agencies for which you collect sales tax, and then set up the tax collecting information, as shown in Figure 16-6.

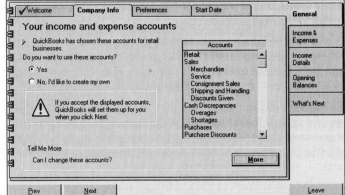

Figure 16-5: Accepting the QuickBooks chart of accounts.

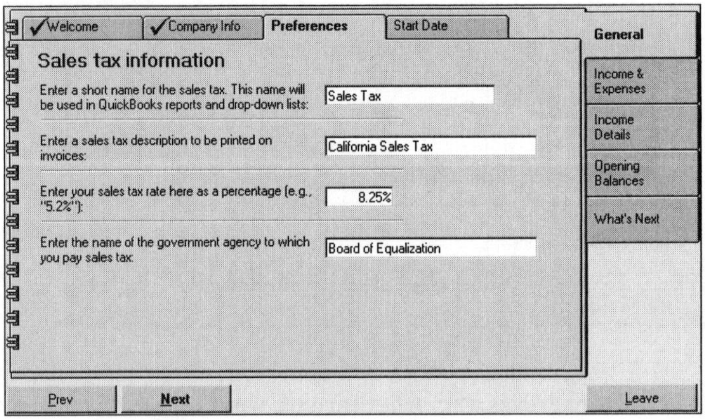

Figure 16-6: Inputting your sales tax information.

10. **Decide whether you want to use QuickBooks to process your payroll.**

    Even if you're the only employee, using QuickBooks payroll information makes things much easier when it comes to filling out your payroll deposits. QuickBooks automatically fills in federal forms for your quarterly tax processing and prints the appropriate form ready for your signature and mailing.

11. **Answer a few more questions including whether you want to use the cash basis or accrual basis of accounting.**

    The *accrual* basis posts sales the minute you write an invoice or post a sales receipt, and posts your expenses as soon as you post the bills into the computer. Accrual basis accounting gives you a clearer picture of where your company is financially than cash basis accounting does. The *cash* basis is when you record bills by writing checks — expenses are posted only when you write the checks. This way of doing business may be simpler, but the only way you'll know how much money you owe is by looking at the pile of bills on your desk.

If you're new to bookkeeping, you may want to go through the interview step-by-step with a tutor at your side. For more details, remember to check out *QuickBooks 2004 For Dummies* — this book can teach you almost everything you need to know about QuickBooks.

12. **If you're comfortable, just click Leave and input the balance of your required information directly into the program without using the interview.**

QuickBooks chart of accounts

After you've finished the EasyStep Interview and have successfully set yourself up in QuickBooks, the program presents a chart of accounts. Think of the *chart of accounts* as an organization system, such as file folders. It keeps all related data in the proper area. When you write a check to pay a bill, it deducts the amount from your checking account, reduces your accounts payable, and perhaps increases your asset or expense accounts.

You have a choice of giving each account a number. These numbers, a kind of bookkeeping shorthand, are standardized throughout bookkeeping; believe it or not, everybody in the industry seems to know what number goes with what item. To keep things less confusing, I like to use titles as well as numbers.

To customize your chart of accounts, follow these steps:

1. **Choose Edit➪Preferences.**

2. **Click the Accounting icon (on the left).**

3. **Click the Company preferences tab and indicate that you'd like to use account numbers.**

   An editable chart of accounts appears, as shown in Figure 16-7. Because QuickBooks doesn't assign account numbers as a default, you'll need to edit the chart to create them.

4. **Go through your QuickBooks chart of accounts and add any missing categories.**

   You may not need all these categories, and you can always add more later. To get an idea of how you can customize the chart of accounts, also look at Figure 16-8, which shows you the chart of accounts from my own business. In Table 16-2, I show you a chart of accounts that a CPA wrote for an eBay business.

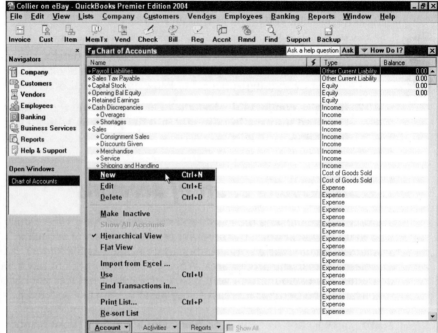

Figure 16-7:
Your chart
of accounts
now has
numbers
generated
by
QuickBooks.

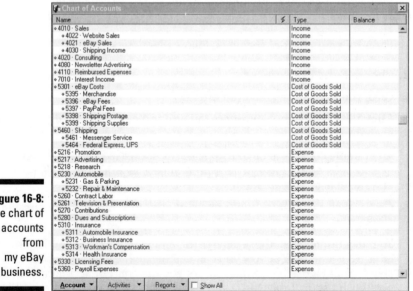

Figure 16-8:
The chart of
accounts
from
my eBay
business.

Table 16-2	eBay Business Chart of Accounts	
Account Number	**Account Name**	**What It Represents**
1001	Checking	All revenue deposited here and all checks drawn upon this account
1002	Money market account	Company savings account
1100	Accounts receivable	For customers to whom you extend credit
1201	Merchandise inventory	Charge to cost of sales as used, or take periodic inventories and adjust at that time
1202	Shipping Supplies	Boxes, tape, labels, and so forth; charge these to cost as used, or take an inventory at the end of the period and adjust to cost of sales
1401	Office Furniture & Equipment	Desk, computer, telephone
1402	Shipping Equipment	Scales, tape dispensers
1403	Vehicles	Your vehicle if it's owned by the company
1501	Accumulated Depreciation	For your accountant's use
1601	Deposits	Security deposits on leases
2001	Accounts Payable	Amounts owed for the stuff you sell, or charged expenses
2100	Payroll Liabilities	Taxes deducted from employees' checks and taxes paid by company on employee earnings
2200	Sales Tax Payable	Sales tax collected at time of sale and owed to the state
2501	Equipment loans	Money borrowed to buy a computer or other equipment
2502	Auto loans	When you get that hot new van for visiting your consignment clients
3000	Owner's capital	Your opening balance
3902	Owner's draw	Your withdrawals for the current year
4001	Merchandise sales	Revenue from sales of your products
4002	Shipping and handling	Paid by the customer

(continued)

Table 16-2 *(continued)*

Account Number	Account Name	What It Represents
4009	Returns	Total dollar amount of returned merchandise
4101	Interest income	From your investments
4201	Other income	Income not otherwise classified
5001	Merchandise purchases	All the merchandise you buy for eBay; you'll probably use subaccounts for individual items
5002	Freight in	Freight and shipping charges you pay for your inventory, not for shipments to customers
5003	Shipping	Shipping to your customers: USPS, FedEx, UPS, and so on
5004	Shipping Supplies	Boxes, labels, tape, bubble pack
6110	Automobile expense	When you use your car for work
6111	Gas and oil	Filling up the tank!
6112	Repairs	When your business owns the car
6120	Bank service charges	Monthly service charges, NSF charges, and so forth
6140	Contributions	Charity
6142	Data services	Do you have an outside firm processing your payroll?
6143	Internet Service Provider	What you pay to your Internet provider
6144	Web site hosting fees	Fees paid to your hosting company
6150	Depreciation expense	For your accountant's use
6151	eBay fees	What you pay eBay every month to stay in business based on your sales
6152	Discounts	Fees you're charged for using eBay and accepting credit card payments; deducted from your revenue and reported to you on your eBay statement
6153	Other auction site fees	You may want to set up subcategories for each site where you do business, such as Yahoo! or Amazon.com

Account Number	Account Name	What It Represents
6156	PayPal fees	Processing fees paid to PayPal
6158	Credit card merchant account fees	If you have a separate merchant account, post those fees here
6160	Dues	If you join an organization that charges membership fees (relating to your business)
6161	Magazines and periodicals	Books and magazines that help you run and expand your business
6170	Equipment rental	Postage meter, occasional van
6180	Insurance	Policies that cover your merchandise or your office
6185	Liability Insurance	Insurance that covers you if someone slips and falls at your place of business (can also be put under Insurance)
6190	Disability Insurance	Insurance that will pay you if you become temporarily or permanently disabled and can't perform your work
6191	Health insurance	If provided for yourself, you may be required to provide it to employees
6200	Interest expense	Credit interest and interest on loans
6220	Loan interest	When you borrow from the bank
6230	Licenses and permits	State and city Licenses
6240	Miscellaneous	Whatever doesn't go anyplace else
6250	Postage and delivery	Stamps used in your regular business
6251	endicia.com fees	Fees for your eBay business postage service
6260	Printing	Your business cards, correspondence stationery, and so on
6265	Filing fees	Fees paid to file legal documents
6270	Professional fees	Fees paid to consultants
6280	Legal fees	If you have to pay a lawyer
6650	Accounting and bookkeeping	Bookkeeper, CAP, or EA

(continued)

Table 16-2 *(continued)*

Account Number	Account Name	What It Represents
6290	Rent	Office, warehouse, and so on
6300	Repairs	Can be the major category for the following subcategories
6310	Building repairs	Repairs to the building where you operate your business
6320	Computer repairs	What you pay the person who sets up your wireless network
6330	Equipment repairs	When the copier or phone needs fixing
6340	Telephone	Regular telephone, FAX lines
6350	Travel and entertainment	Business-related travel, business meals
6360	Entertainment	When you take eBay's CEO out to dinner to benefit your eBay business
6370	Meals	Meals while traveling for your business
6390	Utilities	Major heading for the following subcategories
6391	Electricity and gas	Electricity and gas
6392	Water	Water
6560	Payroll expenses	Wages paid to others
6770	Supplies	Office supplies
6772	Computer	Computer and supplies
6780	Marketing	Advertising or promotional items you purchase to give away
6790	Office	Miscellaneous office expenses, such as bottled water delivery
6820	Taxes	Major category for the following subcategories
6830	Federal	Federal taxes
6840	Local	Local taxes
6850	Property	Property taxes
6860	State	State taxes

QuickBooks integrates with PayPal

PayPal can provide your payment history in QuickBooks format. They even offer a settlement and reconciliation system download that breaks up your PayPal transactions into debits and credits. A handy feature! One warning though: These are only financial transactions. When you use QuickBooks to its fullest, you will have your inventory in the program. When you purchase merchandise to sell, QuickBooks sets up the inventory — and deducts from it each time you input an invoice or a sales receipt. This way your inventory receipts follow GAAP. In my book *eBay Timesaving Techniques For Dummies*, I show you the procedures for posting your weekly (or daily) sales in QuickBooks by using sales receipts.

QuickBooks on the Web

If you want to handle everything on the Web, use QuickBooks online service. The online QuickBooks program offers fewer features than the home version, but if your accounting needs are simple, it may right for you. Before you decide, however, consider that while your accounting needs may be simple now, they may not be so simple later.

Intuit charges $14.95 a month for the service, which is comparable to buying the QuickBooks Pro version. The online version also requires you to have a broadband connection to the Internet so that you're always online (dial-up connections need not apply). The online edition doesn't include integrated payroll, purchase orders, online banking, and bill payments.

Chapter 17

Building an eBay Back Office

In This Chapter

▷ Organizing your stock

▷ Keeping inventory

▷ Exploring shipping materials

▷ Becoming your own post office

The more items you sell, the more confusing things can get. As you build your eBay business, the little side table you use for storing eBay merchandise isn't going to work. You must think industrial. Even part-time sellers can benefit by adding a few professional touches to their business areas.

In this chapter, I emphasize the importance of setting up and organizing your back office. I cover everything from stacking your stock to keeping inventory to indispensable packing materials and online postage services. Organization will be your byword. Dive right in. The sooner you read this chapter, the sooner you can build your eBay back office and get down to business.

The Warehouse: Organizing Your Space

Whether you plan to sell large items or small items, you need space for storing them. As you make savvy purchases, maintaining an item's mint condition will be one of your greatest challenges. Organized storage in itself is an art, so in this section, I cover the details of what you'll need to safeguard your precious stock.

Shelving your profits

Before you stock the shelves, it helps to have some! You also need a place to put the shelves: your garage, a spare room, or somewhere else. You have a choice between two basic kinds of shelves:

- **Plastic:** If you're just starting out, you can always go to the local closet and linen supply store to buy inexpensive plastic shelves. They're light and cheap — and they'll buckle in time.

- **Steel:** If you want to do it right the first time, buy steel shelving. The most versatile steel shelving is the wire kind (versus solid-steel shelves), which is lighter and allows air to circulate around your items. Steel wire shelving assembles easily; I put mine together without help. They come with leveling feet and 4-inch casters, so should you need to move a shelf unit, you can. Installing the casters is up to you. You can combine steel wire shelving units to create a full wall of shelves. Each shelf safely holds as much as 600 pounds of merchandise.

  Search eBay for **shelving** to find sellers offering this kind of industrial shelving. The main problem with ordering this product online is that the shipping usually costs more than the shelving.

To save you time, dear reader, I researched the subject and found some readily available, reasonably priced shelves. Just go to Sam's Club or Costco and look for Seville Classics four-shelf commercial shelving, sold in 36- and 48-inch-wide units. Each shelf will hold up to 500 pounds. These shelves are available also on the Costco Web site, but you have to pay for shipping.

Box 'em or bag 'em?

Packing your items for storage can be a challenge. As long as you're picking up your shelving (see preceding section), pick up some plastic bags in sandwich, quart, and gallon sizes. The sandwich baggies are perfect for storing smaller items. When items are stored in plastic, they can't pick up any smells or become musty before you sell them. The plastic also protects the items from rubbing against each other and causing possible damage. If you package them one item to a bag, you can then just lift one off the shelf and put it directly into a shipping box when the auction is over.

Your bags of items will have to go into boxes for storage on the shelves. Clear plastic storage boxes, the kind you often find at superstores, are great for bulky items. They're usually 26 inches, so before you buy these big plastic containers, be sure that they'll fit on your shelving comfortably and that you'll have easy access to your items. Using cardboard office-type file storage boxes from an office supply store is another option. These cardboard boxes are 10 x 12 x 16 inches, which is a nice size for storing medium-size products. At around $1 each, they're the most economical choice. The downside is that you can't see through cardboard boxes, so if your label falls off, you have to take the box off the shelf and open it to check its contents. Smaller see-through plastic boxes with various compartments, such as the kind home improvement stores carry for storing tools, work great for storing very small items.

 When using these large plastic bins, it's always a good idea to tape a pad of Post-it notes on the end of the box so you can quickly identify the contents. You *can* use regular sticky-labels, but changing them will leave large amounts of paper residue over time, and your storage will look sloppy and icky.

Inventory: Keeping Track of What You Have and Where You Keep It

Savvy eBay sellers have different methods of handling inventory. They use everything from spiral-bound notebooks to sophisticated software programs. Although computerized inventory tracking can simplify this task, starting with a plain ol' handwritten ledger is fine, too. Choose whichever works best for you, but keep in mind that as your eBay business grows, a software program that tracks inventory for you may become necessary.

Most of these systems wouldn't work for a company with a warehouse full of stock but will work nicely in an eBay sales environment. Many sellers tape sheets of paper to their boxes to identify them by number, and use that as a reference to a simple Excel spreadsheet for selling purposes. Excel spreadsheets are perfect for keeping track of your auctions as well, but if you're using a management service or software, you don't need both for physical inventory. After you're running a full-time business, however, you have to keep Uncle Sam happy with a dollars and cents accounting of your inventory, so keep your inventory records in a standardized program such as QuickBooks (discussed in Chapter 16). In Chapter 8, I detail a variety of auction management software and Web sites, many of which include physical inventory tracking features.

You may also want to use Excel spreadsheets for your downloaded PayPal statements, to hold information waiting to transfer to your bookkeeping program.

Planning: The key to good organization

When it became time for me to put my eBay merchandise in order, I was busy with my regular business, so I hired people to organize my eBay area. This decision turned out to be one massive mistake. They organized everything and put all my items in boxes — but didn't label the boxes to indicate what was stored in each.

I still haven't recovered and don't know where a bunch of my stuff is!

A bit of advice: Think things out and plan where you'll put everything. Organize your items by theme, type, or size. If you organize before planning, you might end up with organized disorganization.

The Shipping Department: Packin' It Up

If you've read *eBay For Dummies,* you know all about the various ways to pack your items. I hope you've become an expert! In this section, I review some of the things you must have for a complete, smooth-running shipping department, such as cleaning supplies and packing materials. The *handling fee* portion of your shipping charges pays for these kinds of items. Don't run low on them and pay attention to how you store them. They must be kept in a clean environment.

Packaging clean up

Be sure the items you send out are in tip-top shape. Here are a few everyday chemicals that can gild the lily:

- ✔ **WD-40:** The decades-old lubricant works very well at getting price stickers off plastic and glass without damaging the product. The plastic on a toy box may begin to look nasty, even when stored in a clean environment. A quick wipe with a paper towel with a dash of WD-40 will make it shine like new. It also works incredibly well for untangling jewelry chains and shining up metallic objects.

- ✔ **Goo Gone:** Goo Gone works miracles in cleaning up gooey sticker residue from nonporous items.

- ✔ **un-du:** This amazing liquid easily removes stickers from cardboard, plastic, fabrics and more without causing damage. It comes packaged with a patented mini-scraper top that can be used in any of your sticker cleaning projects. If you can't find un-du, check out my Web site (www.coolebaytools.com) for places to purchase it. You can also use lighter fluid (which is, of course, considerably more dangerous and may damage your item).

Packing materials

So that you can always be sure that your items will arrive at their destinations in one piece, you'll want to keep the following on hand at all times:

- ✔ **Bubble pack:** A clean, puffy product that comes in rolls, bubble pack is available in several sizes. Depending on your product, you may have to carry two sizes of bubble pack to properly protect the goods. Bubble pack can be expensive, but check out vendors at eBay; you'll find quite a lot of them (and possibly a deal). See Figure 17-1.

- ✔ **Styrofoam packing peanuts:** Why they call them peanuts, I'll never know — I guess somebody thought they look like peanuts. Nonetheless, Styrofoam peanuts protect just about everything you ship. Storing them is the tricky part. One of the most ingenious storage solutions I've seen is putting the peanuts into 33-gallon plastic trash bags, and then hanging these bags on cup hooks (available at the hardware store) around the walls in a garage. When packing with peanuts, be sure that you place the item carefully and use enough peanuts to fill the box *completely;* leaving any airspace defeats the point of using the peanuts in the first place.

- ✔ **Plastic bags:** Buy plastic bags in bulk to save money. Make sure you buy various sizes and use them for both shipping and storing. Even large kitchen or trash bags are good for wrapping up posters and large items; the plastic protects the item from inclement weather by water-proofing it.

- ✔ **Two- or three-inch shipping tape:** You'll need clear tape for finishing up packages that go any other way than USPS Priority. You'll also need the clear tape to place over address labels to protect them from scrapes and rain. I once received a package with an address label soaked with rain and barely legible. Don't risk a lost package for want of a few inches of tape. If you're shipping by Priority Mail, the post office will supply you with free preprinted tape. See the following section on boxes for more information.

- ✔ **Bubble envelopes:** If you send items that fit nicely into bubble pack-lined envelopes, use them (see Figure 17-2). This type of envelope — with paper on the outside and bubble pack on the inside — is perfect for mailing small items or clothing using First class mail. The envelopes are available in quantity (an economical choice) and don't take up much storage space. Table 17-1 shows you the industry-standard sizes of bubble envelopes and their suggested uses.

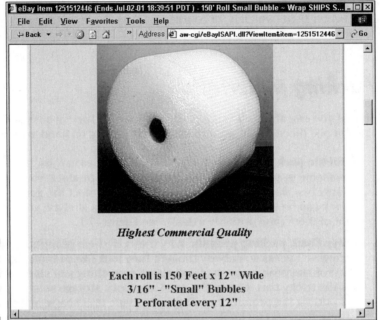

Figure 17-1:
Bubble pack
in its pure
form.

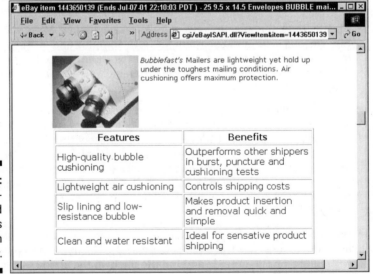

Figure 17-2:
Bubble-
pack-lined
envelopes
for sale on
eBay.

Removing musty odors from apparel items

Clothing can often pick up odors that you just don't notice. I recently bought a designer dress on eBay from a seller who had the typical disclaimer in her description: "No stains, holes, repairs, or odors. Comes from a smoke-free, pet-free home." Unfortunately, the minute I opened the box I could smell the musty odor of an item that had been stored for a long time.

To prevent that icky, storage odor, keep a package of Dryel Fabric Care System around. This is a safe, do-it-yourself dry cleaning product. Just toss your better eBay clothing items in the patented Dryel bag with the special sheet and toss it in the dryer as per the instructions on the box. Your garment will come out smelling clean — and wrinkle free. For more information, visit their Website at www.Dryel.com.

Table 17-1	Standard Bubble-Padded Mailer Sizes	
Size	*Measurements*	*Suggested Items*
#000	4" x 8"	Collector trading cards, jewelry, computer diskettes, coins
#00	5" x 10"	Postcards, paper ephemera
#0	6" x 10"	Doll clothes, CDs, DVDs, Xbox or PS2 games
#1	7¼" x 12"	Cardboard sleeve VHS tapes, jewel-cased CDs, and DVDs
#2	8½" x 12"	Clamshell VHS tapes, books
#3	8½" x 14½"	Toys, clothing, stuffed animals
#4	9½" x 14½"	Small books, trade paperbacks
#5	10½" x 16"	Hardcover books, dolls
#6	12½" x 19"	Clothing, soft boxed items
#7	14¼" x 20"	Much larger packaged items, framed items and plaques

Packaging — the heart of the matter

Depending on the size of the item you sell, you can purchase boxes in bulk at reliable sources. Because you have a resale number (see Chapter 15), look in your local yellow pages for wholesale boxes (you still have to pay tax, but the resale number identifies you as a business and often can get you a lower price). Try to purchase from a manufacturer that specializes in B2B (business to business) sales. Some box companies specialize in selling to the occasional box user. Knowing the size that you need enables you to buy by the case lot.

You can save big money if your items fit into boxes that the post office supplies and you plan on using Priority Mail. The USPS will give you all the boxes and mailing envelopes you need free, and it offers plenty of sizes. See the handy Table 17-2 for available sizes.

Table 17-2 Free Priority Mail Packaging

Size	*Description*	*Minimum Quantity*
8⅝" x 5⅜" x 1⅝"	Small video box	25
9¼" x 6¼" x 2"	Large video box	25
11¼" x 14" x 2¼"	Medium	25
12¼" x 15½" x 3"	Large	25
6" x 38"	Triangle tube	10
7" x 7" x 6"	Small square	25
12" x 12" x 8"	Medium square	25
12½" x 15½"	Tyvek envelope	1
6" x 10"	Cardboard envelope	1
12½" x 9½"	2lb. Flat rate cardboard envelope	1
12½" x 9½"	1lb. Cardboard envelope	25
5" x 10"	Cardboard window envelope	1

Go to `http://supplies.usps.gov/` (see Figure 17-3) to order your packing tape, labels, forms, and just about anything else that you'll need to ship Priority Mail. Be sure to order a month or so before you need the boxes so that you'll have the size you need when you need it.

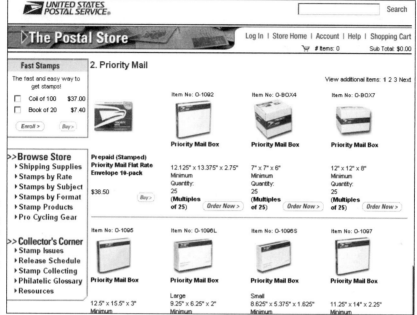

Figure 17-3:
Order
shipping
supplies
from the
USPS.

The Mail Room: Sendin' It Out

In August of 1999, the United States Postal Service announced a new service: information-based indicia (IBI). Targeted at the SOHO (small office/home office) market, IBI is USPS-certified postage that you can print on envelopes and sticker labels right from your PC. In this section, I give you the lowdown on the main Internet postage vendors: Endicia.com, Stamps.com, and Pitney Bowes. You also find out how to ship directly through PayPal.

I'm a savvy consumer and businesswoman. I don't believe in paying for extras, nor do I believe in being a victim of hidden charges. The online postage arena — while providing helpful tools that make running your eBay business easier — is fraught with bargains, deals, and introductory offers. I urge you to read these offers carefully so that you know what you're getting yourself into: Evaluate how much it will cost you to start out and to maintain an ongoing relationship with the company. Although you may initially get some free hardware and pay a low introductory rate, the fine print might tell you that you have agreed to pay unreasonably high monthly prices six months down the line. I always double-check pricing before getting into anything, and I urge you to do the same.

Your old pal the United States Postal now has Web tools that enable you to file for delivery confirmation free of charge (that's right — no more 45 or 55 cents each) and print postage online. One caveat: This is a no-frills online service, and you often get what you pay for. You have to download software to your computer to use this service, and you can't print the labels on a label printer. You must print to regular 8 ½ x 11 paper. For more details, go to

```
www.usps.com/clicknship
```

Printing labels on your printer is convenient until you start sending out a dozen packages at a time — then cutting the paper and taping the label gets a bit too time consuming. I highly recommend you do yourself a favor and get a label printer. Yes, they can be expensive, but you can find some great deals on eBay. I bought my heavy-duty, professional Eltron Zebra 2844 thermal label printer on eBay for one-fourth the retail price. (Search eBay for *zebra 2844*). It's saved me countless hours. Dymo also makes a very good label printer for beginners.

ClickStamp Internet Postage from Pitney Bowes

Pitney Bowes has an online postage service called ClickStamp® that enables you to print postage directly from your computer while online. To register online and download their software, go to the Pitney Bowes Web site at

```
www.pitneyworks.com
```

and click the ClickStamp Internet postage link.

Here are some features of the ClickStamp service:

- ✔ **Zip code check:** The software runs a check on your addresses and corrects any zip code errors you've made.

- ✔ *No* **Media mail:** Unlike the other services, ClickStamp doesn't issue postage for Media mail and the off-beat postage classes. You need Media Mail if you're going to be mailing books or tapes.

- ✔ **Labels:** You must print your package labels on 3.33" x 4" labels.

- ✔ **Purchase postage online:** You can purchase postage with no surcharge, purchasing as little as $10 to a maximum of $500.

- ✔ *No* **delivery confirmations:** You can't print delivery confirmations. An excellent workaround, however, is to use ClickStamp with the delivery confirmations from Shippertools.com (free by paying a monthly fee). For more information, see Chapter 14.

Free USPS package pick up

Yes! Some things *are* free! If you print electronic postage through one of the vendors mentioned in this chapter, you can go the post office Web site at `http://carrierpickup.usps.com/cgi-bin/WebObjects/Carrier` `Pickup.woa` and request a free pick up for all your packages. If the URL is too long to type, go to the Post Office main page and type **carrier pickup** in the search box. You can request a next-day pickup as late as 2 a.m.

The best part? As of this writing, Pitney Bowes offers a 30-day free trial period, and the total monthly fees are only $4.99 a month.

Endicia.com

At the beginning of PC graphics in the early 90s, I attended a cutting-edge industry trade show. I had a successful graphics and advertising business, so I was interested in the latest and greatest innovations to bring my business off the light table and onto my computer. In a smallish booth were a couple of guys peddling new software to enable artists to design direct mail pieces from the desktop. Wow! What an innovation! Their inexpensive software even let you produce your own bar coding for the post office. I fell in love with that software and used it throughout my graphics career.

That program, DAZzle, combined with their patented Dial-A-Zip became the basis for today's software (see Figure 17-4) that is distributed to all Endicia.com customers. There isn't a more robust mailing program on the market.

Endicia.com has all the features of Stamps.com and more:

- ✔ **Buy your postage online:** With a click of your mouse, you can purchase your postage instantly using your credit card or by direct debit from your checking account. You can register your preferences when you sign up with Endicia.com.

- ✔ **Print postage for all classes of mail, including international:** From Anniston, Alabama to Bulawayo, Zimbabwe, the DAZzle software not only prints postage but also lists all your shipping options and applicable rates. For international mailing, it will also advise you as to any prohibitions (for example, no prison-made goods can be mailed to Botswana), restrictions, necessary customs forms, and areas served within the country.

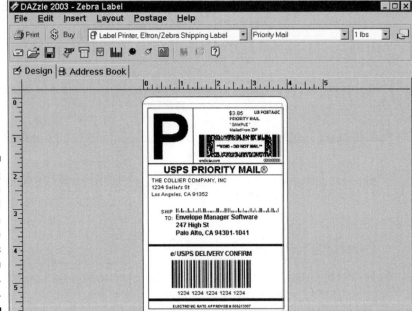

Figure 17-4:
DAZzle, the
label and
design
software
that comes
with
Endicia.
com.

✔ **Free delivery confirmations on Priority mail:** Delivery confirmations may be printed also for First Class, Parcel Post, and Media Mail for only $.13 each (a savings of $.42 from post office purchases).

✔ **Mailpiece design:** Endicia Internet Postage is based on DAZzle, an award-winning mailpiece design tool that lets you design envelopes, postcards, and labels with color graphics, logos, pictures, text messages, and rubber stamps. You can print your mailing label with postage and delivery confirmation on anything from plain paper (tape it on with clear tape) to fancy 4 x 6 labels in a label printer from their extensive list of label templates.

✔ **Integration with U-PIC Insurance:** If you're saving time and money using U-PIC (a private package insurer — see Chapter 14), you can send your monthly insurance logs electronically to U-PIC at the end of the month — a service that's integrated into the DAZzle software. There's no need to print a hard copy and mail in this information.

✔ **No cut-and-paste necessary:** Endicia integrates with most common software programs. With their DAZzle software open on your computer, highlight the buyer's address from an e-mail or the PayPal site and press Ctrl+C. The address automatically appears in the DAZzle postage software. No pasting needed.

Endicia.com offers two levels of service. All the features just listed come with the standard plan. Their premium plan adds customizable e-mail, enhanced online transaction reports and statistics, business reply mail, return shipping labels (prepaid so your customer won't have to pay for the return), and stealth indicias.

The *stealth indicia* (also known as the postage-paid indicia) is an awesome tool for the eBay seller. By using this feature, your customer will not see the exact amount of postage that you paid. This allows you to add reasonable shipping and handling costs and not inflame the buyer when they see the final label.

With all these features, you'd think their service would be expensive, but it's not. The standard plan is $9.95 a month ($99.95 if paid annually), and the premium plan is $15.95 a month ($174.94 annually). For a free 60-day trial just for my readers, go to

```
www.endicia.com/coolebaytools
```

PayPal Shipping Services

PayPal continues to add great features for sellers. Now you can not only buy postage or ship with UPS through PayPal but also print labels on your own printer. If you ship lots of items and use a different service for printing your shipping data (such as the other services mentioned in this chapter), PayPal allows you to input the tracking information on the site. Just click the Details link for the transaction, and then click the Add button that appears, as shown in Figure 17-5. Input the tracking or delivery confirmation information from USPS, UPS, or another shipping company, and PayPal sends an e-mail to your buyer with that information.

The information you added appears in both the record of your PayPal transaction and the buyer's record in their account, as shown in Figure 17-6. (You can check the information by clicking the Details link again.)

PayPal shipping services work great when you're just starting out in your eBay business, but once you get rolling, you need a mailing service that includes e-mail and record keeping, such as Endicia or Stamps.com. When you process your shipping (UPS or USPS) on PayPal, the shipping amount is deducted from your PayPal (sales revenue) balance. This is an important issue.

Figure 17-5:
Click the
Add button
in the
payment
record to
input
tracking
informa-
tion and
generate an
e-mail to
your buyer.

Figure 17-6:
The tracking
information
becomes
part of the
sales record
on PayPal.

If you're starting a business in earnest, you need to keep track of your online expenses separately (see Chapter 16). Allowing PayPal to deduct your shipping costs from your incoming revenue creates a bookkeeping nightmare. You need to have exact figures for expense and income — and it really helps keep confusion to a minimum when your deposits (withdrawals from your PayPal account to your bank) match your sales receipts. If you want to ship through PayPal, be sure you withdraw your sales amount to your checking account *before* you process your shipping. That way, your shipping can be charged to your business credit card for easier tracking.

To purchase postage and print your label for a specific purchase, click the Ship button next to the payment record in your PayPal account overview, as shown in Figure 17-7. You'll be taken through a step-by-step process for paying for your shipping and printing the appropriate label on your printer.

U.S. Business Account Overview

Name: The Collier Company, Inc (Marsha Collier)
Email: ▓▓▓▓▓▓▓▓▓▓▓ (Add email)
Status: Verified (1020)

| Balance: | $88.42 USD | View Limits |

Earn a return on your balance!

PayPal Visa Card
Many
Great
Designs
30-second
Response
Apply Now

Recent Activity | All Activity | Items Won ⓔ**b**Y | Items Sold $ = PayPal Preferred
ⓔ**b**Y   Cashback

Your Recent Activity displays the last 7 days of account activity.

File	Type	To/From	Name/Email	Amount ($)	Date	Status	Details	Action
☐	Payment	From	▓▓▓▓▓▓	$48.93 USD	May 15, 2004	Uncleared	Details	[Accept] [Deny]
☐	Refund	To	▓▓▓▓	-$6.50 USD	May 14, 2004	Completed	Details	
☐	Payment	To	▓▓▓▓	-$22.99 USD	May 14, 2004	Completed	Details	
☐	Payment	From	▓▓▓▓	$47.05 USD	May 14, 2004	Completed	Details	[Ship]
☐	Payment	To	▓▓▓	-$13.81 USD	May 13, 2004	Completed	Details	
				$0.00	May			

Figure 17-7:
Click the
Ship button
to ship your
item through
UPS or the
USPS.

Stamps.com

Stamps.com purchased 31 Internet postage patents from e-stamp, making its services a combination of the best of both sites. (e-stamp discontinued its online postage service late in 2000; I was a big fan.) Many eBay sellers moved their postage business over to Stamps.com, which is shown in Figure 17-8.

Stamps.com works with software that you probably use every day, integrating itself into many programs, such as Microsoft Word, Outlook, and Office, Corel WordPerfect, Palm Desktop, and Quicken. Here are some features you might enjoy:

✔ **Use your printer to print postage:** If your printer allows it, you can even print your envelopes along with bar-coded addresses, your return address, and postage. This saves quite a bit in label costs.

The Stamps.com custom Envelope Wizard permits you to design your own envelopes, including a logo or graphics. You can purchase a box of 500 #10 envelopes for as little as $4.99 at office supply stores. (Endicia.com provides a more robust envelope graphics wizard.)

Figure 17-8:
Stamps.
com.

✔ **Have Stamps.com check that your addresses are valid:** Before printing any postage, the Stamps.com software contacts the USPS database of every valid mailing address in the United States. This Address Matching System (AMS) is updated monthly.

✔ **Have Stamps.com add the extra four digits to your addressee's zip codes:** This nifty feature helps ensure swift delivery while freeing you of the hassle of having to look it up.

Purchasing postage is as easy as going to www.stamps.com and clicking your mouse. Your credit card information is kept secure on its site. With Stamps. com, you don't *need* any extra fancy equipment, although most introductory deals come with a free 5-pound-maximum scale. The scale also functions on its own. Serious users should get a better quality postage scale from a seller on eBay or through Office Depot.

Because Office Depot delivers any order more than $50 free the next day, it's a great place to get paper and labels. Better buys on scales, though, can be found on eBay, especially if you search *postage scale*. I'm using a super small, 13-pound-maximum scale manufactured by Escali that I bought on eBay for only $29.95, complete with a five-year warranty.

To find the Stamps.com deal of the month, visit its Web site. They charge a flat rate of $15.99 per month The site regularly offers sign-up bonuses that include as much as $20 free postage or a free 5-pound-maximum digital postage scale.

Part V
The Part of Tens

"You've opened an insect-clothing shop at eBay? Neat! Where do you get buttons that small?"

In this part . . .

Not everyone is a shooting star at eBay, but it's a good goal to reach for. For your inspiration, I've included profiles on some interesting people — from all walks of life — who've turned eBay into a profitable enterprise, some working only part-time. These are not people in big companies. Instead, they're people like us, working hard to expand their business on eBay. In the second chapter, I provide information on moving merchandise that you think you might never sell.

Chapter 18

Ten Successful eBay Sellers and Their Stories

In This Chapter

▶ People who make their living selling at eBay . . .

▶ . . . and love it!

I enjoy hearing stories about how much people like eBay. I enjoy it even more when I hear that they're doing something that they get pleasure from while earning a good living. One of the best parts of teaching at eBay University is talking to the hundreds of sellers who attend. I get the opportunity to bounce ideas around with them and find out about the creative ways they spend their time at eBay.

I thought you might like to know more about some of the people at eBay too, so I interviewed them; it was so much fun getting to know about each of them. They have different backgrounds and lifestyles — but they all have one thing in common: eBay!

In favor of highlighting some regular folks at eBay, I dispensed with the customary writer thing (you know, finding the largest PowerSellers at eBay to interview). No one's a success overnight, and the people I discuss in this chapter certainly have been plugging away at eBay, increasing their businesses and becoming successful. I dug through some old feedbacks (all the way back to 1997) and contacted sellers to see how they're doing these days. Here are their stories (and their advice).

Abovethemall

Member since April 1998; Feedback 3162; Positive Feedback 99.9%

Aside from being a PowerSeller, pretty, bright, and talented, Marjie Smith is a heck of an eBay seller. She's not only a PowerSeller, she's the founder of the Disabled Online Users Association (DOUA) — her other full-time job.

She discovered eBay when she was running an e-mail discussion group of women who collected Beanies Babies. Many were looking for connections to complete their collections. Being the head "nut" (nicknamed that by the group after the Ty Beanie "Nuts" the Squirrel), it was her job to help them accomplish this goal. The rest, they say, is history.

Marjie runs 50 to 100 auctions a week and keeps her eBay store as stocked as she possibly can. She's an authorized Etienne Aigner representative and has exclusive agreements with several unique gift lines. But she's quick to point out that she'll sell anything! She once found a box of old, beat-up books next to a dumpster outside a thrift shop. She waited till no one was looking and snapped them up and sold them on eBay. That box of books netted her a cool $300 profit.

Just like many of the sellers I profile here, Marjie spends as many as 70 hours a week on her eBay enterprises. Her biggest sale came from a woman who used Buy It Now to purchase more than $1000 worth of lovely Etienne Aigner accessories from her eBay store in one day.

eBay has really changed her life. "Being a successful eBay seller has truly given me my wings. I am independent, self-sufficient, and financially stable. I know I won't get laid off, downsized, or put out to pasture before I'm ready. I'm my own boss, work my own hours, set my own limits, and can readily achieve them thanks to the platform that eBay provides to all sellers. When they say it's a level playing field, believe it."

Aside from an eBay store, Marjie sells from her Web site `www.abovethemall.com` (see Figure 18-1) and runs the site for DOUA, `www.doua.info`.

Figure 18-1:
The Abovethem-all Web site.

Marjie's words for new sellers on eBay? Remember back to when you were a new buyer. Take all the good from the sellers who've helped you along the way, add your own flavor, and always do right by your customers.

BobMill

Member since November 1997; Feedback: 24,162 Positive Feedback: 99.99%

When I first wrote about Bob, he had almost 14,000 feedbacks. If you were to look at his feedback, you'd notice that he has a mass of repeat customers. Although his feedback rating is now more than 24,000, he has more than 70,000 positives — meaning that he's had lots of repeat customers. Pretty darn impressive.

Bob collects stamps, and that's how he found his way to eBay, purchasing stamps for his own collection. Boy does he collect stamps! He has almost all of the 3-, 4-, 5-, 6-, and 8-cent stamp sheets and first-day covers — and that's only part of his collection.

He's a pretty funny guy; I recommend checking out his Web site at

```
www.xmission.com/~emailbox/bob.htm
```

His full-time work (at least 90 hours a week, no kidding) is on eBay, selling stamps.

Because Bob has a unique sense of humor, he often sells things that are a bit "off base." Figure 18-2 shows some stamps from the island of Redonda, a dependency of Antigua and Barbuda. This island in the Caribbean has no human population; it's inhabited by about 40,000 seabirds. The island has no postal system, post office, or even a mailbox. Antigua and Barbuda issued the stamps as a revenue builder.

Bob told me an amazing story about selling a mint sheet of stamps that featured the Final Reunion of the Grand Army of the Republic. The buyer asked him to mail it to a lady recovering from hip surgery. A few days later, he got a handwritten, seven-page letter of thanks. The lady said it brought back such good memories. At age 96, this lady was the only surviving daughter of the last surviving member of the Union Army. She remembered her father's stories of the heat, the noise, and the fear as he and his comrades faced at the charge of General Pickett at the Battle of Gettysburg. Selling an item that gets a response like that can make you feel glad to be alive.

Before I get too warm and fuzzy here, I'll say that Bob's a serious seller who's aware of his business and the competition on eBay, especially the amateurs who sell valuables at whatever price they can get. He uses software to run his business: AuctionSubmit for listing and Auctiva for auction promotion tools.

About this Mint Never Hinged Item:

Rotary International has put Service Above Self for almost a century. When it turned 75, countries throughout the word paid honor to this fine organization with stamps, sets and souvenir sheets. I am breaking down an outstanding collection of items issued in honor of Rotary and present them here for you. Even if you are not a stamp collector, any of these would make a wonderful gift for any Rotarian you know.

Please note that any yellowing is a result of the scan; the photo is not an accurate reflection of the true beauty of this item.

The Fine Print:	**About Bobmill:**
Shipping/handling for all buyers is only $1.00 for up to three items. I do not rip off international customers by charging them outrageous shipping fees.	I am the largest and highest-rated stamp dealer on eBay. Check my feedback, then bid with confidence! Please feel free to <u>email</u> any questions, comments, or to ask for assistance with your collection.

Figure 18-2:
Some of BobMill's unique stamps.

Bob's #1 tip for new sellers at eBay: "Listen to your customers. Nothing is more important, but fast shipping is a close second."

Bubblefast

Member since May 1999; Feedback: 11,725; Positive Feedback 99.9%

I first met the Bubblefast "family" when I needed to move my mother's things from Florida to California. When I got the price quote from the moving company for rolls of cushioning, it was so high I nearly fell over! I knew that I could find a better price at eBay — and I did. Bubblefast prices were 50 percent less than the moving company had quoted, and they shipped the wrap directly to my mom's house so that I could meet it there to wrap her valuables.

The Bubblefast business began with Robin and her husband Alan. Their first transaction at eBay took place in early 1999, when Alan bought a Macintosh computer. When it came to finally selling, Alan figured that all eBay sellers would need shipping supplies. At first, they sold just one product, a 150' roll of ³⁄₁₆" (small size) bubble cushioning. Now they sell more than 65 variations of 8 or 9 products: bubble cushioning, antistatic bubble, bubble bags, bubble-lined mailers, rolled shipping foam, boxes, sealing tape, and stretch film.

Alan passed away in 2001, and Robin and her family carried on the business. On the bright side, Robin remarried and now (with a combined family) they have even more indentured employees. The Le Vine Family — Robin, Mark, Jenny 16, Steven 11, Sara 9, Michelle 20, and Grandma Gloria — and family friends Syble and Billy work closely together, putting in 70 to 80 hours a week.

A seller with many repeat customers (more than 21,000 positives; repeat customers help build businesses!), they decided to branch out and go into consignment selling. They registered on eBay as Trading Assistants and now they're "up to their eyeballs in new business." It works out real well for them, because they're already in the shipping supply business. No package is a challenge!

Mark uses Turbo Lister for the Bubblefast auctions. Fashion mavens Jenny and Michelle scrutinize and help write descriptions for consignment listings. Jenny also posts feedback several times a week. Robin still handles order entry and answers the phone and e-mail. Grandma Gloria, her friend Syble, and elf Billy handle the packing and shipping. They ship anywhere from 100 to 200 orders a day — their total shipping bill runs between $25 to $30K a month. The family has customers from around the world — they've shipped to every state in the U.S. and internationally as far as Japan — who buy from their auctions (see Figure 18-3), eBay store, and Web site (www.bubblefast.com). Last year their business grossed $650,000. The profit margin in the Bubblefast products is low, so they have to make it up in volume.

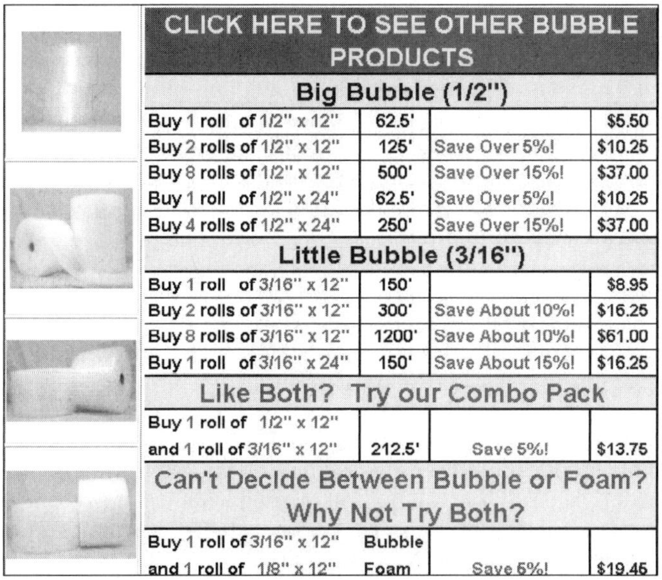

Figure 18-3:
A Bubblefast store link.

CLICK HERE TO SEE OTHER BUBBLE PRODUCTS			
Big Bubble (1/2")			
Buy 1 roll of 1/2" x 12"	62.5'		$5.50
Buy 2 rolls of 1/2" x 12"	125'	Save Over 5%!	$10.25
Buy 8 rolls of 1/2" x 12"	500'	Save Over 15%!	$37.00
Buy 1 roll of 1/2" x 24"	62.5'	Save Over 5%!	$10.25
Buy 4 rolls of 1/2" x 24"	250'	Save Over 15%!	$37.00
Little Bubble (3/16")			
Buy 1 roll of 3/16" x 12"	150'		$8.95
Buy 2 rolls of 3/16" x 12"	300'	Save About 10%!	$16.25
Buy 8 rolls of 3/16" x 12"	1200'	Save About 10%!	$61.00
Buy 1 roll of 3/16" x 24"	150'	Save About 15%!	$16.25
Like Both? Try our Combo Pack			
Buy 1 roll of 1/2" x 12" and 1 roll of 3/16" x 12"	212.5'	Save 5%!	$13.75
Can't Decide Between Bubble or Foam? Why Not Try Both?			
Buy 1 roll of 3/16" x 12" and 1 roll of 1/8" x 12"	Bubble Foam	Save 5%!	$19.45

eBay has totally changed this family's lives. Alan used to say "Our family is together all the time now; we've learned to pull together for a common goal." It's still true today with the family business he started.

The Le Vine family's tip for eBay sellers: "If you want to create a thriving eBay business and are willing to put the time and energy into it, the possibilities are endless. With a minimal investment of money, you have the potential to reach the world! Treat every customer like you want to be treated. After all this time, the customer is still always right."

Cardking4

Member since September 1998; Feedback: 3,155 Positive Feedback: 99.9%

This seller is one of my favorite people in the world. I knew Ken Tate long before he discovered eBay. He was the sports card king of the San Fernando Valley (a suburb of Los Angeles), selling cards wholesale to various sports card shops in the area, which is his retirement dream job. After years of working with Caltech, Fairchild, and JPL (deep space networks), this renowned engineer settled down to selling baseball cards in 1986 and found an outlet at eBay over a decade later. Ken is 81.

A visit to Ken's warehouse is a collector's dream come true. He has all the real stuff, and things signed by all the greats: Mantle, Williams, Cobb, Ali — you name the sports memorabilia, he either owns it or has seen it. This man knows his stuff. Check out Figure 18-4 for an example of one of Ken's auctions. From his ever-growing stock and collection of hockey sticks, signed bats, tobacco cards, and cases and cases of sports cards come his eBay sales — his full-time work. He's an expert when it comes to his collectibles, and he has an entire room of reference books about almost any collectible item you can imagine. His place is part museum, part library, and part Disneyland all rolled into one.

Ken collects and sells coins, too. He has currency and coins from all over, mostly uncirculated American coins. His was the first place where I ever saw an ancient Sassanian coin from A.D. 459. He works part-time at local coin shows, evaluating coins for the participants.

Ken is an eBay PowerSeller and uses Quicken to keep his books. eBay has changed his life for the better. He no longer has time to watch TV because he's always busy studying the market, seeing what the new trends are, and making deals for new merchandise. He's constantly learning and studies eBay the way some people study the stock market. His lovely wife Dot is a painter, and he has convinced her to dabble a bit on eBay as well.

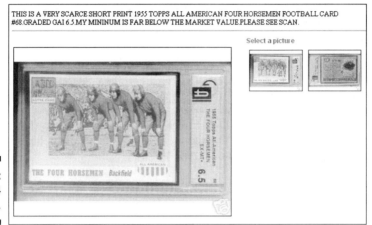

THIS IS A VERY SCARCE SHORT PRINT 1955 TOPPS ALL AMERICAN FOUR HORSEMEN FOOTBALL CARD #68.GRADED GAI 6.5.MY MININUM IS FAR BELOW THE MARKET VALUE.PLEASE SEE SCAN.

Figure 18-4:
A Cardking4
auction.

Ken's tip for sellers: "Start off slowly, study your market, and see what's selling."

ListingRover

Member since December 1999; Feedback 612; Positive Feedback 100%

In late 1998, a buddy of Steve Lindhorst purchased six green computer keyboards on eBay. He needed only one, so he sold the other five and made a pretty good profit on the deal. This got Steve's interest, and he registered and dove straight into selling. His first positive feedback came from selling a sales brochure for 1960 Ford delivery vans. He bought it at a used book store for less than $2.00 and sold it for $9.99.

I met Steve when teaching at eBay University. He's an instructor too and does a great job selling merchandise he buys in wholesale lots and as a Trading Assistant (selling items for other people). He's a creative seller too. His most memorable transaction involved a die-cast Shelby Cobra made by the Franklin Mint and signed by Carroll Shelby.

"I was working at an auto show for eBay and during a break decided to stroll through the vendor's booths. I was hoping to meet the legendary Carroll Shelby, who was appearing at the show. At a booth I noticed a model of the Shelby Cobra. It had a price tag of $120. I put two and two together and thought, 'I'll bet Mr. Shelby would autograph that if I ask him.' I took a chance on my wife's loving understanding and purchased the little car. I really felt like I was taking a chance and was a little scared to lay that money down."

Later Steve met Mr. Shelby and took a picture of him signing the car. He listed the Cobra with a reserve of $120 and hoped for the best. It sold for $420 to a woman who purchased it for her husband's anniversary present.

"This taught me two very important lessons. First, know the community and you can learn to depend on eBay as a marketplace. Second, be willing to take risks. If you know the community, it's a calculated risk."

Steve loves getting up and listing his items on eBay, knowing that they will sell. He promotes his eBay consignment selling business on his own Web site, www.listingrover.com (see Figure 18-5).

Steve's motto when it comes to eBay? "Think! Be observant! Never give up! Have a good time!"

Figure 18-5: Listing Rover's Web site lures in new eBay consignment customers.

Magic-By-Mail

Member since October 2001; Feedback 2729; Positive Feedback 99.9%

After 20 years on the job, Jonathan retired from his position as a police officer in England, came to America, and met his lovely wife Ellen. They discovered eBay together. Jonathan's lifelong hobby was magic, so he developed his own magic products and put them up for sale — they sold immediately. What started as a means to supplement Jonathan's pension became a burgeoning full-time business. Two years ago, they even opened their own Web site, www.magicbymail.biz.

The best day they ever had on eBay was recently when they sold more than $3500 of magic in 10 hours! They once made a $1000 plus sale to a magician in Australia and have had several other single sales between $500 and $900. Take a look at one of magic-by-mail's auctions in Figure 18-6.

FOLDING 3 in 1 QUARTER

It's a Biting Coin

It's the Coin in the Bottle

It's a Flipper

This is a must for any magician - A precision machined Laser Cut Folding US Quarter This is a real stunner.

You are bidding on a Brand New, Precision engineered, single fold Genuine US. 4 in 1 Folding Quarter Coin.

Bite a Coin in half - David Blaine did it - Now you can too

Figure 18-6: Magic secret tricks sold by magic-by-mail.

Although they devote many hours a day to their eBay business, it has allowed them to be flexible with their schedules. Ellen is just finishing her Bachelors degree in Professional Business Communication. She's applied much of what she's learned to their eBay business.

They enjoy buying on eBay too. Their most treasured purchase was an 1857 first edition magic book, "Magician's Own Book," which had been previously owned by a relative of Martha Washington (the wife of America's first president).

The biggest challenge in their business is keeping up with its growth! They've had such a steady increase in monthly sales that they're looking to move their business to larger quarters. That's a tough problem to have.

Magic-by-mail's tip for new sellers: "Plan ahead, start small, and let your business grow. Look after your customers; they are your single biggest asset. Without customers you would not have a business." I think those are good words to live by.

Melrose_Stamp

Member since March 1998; Feedback 4755; Positive Feedback 100%

A while back, I needed a rubber stamp or two for my business and didn't have time to go out to a printing store and place an order. I thought surely someone on eBay sells custom rubber stamps! I was right. That's when I met Jeff Stannard of Melrose Stamp Company. He specializes in self-inking custom rubber stamps and also sells stock design stamps.

Jeff was an assistant in a New York State economic development agency when he started his part-time business on eBay. Being around entrepreneurs gave him the inspiration he needed to quit his job and take his part-time sales to the next level.

He's had his eBay store since 2001 (see Figure 18-7) and works the business himself with no employees. His biggest sale came from a Chamber of Commerce in South Carolina. They ordered 65 custom stamps to use for a promotional day, where various merchants stamp a customer's card indicating the customer visited the store during the promotional day.

Figure 18-7:
Just one
category
from
Melrose_
Stamp's
eBay store.

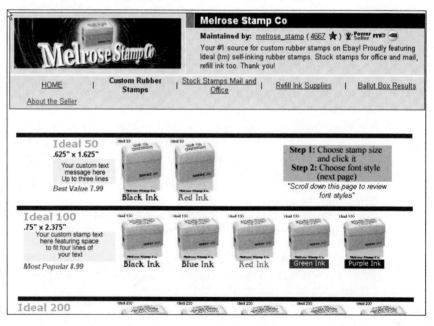

eBay has certainly changed his life. No longer a nine-to-fiver, Jeff works more than 60 hours a week. All his life he wanted to run his own business. "My business model would fail if it were locally based only. With eBay, I'm living my dream and selling my products globally. It's a life of independence, free from the corporate rat race!"

Jeff's advice to new eBay sellers? "Invest time to create a business plan. A business plan will help you identify your strengths and weaknesses, threats and opportunities. Build into the plan a set of financial projections as well; this will help you to clearly identify investment and working capital needs. Treat your eBay operation as a real, sustainable business and you will go far!"

Noblespirit

Member since September 1998, Feedback 10,4251; Positive Feedback 99.1%

Joe Cortese is a funny and creative guy, but I always wondered where his user ID came from. Joe was very close to his father, who passed away in 1995. His user ID at eBay was conceived as a tribute to his Dad, a "noble spirit." Joe says "through this name he is with me every day and guides me still."

Now that I've got you all misty-eyed, let me tell you how Joe got started on eBay. Joe's business was (and still is) centered around purchasing large estates and selling the contents to various dealers around the world. In 1997, on a train trip to Florida, he chatted with a fellow passenger who collected World War II memorabilia. The gentleman had a side business, selling pieces from his collection (and others) on eBay — something that Joe had never heard of.

About a year later, Joe decided to give this eBay thing a whirl. A local auctioneer was helping sell off some of the contents of Joe's house, including a Civil War vest pocket bible with dated notations about battles. The auctioneer told Joe that it was worth only about $15. Doubting the proposed value, Joe decided to sell the bible on eBay. When it sold for $375.00, he was hooked.

Joe is now the largest eBay seller of collectibles on eBay — specializing in coins and stamps. He acquires merchandise and also takes collections on consignment. All his auctions are run with no reserve price (see Figure 18-8), "Selling at no reserve is the most exciting aspect but it requires fortitude, consistency, and diversity. We might sell a Barbie doll one day and a $10,000 Ming Dynasty vase the next," quips Joe.

Joe even found time to develop with a programmer his own proprietary software, Meridian, to automate his auction business. You can read more about that on his Web site, www.noblespirit.com.

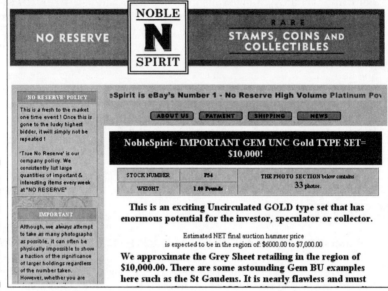

Figure 18-8:
One of
Noblespirit's
fascinating
auctions —
without a
reserve!

Joe's tip for new sellers mirrors my thoughts exactly: "Sell what you know, sell what you love. Those are the things you will sell best. Don't view eBay as a blanket golden opportunity to start a business unless you are prepared to make the same investment that you would be making to start that business in the real world."

PreservationPublishing

Member since April 1998; Feedback 642; Positive Feedback: 99.8%

Jillian Cline is not only a part-time seller on eBay, she trains dogs, writes books, and sells original dog products (books, cards, t-shirts, and other specialty items) through her own dealer network at dog shows throughout the country and through ads in magazines. eBay is a natural extension of her business.

She's also a collector and veteran eBay shopper. Her first transaction was buying a small bronze bulldog that was signed on the collar. She purchased it for half of what she had previously paid in an antique store for others. She now haunts eBay regularly for small bronze and metal bulldogs. She also purchased a framed, signed, and numbered Blue Dog lithograph by Louisiana artist George Rodrigue. She paid $1800 on eBay and had it appraised recently for $8000!

Her own eBay store is open 24/7, even though running her business can be difficult. Her husband is often transferred, forcing her to move. It would be impossible for her to have a traditional job, but eBay allows her to conduct business wherever they go.

She can run auctions (as in Figure 18-9) any time she likes. She used to have to spend her weekends schlepping her merchandise to dog shows and setting up a booth. With eBay she can display her pet products online and handle orders as they come in. Jillian also sells from her Web site:

www.preservationpublishing.com

Jillian says "Don't give up! Keep listing different items in auctions to draw people to your eBay store. Use cross-promotions and take advantage of eBay's occasional listing sale days. On those days test new products — and lots of them!"

Elegant Vintage Pit Bull blank Greeting cards

This lot consists of 2 beautiful, top quality 5"x7" (finished size) cards are blank inside, so you can compose your personal messages - with matching envelopes. They're also ideal to frame and hang in your home as reminders of days gone by. *They make great gifts too!*

Buyer to pay shipping & handling via First Class Mail of $1.75 (Add up to five additional packs for a low Priority Mail shipping rate of $4. Winner must submit payment within a week of winning the item.

Figure 18-9: A Preservation Publishing auction.

SallyJo

Member since January 1998; Feedback: 5118 Positive Feedback: 99.9%

Sally Severance is an eBay PowerSeller, a mother of four valedictorians, a rancher specializing in purebred Charolais cattle (her ranch Web site is www.sdcbulls.com), and runs a North Dakota farm with her husband. She gave up a successful ten-year banking career to stay home with her family, and by the way, she buys and sells at eBay.

From her ranch in North Dakota, Sally sells collectibles (see Figure 18-10) and general merchandise on eBay to supplement her income. The 25 to 30 hours a week that she spends on eBay earn her the money to buy things that she and her kids want.

Figure 18-10: A SallyJo auction.

USA FLAG ～ ABSOLUTELY PRECIOUS!

You are bidding on a beautiful USA flag. This is highest quality, American flag ever made! It is a beautiful, brand new American flag, made in the USA, with vibrant contrasting colors. It is a large, full size flag that measures 3X5 feet. It is constructed of 100% high quality 2-ply poly fabric, which combines durability, strength and flyability. It has all-sewn stripes and embroidered stars with a canvas header. It has 4 lines in the fly end, w/rope and 2 large brass grommets on the other end. Each flag is individually packaged. If you want to fly the highest quality, most beautiful flag ever made, this is the flag for YOU! The suggested retail price is $49.99. With a son who just spent almost a year in Iraq, I searched for the best flag to fly on our North Dakota ranch...and this is it!

Please check out my other items up for auction and SAVE on postage.

YOU WILL LOVE IT

Sally also shops for her family on eBay and considers that part of her business. She can save money by finding some special things for her children and grand-children. She has one daughter, Robyn, who is married with two children, and three sons: Ryan, an engineer; Randy, a recent college graduate working on the farm; and Rod, in the Army and recently returned after serving 11 months in Iraq. She has made many friends on eBay and really enjoys personal contact with customers.

Sally spent an entire year using her eBay earnings sending weekly care pack-ages to our troops in Iraq.

Her new eBay store is slowly filling with items. She does not use software to list her auctions because she feels that they're more personal when she does them herself.

Sally's tip for eBay sellers: "My #1 tip on setting up a business on eBay is to be honest, especially when writing up a description of what you are selling!"

Chapter 19

Ten Other Places to Move Merchandise

In This Chapter

▶ Giving it away: Charitable donations

▶ Going to garage sales, swap meets, the local antique mall, and community events

▶ Unloading on other eBay sellers

▶ Going, going, gone: Turning over your goods to a live auctioneer

▶ Finding a place that specializes

▶ Placing a classified ad

▶ Selling it cheap: A last-ditch effort

*W*hen a corner of your eBay storage area becomes the graveyard of unsold stuff (at some point it will — believe me), whatcha gonna do? Inevitably, you'll find yourself holding onto some merchandise that you feel may never scrape together a profit, and you'll become sick of looking at it. Whether thousands of those salad spinners that you bought to sell on eBay are suddenly appearing in multiple auctions or you jumped on the opportunity to buy a truckload (literally) of bargain-priced cat scratching posts, you have to make room for this stuff immediately or sell it fast.

Every business has a problem with excess inventory, so don't feel bad about it. You can't expect to bat .300 every time you choose a product to sell. The key is getting rid of excess products while losing nothing on your investment. None of your merchandise is trash — I hope — so someone out there may want it and will pay *something* for it. If not, you can always give it away. In this chapter, I highlight the top ten ways to move that superfluous merchandise and still save your investment.

Donate to Charitable Organizations

Charitable donating is my personal favorite way of unloading unwanted items. Not only are you doing something good for someone else, but your donation may be a 100 percent business write-off. My community has many private schools, churches, and synagogues. What these places all have in common are putting on fundraisers (auctions, raffles, tournaments, bingo) and welcoming donations. You have to give the best stuff to your schools or churches — especially if your item will be some sort of prize. Many charities often gratefully take boxes of miscellaneous stuff (think Salvation Army and Goodwill).

Classy gifting

Something I like to do is put together little gift baskets for charity auctions. I'll take a bunch of female-related, male-related, or kids' items and put them in a basket on a base of shredded Sunday comics. I keep a roll of clear cellophane on hand to wrap the entire thing. I then top it off with a nice big bow. It's always an appreciated donation and, wrapped up this way, it always gets a higher price at bazaars or silent auctions.

Online charities

One of my favorite Web sites, MissionFish.com (see Figure 19-1) recently joined with eBay to organize eBay Giving Works. MissionFish helps non-profit organizations support their missions by teaching them to fish and to build their own fisheries (to paraphrase the parable). Select your charity, and MissionFish does the rest. See Chapter 2 for more on charity auctions on eBay.

When an item sells, you (the donor) are responsible for shipping the item. You must use a shipping company that supplies a tracking number, which you submit to eBay Giving Works. (In addition to the item, the entire cost of shipping is tax deductible.) After the winner receives the item, all proceeds are sent from MissionFish to the designated non-profit. You then receive a thank-you letter as proof of your gift for IRS tax purposes. You'll have a write-off, and you'll feel good about what you did to help others.

Many other charities accept *gifts-in-kind*; items that are new or gently used that they resell to raise funds. I've brought excess eBay inventory to the American Cancer Society's Discovery Shop, and they've been very gracious about the donations. Now they also sell on eBay (aside from their many retail locations) under their own user ID.

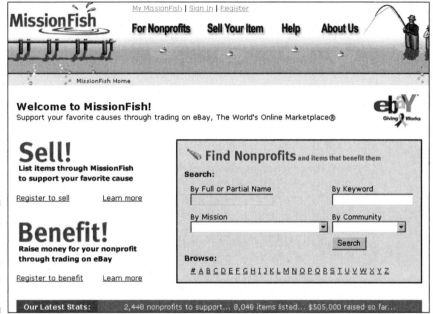

Figure 19-1:
The
MissionFish.
com charity
auctions
home page.

Have a Garage Sale

Sell your items to other eBay sellers. Hee hee, only kidding (maybe not). Perhaps some of the stuff you have may appeal to the locals (some of whom probably do sell on eBay). Garage sales draw big crowds when promoted properly, and you'll be surprised at the amount of stuff you'll unload. An especially good time to have a garage sale is late fall or early winter — just in time for the holidays.

Because you've probably been to a bunch of garage sales but maybe haven't given one in a long, long time, here are a few reminders:

- **Plan the sale at least three weeks in advance:** Decide on the weekend of your sale well beforehand and be sure to set a specific opening time. If you welcome *early birds* (people who like to show up at 6 or 7 a.m.), be sure to put that in your ad and flyers.

- **Invite neighbors to participate:** The more the merrier, right? Also, the bigger the sale, the more customers you're likely to entice. Everyone can drum up at least a few items for a garage sale.

- **Gather and price items to go in the sale:** After you set a date, immediately start putting things aside and pricing them with sticky tags. This way, you won't have to scramble the day before to find things.

- ✔ **Place a classified ad:** Call your local newspaper a week before the sale and ask the friendly classified department people when the best time is to run an ad. Take their advice — they know what they're talking about!

- ✔ **Make flyers to post around the neighborhood:** Fire up your computer and make a flyer; include your address, a map, the date, and the starting time. Be sure to mention special items that you've thrown into the sale to bring 'em in and mention also that many items are new. If two or three families are participating in the sale, mention that too. If you have small throwaway types of items, include the line "Prices start at 25 cents." Hang the flyer in conspicuous places around your neighborhood.

- ✔ **Post large signs on nearby corners:** The day before the sale, put up *large* posters advertising the sale. (You can pick up 22 x 28 poster board from an art store or office supply store.) When you make the posters, use thick black shipping markers on a light board. Use few words, including only the basic details, for example: "Garage Sale June 22-24, 8 a.m., Tons of Stuff, 1234 Extra Cash Blvd." Also make a sign to hang at the sale location "Sale Continues tomorrow, New Items will be Added!"

- ✔ **Clean up any dusty or dirty items:** If you want someone to buy it, you have to make it look good.

- ✔ **Gather supplies:** Get lots of change; make sure you have plenty of tens, fives, a ton of singles, and several rolls of coins. Get a calculator for each person who will be taking money. Set aside a box to use as the cash box. Collect all the supermarket shopping bags that you can for those with multiple purchases.

- ✔ **Hang helium balloons to draw attention to your signs:** The day of the sale, go to the busiest corner near your sale and tie some helium balloons to your sign — that's sure to attract attention. Do the same thing at the corner near your sale and also at the curb of the sale.

- ✔ **Display everything in an orderly fashion:** Pull out your old card tables and arrange items so that people can easily see what's there; a literal pile of junk'll turn them off. Hang clothes on a temporary rack (or use a clothesline on the day of the sale).

- ✔ **Get ready to negotiate:** Talk to people when they approach and *make that sale!*

Rent a Table at the Local Swap Meet

Local *swap meets* (regularly scheduled events where you can rent space for a token fee and sell your wares) can be a great place to meet other eBay sellers. But whatever you do, don't mention that you sell on eBay. Let the customers think that you're a rube and that they can get the best of you. Offer great deals; give 'em a discount if they buy a ton of stuff. Just like with a garage sale (see preceding section), you can move lots of merchandise here.

Don't forget to try to unload your goods to other sellers; perhaps they can do with a little extra inventory. Check the classifieds of local newspapers for swap meets; you should be able to find ads listing these types of sales, which occur once a month in some towns.

Consign Merchandise to the Local Antique Mall

An *antique mall* is a retail store that's often run by several people who take your merchandise on consignment. You can probably find a few in your area. Your items are sold in the store (good for you), and the storeowners take a commission on each sale (good for them). They take your items, tag them with your own identifying tag, and display them for sale. Antique malls usually see an enormous amount of foot traffic, and this may be as close to having a retail store that you'll ever get.

Take a Booth at a Community Event

Where I live, the local business community often holds special events: street fairs, Fourth of July extravaganzas, pumpkin festivals, and others I can't think of right now. As a vendor, you can buy a booth at such events to peddle your wares. For seasonal events, purchasing a bunch of holiday-related items to make your table match the festivities is a savvy marketing idea. Your excess eBay inventory will just be part of the display — and a big part of your sales. You might even consider donating a percentage of your sales to a local non-profit to help boost traffic.

If the event is in the evening, purchase a few hundred glow-in-the-dark bracelets on eBay (you can often get 100 for $20). The kids love them and will drag their parents to your booth. Be creative and think of other ways to make your booth stand out. Support your community, have a barrel of fun, and make some money!

Resell to Sellers on eBay

Package up your items into related lots that will appeal to sellers who are looking for merchandise online. Take a tip from the successful eBay seller that often combines many lost packages into single lots to sell on eBay: the Post Office Mail Recovery Center. If you're overstocked with stuffed animals, put together a lot of a dozen. If you don't have a dozen of any one item, make packages of related items that will appeal to a certain type of seller.

Be sure to use the words *liquidation, wholesale,* or *resale* (or all three) in your title. A world of savvy sellers is out there looking for items to sell. Maybe another seller can move the items later or in a different venue.

Note that eBay has Wholesale subcategories for almost every sort of merchandise.

Visit a Local Auctioneer

Yes, when I say you should visit a local auctioneer, I mean a real live auctioneer, one who holds live auctions at real auction houses that real people attend. Many people enjoy going to live auctions. (I recommend that you go occasionally to acquire unique items to resell on eBay.) Shopping at auctions can be addictive (duh), and live auctions attract an elite group of knowledgeable buyers.

The basic idea is to bring your stuff to an auctioneer, who auctions off lots for you. Good auctioneers, such as those at the Los Angeles Bonhams & Butterfields (www.butterfields.com) can get a crowd going, bidding far more than an item was expected to sell for. Bonhams & Butterfields appraisal page is shown in Figure 19-2.

Figure 19-2: Bonhams & Butterfields consignment information.

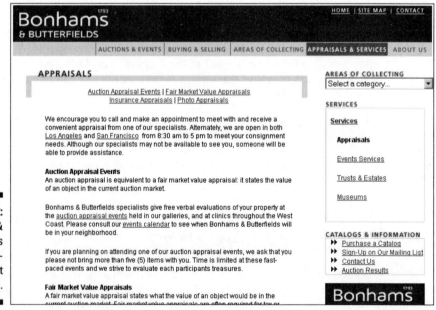

Here are a few facts about real live auctioneers and some pointers to keep in mind when looking for one:

- ✔ **Make sure that the auction house you choose is licensed to hold auctions in your state, insured, and bonded (more about bonding in Chapter 9).** You don't want to leave your fine merchandise with someone who will pack up and disappear with your stuff before the auction.

- ✔ **Get the details before agreeing to the consignment.** Many auction houses give you at least 75 percent of the final hammer price. Before you consign your items, ask the auctioneer's representative about the details, such as

  - When will the auction be held?

  - How often are the auctions held?

  - Have you sold items like this before? If so, how much have they sold for in the past?

  - Will there be a printed catalog for the sale, and will my piece be shown in it?

  Get the terms and conditions in writing and have the rep walk you through every point so that you thoroughly understand each.

- ✔ **Search the Internet.** Type **licensed auctions** and see what you come up with; it can't hurt.

- ✔ **Contact local auctioneers.** If your items are of good quality, a local auction house may be interested in taking them on consignment.

Find Specialty Auction Sites

If you have some specialized items that just don't sell very well on eBay, you might look for a different venue. Although eBay is the best all-purpose selling site in the world, you may have an item that only a specialist in the field can appreciate.

For example, I've seen some fine works of art not sell on eBay. But don't fret, you'll find many other places online where you can sell these items. For example, I searched Yahoo! for **art auctions**. Under the <u>Web Results heading,</u> I found more than 6 million Web sites that auction artwork. You might want to redefine your search with your telephone area code so that you find auction locations in your immediate area.

You may find an online auctioneer who specializes in the particular item you have for sale, something too esoteric for the eBay crowd. I've found some incredible bargains for myself on elegant new sunglasses made by a company in Italy called Persol, a company world famous for crystal lenses and ultra-fine quality. The super-famous wear these sunglasses: Robert De Niro, Tom Cruise, Donald Trump, Sharon Stone, Mel Gibson, and Cindy Crawford. These sunglasses normally retail from $150–$300 a pair, but you can sometimes find them on eBay for as low as $40. Unless you're buying them dirt cheap, you're not making your profits on eBay. Maybe the crowd just doesn't know about them, but they sell well elsewhere.

Run a Classified Liquidation Ad

Sell your special items in the appropriate categories of the classifieds. Sell the rest of them in preassigned bulk lots for other sellers. When you write the ad, make your lots sound fantastic; give the reader a reason to call you. When they call, be excited about your merchandise. But be honest and tell them you're just selling the stuff to raise cash.

Sell Everything on eBay for a $.99 Opening Bid . . .

. . . and take what you get.

Part VI
Appendixes

The 5th Wave — By Rich Tennant

"How many times have I told you that you can't sell your brother at eBay?"

In this part . . .

Appendix A is my random glossary of words that may be new to you, but will soon become part of your day-to-day vocabulary; refer to it often as you peruse other parts of the book. In Appendix B, I briefly discuss home networking: how it can work for you, what it is, the benefits, and how to set one up.

Appendix A

Glossary

1099: An end-of-year form that you file with the IRS to record your payments to outside contractors. A 1099 must be filed for anyone to whom you pay more than $600 in a calendar year.

About Me page: The free Web page given to every eBay user. An excellent promotional tool.

absentee bid: A bid that an auction house employee places on a lot (or lots) — up to a maximum amount that you designate — in your absence. When you want to participate in a live auction but can't attend it physically, you can pre-arrange to have the auction house place absentee bids for you.

accounts payable: The amount your business owes to vendors, office supply stores, your credit card charges, and the like. This includes any money your business owes.

accounts receivable: The money people owe you, such as the checks and money orders you're expecting in the mail; the money sitting in your PayPal account that you haven't transferred to your checking account.

announcements pages: eBay pages where you get all the latest eBay information. You need to check these pages periodically. If you follow the Announcements link, which is at the bottom of every eBay page, you end up at the Community announcements page at www2.ebay.com/aw/marketing.shtml. If you're wondering whether it's your computer's problem or an eBay problem when the search engine isn't working, check out the System Status Announcements Board at www2.ebay.com/aw/announce.shtml.

as is/where is: An item that comes with no warranty, implied or otherwise, speaking to the merchantability of the product.

bid increment: The amount that a bid must advance, based on the auction's high bid.

bid retraction: A cancelled auction bid. Retractions can occur only under extreme circumstances (such as when you type the wrong numerals).

bid shielding: An illegal process wherein two bidders work together to defraud a seller out of high bids by retracting a bid at the last minute and granting a confederate's low bid the win. Not as much of an issue anymore due to eBay's new bid retraction policy; *see also* bid retraction.

bonding: A surety bond can be issued by a third party (usually an insurance company) to guarantee a seller's performance in a transaction.

card not present: Credit card services use this term to describe transactions that typically happen over the Internet or by mail order. It means that the seller hasn't seen the actual card.

caveat emptor: Latin for *let the buyer beware.* If you see this posted anywhere, proceed cautiously — you're responsible for the outcome of any transaction in which you take part.

chargeback: When someone calls his or her credit card company and refuses to pay for a transaction. The credit card company will credit the card in question while making you pay back the amount.

consignment: When someone hands over merchandise to you, which you then auction on eBay. You make a little commission and the other person sells something without the hassle.

cookie: A small text file that may be left on your computer to personalize your experience on a particular Web site. When you sign on to eBay, a cookie is placed on your computer that keeps your user ID and password active for as long as you're on the site.

corporation: A separate entity set up to do business.

CPA: Certified Public Accountant. Someone who has been educated in accounting and has passed a certification test. CPAs are at the top of the accounting professional heap.

DBA: Doing business as. These letters appear next to the common name of a business entity, sole proprietorship, partnership, or corporation that conducts business under a fictitious name.

DOA: Dead on arrival. The product you purchased doesn't work from the moment you opened the package.

DUNS number: Data Universal Numbering System number. An identification number issued to businesses from a database maintained by the great and powerful Dun and Bradstreet. These numbers are issued to allow your business to register with more than 50 global, industry, and trade associations, including the United Nations, the U.S. Federal Government, the Australian

Government, and the European Commission. My business has had a DUNS number for years. You can get yours at no cost by calling Dun and Bradstreet at 800-333-0505 (`https://eupdate.dnb.com/requestoptions.html`).

EIN: Employer identification number. If you run your business as a partnership or a corporation, you need an EIN number from the IRS. If you're a sole proprietor, your Social Security number is your EIN because you file all your business in your personal tax return.

entrepreneur: That's you! An entrepreneur is someone who takes the financial risk to start a business. Even if you're buying and reselling garage sale items, you're still an entrepreneur.

FOB: Free on board. When you begin purchasing large lots of merchandise to sell, you'll encounter this term. The FOB location technically means the place where the seller delivers the goods. If the price you're quoted is FOB Chicago, you're responsible for all shipping costs to get the goods from Chicago to your home city.

FTP: File Transfer Protocol. The protocol used to transfer files from one server to another.

hammer fee: A fee that the auction house charges at a live auction. Be sure to read the information package *before* you bid on an item in a live auction. Hammer fees usually add 10–15 percent to the amount of your bid.

HTF: Hard to find. An abbreviation that commonly appears in eBay auction titles to describe items that are, uh, hard to find.

invoice: A bill that outlines the items in a specific transaction; who the item is sold to, and all costs involved.

ISBN number: International Standard Book Number. Just like a car's VIN number or the UPC code on a can of beans, the ISBN identifies a book by a universal number.

keystone: In the brick-and-mortar retailing world, 100 percent markup. A product sells for keystone if it sells for twice the wholesale price. Products that you can sell at keystone are very nice to find.

live auctions: Auctions held online in real time. Check out `www.ebayliveauctions.com`.

mannequin. A representation of the human form made of wood, fiberglass, or plastic. Essential for modeling clothing for your eBay apparel sales.

MIB: Mint in box. Okay, the item inside the box is mint, but the box looks like a sixteen-wheeler ran over it.

MIMB: Mint in mint box. Not only is the item in mint condition, but it's in a perfect box as well.

mint: An item in perfect condition is described as mint. This is truly a subjective opinion, usually based on individual standards.

MSRP: Manufacturers suggested retail price. The price hardly anybody pays.

NARU: Not a registered user. A user of eBay or other online community who has been suspended for any number of reasons.

OOP: Out of print. When a book or CD is being published, it usually has its own lifetime in the manufacturing process. When it is no longer being made, it's out of print, or OOP.

provenance: The story behind an item, including who owned it and where it came from. If you have an interesting provenance for one of your items, be sure to put it in the auction description because it adds considerable value to the item.

QuickBooks: A top-of-the-heap accounting program that helps you keep your records straight.

register: Similar to a checkbook account listing, QuickBooks keeps registers that go up and down depending on the amount of flow in an account balance.

ROI: Return on investment. A figure expressed as a percentage that stands for your net profit after taxes and your own equity.

sniping: The act (or fine art) of bidding at the very last possible second of an auction.

sole proprietorship: A business that's owned by only one person, and the profits and losses are recorded on that person's personal tax return.

split transaction: A transaction that you must assign to more than one category. If you pay a credit card bill and a portion of the bill went to purchased merchandise, a portion to gas for business-related outings, and yet another portion to eBay fees, you must post each amount to its own category.

tax deduction: An expenditure on your part that represents a normal and necessary expense for your business. Before you get carried away and assume that *every* penny you spend is a write-off (deduction), check with your tax professional to outline exactly what is and what isn't.

TOS: Terms of service. eBay has a TOS agreement; check it out at `pages.ebay.com/help/policies/user-agreement.html`.

W-9: A form that must be filled out by any outside contractor you pay for services. This form includes the contractor's Social Security number and address. Your outside contractors must give you an invoice for each payment that you make to them. You use the information from this form to issue your 1099s at the end of the year. *See also* 1099.

wholesale: Products sold to retailers (that's you) at a price above the manufacturer's cost, allowing for a mark-up to retail. I hope you buy most of your merchandise at wholesale. Stores such as Costco or Sam's Club sell items in bulk at prices marginally over wholesale. You must get a resale number from your state to buy at true wholesale.

Appendix B

The Hows and Whys of a Home Network

● ●

*W*hat is a network? A *network* is a way to connect computers so that they can communicate with each other — as if they were one giant computer with different terminals. The best part is that a network enables high-speed Internet connection sharing, as well as the sharing of printers and other peripherals. By setting up a computer network, one computer might run bookkeeping, another might run a graphics server, and others might be used as personal PCs for different users. From each networked computer, it's possible to access programs and files on all other networked computers.

Today's technologies allow you to perform this same miracle on the *home network*. You can connect as many computers as you like, and run your business from anywhere in your home — you can even hook up your laptop from the bedroom if you don't feel like getting out of bed.

Now for the *whys* of a home network. A network is a convenient way to run a business. All big companies use them, and so should you. You can print your postage, for example, on one printer from any computer in your home or office. You can extend your DSL line or Internet cable connection so that you can use it anywhere in your home — as well as in your office.

In a network, you can set certain directories in each computer to be *shared*. That way, other computers on the network can access those directories. You can also password-protect certain files and directories to prevent others — your children or your employees — from accessing them.

I devote the rest of this appendix to a quick and dirty discussion of home networks installed on Windows-based PCs. I give you a lesson on what I know works for most people. (Hey, if it doesn't work, don't e-mail me — head back to the store and get your money back!)

At this point, I want to remind you that I'm not a techno-whiz (just like I'm not a lawyer or an accountant). For more information about anything you'd think to ask about home networking, I defer to Kathy Ivens, author of *Home Networking For Dummies* (published by Wiley).

What I know about home networks, I've found out the hard way — from the school of hard knocks. A lot of research went into this appendix as well, so humor me and read on.

Variations of a Home Network

You have a choice of four types of home networks: Ethernet, powerline, home phoneline, and wireless. See Table B-1 for a quick rundown of some pros and cons of each.

Table B-1	Types of Networks Pros and Cons	
Type	*Pros*	*Cons*
Traditional Ethernet*	Fast, cheap, and easy setup	Computers and printers must be hardwired; cables run everywhere
Home phoneline	Fast; runs over your home phone lines	Old wiring or not enough phone jacks may be a drawback
Powerline	Fast; your home is already prewired with outlets	Electrical interference may degrade the signal
Wireless network**	Pretty fast; wireless (no ugly cords to deal with)	Expensive; may not be reliable because of interference from home electrical devices

*Connects computers with high quality cable over a maximum of 328 feet of cabling.
**Several flavors of wireless are available. See "Hooking Up with Wireless" later in this chapter.

The home phoneline network is fading in popularity because people don't have enough phone jacks in their house to make it an easy proposition.

The wireless network is currently the hot ticket and highly touted by the geek gurus. However, the wireless signal may experience interference because the network runs with the same 2.4 GHz technology as some home wireless telephones. I have a wireless network as a secondary network, and it works, kinda. My primary network is a hybrid, combining Ethernet, home phoneline, and wireless.

With broadband over powerline, you get high-speed Internet directly into your home electrical system. Just plug in your powerline boxes (more on that later) and you're up and running!

All networks need the following two devices:

✔ **Router:** A router allows you to share a single Internet IP address among multiple computers. A router does exactly what its name implies; it routes signals and data to the different computers on your network. If you have one computer, the router can act as a firewall or even a network device leading to a print server (a gizmo that attaches to your router and allows you to print directly to a printer without having another computer on).

✔ **Modem:** You need a modem for Internet connection. You get one from your cable or phone company and plug it into an outlet with cable (just like your TV) or into a special phone jack if you have DSL. The modem connects to your router with an Ethernet cable.

If you have broadband, you don't even need to have a main computer turned on to access the connection anywhere in the house. If you keep a printer turned on (and have a print server), you can also connect that to your router and print from your laptop in another room — right through the network.

Before touching your network card or opening your computer to install anything, touch a grounded metal object to free yourself of static electricity Otherwise, a spark could go from your hand to the delicate components on the network card or another card, thereby rendering the card useless. Better yet, go to an electronics store and purchase a wrist grounding strap that has a cord with a gator clip, which you clip to a metal part of the computer before touching anything inside for safety.

Powerline network

An ingenious invention, a powerline network uses your existing home powerlines to carry your network and your high-speed Internet connection. You access the network by plugging a powerline adapter from your computer into an electrical outlet on the wall. Powerline networks have been around for a while and are in the second round of technological advances.

Hooking up a powerline network is so easy that it's a bit disappointing — you'll wonder why it isn't more complicated. Most installations work immediately right out of the box. Figure B-1 shows you the base setup. Computers in any other rooms need only a powerline bridge adapter with an Ethernet cable to a network card.

To set up a powerline network, you'll need the following (in addition to a router and modem):

✔ **Electrical outlets:** I'll bet you have more than one in each room of your house.

✔ **An Ethernet card for each computer:** Many new computers already have an Ethernet card. If yours doesn't, you can get inexpensive Ethernet cards for around $10.

✔ **Powerline Ethernet bridge for each computer:** You plug an Ethernet cable from your computer into the powerline Ethernet bridge, and then plug Netgear's Ethernet bridge into a wall outlet. See Figure B-2.

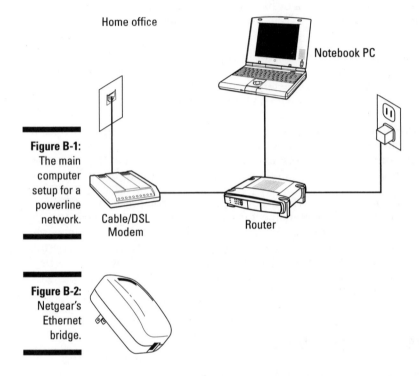

Home office

Notebook PC

Figure B-1:
The main
computer
setup for a
powerline
network.

Cable/DSL
Modem

Router

Figure B-2:
Netgear's
Ethernet
bridge.

Hooking up the powerline network goes like this:

1. **The high-speed connection comes in through your DSL or cable line.**

2. **Plug the cable line (or phoneline for DSL) into your modem.**

3. **Connect one "in" Ethernet cable from your modem to a router.**

4. **Connect one "out" Ethernet cable from the router to a local computer.**

5. **Connect another "out" Ethernet cable to the powerline adapter.**

6. **Plug the powerline box into a convenient wall outlet.**

Home phoneline

According to the Home Phoneline Networking Alliance (HPNA) — the association that works with hardware companies to develop a single net-working standard — tests indicate that phoneline network technology can be successfully installed and operational in 99 percent of today's homes. In real life, how your home is wired and the quality of those wires dictates that success.

I can hook up to my network successfully from 90 percent of the phone jacks in my house. The wall telephone cabling contains four wires, and your telephone uses only a portion of two. There's plenty more room in the cable for your network. Figure B-3 shows you what the typical home phoneline setup looks like.

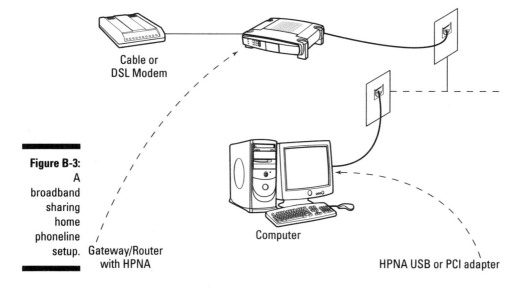

Figure B-3:
A broadband sharing home phoneline setup.

Cable or DSL Modem

Gateway/Router with HPNA

Computer

HPNA USB or PCI adapter

The phoneline network sends data at a speedy 10MB per second (the same speed as a regular Ethernet network) and can operate with computers or other equipment placed as far as 1000 feet apart and will work in homes as large as 10,000 square feet. Best of all, you can talk on the same phoneline without causing any interference.

Take a look at the jacks at the end of all your phone cords; if you see only two copper-colored wires in the plastic jack, toss the cord. The ones that you need to carry your full load must have *four* wires visible in the clear plastic end of the jack.

To set up your network to carry files and your high-speed connection throughout your house, you need some extra hardware:

> ✔ **Bridge:** A device that connects your Ethernet (router connection) with your powerline network. You can get a device that combines the router and the bridge.

✔ **HPNA network adapter for each computer:** You need an adapter that enables your computer to become one with other computers on the network. These adapters are available also as a USB device, eliminating the need to install a card in your computer.

✔ **Phone jacks:** Kind of essential for plugging in the phone wire from the adapter.

To install a home phoneline network, just follow these steps (be sure to follow your manufacturer's instructions if they vary from this information).

If you're installing a USB (universal serial bus) adapter, don't bother trying to open your computer. Just plug in the adapter to an available USB port and proceed to Step 5.

1. **Turn off your computer and disconnect its power cord.**

2. **Open the cover of your computer.**

3. **Install the network card in an available slot.**

   Touch the card only by the metal part on its outside edge. When installing the card, press firmly down on the top of the card with your thumb to properly seat the card in the slot. Fasten the card to the chassis by tightening the screw on the metal edge.

4. **Replace the cover on your PC and reconnect the power cord.**

5. **Connect one end of the (RJ-11) telephone cord that came with your network card to the port labeled *To Wall* on the card, and plug the other end into a convenient wall telephone jack.**

   If you have a telephone that needs to use that wall jack, connect the cord to the port labeled *To Phone;* your telephone will work through the network card.

6. **Power up your computer.**

   If you're lucky, your computer will see the new hardware and ask you to install the driver. If you're not lucky, check the instructions (as a last-ditch effort, you can always read the instructions!) for troubleshooting tips.

7. **When asked, insert the CD or the disk that came with the card (containing those tricky drivers) and follow the on-screen instructions.**

   As you go through the instructions, decide on a name for each computer that you want to install on the network.

8. **Set up directories that you want shared on the network.**

   Go to My Computer, select the directories (denoted by folder icons) that you want to share, right-click, and indicate that you want to share these directories with other computers on the network. Do the same with your local printers.

9. **Repeat Steps 1–8 on each computer.**

   As you add a computer, double-check that it can communicate with the other computers that you've already installed on the network by trying to open a shared directory on a remote computer and printing a test page on a remote printer.

10. **If your network is not functioning properly after you complete all recommended steps, call tech support as many times as necessary to get your network up and running.**

    When your network connection is flying and working flawlessly, it's time to add your broadband.

11. **To install the broadband connection, take the Ethernet cable from the modem and connect it to the back of your router. Then connect another Ethernet cable from the router to the phoneline network bridge.**

12. **Connect the phoneline that comes with your bridge from the bridge to a telephone wall jack.**

    Voila — you should be good to go with your Internet connection on all the computers in your network.

The wall connectors each have an outlet for a telephone cord that you plug into your wall jack. (I cheated in one room and connected two computers to one phone jack with a splitter that makes two jacks out of one.)

Hooking up with wireless

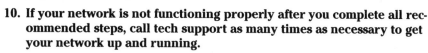

Wireless networking — also known as WiFi or, to the more technically inclined, IEEE 802.11 — is the hot new technology for all kinds of networks. It's an impressive system when it works, with no cables or connectors to bog you down.

If you're worried about your next-door neighbor hacking into your computer through your wireless connection — stop worrying. Wireless networks are protected by their own brand of security, called WEP (or Wired Equivalent Privacy). WEP encrypts your wireless transmissions and prevent others from getting into your network. Although super-hackers have cracked this system, it's the best possible until a new security system is invented.

To link your laptop or desktop to a wireless network with WEP encryption, you have to enter a key code from the wireless access point. Just enter it into your wireless card software on every computer that uses the network, and you should be good to go.

You may get confused when you see the different types of wireless available. Here's the lowdown on the variations:

✔ **802.11a:** This wireless format works really well — fast with good connectivity. It's also very expensive. This format is used when you have to connect a large group, such as at a convention center or in a dormitory. It delivers data at speeds as high as 54 Mbps (megabits per second). It runs at the 5 GHz band (hence its nickname WiFi5), so it doesn't have any competition for bandwidth with wireless phones or microwave ovens.

✔ **802.11b:** My laptop has a built-in 802.11b card, so I can connect to the popular HotSpots in Starbucks and airports. It's the most common wireless type, and it's used on the most platforms. It travels over the 2.4 GHz band. The 802.11b version is slower than the 802.11a version, transferring data at only 11 Mbps. It's a solid, low-cost solution when you have no more than 32 users per access point.

The lower frequency of 2.4 GHz drains less power from laptops and other portable devices, so laptop batteries will last longer. Also, 2.4 GHz signals travel farther and can work through walls and floors more effectively than 5 GHz signals.

✔ **802.11g:** This is the newest flavor based on the 2.4 GHz band. It speeds data up to a possible 54 Mbps, and it's backward compatible with 802.11b service.

Installing your wireless network isn't a gut-wrenching experience either (although it can be if the signal doesn't reach where you want it). You hook up your computer (a laptop works best) to the wireless access point (the gizmo with the antenna that broadcasts your signal throughout your home or office) to perform some setup tasks such as choosing your channel and setting up your WEP code. (The wireless access point will come with its own instructions.)

After you complete the setup and turn on your wireless access point, you have a WiFi hotspot in your home or office. Typically, a hotspot provides coverage for about 100 feet in all directions, although walls and floors cut down on the range.

Here are some simplified steps on configuring your network:

1. **Run a cable from your cable connection or a phone cord from your DSL line to your modem.**

2. **Connect one Ethernet cable from your modem to your router.**

3. **Connect one Ethernet cable to your wireless access point.**

Take a look at this network diagram from Netgear in Figure B-4.

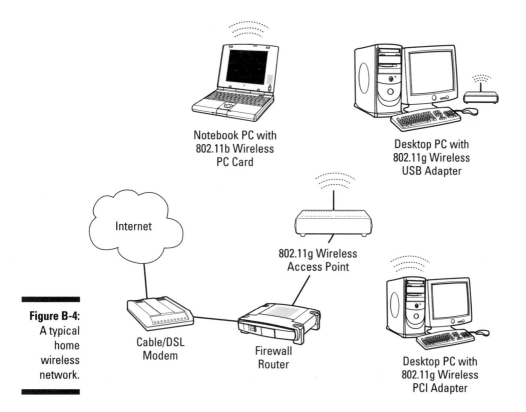

Notebook PC with
802.11b Wireless
PC Card

Desktop PC with
802.11g Wireless
USB Adapter

Internet

802.11g Wireless
Access Point

Figure B-4:
A typical
home
wireless
network.

Cable/DSL
Modem

Firewall
Router

Desktop PC with
802.11g Wireless
PCI Adapter

Internet Security and Your Home Network

A dial-up connection exposes your computer to the Internet only when you dial up and get connected. Most broadband Internet connections are always on, which means your computer is always exposed. You should shield your computer with a strong firewall and an antivirus program.

Firewall software

When you're connected to the Internet, you're exposed not only to hackers but also to threats such as *Trojan horses,* programs that can get into your computer when you innocently view an infected Web site. Once inside your computer, the Trojan horse, like ET, phones home. From there, an evil-deed-doer, now with a direct line to your computer, may be able to wreak havoc with your precious data.

If you're technically inclined — and even if you're not — visit the Web site for Gibson Research Corporation (www.grc.com). Gibson Research is the brain-child of an early PC pioneer, Steve Gibson, who's renowned as a genius in the world of codes and programming. Steve is *the* expert when it comes to expos-ing the vulnerabilities of systems over the Internet. A few free diagnostic pro-grams on this site will check your computer's vulnerability to Internet threats.

Shields Up and LeakTest are programs that test your computer and terrify you with results that expose the vulnerability of your Internet connection. I learned about ZoneAlarm on Steve's site. This free program (the Pro version costs $39.95) has won every major award in the industry as the most secure software firewall. If your main concern is safety, visit www.zonelabs.com for a free download of ZoneAlarm.

Antivirus software

You're still going to need antivirus software to protect you from the idiots who think it's fun to send destructive code through e-mail. The leading pro-grams in this area are Norton AntiVirus and McAfee. One of the problems inherent in buying software is that you might be urged to load much more than you need onto your computer. If all you need is an antivirus software, purchase only an antivirus software. But don't delay. Buy it now and be sure to update the antivirus files each week so that you're fully protected from the latest viruses.

Index

Symbols and Numerics

* (asterisk) search operator, 148
@1 (at sign, one) search operator, 148
, (comma) search operator, 148
- (minus sign) search operator, 148
# of Watchers (Number of Watchers) feature, 64
{ } (parentheses) search delimiters, 148
" " (quotation marks) search delimiters, 148
99¢ Only store, acquiring merchandise at, 126
7-Eleven money order, 240
1099 form, 351
30-day Federal Trade Commission rule, 52
24-hour auction, 46

• A •

AAASeller.com Web site, 189, 190, 226
About Me page, 27, 54, 55, 71–73, 110
About the Seller page, 110, 120
Abovethemall (eBay seller), 327–329
access-restricted auction, 39, 42
account summary page, 69–70
accounting, double-entry, 291
accounts payable/receivable, 351
Accredited Registrar Directory, 169
Action Figure Digest, 152
action figures, selling, 17, 132, 152
Address Verification Service (AVS), 249
Adult Only area, 39, 42
age of bidder
  determining, 84
  reporting underage bidder, 98–99
alcohol, selling, 84, 86, 87, 88
All Bidding area, 58
All Buying area, 59, 60–64
All Favorites area, 58, 67–69

All Selling area, 58, 59–60, 65, 74, 253
Amazon.com Web site, 108, 151
America Online (AOL) Web site hosting, 159, 160, 226
American Merchandise Liquidators Web site, 135
American Philatelic Society, 155
AmeriSurplus Web site, 135
ammunition, selling, 86
AMNACS (American Numismatic Association Certification Service), 155
ándale Web site, 190
animals, selling, 86
announcement pages, 351
announcing future auction, 50
antique mall, liquidating merchandise at, 345
Antique Trader, 152
AOL (America Online) Web site hosting, 159, 160, 226
API (application program interface), 47, 190, 269, 271
appraisal, online, 154
artifacts, selling, 88
artprice.com Web site, 153
as is/where is, 351
asterisk (*) search operator, 148
at sign, one (@1) search operator, 148
AT&T WorldNet Web site hosting, 159
Auction Advisor seminar series, 81
Auction Tamer software, 193
auction, traditional
  acquiring merchandise at, 129–132
  consignment clinic, 154
  liquidating merchandise at, 346–347
  selling by auction house on eBay, 34–35
Auction Wizard 2000 software, 189, 194–195
AuctionHawk Web site, 190, 226
AuctionHelper Web site, 189, 190
AuctionPayments.com Web site, 241–242

AuctionWeb Web site, 10
AuctionWorks Web site (MarketWorks. com), 189, 191–192
Auctiva Web site, 190
authenticating item, 154–156
author contact information, 6
Autograph Collector, 152
autographs, selling, 88, 152, 153, 155
AVS (Address Verification Service), 249

• B •

Ballista template listing system, 192
bank debit, payment by, 245
banner advertising, 114, 166, 170–172
Barbie Bazaar, 152
baseline, 12
Basic Search Options page, 149–150
batteries, selling, 88
Beanie Babies, selling, 52, 133
bidding
  absentee, 351
  age of bidder, determining, 84
  All Bidding area, 58
  annotating bid, 62
  blocking bidder, 75, 94
  canceling bid, 73–74, 76, 351
  contract, bid as legally binding, 95
  Dutch auction, 40, 61
  highest bid, displaying, 61
  history of bidder, researching, 75, 76–77
  increment, 351
  live auction, 35
  management tool overview, 73–75
  minimum bid amount, 74
  preapproving bidder, 75
  proxy, 44–45, 94
  retracting (canceling), 73–74, 76, 351
  shielding, 94
  shill, 92
  sniping, 354
  starting, 39, 40, 44–45
  stealing bidder, 91
  store, online, 119
  total, displaying, 61
  tracking, 60–61, 64–65
  underage bidder, reporting, 98–99
  unwelcome bidder, 94–95
  winning bid, displaying, 61, 62–63

BidPay.com Web site (AuctionPayments. com), 241–242
Big Lots, acquiring merchandise at, 126–127
blocking bidder, 75, 94
BobMill (eBay seller), 329–330
boldface listing option, 121, 202, 206, 211
bonding transaction, 103, 245, 247
Bonhams & Butterfields auction house, 346
bonus policy, 52, 86
bookkeeping. *See also* tax
  accounting, double-entry, 291
  accounts payable/receivable, 351
  accrual basis, 300
  calendar, keeping daily, 293
  cash basis, 300
  checkbook, reconciling, 296
  credit card, 293–294
  expense, posting, 290–291, 293–294
  QuickBooks bookkeeping chart of account, 305
  software, 26, 290, 295–296
  standards, 291
  supporting information, 293–294
  time period to keep documentation, 294–295
books, selling, 17–18, 31
bottles, selling, 84, 87
Bowers and Merena Auctions Web site, 154
broadbandreports.com Web site, 20
B2B (business to business) transaction, 139
Bubblefast (eBay seller), 23, 330–332
bulk, buying product in, 14
business license, 284–287
Buy It Now feature, 45, 76, 119, 208–210, 211
Buyer Community Participation Number, 250
buyer's premium auction fee, 130
buySAFE service, 247

• C •

cable TV descramblers, selling, 87
calendar, keeping daily, 293
canceling
  auction, 73, 74
  bid, 73–74, 76, 351

Cardking4 (eBay seller), 332–333
Carfax automotive service, 32–33
cars, selling, 31–34, 131, 212
cash on delivery (C.O.D.), 242
catalogs, selling, 86
category
  changing mid-auction, 201
  choosing, 30–31, 201
  Clothing Shoes & Accessories, 31
  Collectibles, 15, 30
  custom, 118
  Find a Main Category feature, 30–31
  Mature Audiences, 42, 89
  Merchant Kit, 48
  Motors, 31–34
  multiple categories, listing auction in, 51,
    201, 211
  Other Items, 118
  Overview page, 30
  searching, 147
  specializing in, 14, 145
  store, online, 114, 118
  Toys & Hobbies, 30
caveat emptor, 352
CDs, selling, 152
cell phone, sending End of Auction notice
  to, 70
Certified Developer, 190
Certified Public Accountant (CPA), 290
CGC (Comics Guaranty, LLC), 155
ChannelAdvisor.com Web site, 189, 190–191
chargeback, 248, 249, 251
charity auction, 54, 130, 132
check, payment by
  cashier's check, 239
  e-check, 244–245
  Escrow.com check handling, 245, 246
  PayPal check handling, 244–245, 250
  personal check, 80, 243–245
  reconciling checkbook, 296
checkout, automating, 187
choice auction, 51
choosing product line, 13–18
Christmas merchandise, acquiring, 125
cigarettes, selling, 87
cigars, selling, 87
city tax registration certificate, 284–285
classified liquidation ad, running, 348

cleaning item for sale, 220, 221, 223,
  312–313, 315
ClickStamp postage printing service,
  318–319
Cline, Jillian (eBay seller), 338–339
Closeout Specialists Web site, 135
closing
  auction, 47, 146
  vacation, online store for, 111
clothing, selling
  acquiring merchandise, 14, 129
  category, 31
  children's clothing, 18
  cleaning, 220, 315
  introduced, 14–15
  lingerie, 39
  mannequin, 219–220
  photographing, 16, 219–220
  steamer, 220
  used clothing, 89
Cloud Dome (photography tool), 218, 222
C.O.D. (cash on delivery), 242
coins, selling, 152, 154, 155
collectibles, selling. *See also specific
  collectible*
  acquiring merchandise, 128, 129, 130
  category, 15, 30
  introduced, 14
  ten-day auction, 46
  value, determining, 145, 152–153
Collector Editions, 152
Collectors Universe Web site, 153
Collier, Marsha
  contact information, 6
  *eBay Timesaving Techniques For
    Dummies*, 46, 143, 183, 264
comic books, selling, 153, 155
Comics Guaranty, LLC (CGC), 155
comma (,) search operator, 148
community event, liquidating merchandise
  at, 345
community values, 83–84
Compare Items feature, 182
competition, researching, 64, 69, 151
computer hardware needed, 20
comScore Web site, 108
connecting to Internet, 20–22
consignment, 141–143, 154, 193, 195
consumerism, responsible, 83

contract
  bid as legally binding, 95
  consignment agreement, 141
  partnership agreement, 281
  selling, 88
cookie system, 57
Cool eBay Tools Web site, 6, 183, 215, 229
Corel Web Designer software, 159
corporation, running business as, 282–283
Cortese, Joe (eBay seller), 192, 337–338
cost
  auction management service, online, 192
  auction management software, 188–189
  banner, 114, 166
  boldface listing option, 121, 206, 211
  bonding transaction, 247
  Buy It Now feature, 211
  buyer's premium, 130
  buySAFE service, 247
  camera, digital, 217
  car fee list, 34
  categories, listing in multiple, 211
  check, cashier's, 239
  ClickStamp postage printing service, 319
  consignment selling, 142–143
  credit card, 247–248, 259
  CuteFTP, 179
  domain name registration, 169
  Endicia.com postage printing service, 320, 321
  Escrow.com, 246
  FedEx, 264, 267
  fee avoidance, 93
  fixed-price sale fee list, 38
  FVF, 34, 38, 50, 194, 212
  gallery, 121, 208, 211
  hammer fee, 130
  highlight option, 121, 202, 205, 211
  home-page featured auction, 202, 211
  ID Verify, 76
  insertion (listing) fee, 37–38, 40, 108, 119, 210–211
  ISP, 21, 22
  lighting, studio, 218
  Listing Designer option, 121, 205, 211
  listing, scheduled, 211
  merchant account, 27, 257–258
  money order, 239–240, 241
  Paint Shop Pro, 225

  payment service, online, 26, 248
  PayPal, 250, 251, 252
  QuickBooks, 296, 307
  real estate fee overview, 37
  reserve price auction, 41
  scanner, 224
  search engine submission service, 172
  Selling Manager feature, 189, 194
  shipping, 13
  SquareTrade seal, 103
  Stamps.com, 324
  steamer, 220
  store, online, 108, 113, 119
  subtitle, 121, 211
  ten-day auction, 46, 211
  tripod, 217
  U-PIC, 275
  UPS, 264, 268, 269, 275
  USPS, 264, 271, 273, 275, 317
  VeriSign, 261
  Web site, 162, 163, 167, 169, 186
  Yahoo! Express, 173
  Yahoo! PayDirect, 255–256
  ZoneAlarm, 366
cost of item, determining. *See* value of
    item, determining
Costco, 128, 257, 258–260
countdown timer, 63
counter, 206–207
counterfeit merchandise, selling, 86, 90
CPA (Certified Public Accountant), 290
credit card
  bookkeeping, 293–294
  changing credit card information, 70
  chargeback, 248, 249, 251
  cost, 247–248, 259
  Costco, 258–260
  CVV2, 255
  debit by eBay, viewing, 69
  Escrow.com, handling by, 245, 246
  importance of accepting, 26
  insurance, 81
  merchant account, 26–27, 247, 256–258
  payment service, online, 26, 248
  random charge check, 255
  security, 26
  selling, 86
  SET, 249
  transaction, card not present, 352

Verified by Visa acceptance, 249
VeriSign transaction processing, 76,
    260–261
cruises, selling, 87
currency
  counterfeit, selling, 86
  value of item, currency considerations
    when determining, 145
customer service, 118, 231–238
CuteFTP software, 160–161, 179
CuteHTML software, 25
CVV2 credit card security, 255

• D •

Data Universal Numbering System (DUNS)
    number, 352–353
DAZzle software, 319–320
DBA (doing business as), 352
dead on arrival (DOA), 352
DEK Auction Manager software, 193
Department of the Treasury property
    auction, 131
Dependable Auto Shippers, 33
description area, 112, 213–214, 229, 232
Dial-A-Zip software, 319
Didn't Win page, 61
Digital Subscriber Line (DSL), 21–22, 359,
    360, 364
Disabled Online Users Association (DOUA),
    327, 328
discount club store, acquiring
    merchandise at, 127–128
display stand, 220–221
dispute resolution, SquareTrade, 76, 77, 87,
    100–104
DOA (dead on arrival), 352
dog-related merchandise, selling, 338–339
doing business as (DBA), 352
Doll Reader, 152
dollar store, acquiring merchandise at,
    126–127
dolls, selling, 40, 129, 152
DOUA (Disabled Online Users Association),
    327, 328
double-entry accounting, 291
drop-down box policy, 90
drop-ship service, 136
drugs, selling, 86, 87, 280–281

DSL (Digital Subscriber Line), 21–22, 359,
    360, 364
DUNS (Data Universal Numbering System)
    number, 352–353
duplicate auction, 51–52
Dutch auction
  bidding, 40, 61
  categories, running in multiple, 51
  color coding, 64
  described, 39–40
  featured auction listing, 40
  insertion (listing) fee, 40, 211
  non-paying buyer alert, 98
  reserve price option, 42
  Second Chance feature, 50
DVDs, selling, 31, 128

• E •

EA (enrolled agent), 290
e-appraisal, 154
Earthlink Web site hosting, 159
eBay Motors, 33–34
eBay Timesaving Techniques For Dummies
    (Collier), 46, 143, 183, 264
eBay University, 81, 201
e-check, payment by, 244–245
EIN (employer identification number), 353
electronic equipment, selling, 88
e-mail
  address, changing, 70, 76
  address, keeping current, 98
  address, privacy of seller's, 24
  address, wireless, 70
  auction cancellation notice, e-mailing, 74
  automating, 181, 235
  buyer, written communication with,
    234–238
  eBay employee, verifying e-mail from, 99
  forwarding, 24, 186
  link opening e-mail window, 53
  notification preference, setting, 85
  PayPal, from, 97, 187
  phishing, 97
  reporting fraudulent, 97
  search result, e-mailing, 69
  Selling Manager feature, sending
    from, 194
  signature, 234

e-mail *(continued)*
  sorting, 181
  spam, 135
  transaction interception, 93
  winner notification, 187, 235–236
embargoed merchandise from prohibited
    country, selling, 89
employee payroll processing, 288, 300,
    303, 306
employer identification number (EIN), 353
e-names.org Web site, 169
End of Auction notice, 70
Endicia.com postage printing service, 271,
    305, 319–321
enrolled agent (EA), 290
entrepreneur, 353
Escrow.com Web site, 245–247
estate auction, acquiring merchandise
    at, 130
Ethernet networking standard, 358, 360
event tickets, selling, 88
Excel software, 26, 187, 296, 311
existing business, bringing to eBay, 18–19
expert eBay seller, 185
extension, FrontPage, 160

• F •

family business, running on eBay, 17–18,
    330–332
Favorite Sellers area, 69
favorites, 58, 67–69
featured auction listing, 40, 202–204, 211
Federal Employee Tax ID number, 288
Federal Trade Commission 30-day rule, 52
Federal wire-fraud statute, 92
Federation of Tax Administrators
    Web site, 288
FedEx (Federal Express), 264–267, 274
fee avoidance, 93
feedback
  accessing, 76
  automating, 188, 196
  boosting feedback rating via buying from
    yourself, 24
  Buy It Now feature, feedback rating
    needed for, 208
  buyer feedback, 24, 66, 76–77, 94, 237

  duration, 76
  e-mail address change recorded in, 76
  icon, 67
  introduced, 24
  leaving, 67, 77–78, 188, 194, 237
  Mutual Feedback Withdrawal, filing for, 77
  negative, 77, 78, 94, 103
  payment reminder, checking feedback
    before sending, 236
  PayPal, 250
  PowerSeller requirement, 79
  responding to, 78–79
  Second Chance Offer scenario, 50
  seller feedback, 24
  SquareTrade mediation, 77
  SquareTrade membership, effect on, 103
  star color-coding, 76
  transaction, on, 78
  user ID change recorded in, 76
fictitious business name statement,
    filing, 284
File Transfer Protocol (FTP), 160,
    178–179, 226
final value fee (FVF), 34, 38, 50, 194, 212
Financial Accounting Standards Board, 291
Find a Main Category feature, 30–31
Find Items page, 148. *See also* searching
firearms, selling, 86
firewall, 365–366
fireworks, selling, 86
five-day auction, 45
fixed-price sale, 37–38
flatbed scanner, 224
flooding market, 138
FOB (free on board), 137
font, 48, 53
food, selling, 88
format, business, 279–283
fraud protection program, 50, 80–81, 245
freight on board. *See* FOB (free on board)
freight, selling unclaimed, 134, 135
freon, selling, 88
FrontPage software, 25, 160
FTP (File Transfer Protocol), 160,
    178–179, 226
future auction, announcing, 50
FVF (final value fee), 34, 38, 50, 194, 212

• G •

GAAP (Generally Accepted Accounting
Procedures), 291
gallery, 115–116, 121, 179–181, 207–208, 211
garage sale, 128–129, 343–344
gateway, merchant account, 257
General Services Administration
auction, 131
generalist seller, 214
Generally Accepted Accounting
Procedures (GAAP), 291
GeoCities Web site hosting, 159, 160,
166, 172
Gibson Research Corporation Web site, 366
giveaway policy, 52
Giving Works auction, 54, 342
glasses, selling advertising, 153
going-out-of-business sale, acquiring
merchandise at, 129
Goldmine, 152
Goodwill, acquiring merchandise at, 14,
132–133
Google, submitting Web site to, 173
grading item, 154, 155
guns, selling, 86

• H •

hair, selling, 87
hammer fee, 130
hard drive size needed, 20
hard to find (HTF), 353
hazardous material, selling, 89
hidden text, policy regarding, 90
highlight listing option, 121, 202, 205, 211
hobby, turning into business, 14–16
holiday, closing auction on, 47
Home Networking For Dummies (Ivens), 357
home page, eBay, 12–13, 40, 202–204, 211
hosting, Web site, 159, 161–167, 172, 186
HTF (hard to find), 353
HTML (HyperText Markup Language)
cutting and pasting, 183
editor, 25–26, 159
font, 48, 53
generating, 117, 160, 182–183, 229
hyperlink, 159

image-related, 180, 183
Merchant Kit, 47–48, 49
store, online, 117
template, 11, 117, 192, 196
text, hidden, 90
human parts and remains, selling, 86, 87
hyperlink, 159. *See also* linking
HyperText Markup Language. *See* HTML

• I •

IBI (information-based indicia), 317
ICANN (Internet Corporation for Assigned
Names and Numbers), 168–169, 170
icon overview, 67
ID Verify feature, 75, 76, 208
IDs, selling government, 86
income splitting, 282
incorporation, 282–283
InexpensiveDomains.com Web site, 169
information-based indicia (IBI), 317
Inkfrog Web site, 189, 190, 226
insertion (listing) fee, 37–38, 40, 108, 119,
210–211
insurance
credit card, 81
QuickBooks insurance charts of
account, 305
shipping, 80, 267, 270, 274–276, 320
Interland.com Web site hosting, 163,
164–165, 167
Internal Revenue Service (IRS), 131, 292,
294, 295, 351
international selling, 89, 240, 252, 255
International Standard Book Number
(ISBN), 353
Internet connection, 20–22, 357, 358–359
Internet Corporation for Assigned Names
and Numbers (ICANN), 168–169, 170
InterNIC Web site, 169
inventory, 182, 191, 192, 303, 311
invoice
defined, 353
printing, 194
IP (Internet Protocol) address tracing, 92
IRS (Internal Revenue Service), 131, 292,
294, 295, 351
ISBN (International Standard Book
Number), 353

ISP (Internet Service Provider), 20–22, 92, 157, 159–160, 226
item number, 62
Items I'm Selling area, 64–65
Items I'm Watching area, 63–64
Items I've Sold area, 65–67
Items I've Won area, 61, 62–63
Ivens, Kathy (*Home Networking For Dummies*), 357

• J •

Jasc Paint Shop Pro software, 225
jewelry, selling, 220–221
job lot merchandise, acquiring, 138

• K •

keystone, 353
keyword
  online store description, 112
  spamming, 53, 88, 89–90
  Web site, 172
knives (weapons), selling, 89

• L •

label printing. *See* printing label
law enforcement
  buyer, reporting to, 100
  eBay cooperation with, 90
  police-related merchandise, selling, 89
  stolen merchandise auction, 131
Le Vine Family (eBay sellers), 330–332
LeakTest software, 366
ledger book, 24
legality
  age of buyer, determining, 84
  bid as legally binding contract, 95
  bonus, offering regulated item as, 86
  check, passing bad, 244
  document preparation, online, 283
  Federal wire-fraud statute, 92
  illegal item, linking to site offering, 55
  illegal item, reporting seller offering, 99
  jurisdiction, 84
  liability, 280–281, 282

payment, refusing to accept from winning bidder, 93
  prohibited item policy, 86–87
  trademark usage, improper, 90, 91
  trading violation, 91–96, 98–99
  transaction interception, 93
LegalZoom Web site, 283
liability, 280–281, 282
license
  agreement, 48
  business license, 284–287
  selling, 86
limited liability company (LLC), 282
Lindhorst, Steve (eBay seller), 333–334
Lindsell-Roberts, Sheryl (*Writing Business Letters For Dummies*), 233
LinkExchange network, 166
linking
  About Me page, from, 55
  auction, to another, 53
  e-mail window, opening via link, 53
  illegal item, to site offering, 55
  online store, linking from auction, 119
  photograph, to, 53, 181
  policy, 50, 53, 55
  TipLink buttons, 49–50
  vendor, to third-party, 53
  Web site, linking to eBay auction from external, 47–49
  Web site, linking to external from eBay auction, 27, 50, 53, 55
liquidating unsold merchandise, 341–348
liquidation merchandise, acquiring, 130, 131, 134–135, 136, 138
Liquidation.com Web site, 138
lister, 28
listing
  boldface option, 121, 202, 206, 211
  categories, in multiple, 51, 201, 211
  ending early, 73, 74
  error, correcting, 74
  featured auction, 40, 202–204
  highlight option, 121, 202, 205, 211
  identical listings, maximum permitted, 51
  insertion fee, 37–38, 40, 108, 119, 210–211
  online store listing header, custom, 118
  policy, 51–53
  PowerSeller listing volume requirement, 79

pre-sale, 52, 89
relisting, 11, 67, 183
scheduling unattended, 184, 196, 211
searching for new, 68–69
Sell Similar feature, 11, 183–184
Seller's Assistant software, using, 189, 195–196
shipping quote, including, 232
Turbo Lister software, using, 80, 184, 197
upload, bulk, 184
Listing Designer option, 121, 205–206, 211
ListingRover (eBay seller), 333–334
live auction, 34–35
LLC (limited liability company), 282
lockpicking devices, selling, 86
lodging, selling, 87
logging off, 57
lottery tickets, selling, 86
Lyn Knight Currency Auctions
Web site, 154

• *M* •

Magic-By-Mail (eBay seller), 334–335
mail order business, bringing to eBay, 19
mailing list
  marketing on, 47
  selling, 86
ManageAuctions.com Web site, 207, 226
manufacturers suggested retail price
  (MSRP), 354
MarketWorks.com Web site, 189, 191–192
Mature Audiences category, 39, 42, 89
Mavica camera, 216
McAfee software, 366
mediation, 77, 102. *See also* SquareTrade
  dispute resolution
medical devices, selling used, 89
mega pixel, 215
Melrose_Stamp (eBay seller), 336–337
Member Profile, 62
membership suspension, 95
merchant account, 26–27, 247, 256–258
Merchant Kit feature, 47–48
Meridian software/Web site, 189, 192–193
meta tag, 172
MIB (mint in box), 354
Microsoft Web site hosting, 163, 165–166, 172

Microsoft Works software, 296
militaria, selling, 86
Mill, Bob (eBay seller), 329–330
MIMB (mint in mint box), 354
mint, 354
mint in box (MIB), 354
minus sign (-) search operator, 148
MissionFish.com Web site, 342, 343
modem, 21, 359
money order, payment by, 239–242, 246
money, selling counterfeit, 86
More Search Options page, 200
Motors category, 31–34
movie-related merchandise, selling
  DVD, 31, 128
  memorabilia, 30, 46, 132, 133, 145
  posters, 46, 153
  VHS tape, 48
MSN Web site hosting, 159
msnTV Web site hosting, 159
MSRP (manufacturers suggested retail
  price), 354
Multistate Tax Commission Web site, 288
municipal tax registration certificate,
  284–285
music
  background, 182
  selling, 18, 152
Mutual Feedback Withdrawal, filing for, 77
My Account area, 58, 69–71, 78, 85
My eBay page
  accessing, 58
  All Bidding area, 58
  All Buying area, 59, 60–64
  All Favorites area, 58, 67–69
  All Selling area, 58, 59–60, 65, 74, 253
  customer service tool, as, 232
  desktop shortcut to, creating, 58
  Items I'm Selling area, 64–65
  Items I'm Watching area, 63–64
  Items I've Sold area, 65–67
  Items I've Won area, 61, 62–63
  Personal Information area, 70
  Preferences area, 57, 70–71
  Views box, 63, 65
My Summary area, 58, 59
My Web Wholesaler Web site, 135

• N •

NameProtect.com Web site, 168
NamesAreCheap.com Web site, 168, 169
NARU (not a registered user), 354
National Check Fraud Center, 244
National Fraud Information Center
    (NFIC), 100
navigation bar, 58
Nelson, Stephen L. (*QuickBooks 2004 For Dummies*), 297
network, home, 355, 357–366
Network Solutions Web site, 168, 169
neutraceuticals, selling, 280–281
newsgroup, marketing on, 47
NFIC (National Fraud Information
    Center), 100
NGCA (Numismatic Guaranty Corporation
    of America), 155
99¢ Only store, acquiring merchandise
    at, 126
Noblespirit (eBay seller), 337–338
Nolo Web site, 279
Norton AntiVirus software, 366
not a registered user (NARU), 354
NPB (non-paying buyer), 50, 95–96, 98,
    194, 237
number, item, 62
Number of Watchers (# of Watchers)
    feature, 64
Numismatic Guaranty Corporation of
    America (NGCA), 155
Numismatic News, 152

• O •

ODR (online dispute resolution), 102
offensive material, selling, 89
office, home, 27–28. *See also* storage space
Omidyar, Pierre (eBay AuctionWeb co-
    founder), 10
1099 form, 351
one-day auction, 45
Online Authentics Web site, 155
online dispute resolution (ODR), 102
online store. *See* store, online
OOP (out of print), 354
Other Items category, 118

• P •

Pacific Bell DSL Web site hosting, 159
packaging
    selling packaging material, 330–331
    shipment, needed for, 13, 312–317
Paint Shop Pro software, 225
Pair Networks Web site hosting, 186
pallet, acquiring merchandise by, 136–137
paperwork, 24
parentheses ({ }) search delimiters, 148
partnership, running business as, 279,
    280, 281
password, 57, 70
payment. *See also* credit card; PayPal
    payment service
    bank debit, 245
    cash, 243
    check, cashier's, 239
    check, personal, 80, 243–245
    C.O.D., 242
    e-check, 244–245
    escrow service, 245–247
    international, 240
    marking item paid manually, 67
    money order, 239–242, 246
    NPB, 50, 95–96, 98, 194, 237
    received notice, 237–238
    refusing to accept from winning
        bidder, 93
    reminder, 236–237
    search result, limiting by payment
        option, 149
    service, online, 26, 248
    status, displaying, 67
    store, online, 121
    transfer, instant, 244–245
    winner notification, including payment
        information in, 235
    Yahoo! PayDirect, 245, 255–256
PayPal payment service
    account needed to use, 250
    accounts, payment from multiple, 252
    adding to auction, 49
    address confirmation, 251
    AVS, 249
    Buyer Community Participation
        Number, 250
    chargeback, 249, 251

check handling, 244–245, 250
cost, 250, 251, 252
CVV2 support, 255
debit card, 250
deposit, 250
downloading data from, 187, 252–253
e-check, 244–245
e-mail from, 97, 187
feedback system, 250
home page, 250
interest paid on cash balance, 255
international payment, 252, 255
introduced, 26
label printing, 321, 322
membership, verified, 251
phishing, 97
QuickBooks, integration with, 305, 307
random charge check, 255
receipt, 67
registering with, 253–255
search result, limiting to, 149
Seller Overview page, 253
Seller Protection policy, 251–252
shipping service, 238, 321–323
transfer, instant, 244–245
Web site support, 161, 162
withdrawal, 250, 251, 255
payroll processing, 288, 300, 303, 306
PCGA (Promotional Glass Collectors
    Association) Web site, 153
PCGS (Professional Coin Grading Service),
    154, 155
PCI Coin Grading Service, 155
personal information
  importance of introducing yourself, 233
  My eBay page Personal Information
      area, 70
  selling, 86
pesticide, selling, 89
phishing, 97
photograph
  background, 222, 223
  camera, digital, 215–217
  clothing, 16, 219–220
  Cloud Dome, 218, 222
  cropping, 208, 228
  description area, in, 229
  display stand, 220–221
  editing software, 224–225

file format, 224
file size, 232
gallery, 115–116, 121, 179–181,
    207–208, 211
hosting, 186, 191, 192, 225–226
HTML, image-related, 180, 183
jewelry, 220–221
lighting, 218
linking to, 53, 181
macro, 216
page-top option, 227
Picture Services feature, 226–228
prop, 219
riser, 220
rotating, 228
scanning, 224
seamless (background), 222
search result, displaying in, 149
stage, 214, 222
studio, 214–222
supporting item for, 220–222
tripod, 216, 217
uploading, 178–179, 191, 192, 195, 227
Photoshop software, 225
picture. *See* photograph
Picture Services feature, 226–228
Pitney Bowes ClickStamp postage printing
    service, 318–319
plain old telephone service (POTS), 22
plants, selling, 87
police
  buyer, reporting to, 100
  eBay cooperation with, 90
  selling police-related merchandise, 89
  stolen merchandise auction, 131
policy
  bid shielding, 94
  bonus, offering, 52, 86
  choice auction, 51
  drop-down box, 90
  duplicate auction, 51–52
  fee avoidance, 93
  giveaway, offering, 52
  keyword spamming, 53, 88, 89–90
  linking, 50, 53, 55
  listing policy, 51–53
  payment, refusing to accept from winning
      bidder, 93
  PayPal Seller Protection policy, 251

policy *(continued)*
  potentially infringing item, 89–91
  privacy, 24, 85
  prize, offering, 52
  prohibited item, 86–87
  questionable item, 87–89
  Second Chance feature, 33, 50
  store, online, 110, 117, 118
  text, hidden, 90
  trading violation, 91–96, 98–99
postage
  meters, selling, 87
  printing using Web-based service, 271, 318–320, 323–324
Postal Service. *See* USPS (United States Postal Service)
posters, selling, 46, 153
potentially infringing item policy, 89–91
POTS (plain old telephone service), 22
PowerSeller, 12, 79–80
Preferences area, 57, 70–71
Preferred Solution Provider, 190
pre-sale listing, 52, 89
prescription devices, selling, 87
PreservationPublishing (eBay seller), 338–339
price of item, determining. *See* value of item, determining
printing invoice, 194
printing label
  automating, 187
  ChannelAdvisor, 191
  DAZzle, 320
  Endicia.com, 320
  FedEx, 267
  Items I've Sold page, from, 67
  Meridian, 193
  PayPal, 321, 322
  printer, 318
  Seller's Assistant, 196
  Selling Manager, 194
  Stamps.com, 323
  UPS, 268
printing postage using Web-based service, 271, 318–320, 323–324
Priority eSupport PowerSeller service, 80

privacy
  domain registration information, 170
  policy, 24, 85
private auction, 39, 43
prize policy, 52
processor (transaction clearinghouse), 257
product line, choosing, 13–18
Professional Coin Grading Service (PCGS), 154, 155
Professional Sports Authenticator (PSA), 155
profiling buyer, 146
prohibited item policy, 86–87
promotion freebie, selling, 133
Promotional Glass Collectors Association (PCGA) Web site, 153
Propertybureau.com Web site, 131
proprietorship, sole, 280–281
provenance, 354
proxy bidding, 44–45, 94
PSA (Professional Sports Authenticator), 155
Purchase Protection program, 32, 51

• *Q* •

questionable item policy, 87–89
QuickBooks software
  balance display, 297
  chart of accounts, 301–306
  Company preferences tab, 301
  cost, 296, 307
  EasyStep Interview feature, 298–301
  introduced, 26
  inventory processing, 182, 303
  online service, 307
  PayPal, integration with, 305, 307
  payroll processing, 300, 303, 306
  Pro version, 296–298
  register, 354
  reporting, 297
  sales tax processing, 299, 303
QuickBooks 2004 For Dummies (Nelson), 297, 301
quotation marks (" ") search delimiters, 148

• R •

random charge credit card check, 255
ReadyHosting.com Web site hosting, 163–164
real estate, selling, 19, 35–37, 212
recalled merchandise, selling, 87
record-keeping. *See* bookkeeping
records, selling vinyl, 152
redundancy, 162
refrigerant, selling, 88
Related Links box, 59
relisting item, 11, 67, 183
report, generating, 187, 192, 193, 196, 297
reporting
  bidder, underage, 98–99
  e-mail, fraudulent, 97
  illegal item, seller offering, 99
  NFIC, fraudulent activity to, 100
  police, buyer to, 100
  trading violation, 91, 95–96, 100, 104–105
Request to Provide (RTP) form, 274
resale certificate (sales tax), 134, 139, 287
resale store, acquiring merchandise at, 132–133
reselling item bought on eBay, 64, 69, 139–141, 345–346
reserve price auction, 33, 40–42, 74, 210–211
responsible consumerism, 83
restricted access auction, 39, 42
returns
  acquiring merchandise via buying, 134–135
  store, online, 118
Review Payments page, 121
riser (photography prop), 220
Road Runner Web site hosting, 159, 160
rock and roll memorabilia, selling, 154
router, 359
RTP (Request to Provide) form, 274

• S •

sales tax, 118, 134, 287–288, 299, 303
SallyJo (eBay seller), 339–340
salvage merchandise, acquiring, 134, 135
salvagecloseouts.com Web site, 135

Salvation Army, acquiring merchandise at, 132–133
Sam's Club, acquiring merchandise at, 127
satellite descramblers, selling, 87
scanning photograph, 224
SCG (Sportscard Guarantee), 155
scheduling unattended listing, 184, 196, 211
seamless (photography background), 222
searching
  article, avoiding, 147
  auctions, completed, 44, 150, 200
  Basic Search Options page, 149–150
  case sensitivity, 147
  category, 147
  combining words, 148
  Compare Items feature, 182
  conjunction, avoiding, 147
  e-mailing search result, 69
  engine, eBay, 31
  engine, Internet, 172–173
  excluding word, 148
  favorite searching, 68–69
  listing, new, 68–69
  location, limiting by, 149
  More Search Options page, 200
  payment option, limiting by, 149
  photograph display in search result, 149
  phrase, 148
  quantity, limiting by, 149
  seller, limiting by, 151
  sorting search result, 149
  spelling variation, 148
  store, online, 118, 119, 121
  syntax, 146, 148
  Titles and Descriptions option, 147
  trademark, 168
  value of item, determining via, 44, 150–151
  wholesale merchandise, for, 139–140
  wild card, 148
seasonal merchandise, acquiring, 125, 135
Second Chance feature, 33, 50, 67
Secure Electronic Transactions (SET), 249
securities, selling, 87
Security Center area, 100, 104–105
seeds, selling, 87
self discipline, 10
Sell Similar feature, 11, 183–184

Sell your item page, 30–31, 183, 227, 229–230
Sellathon ViewTracker service, 185
seller feedback, 24
Seller's Assistant software, 189, 195–196
Selling Manager feature, 65, 80, 189, 194
Selling-Related Links box, 60
seminar series, 81
SET (Secure Electronic Transactions), 249
seven-day auction, 46
7-Eleven money order, 240
Severance, Sally (eBay seller), 339–340
shelf-pull merchandise, acquiring, 135
shelving, 310
Shields Up software, 366
shill bidding, 92
Shippertools.com Web site, 272–273
shipping. *See also* printing label; *specific carrier*
  calculator, 232
  car, 33, 34
  carrier, choosing, 263–264
  check, clearing before, 80
  cost, 13
  drop-ship service, 136
  Escrow.com requirement, 246
  FOB, 137
  heavy item, 265
  insurance, 80, 267, 270, 274–276, 320
  limiting by location, 94, 118
  listing, including shipping quote in, 232
  manifest, 134
  marking item shipped, 67
  notice, 237–238
  packaging, 13, 312–317
  pallet merchandise, 137
  PayPal shipping service, 238, 321–323
  QuickBooks shipping charts of accounts, 303, 304
  store, online, 118, 122
  tracking, 238, 252, 267, 270
Shooting Star software/Web site, 189, 193
signature, e-mail, 234
signing out of eBay, 57
Skoll, Jeff (eBay AuctionWeb co-founder), 10
slot machines, selling, 89
Small Business Center Web site hosting, 163, 165–166, 172

Small Business/Self-Employed Web site, 292
Smith, Marjie (eBay seller), 327–329
sniping, 354
sole proprietorship, 280–281
Sony Mavica camera, 216
Sothebys Web site, 153
spam
  e-mail, 135
  keyword spamming, 53, 88, 89–90
SpareDollar.com Web site, 189
specializing in specific category, 14, 145
spelling, 46, 148
spider, Internet search engine, 172
SpoonFeeder software/Web site, 189, 193
sport merchandise, selling
  collectibles, 153, 155, 332–333
  equipment, 16, 125
Sports Collectors Digest, 153
Sportscard Guarantee (SCG), 155
spreadsheet software, 26, 296
SquareTrade dispute resolution, 76, 77, 87, 100–104, 118
Stamp Collector, 153
stamps (postage), selling
  collectible, 153, 155, 329
  counterfeit, 86
stamps (rubber), selling, 336–337
Stamps.com, 323–324
Stannard, Jeff (eBay seller), 336–337
"Starting a Business and Keeping Records" (IRS), 295
State Employer number, 288
statistics
  auction, 184–186
  Web site, 162
stealing bidder, 91
stealitback.com Web site, 131
stealth indicia service, 321
steamer, 220
stock, acquiring. *See* merchandise, acquiring
stocks (securities), selling, 87
stolen property
  buying at police auction, 131
  selling, 87
storage space, 13, 27, 28, 309–311
Store Builder feature, 115

store, online
  About the Seller page, 110, 120
  auction, linking from, 119
  banner, 114
  bidding, 119
  branding, 110, 111, 167
  Buy It Now feature, 45, 76, 119, 208–210
  category, choosing, 114, 118
  color theme, 111
  commitment needed, 111
  cost, 108, 113, 119
  creating, 111–114
  customer service, 118
  description, entering keyword
    information in, 112
  exchange, 118
  Gallery feature, 121
  HTML, 117
  listing header, custom, 118
  logo, 118
  naming, 109–110, 112, 113
  payment, 121
  policy, 110, 117, 118
  promotion, 120
  refund, 118
  returns, 118
  sales tax, 118
  searching, 118, 119, 121
  Seller's hub, 110–111
  shipping, 118, 122
  sorting, 115
  SquareTrade membership, 118
  template, 117
  title features, optional, 121
  transaction, 121–122
  vacation, closing for, 111
  Web site, using in conjunction with, 110
Storefront feature
  eBay, 98
  MarketWorks, 192
Stores page
  accessing, 108
  Create New Page link, 117
  cross-promotion box, 120
  gallery view, 115–116
  list view, 115
  Open a Store link, 111
  opening page, 109
  Seller Manage Store link, 115

  Sellers link, 110
  Store Editing/Branding list, 115
Submit It! search engine submission
    service, 172–173
subtitle, 121, 204–205, 211
surety bonding, 103, 245, 247
surveillance equipment, selling, 87
suspension of membership, 95
swap meet, liquidating merchandise at,
    344–345
syntax, search, 146
System Status Announcements Board, 351

• *T* •

Tate, Ken (eBay seller), 332–333
tax. *See also* bookkeeping
  accountant, hiring, 290
  calendar, keeping daily, 293
  city tax registration certificate, 284–285
  corporation, 282–283
  deduction, 354
  EA, hiring, 290
  employee tax withholding, 288
  Federal Employee Tax ID number, 288
  income splitting, 282
  LLC, 282
  partnership-run business, 281
  QuickBooks tax charts of account, 306
  sales tax, 118, 134, 287–288, 299, 303
  sole proprietorship, 280
  State Employer number, 288
  supporting information, 293–294
  1099 form, 351
  W-9 form, 355
Tax Information for Business Web site, 294
tdwcloseouts.com Web site, 135
Teddy Bear Review, 153
teddy bears, selling, 153
template, HTML, 11, 117, 192, 196
Template studio software, 196
ten-day auction, 46, 211
terms of service (TOS), 355
text
  boldface listing option, 121, 202, 206, 211
  case sensitivity when searching, 147
  font, 48, 53
  grammar, 233
  hidden, 90

text *(continued)*
  punctuation, 233
  size, 232
  spelling, 46, 148
  writing auction description, 112,
    213–214, 232
30-day Federal Trade Commission rule, 52
three-day auction, 45
thrift store, acquiring merchandise at,
    132–133
tickets, selling
  event tickets, 88
  lottery tickets, 86
  travel tickets, 87
timing, 45–47
TipLink buttons, 49–50
title, auction, 62
tobacco, selling, 87
TOPHOSTS.COM Web site, 163
TOS (terms of service), 355
toys, selling
  acquiring merchandise, 129
  action figures, 17, 132, 152
  category, 30
  dolls, 40, 129, 152
  introduced, 17–18
  teddy bears, 153
tracking
  bidding, 60–61, 64–65
  buyer, 187
  shipping, 238, 252, 267, 270
trademark
  searching, 168
  usage, improper, 90, 91
  Web site name, 168
TrademarkSearchForFree.com
    Web site, 168
Trading Assistant seller, 142
transaction
  bonding, 103, 245, 247
  B2B, 139
  contacting buyer, 100
  feedback, 78
  interception, 93
  interference, 92
  processor, 257

removing completed, 63
security, 26
split, 354
store, online, 121–122
VeriSign transaction processing, 76,
    260–261
travel packages, selling, 87
Treasury Department property
    auction, 131
Tuesday Morning, acquiring merchandise
    at, 127
Turbo Lister software, 11, 80, 184, 197
TV descramblers, selling, 87
24-hour auction, 46

• U •

United Parcel Service (UPS), 264, 268–270,
    274, 275
United States Postal Service. *See* USPS
Universal Resource Locator (URL), 158
University, eBay, 81, 201
unwelcome bidder, 94–95
U-PIC (Universal Parcel Insurance
    Coverage), 274–276, 320
uploader, 178, 184. *See also* FTP (File
    Transfer Protocol)
UPS (United Parcel Service), 264, 268–270,
    274, 275
uptime, 161
URL (Universal Resource Locator), 158, 169
User Agreement, 51, 85, 279
user ID
  changing, 24, 70, 76
  choosing, 22–23
  multiple, having, 57
  store name, using as, 109
  transferring to third party, 279
USPS (United States Postal Service)
  API, 271
  auction, lost package, 131
  Click-N-Ship, 271, 318
  cost, 264, 271, 273, 275, 317
  delivery confirmation, 272–273, 318, 320
  IBI, 317

insurance, 80, 274, 275
Media Mail, 264, 271, 318
money order, 240–241
package pick up, 319
packaging supplies, 316–317
Parcel Post, 264, 271
postage, printing using Web-based
    service, 271, 318–320, 323–324
Priority Mail, 264, 271, 272, 316–317, 320
rate calculator, 270
selling on eBay by, 30
vehicle, buying from, 131
Web site, 270

● *V* ●

vacation
  closing online store for, 111
  selling vacation package, 87
value of item, determining
  action figure, 152
  Amazon auction result, via checking, 151
  antique, 152
  appraisal, online, 154
  autograph, 152
  CD, 152
  coin, 152, 154, 155
  collectible, 145, 152–153
  competitor auction, via checking, 151
  consignment clinic, 154
  currency considerations, 145
  doll, 152
  market fluctuation, 145
  profiling buyer, 146
  record, vinyl, 152
  reference resource overview, 152–154
  searching eBay, via, 44, 150–151
  sport-related merchandise, 155
  stamp, 153
  teddy bear, 153
  Yahoo! auction result, via checking, 151
values, community, 83–84
Vehicle Identification Number (VIN), 33
Vehicle Purchase Protection program, 32
vehicles, selling, 31–34, 131, 212

Vendio Web site, 189
vendor, linking to third-party, 53
VeriSign transaction processing,
    76, 260–261
VeRO (Verified Rights Owners) program, 90
VHS tapes, selling, 48
view counter, 206–207
ViewTracker service, 185
VIN (Vehicle Identification Number), 33
virus protection, 366
visitor volume, eBay total, 108
vitamins, selling, 280–281

● *W* ●

watching item, 63–64
weapons, selling, 86, 89
Web Easy 5 software, 159
Web site
  backing up, 162
  banner advertising, 166, 170–172
  cost, 162, 163, 167, 169, 186
  data transfer limit, 162
  domain, 168–170
  hosting, 159, 161–167, 172, 186
  importance of, 157–158
  keyword, assigning, 172
  linking to eBay auction from external
      site, 47–49
  linking to external site from eBay auction,
      27, 50, 53, 55
  marketing, 166, 170–173
  meta tag, 172
  music, background, 182
  naming, 167–168
  online store, using in conjunction
      with, 110
  PayPal support, 161, 162
  redundancy, 162
  search engine, submitting to, 172–173
  shopping cart support, 162
  space, free, 158–161
  space, paid, 161–167
  statistics, 162
  technical support, 162

Web site *(continued)*
  trademarking name, 168
  transferring files, 160–161
  uptime, 161
  URL, 158
  winner notification e-mail, including Web
    site offer in, 236
Webhostdirectory Web site, 163
weekend browsing, 46
Western Union money order, 240, 241–242
WHOIS database, 170
Wholesale Central Web site, 135
wholesale merchandise, acquiring,
    138–140, 143
wildlife products, selling, 86
wire-fraud statute, Federal, 92
withholding form, tax, 288
W-9 form, 355
workshop, online, 81
WorldNet Web site hosting, 159
Writing Business Letters For Dummies
    (Lindsell-Roberts), 233

• *Y* •

Yahoo!
  auction result, checking to determine
    item value, 151
  Express feature, 173
  PayDirect service, 245, 255–256
  search engine, 173
  store, online, 108
  Web site hosting, 159, 163, 166–167, 172
  Yellow Pages, 152
youreallycan.com Web site, 167

• *Z* •

ZoneAlarm software, 366
Zoovy.com Web site, 189, 190

FOR DUMMIES®

The easy way to get more done and have more fun

ONAL FINANCE & BUSINESS

nvesting
0-7645-2431-3

Home Buying
A Reference for the Rest of Us!
0-7645-5331-3

Grant Writing
A Reference for the Rest of Us!
0-7645-5307-0

Also available:

Accounting For Dummies
(0-7645-5314-3)

Business Plans Kit For Dummies
(0-7645-5365-8)

Managing For Dummies
(1-5688-4858-7)

Mutual Funds For Dummies
(0-7645-5329-1)

QuickBooks All-in-One Desk Reference For Dummies
(0-7645-1963-8)

Resumes For Dummies
(0-7645-5471-9)

Small Business Kit For Dummies
(0-7645-5093-4)

Starting an eBay Business For Dummies
(0-7645-1547-0)

Taxes For Dummies 2003
(0-7645-5475-1)

E, GARDEN, FOOD & WINE

Feng Shui
eference for the Rest of Us!
-7645-5295-3

Gardening
A Reference for the Rest of Us!
0-7645-5130-2

Cooking
A Reference for the Rest of Us!
0-7645-5250-3

Also available:

Bartending For Dummies
(0-7645-5051-9)

Christmas Cooking For Dummies
(0-7645-5407-7)

Cookies For Dummies
(0-7645-5390-9)

Diabetes Cookbook For Dummies
(0-7645-5230-9)

Grilling For Dummies
(0-7645-5076-4)

Home Maintenance For Dummies
(0-7645-5215-5)

Slow Cookers For Dummies
(0-7645-5240-6)

Wine For Dummies
(0-7645-5114-0)

ESS, SPORTS, HOBBIES & PETS

Fitness
eference for the Rest of Us!
-7645-5167-1

Golf
A Reference for the Rest of Us!
0-7645-5146-9

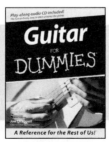

Guitar
A Reference for the Rest of Us!
0-7645-5106-X

Also available:

Cats For Dummies
(0-7645-5275-9)

Chess For Dummies
(0-7645-5003-9)

Dog Training For Dummies
(0-7645-5286-4)

Labrador Retrievers For Dummies
(0-7645-5281-3)

Martial Arts For Dummies
(0-7645-5358-5)

Piano For Dummies
(0-7645-5105-1)

Pilates For Dummies
(0-7645-5397-6)

Power Yoga For Dummies
(0-7645-5342-9)

Puppies For Dummies
(0-7645-5255-4)

Quilting For Dummies
(0-7645-5118-3)

Rock Guitar For Dummies
(0-7645-5356-9)

Weight Training For Dummies
(0-7645-5168-X)

---

able wherever books are sold.
www.dummies.com or call 1-877-762-2974 to order direct

FOR DUMMIES®

A world of resources to help you grow

TRAVEL

0-7645-5453-0

0-7645-5438-7

0-7645-5444-1

Also available:

America's National Parks For Dummies
(0-7645-6204-5)

Caribbean For Dummies
(0-7645-5445-X)

Cruise Vacations For Dummies 2003
(0-7645-5459-X)

Europe For Dummies
(0-7645-5456-5)

Ireland For Dummies
(0-7645-6199-5)

France For Dummies
(0-7645-6292-4)

Las Vegas For Dummies
(0-7645-5448-4)

London For Dummies
(0-7645-5416-6)

Mexico's Beach Resorts For Dummies
(0-7645-6262-2)

Paris For Dummies
(0-7645-5494-8)

RV Vacations For Dummi
(0-7645-5443-3)

EDUCATION & TEST PREPARATION

0-7645-5194-9

0-7645-5325-9

0-7645-5249-X

Also available:

The ACT For Dummies
(0-7645-5210-4)

Chemistry For Dummies
(0-7645-5430-1)

English Grammar For Dummies
(0-7645-5322-4)

French For Dummies
(0-7645-5193-0)

GMAT For Dummies
(0-7645-5251-1)

Inglés Para Dummies
(0-7645-5427-1)

Italian For Dummies
(0-7645-5196-5)

Research Papers For Dum
(0-7645-5426-3)

SAT I For Dummies
(0-7645-5472-7)

U.S. History For Dummie
(0-7645-5249-X)

World History For Dumm
(0-7645-5242-2)

HEALTH, SELF-HELP & SPIRITUALITY

0-7645-5154-X

0-7645-5302-X

0-7645-5418-2

Also available:

The Bible For Dummies
(0-7645-5296-1)

Controlling Cholesterol For Dummies
(0-7645-5440-9)

Dating For Dummies
(0-7645-5072-1)

Dieting For Dummies
(0-7645-5126-4)

High Blood Pressure For Dummies
(0-7645-5424-7)

Judaism For Dummies
(0-7645-5299-6)

Menopause For Dummie
(0-7645-5458-1)

Nutrition For Dummies
(0-7645-5180-9)

Potty Training For Dumm
(0-7645-5417-4)

Pregnancy For Dummies
(0-7645-5074-8)

Rekindling Romance For Dummies
(0-7645-5303-8)

Religion For Dummies
(0-7645-5264-3)

Available wherever books are sold. Go to www.dummies.com or call 1-877-762-2974 to order direct

FOR DUMMIES®

Helping you expand your horizons and realize your potential

GRAPHICS & WEB SITE DEVELOPMENT

0-7645-1651-5

0-7645-1643-4

0-7645-0895-4

Also available:

Adobe Acrobat 5 PDF
For Dummies
(0-7645-1652-3)
ASP.NET For Dummies
(0-7645-0866-0)
ColdFusion MX For Dummies
(0-7645-1672-8)
Dreamweaver MX For
Dummies
(0-7645-1630-2)
FrontPage 2002 For Dummies
(0-7645-0821-0)

HTML 4 For Dummies
(0-7645-0723-0)
Illustrator 10 For Dummies
(0-7645-3636-2)
PowerPoint 2002 For
Dummies
(0-7645-0817-2)
Web Design For Dummies
(0-7645-0823-7)

PROGRAMMING & DATABASES

0-7645-0746-X

0-7645-1626-4

0-7645-1657-4

Also available:

Access 2002 For Dummies
(0-7645-0818-0)
Beginning Programming
For Dummies
(0-7645-0835-0)
Crystal Reports 9 For
Dummies
(0-7645-1641-8)
Java & XML For Dummies
(0-7645-1658-2)
Java 2 For Dummies
(0-7645-0765-6)

JavaScript For Dummies
(0-7645-0633-1)
Oracle9i For Dummies
(0-7645-0880-6)
Perl For Dummies
(0-7645-0776-1)
PHP and MySQL For
Dummies
(0-7645-1650-7)
SQL For Dummies
(0-7645-0737-0)
Visual Basic .NET For
Dummies
(0-7645-0867-9)

LINUX, NETWORKING & CERTIFICATION

0-7645-1545-4

0-7645-1760-0

0-7645-0772-9

Also available:

A+ Certification For Dummies
(0-7645-0812-1)
CCNP All-in-One Certification
For Dummies
(0-7645-1648-5)
Cisco Networking For
Dummies
(0-7645-1668-X)
CISSP For Dummies
(0-7645-1670-1)
CIW Foundations For
Dummies
(0-7645-1635-3)

Firewalls For Dummies
(0-7645-0884-9)
Home Networking For
Dummies
(0-7645-0857-1)
Red Hat Linux All-in-One
Desk Reference For Dummies
(0-7645-2442-9)
UNIX For Dummies
(0-7645-0419-3)

Available wherever books are sold.
Go to www.dummies.com or call 1-877-762-2974 to order direct